The Media
and the
Mayor's Race

The Media
and the
Mayor's Race

❧ THE FAILURE OF
URBAN POLITICAL
REPORTING ❧

Phyllis Kaniss

INDIANA UNIVERSITY PRESS
BLOOMINGTON and INDIANAPOLIS

The paper used in this publication meets the minimum requirements of American National Standard for Information Sciences—Permanence of Paper for Printed Library Materials, ANSI Z39.48-1984.

Manufactured in the United States of America

Library of Congress Cataloging-in-Publication Data

Kaniss, Phyllis C.
    The media and the mayor's race : the failure of urban political reporting / Phyllis Kaniss.
        p.   cm.
    Includes bibliographical references (p.) and index.
    ISBN 0-253-33114-5 (alk. paper). — ISBN 0-253-20932-3 (pbk. : alk. paper)
    1. Press and politics—Pennsylvania—Philadelphia. 2. Reporters and reporting—Pennsylvania—Philadelphia. 3. Elections—Pennsylvania—Philadelphia. 4. Philadelphia (Pa.)—Politics and government—1865–   I. Title.
PN4899.P5K36   1995
070.4′49324974811—dc20   94-13043

1 2 3 4 5 00 99 98 97 96 95

For my parents, Samuel and Norma Kaniss

Contents

Acknowledgments

🌀 In 1991, I was fortunate to witness firsthand the excitement, intrigue, and drama of a big-city mayoral campaign and to observe the work of the reporters who covered the campaign. I could not have written this book without the extraordinary access I was granted by those journalists. I am particularly indebted to Dave Davies, Tia O'Brien, and Sal Paolantonio for allowing me to follow them on the campaign trail and for giving generously of their time throughout the year to answer my many questions. Others might resent or shun the intrusion of an observer who was quite likely to be critical of their efforts. But these three reporters were unfailingly open to my questions and more than willing to reflect on the strengths and weaknesses of their profession.

Many other individuals also contributed important insights, either in private interviews with me or with my students. From the media, I would like to thank David Boldt, Drew Berry, Cynthia Burton, Harvey Clark, Russell Cooke, Lisa DePaulo, Marc Duvoisin, Barbara Grant, Laurie Hollman, Larry Kane, Wally Kennedy, Donald Kimmelman, Max King, Acel Moore, Rick Nichols, Vernon Odom, Charlie Thomson, and Dale Wilcox. From the campaigns, I would like to acknowledge Lucien Blackwell, George Burrell, Judy Castille, David Cohen, Joe Egan, Harriet Garrett, Peter Hearn, Sam Katz, Bob Kutler, Laura Linton, Neil Oxman, Ed Rendell, Chris Mottola, Joe Sanchez, Shanin Specter, Joe Torsella, and Marty Weinberg.

I would like to thank my dear friend and distinguished journalist Donald Drake for his encouragement and advice throughout this project and for providing valuable criticism and direction after reading the manuscript. I am also indebted to another friend, Ernie Leonardo, division chief of comprehensive planning for the Philadelphia City Planning Commission, for patiently guiding me through the technical issues discussed in Chapter 29 and for sharing his insights on urban problems and prospects.

Dean Kathleen Hall Jamieson and the Annenberg School for Communication provided a supportive home for my research, and the students in my Media and Urban Policy course, who lived and breathed the mayoral campaign along with me in 1991, contributed many ideas to this book. My research assistants during that year—Sarah Dupret and Patty Chang— were superb, and I owe my description of the "third-base coach" to Tereza Nemessanyi's perceptive observations. I would also like to thank Steven Pessagno, Jonathan Cutler, and Jefrey Dubard for their assistance in completing the manuscript.

At Indiana University Press, I would like to express my appreciation to editor Robert Sloan for believing in the value of a case study of the media coverage of one city's election, and to Elaine Otto for her skillful editing.

Authors often acknowledge the love and devotion of their spouses, but it is hard for me to imagine any mate having more active involvement with a book than my husband, Paul Wheeling, had with this one. He was my computer guru, my data base consultant, and my finest and most perceptive editor—not to mention, the resourceful entertainer of our sons, Josh and Max, on the snowy days when I was finishing the manuscript. The only time he ever overstepped his role was when he tried to subject my prose to a computerized grammar checker.

Finally, I would like to thank my parents, Samuel and Norma Kaniss, for instilling in all their children a passion for learning and discovering new ideas. It is to them, with love, that this book is dedicated.

PART I

The Primary

1 From the Ritz to the Roller Rink

January 23, 1991 5:30 P.M.

✿ The KYW-TV car pulled up to the entrance of the Ritz Carlton Hotel at Seventeenth and Chestnut Streets in downtown Philadelphia, and reporter Tia O'Brien and her cameraman got out and began to unload their equipment in the winter dusk. O'Brien paused to admire the elegant entrance of the newly opened hotel, where two uniformed doormen stood at attention. The hotel was one of the last jewels to adorn Liberty Place, the expensive new retail and office complex whose prismed glass tower had so dramatically altered the city's skyline. Not bad for Philadelphia, she thought.

Standing in this spot, it was hard to believe that this was a city on the verge of bankruptcy. For months, O'Brien had been covering the dismal twists and turns in the city's fiscal crisis. In the fall of 1990, a major city bond deal had fallen through, and as a result the government had only narrowly averted payless paydays for city workers. A piecemeal solution had been found, but new shortfalls loomed only months away. It was only in the last week that O'Brien's stories about the city's financial woes had been pushed off the evening newscast. Since the United States attacked Iraqi forces occupying Kuwait one week ago, both the national and local news programs were dominated by the war.

But in the lobby of the Ritz Carlton, the war and the city's financial problems seemed very far away. As the reporter and her cameraman hurried through the hotel's cocktail lounge, they passed a business crowd relaxing over drinks in lushly upholstered armchairs, the soft strains of piano music in the background. O'Brien was headed toward a small meeting room around the corner from the bar where politics was the order of the day. She was set to go live on the six o'clock newscast to cover the unveiling of a new set of television commercials by mayoral hopeful Sam Katz, a successful financial consultant and relative newcomer to city politics, who was running hard for the Republican nomination for mayor of Philadelphia.

The next mayor was going to face a complex set of problems, she knew. In 1991, Philadelphia was at a crossroads. Its downtown had never looked better. The Liberty Place tower, which had broken the city's longstanding "gentleman's agreement" on height limitation, had set the stage for the transformation of the west side of City Hall. Several other striking office towers were now going up, alongside elegant new shops and a sophisticated restaurant scene. But as with many other cities, Philadelphia's downtown was deceiving when it came to any assessment of the economic and social health of the city. The near-bankruptcy of city government reflected underlying structural problems that could not be easily papered over, even if bonds could be floated to get over the latest shortfall. Philadelphia, like many other central cities, had been steadily witnessing the erosion of its tax base as businesses and residents continued to flee the city. In the 1980s, the city had lost a staggering 13 percent of its middle-class residents, and in the last two years alone, the employment base was down by 35,000 jobs. At the same time, powerful city labor unions had won any number of battles to keep their membership intact and their wages and benefits high. The next mayor of Philadelphia was going to have to deal not simply with the short-term problem of fiscal solvency but with the longer-term issues of economic development and labor concessions, whether he was a Democrat or Republican.

Although Philadelphia had not seen a Republican in the mayor's office since 1951, the party had a reason to be hopeful. Two years ago, they had succeeded in electing a Republican citywide as District Attorney: the popular Vietnam war veteran, Ron Castille. And now they were running against the legacy of W. Wilson Goode, the city's first black mayor, who was completing his second and final term in office. Goode had presided over one of the worst disasters in the city's history: the ill-fated attempt to evict the radical MOVE cult from a West Philadelphia row house by dropping a bomb on it from a police helicopter. The bomb started a fire that killed eleven MOVE members, including five children, and destroyed sixty-one homes. Although Goode had narrowly won re-election in 1987, the MOVE disaster cast a shadow over his administration that had only deepened as the city teetered on the brink of financial disaster. Even though the Democrats had almost six times as many voters as the Republicans, the party members in attendance at Sam Katz's fundraiser had good reason to be optimistic on this cold January evening.

But Sam Katz was not the only man hoping to throw the Democrats out of City Hall. In the battle to win the Republican nomination, Katz faced a formidable opponent: Frank L. Rizzo. Rizzo had been a larger-than-life Philadelphia legend for over two decades, a tough-talking former police commissioner who had used a law-and-order theme to win two terms as mayor of the city in the 1970s. After losing an attempt to change the city charter so that he could serve a third term, Rizzo had tried twice in the following decade to make a comeback, first as a Democrat in a primary fight with Wilson Goode, and then in 1987, as a Republican challenging Goode in the general election. Both times Rizzo had failed, although in his last run he had come within 17,000 votes of beating Goode. Now, at age seventy, he was taking his last crack at the mayor's office, vying with Katz for the all-important endorsement of Republican party boss William A. (Billy) Meehan. Meehan was said to be favoring District Attorney Ron Castille, but Castille was reluctant to run.

Sam Katz had scheduled his campaign event on the evening that Frank Rizzo was to publicly announce his candidacy for mayor. The Katz cocktail party began at 5:30, the Rizzo announcement was slated for 7:00. If the Katz team had calculated correctly, the drinks, hors d'oeuvres, and screening of the ads would serve more than to raise money for the campaign. They would steal valuable media time away from Rizzo on his big night. In 1991, with more and more Philadelphians abandoning newspapers for local television newscasts, the outcome of the election was going to have a lot to do with attracting the attention of television cameras. But with local stations increasingly turning from politics to "news-you-can-use," getting on the evening news was going to prove no easy matter.

As O'Brien entered the Katz fundraiser, she passed a table set up with campaign literature. One handout was an article headlined "Katz Claims He Can Beat Rizzo with GOP's Blessing," from that day's *Daily News,* the city tabloid that was co-owned along with the *Philadelphia Inquirer* by Knight-Ridder, the second largest newspaper chain in the country. The article described a poll commissioned by Katz showing that he had considerable name recognition and that he could win a primary contest against Rizzo if he had the endorsement of the Republican party. O'Brien ignored the handouts and, with her cameraman trailing behind her, began moving through the room with her microphone, weaving her way through the small crowd of well-dressed supporters who were sipping white wine and nibbling crab hors d'oeuvres.

Unlike the other television reporter present, veteran Harvey Clark from WCAU, who stood looking faintly bored in the middle of the room, O'Brien set out reporting immediately. Although barely more than five feet tall, her razor-sharp questions and her insider's sense of what was really going down in city hall had earned her respect and even fear from local politicians. She was one of an ever-shrinking breed in the world of local television news, a specialized political reporter who actually cultivated her own sources and did her own research. Tonight she headed over to Donald Jamieson, a key player in the city's Republican party. "Can you tell us which candidate the party is leaning toward? Does Sam Katz have a chance here?" Her interview was soon being overheard by another reporter who had wandered in, Sal Paolantonio, the *Philadelphia Inquirer*'s lead political writer for the election, who jotted a few comments into his notebook.

Soon, the 41-year-old Katz, wearing a dark conservative suit and horn-rimmed glasses, arrived with little fanfare with his wife and their four young children. Connie Katz, with her twinkling eyes and bubbly laugh, worked the crowd as if welcoming people to her son's bar mitzvah. She paused to say hello to Harvey Clark and kidded him about an earlier campaign appearance he had covered, then moved on to talk exuberantly about how much fun she and the kids had making the campaign's family commercial.

"Ladies and gentlemen," Katz said when he finally took to the podium, "I want to thank you all for coming this evening and for your generous support of my campaign. As you all know, I am running for mayor because I believe I am the best qualified individual to address the severe financial problems facing this city . . . " As he spoke, his remarks were conspicuously ignored by the television cameramen. They had been instructed by their reporters to get video and sound not of the candidate himself but of the campaign commercials he was releasing, in case the tape of the ads wasn't ready in time for reporters. Whatever Katz might choose to say from the lectern that evening about the city's problems was not news. Only the ads were news. In the ever-evolving calculus of what was worth covering on local television, speeches were out and ad campaigns— with their good visuals, short, sexy sound-bites, and scathing attacks against opponents—were in. Prescriptions for solutions to the complex problems facing the nation's cities, pronounced from behind a lectern, were a story that TV cameras were increasingly ignoring.

As Katz introduced the series of commercials, the three cameramen (one accompanying O'Brien from KYW, the local NBC affiliate, one with Clark from WCAU, the CBS affiliate, and a third attending alone from WTXF, the independent Fox affiliate) crowded to the front of the room to shoot the television screen. The campaign contributors, who were shunted to the back of the room, jokingly complained that they couldn't see the ads. "We'll show them again after the TV people leave," Katz announced with a broad smile. And, sure enough, as soon as the ads were over, even as Katz's wife and children were theatrically mugging for the crowd over their roles as stars, the "TV people" were packing up their equipment and preparing to move on to the next event on the evening's calendar: Frank Rizzo's announcement.

In the KYW car heading up the Schuylkill Expressway, O'Brien chatted with her cameraman, who was at the wheel, about the traffic and the war, but she said little about the event they had just covered. Her live shot from the Ritz had been killed at the last minute because of all the war news and because it had been difficult to get a cable out of the third floor of the hotel. She had been disappointed by her interview with Katz. "He's not launching any nasty attacks on Rizzo, which is a shame." The ads she had found kind of flat. In most of the spots, Katz had stood behind a desk and talked about how he could solve the city's fiscal problems.

O'Brien was more interested in discussing an article that had appeared in that day's *Daily News*—not about the mayoral campaign but about her own station. The newspaper described contract talks between Group W (Westinghouse Broadcasting), KYW's corporate owner, and news anchors, reporters, and writers at the TV station and KYW Newsradio. The story noted that television stations throughout the country were taking steps to cut costs and that KYW-TV was particularly vulnerable since it had the lowest-rated news in the latest ratings period. As part of the cost-cutting ideas at KYW, the article added, there was talk of management eliminating one of the station's newscasts. Reporters at the station were dismayed at the thought of what lengths the station might go to save money and skeptical about the need for all the economies, since word had it that KYW had been returning a nice rate of profit to Westinghouse.

"Why are our ratings so low, do you think?" O'Brien asked her cameraman as they left the center-city skyscrapers behind, passing the decaying industrial buildings left over from the city's manufacturing heyday. "I don't think our product is any worse than what the other stations are doing, do you?"

In the past two decades, KYW had traveled the curious odyssey of many local television stations, moving from format to format, hiring and firing anchor teams with the regularity of off-season baseball trades, all in the search for higher ratings. In their salad days they had led the pack with the beautiful, blonde Jessica Savitch occupying the anchor's chair, alongside the steady, sure Mort Krim. But with Savitch's departure for the network, the station had fallen on harder times. "Happy talk" had given way to "Eyewitness News," with even a brief foray into hard-edged investigative reporting with a unit called the "I-team." But none of the changes had much effect on the ratings. In the eighties the station had paid big money to lure *Good Morning America* newsman Steve Bell to local news as their chief anchor, but the gamble had not paid off. After years of covering wars, Congressional hearings, and Supreme Court decisions, Bell had looked distinctly uncomfortable reading copy about inner-city murders and suburban school strikes. He had never connected with the Philadelphia audience, and KYW's ratings stayed in the cellar.

When news director Randy Covington was fired and his successor Scott Herman brought in, the charge was clear. Major changes had to be made with the goal of making the news operation more profitable to the station and to Westinghouse. The managers were said to be kicking around ideas for replacing newscasts with "infomercials," 30-minute commercials that masqueraded as informational programming. They were even rumored to be considering using their news anchors to help sell products for the station's advertisers. Plans were also being made to revamp the newscasts that remained after the cuts. A number of format "prototypes" were being tested with audience research. One idea floating around was to do a news show that ran stories chronologically, according to when in the day they occurred—a concept that had drawn derision and horror from many in the newsroom.

"The thing is, we've worked hard to get the product what it is," O'Brien said, as the car began making its way up Roosevelt Boulevard, past miles of narrow, tidy row houses and the tree-lined streets of the city's "Great Northeast."

Soon they arrived at the roller-skating rink, the United Skates of America, where Frank Rizzo was announcing his candidacy. The rink was just below Cottman Avenue, the informal dividing line between the older and newer sections of the Northeast. Both were almost exclusively white, and much of the area was considered a Rizzo stronghold. The rink itself was a massive facility with neon signs directing its usual clientele to skates and lockers, the pro shop and the cafe. At the front of the hall was a podium covered by a "Frank in '91" banner, and behind all was a huge American flag, which would serve as a backdrop for Rizzo's speech.

The crowd was made up of the same kind of people who came out in droves for the Mummer's Parade down South Broad Street on New Year's Day, the Italians and Irish who were at the core of Rizzo's support. It was hard to believe that these people were registered in the same party as those who had attended the Katz fundraiser. No pinstripe suits or earth tone silks at this event. Here the men were dressed in leather jackets and rayon slacks, the younger ones in stone-washed jeans and sweatshirts. The women wore fake furs and high-heeled cowboy boots. There were lots of children at the Rizzo event, encouraged by organizers to emphasize the campaign's "family theme": from the little freckle-faced girls in Catholic school uniforms and braces to Rizzo's grandson Joey in a little boy's sober, suit.

And the reporters were there, too. Tia O'Brien and Harvey Clark were joined by several others, including anchor Marc Howard from WPVI, the ratings leader among the Philadelphia stations, and Barbara Grant, a reporter for the Fox affiliate, Channel 29. While most of the reporters were hovering near an elevated platform midway back from the podium—from which the cameramen would shoot Rizzo's speech—Howard mingled with Rizzo staffers up by the podium itself. Howard was one of a handful of TV reporters in Philadelphia who seemed to enjoy a special relationship with Frank Rizzo.

Tia O'Brien spent most of her time before the speech scoping the hall, figuring out the logistics of where she wanted her cameraman to be located from beginning to end to get the pictures she needed and where she herself would stand. She was particularly concerned about how she was going to get her microphone from the podium, where it was lined up with the other television and radio stations' mikes, back into her hands after the speech so that she could get an interview with Rizzo immediately afterward. In the midst of this maneuvering she stopped for a minute and rolled her eyes. "And I'm supposed to get all this and Sam Katz in a minute-thirty?" she asked, referring to the ninety seconds of news time that these four hours of reporting were being allotted by her producer.

The Inquirer's Paolantonio, meanwhile, worked the crowd. He wanted to know who the people were and why they were here. As far as he was concerned, the real story was the crowd, not what was going to happen on the podium. He was fascinated by the people's answers to his question of why they had turned out for Rizzo, especially the younger ones. They sounded almost nostalgic for a safer, less threatening city that they could only imagine, having been little more than children when Rizzo last held office. Part of his fascination with the scene came from the fact that, as a relative newcomer to Philadelphia politics, this was the first time he had covered the legendary Rizzo at one of his full-blown media events surrounded by his adoring supporters. For veteran reporters like O'Brien, it was an all too familiar—and rather tired—scene.

As Paolantonio took a break in his interviewing, he was joined by another *Inquirer* reporter, Daniel Rubin, the beat reporter for the Northeast. Rubin was not covering tonight's event. He had come to get a feel for the residents of a neighborhood he had just been assigned to cover, having been recently transferred from one of the newspaper's suburban bureaus. Up until a few months ago, the *Inquirer* had put out a twice-a-week tabloid insert for this neighborhood called "Northeast Neighbors." Like other metropolitan newspapers throughout the country, the *Inquirer* was aggressively "zoning" its news sections in an attempt to retain the suburban readers who had become the major target of its advertisers.

With the massive postwar exodus from central cities, metro newspapers had found that suburbanites were no longer all that interested in the depressing news of the cities they had fled; what they really wanted were stories about their own school boards and zoning commissions. The problem was that there were hundreds of these small communities, each with their own governing bodies. While readers cared very much about the news of their own townships, they were fairly indifferent to what was happening several boroughs away. To solve the dilemma, newspapers had come up with the idea of zoning. They produced different local news supplements, such as the *Inquirer*'s Neighbors sections, for each suburban area that possessed enough disposable income to attract sufficient retail advertising.

In Philadelphia, the Northeast had often been considered a suburb-within-the-city, a vast tract of land developed after World War II that lay within the physical boundaries of the city. It had come to attract a large, stable population that was half Jewish, half Catholic, part elderly and comfortable, part young and working class. It was a neighborhood that in recent years had felt forgotten by city hall once its taxes were collected and once election time had passed. And that feeling had only intensified under a black mayor, who seemed to many to care more about affirmative action and set-aside programs than about making sure the trash was collected on time. But it was also true that they often felt forgotten by the city's big newspapers, as if the newspapers seemed to find the middle-class neighborhood's day-to-day concerns too mundane to cover.

Because of this sense of alienation, many Northeast residents were abandoning the two major dailies and turning instead to smaller papers, like the *Northeast Times* and the *News Gleaner*. Advertisers from the area's malls were following, attracted by the lower ad rates and higher household penetrations of the community newspapers. In the attempt to fight back, the *Inquirer* had given the Northeast its own Neighbors section. But in the last year, with advertising linage down because of the recession and the *Inquirer* under pressure from its corporate owner, Knight-Ridder, to cut costs, Northeast Neighbors had been dropped. Coverage of the area was being delegated to beat reporter Rubin for inclusion in the main paper when space permitted.

Although tonight Frank Rizzo was symbolically telling the people of this huge neighborhood that he would not forget their needs, their metropolitan newspaper had, in a sense, turned away because residents did not have as much disposable income as some of their suburban neighbors. Economic necessity was forcing the *Inquirer* and many other metropolitan newspapers to provide more detailed local news coverage for some segments of their audience than for others. More and more, the key to survival rested with meeting the news needs of suburbanites, not city dwellers. It was this new concern with the suburban audience that was threatening to push Paolantonio's stories about the mayoral campaign off the front page, where city election stories had been routinely played in the last mayoral election, and back into the Metro section. Only particularly dramatic articles about the campaign, with appeal to people who weren't voting in the election, would make the front page in 1991.

As Paolantonio continued his interviews with people in the crowd, the lights in the hall dimmed and a tape of the song "Proud to Be an American" began to play. A spotlight followed Frank Rizzo as he made his way through the cheering crowd to the podium. The cameramen crowded around to shoot Rizzo's entrance, then raced back to their positions on the platform, lining up to shoot the speech. Their reporters hung over their shoulders, coaching them on which shot and which sound-bite they wanted, having already read the text of the speech handed to them by Rizzo's aides.

Although the reporters had quickly concluded that the speech would offer "nothing new," Rizzo was actually planning to put a slightly new twist on his old familiar themes. Rather than risk being upstaged by the war with Iraq, he would use the war to his advantage. "Tonight," Rizzo began, "and for the next few months, a lot will be said about the character, ability, and dedication it takes to lead this city. This past week, we have all learned a great lesson about real leadership and real character . . . a lesson taught by our brave men and women fighting in the Persian Gulf. May God bless them, keep them healthy, and bring them home." Deafening applause followed his benediction.

And then, with the image of the troops in the background, Rizzo began to align his tough-guy message with the hard line exhibited by President George Bush in attacking Iraq. "From this day on," he said, pronouncing each word with emphasis, "we will take back the streets from the crack dealers who prey on innocent mothers . . . from the thugs who terrorize our senior citizens . . . from the wolf packs who have victimized our city." Riding the crest of patriotism, Rizzo was making it seem as if the two battles—one to cure the economic and social problems of an aging city, the other to evict an aggressor from foreign soil—were similar.

In truth, the resources going to the Persian Gulf were only going to make it harder for cities like Philadelphia to dig their way out of the morass in which they found themselves in 1991. In the Reagan and Bush years, the federal government had drastically cut back on the funds allocated to the nation's cities. Now, with the federal deficit growing each year and the United States fighting a war, the hope for more urban aid was dwindling. But tonight, with flags waving in joyous triumph, the crowd was eager to hear that the problems of their city could be eliminated by tough action, just as Americans, by and large, were eager to think that the problems of the Mideast could be solved by getting tough with Saddam Hussein. And so they roared their approval as Rizzo said to them, with his reassuringly commanding voice, "Do not despair. These times are tough. But we are tougher. We will not lose another generation to the streets of Philadelphia."

Before the speech ended, Tia O'Brien made her way doggedly through the crushing crowd to the back of the podium. She was moving quickly and had just reached the grandstand as Rizzo spoke his final lines.

"From this moment on, go out and tell your parents. Tell your neighbors. Tell your friends. Tell your children. Frank Rizzo is back, and so is Philadelphia." Ignoring the cheering crowds, O'Brien motioned to Rizzo's campaign manager, Marty Weinberg, that she needed to get her microphone. Rizzo himself was being gingerly hoisted down off the platform, looking momentarily shaken after he lost his balance descending into the crush of admirers. But by the time the TV cameras caught up with him, he had regained his composure. The sound system began blaring, with a tape of Martha and the Vandellas singing "Dancing in the Streets" and Diana Ross following with "There's No Stopping Us Now." Motown music hardly fit the old Rizzo white-ethnic image, but it was effective in stirring up the crowd for good background noise or the "nat[ural] sound" that TV reporters loved to include in their pieces. Through the deafening roar of music and cheering, O'Brien grabbed her microphone and pushed into the center of the crowd to get her interview with Rizzo. When she finally reached his side, she called out to him, "Mr. Mayor? Mr. Mayor, would you still run without party endorsement? Wouldn't that hurt party unity?"

It was a perceptive insider's question that had little to do with the trappings of the media event, the kind of question that a political reporter, not a general assignment reporter, would think to ask. Rizzo responded angrily, shouting over the roar of the crowd, "Anybody, anybody, has the right to run for public office. That doesn't divide anything."

Rizzo's aides hurriedly ushered the candidate away, and O'Brien moved on to interview people in the crowd. Each of the three women she stopped were happy to oblige her with predictable comments about how they loved the ex-mayor and knew he could win. When the interviews were over, one of the women asked a stander-by, "What station is she with, anyway?" Seen on the lowest-rated of the three Philadelphia affiliates, Tia O'Brien's face was not one that drew instant recognition.

O'Brien searched for Rizzo for one more question but with no success. She settled for finding a good backdrop for her "stand-up," the on-site summary of the event that she would use to close her piece. As she got ready to go on-camera, she rummaged through her big canvas tote bag to find a hairbrush, removed the combs that held her hair away from her face, and quickly, roughly, brushed her hair a few times, with a slight grimace. Looking obligingly at a small hand mirror, she applied a bit of lipstick, and as quickly put it away, all the while rehearsing aloud what she would say in the ad-libbed stand-up. Her on-air appearance was not something that much concerned her. She sometimes joked that the major hurdle in her jump from public radio to TV had been her ultrafine hair, which had made even skilled fashion consultants throw up their hands in despair. "I'll never have TV hair," she once noted, with very little sign of regret.

O'Brien did her stand-up four times in the din of the crowd at the restaurant next door to the roller rink, where Rizzo supporters had gone to celebrate, ending each one with her formulaic close, "This is Tia O'Brien, Channel 3 News, Nightcast." She said nothing about Rizzo's message or his appeal to the crowd. Rather, she talked about his chances of winning Billy Meehan's endorsement and whether or not the Republican party would blow its best chance in forty years to regain city hall.

O'Brien then headed for the car. Just as her cameraman was loading his equipment into the trunk, she saw Rizzo emerging from the rink on his way to the restaurant. "Gee," she said, "he's going to walk right past us." For a minute, she thought of waiting, tempted by the easy access to the prey she had been stalking all evening, the star of the night. But just as quickly she abandoned the idea and got into the passenger seat. She had her package.

In the car, she discussed the shots with her cameraman. Did you get him wide? Did you get good shots of him coming in? Did you get the crowd? Yes. Yes. Great shot of a woman actually crying at Frank's words. They discussed the number of people who were there. "What do you think? About 300?" "Yeh, 300 sounds right." (The *Daily News* would call it 500, the *Inquirer*, 800.) As the car raced down I-95 toward the lights of the center-city skyscrapers, O'Brien picked up the car phone to check in with her producer at the station. She argued the case that she had two events here—Rizzo's announcement and Katz's commercials—and that it was going to be hard to fit them both into one piece. She listened for a few minutes, then said, "Sure, I understand, I can fit it into one piece. I was just saying it's going to take some maneuvering." When she hung up, she told her cameraman, "Well, there's nine minutes of war news. I guess you can't argue with that. But I am up to 1:45."

One minute and forty-five seconds was just about all that the million or so television viewers in the Delaware Valley would see about the campaign, no matter which of the three eleven o'clock newscasts they tuned into that night. Despite the different reporting styles of the journalists—O'Brien, intense and aggressive, Clark, aloof and patient, Howard, manically friendly—viewers would see three relatively similar reports. Each report emphasized the theatricality of Rizzo's announcement (O'Brien: "It could've been a rock star, but it was Philadelphia's own Frank Rizzo"; Clark: "It was a production straight out of Hollywood"; Howard: "It was vintage Frank Rizzo, it took him ten minutes just to wade through the crowd"). And each chose one or two ten-second fragments of Rizzo's speech for their sound-bites to convey his message. They all referred to the emotional and unwavering quality of Rizzo supporters before describing Rizzo's tough fight for Meehan's endorsement.

But while the television reporters reveled in the colorful trappings of the announcement, they all suggested that Rizzo had nothing new to offer voters or, for that matter, the reporters who were covering him. O'Brien talked about the need to "bring him back to political life" and the fact that "he sounded a message Philadelphians have heard many times before," and Harvey Clark echoed her. "The message was the same today as it was back then," he said and included his question to Rizzo, "Seventy years old? You up to it?" Marc Howard pointed out that while many believed Rizzo could win a half-million votes in the Delaware Valley, the problem was that "many of those voters, including some here tonight, do not live in Philadelphia." The description could have as easily been made of Howard's viewers, many of whom were suburbanites who lapped up news coverage about the Big Bambino but couldn't vote for him.

While Rizzo was being subtly knocked in the reports, Sam Katz was succeeding in his ploy to take coverage away from the ex-mayor. All three stations talked about the Katz ads in what otherwise would have been exclusively Rizzo stories. Even more importantly, they seemed to use Katz as a positive counterpoint to Rizzo. Tia O'Brien followed a sound-bite of an angry Frank Rizzo bellowing, "Anybody, anybody has the right to run for public office. That doesn't divide anything," with a placid Sam Katz reciting in a calm, measured voice, "I think Philadelphia needs a leader who's looking to the future and who's not wedded to the past." And Channel 6 noted that "Sam Katz shows off a new TV ad campaign on the night that Frank Rizzo enters the race."

In the newspapers, it would be a slightly different picture. In the next morning's *Inquirer,* Sal Paolantonio would relegate Sam Katz's fundraiser to two paragraphs midway through his story about Rizzo's "vintage speech" and use Katz's poll as evidence that Rizzo was "well positioned to win the primary." And in the *Daily News,* which hit the streets a few hours later, reporter Cynthia Burton's rendition of the Rizzo announcement would be spread across four columns of the paper, dwarfing a one-column article about Katz's new ads.

But no matter how he fared in the newspapers, there was no question that on the all-important medium of television, Sam Katz had scored a bull's eye. He had not simply won coverage, he had been put on a par with the city's ultimate media darling. And the coverage he received that January night was no lucky break. Unlike the other candidates, Katz was making it onto television news regularly in reports that made him look good. One night he would be on Action News "taking his message to the people"; trusted anchor Jim Gardner would describe Katz as "the municipal finance expert" who said that neighborhood meetings "give the people a chance to address what he calls the good, the bad, and the ugly of Philadelphia." A few days later, he was popping up on Channel 3, talking about his plans for improving city policing. "Republican Sam Katz says that the key to keeping more officers on the roads is to keep their cars on the road. Katz says that private garages can provide better maintenance for police cars than city garages currently do," read anchor Steve Bell, before he let Katz describe how city workers would not be hurt by the move.

Frank Rizzo may have always known how to draw the attention of reporters, but his young challenger was not doing at all badly for a political novice. Although the very antithesis of Rizzo in many ways—Big Frank, the last of the charismatic old-style pols with a die-hard political base, Katz, the youthful idea-man who often put audiences to sleep—Katz was mastering the art of attracting the attention of local television stations. He would never be as colorful as his most lionized opponent, but he was proving that he too could come up with the kind of campaign themes and all-important sound-bites that would make him stand out in the newscasts of the '90s. He was a new face talking about a new problem to a medium crazy for new—and simple—themes. Even though he looked a little like the class nerd when he appeared on the TV screen, he had a message that had been refined into utter simplicity. In those campaign spots he unveiled that January night, he said earnestly: "I know how to manage money. I will solve Philadelphia's fiscal problems."

And because so many Philadelphians were riveted to their television sets to find out the latest on the Iraqi war, it was a message that was to have particular strength as the campaign wore on.

With Frank Rizzo's official entry into the campaign that January night, the race for mayor began in full force. And with it came the race to cover the race—by the four local television stations, by the two major daily newspapers, and by the five or six radio stations with news operations.

For the next several months, Tia O'Brien, Sal Paolantonio, and the other reporters assigned to cover the election would find themselves alternately pursuing and being pursued by the campaign staffs. Reporters would court and cajole and massage their private sources in the hopes of getting a scoop on the hard-won endorsements, the fundraising strategies, and the backroom deals. But they would also be besieged by press releases, position papers, court documents, and phone messages left by campaign managers, press secretaries, and the scores of other political operatives who were all trying to put their spin on the coverage.

At the same time, the reporters would be confronted with the ever-changing demands of news organizations affected by the short-run crunch of a recession and the long-term loss of audiences and advertisers to an increasing array of competitors. The *Inquirer* was facing competition from suburban dailies, community weeklies, and direct mail, while local television stations were losing more and more viewers to cable. Management was also increasingly concerned with demographics. The reporters would be covering the election of the man who would govern a city of some 1.5 million people at a time of unprecedented social and economic upheaval. But they would be producing stories for television stations and newspapers whose target audiences were increasingly suburban—people who were affected less and less by city elections.

Over the next several months, millions of dollars would be spent on television and radio advertising, and countless hours would be put into public appearances at forums, community meetings, transit stops, and churches. But news coverage would send the most powerful messages, influencing how voters cast their ballots—or whether they would even go to the polls come election day.

It would be a campaign in which television played an unprecedented role, as more and more Philadelphians turned to local newscasts for information. But it would also be a time when local stations were cutting staff, trading in experienced veterans for lower-salaried newcomers, and turning away from the kind of news that consultants claimed didn't sell: stories about politics and government. If candidates couldn't supply the drama and emotion of a five-year-old's murder by a drive-by shooter or the ultrasimplified prescriptions of a consumer or health report, then they were not going to be seen much on television news in 1991.

To save time and money, television would rely more than ever on the city's metropolitan newspaper for direction. In the 1991 Philadelphia mayoral race, broadcast journalists would take their cues almost exclusively from a single individual: the *Inquirer*'s political reporter, Sal Paolantonio. Although that reporter would be accused of everything from harboring a personal vendetta against one of the candidates, to letting the drive to get onto page 1 distort his coverage, that would not stop his stories from sending powerful signals to campaign contributors, city voters, and many time-pressed television reporters.

It would be an election in which the voters of Philadelphia faced an unprecedented degree of choice and in which the issues facing the city had never been more serious. But in the media, campaign strategy, poll results, and personal attacks would take precedence over plans and proposals. Informed debate over the hard decisions facing a bankrupt city would be submerged beneath the question of whether one of the candidates was a drunk. And the wide range of candidates offering themselves to voters would be effectively narrowed down by an unspoken media consensus that some candidates were worth covering while others could be safely ignored.

It would be an election in which the problems of the city had never been more complex but in which the themes of the media coverage would never be simpler. "New faces" would be pitted against "old faces," while old-fashioned mudslinging would be played off against newfangled techno-speak. White candidates would be dogged by issues of "character," while African American candidates would only be asked about whether one or more of them would drop out of the race in the interest of black unity. Candidates would all but do cartwheels off City Hall tower to draw reporters to their press conferences, but if they let on that they would be speaking about the problems of the city, the TV stations would ignore them.

In the course of the campaign, Philadelphia's newspapers and television stations would not simply be covering an election for mayor. They would also be experimenting with any number of changes to maintain their dwindling audiences in the face of new competition. All too often, the changes would not improve the way citizens were being informed about government in the nation's increasingly troubled central cities. Instead of stimulating civic involvement, news coverage of local elections would foster cynicism and indifference.

In Philadelphia the message would be clear. The 1991 mayoral campaign would fascinate newspaper readers and television viewers more than any other campaign in recent memory. But it would also turn out to be a year in which record numbers of voters would sit out election day because they were so disenchanted with what they had read and watched as the media made hay of the mayor's race.

2 It's a Users' Business

January 1991

🎐 Frank Rizzo wasn't the only veteran politician attempting a comeback in 1991. Democrat Edward G. Rendell was making what could be his last run for elected office. Rendell's political career had been a history of ups and downs. In 1977, he triumphed over the entrenched leadership of the Democratic party by defeating incumbent district attorney Emmet Fitzpatrick in a surprise upset, and he easily won re-election in 1981. But then in 1986 he suffered a crushing defeat when he ran in the Democratic primary for governor against Bob Casey. The following year, he lost another primary challenge, this time to Wilson Goode for mayor of Philadelphia.

Rendell was all too aware that if he lost this time, his career in politics was over. And he was determined not to lose. Rendell had started planning his campaign almost two years before the election, and at its heart was a media strategy calculated down to the last detail. Rendell understood what made reporters tick almost well enough to write a primer. As district attorney, he had been adept at using the media to whip up public opinion to change laws and to deter criminals and, not incidentally, to make himself look good. He had learned from a shrewd press secretary that you didn't get anything on TV without serving up nice, tidy pictures. If you wanted to publicize a police sting on credit card fraud by downtown merchants, you had to display confiscated tape players and gold jewelry at a press conference. When you wanted to hawk a new program to fingerprint children to prevent abductions, you fingerprinted your own son to get the TV cameras out. (Rendell had been amazed at how much media attention that little gimmick had attracted.) If you were in a hurry, but they needed some extra time for set-ups, then you stayed to give them their set-ups. You wanted them to know that you understood their needs so that they'd understand yours.

But Rendell had learned in his last two unsuccessful bids that getting the kind of coverage that gets you elected to office was a different ball game from getting good ink as an officeholder. So this time around, he had attracted high-priced talent: attorney David L. Cohen to serve as his campaign manager and veteran consultant Neil Oxman to develop his media strategy. Rendell was determined to use what he already knew about the press and follow the orders of Cohen and Oxman when it came to things he wasn't so good at. He knew the basics, like maintaining accessibility. From the outset of his campaign, it was decided that David Cohen would be available to answer reporters' questions at any minute of the day, whether from the office or through his beeper. There would never be a time when reporters could not get their questions answered.

Cohen and Oxman forced on Rendell a second key tenet: Never talk politics to reporters. There were few topics Rendell liked better than politics, but talking politics would reinforce his image as an old pol, a hack, and keep him from looking "mayoral." So it was decided that all questions about politics or strategy—a reaction to the latest poll, an explanation of the new advertising spot, a prediction about the black vote—would be handled by David Cohen. In this way, the media would get their questions answered—and Cohen was a master at providing reporters with succinct information that cast his candidate in the best light—and Rendell would only be shown discussing the city's problems.

But those ground rules were only the beginning. Figuring out how to get covered for what he wanted to be covered for was much more complex. Rendell knew he was not and would never be a Frank Rizzo, who regaled the local press corps with his colorful quotes and outrageous statements. A headline with Ed Rendell's name in it would never sell papers the way Frank Rizzo's could. But he also knew that with all of Rizzo's skill in attracting publicity, the headlines and sound-bites hadn't always worked in the former mayor's interest. The famous Rizzoisms—he had once claimed that he would make "Attila the Hun look like a faggot"—had gotten him quoted frequently but had also helped lose him his last three electoral bids.

Not only did Rizzo have a talent for putting words together like few others, he offered something else reporters loved: controversy. Rendell knew that you could always make headlines if you were willing to be controversial. But he also knew that if you were a public official, more often than not you were going to land on the wrong side of the controversy, with little recourse to making your case. When Rendell looked at a newspaper reporter, he didn't see someone with the noble goal of informing the electorate. He saw someone hungry for the ultimate journalistic coup, making page 1. What bothered him most about reporters was how they would figure out a preconceived story line in any controversy and then emphasize the facts that supported the preconception while ignoring facts that weakened it.

Like the story of his parking tickets. Toward the end of his second term as D.A., reporters found out that Rendell had gotten a number of tickets discharged, including several he had received while on personal errands. Rendell knew he had made a mistake by lumping together tickets he had gotten while at a crime scene with those he'd received while taking a midday break with his son at the swim club, and he knew it was fair game for the media to report it. But he wished they had printed what he had said in his defense. For eight years he had been the only high-ranking city official to refuse a driver and bodyguards. By driving himself, he had incurred some $900 in parking tickets, but he had also saved the city at least a quarter of a million dollars, he estimated. But reporters were hot to use the incident as another example of a public official ripping off the city, and they refused to consider all the facts.

When it came to covering the election, Rendell knew that reporters would need an angle to get on page 1. At a journalist's newspaper like the *Inquirer,* political reporting no longer meant reporting what candidates said about issues of substance. Even though Rendell planned to focus his campaign on the issues, generating position papers on all of the city's problems, he knew those positions would not get much ink. Instead, the reporters would analyze why candidates said what they did. Or worse, they would not even report what the candidates said, at least not in any comprehensive way, but rather would pick out an isolated sentence here and there with which to stir up controversy where none existed, to make the election more interesting.

He knew exactly how reporters would try to make good copy of this primary. At least initially, they would divide the field of candidates along "old face/new face" lines. Eight years in office as a respected district attorney and four campaigns under his belt would not qualify Rendell to be the "experienced former official." It would simply leave him tinged with the aura of the veteran political hack. Sure enough, in Sal Paolantonio's story about Rendell's announcement in October 1990, he had begun, "Edward G. Rendell, the former district attorney who has not won an election in nine years, yesterday became the first official candidate in the 1991 mayoral campaign."

The treatment would be different, Rendell knew, for one of his opponents, Peter Hearn. Hearn was a prominent center-city lawyer who had
never run for office and who was trying to fashion himself as an "outsider"
untainted by the deal making and corruption of politics. Three times in
1990, Hearn's campaign—and his ability to raise money—had taken off
almost as a direct result of the angle of Sal Paolantonio's stories about him.
The first had run in March, when the reporter described Hearn's successful
fundraising visit to a wealthy businessman. And then in November, when
Hearn became the first mayoral candidate to go on television with ads—
telling Philadelphians that he was different, that he was not one of the
politicians who had brought this city to the brink, and that this was "no
time for politics as usual"—two more Paolantonio stories had touted the
popularity of the Hearn "outsider" theme with Philadelphians.

To Rendell, Peter Hearn was hardly an outsider. He knew Hearn as a
politically connected lawyer with a major law firm in Philadelphia who
had played the political game that all lawyers in that position play, bankrolling candidates for office. Hearn had even served as Wilson Goode's
inaugural chairman in 1987. But Rendell, Cohen, and Oxman recognized
that the "outsider" message had struck a chord with voters—polls showed
Hearn's ratings with likely Democratic voters burgeoned after the ads
ran—and, perhaps even more importantly, that the message had struck a
chord with the reporters covering the campaign. Fresh faces were always
going to get better play than veterans.

The "old face/new face" refrain was not going to be the only theme to
dominate campaign coverage, however. In a city in which a majority of the
Democratic party was now African American, race was going to be a
major factor in the outcome of the primary. And in 1991, not one but
three black candidates were considering a run for the Democratic nomination. The most formidable was expected to be George Burrell, a former
deputy mayor who had recently resigned from his city council seat to
make a run for the city's top office. Burrell enjoyed the support of Congressman William Gray, who as majority whip of the U.S. House of Representatives could bring both money and political expertise to Burrell's
campaign. But another city councilman, Lucien Blackwell, a longtime foe
of both Burrell and Gray, was also eyeing the field. Whereas Burrell held
an at-large Council seat with both white and black constituents, Blackwell
represented predominantly black, lower-middle-class West Philadelphia
and had strong union ties in the city. And then there was James White,
Wilson Goode's managing director for five years, who had the support of
the city's municipal unions.

With the possibility of two or even three black candidates entering the race, Rendell knew the other media theme would center on racial polariza-tion. No matter how much he would try to argue that he could be the consensus candidate to bring Philadelphians of all races together, Rendell would constantly be dogged by claims that he was unable to draw black votes away from a black candidate. They would bring up again and again the so-called promise he had been accused of breaking to Philadelphia's black clergy when he was running for governor. (The clergy claimed Rendell had promised that, in return for their support in the governor's race, he would never challenge Wilson Goode for mayor. He claimed he never made such a promise.) He would have to fight the media's natural gravitation to both themes—Hearn's appeal as the "outsider" and the no-tion that blacks would repudiate any white candidate—if he was going to get the kind of news coverage that would help him win votes.

And there was only one way that Rendell, Cohen, and Oxman could counteract this. They would appeal to the media's preoccupation with the horse race and reporters' unquestioning reverence for numbers. They would use polls. Reporters don't want your housing program, Rendell would say, but they love to talk about polls. And so Rendell and his media strategists determined at the outset of the campaign to use polls to their advantage. They would try to make it seem that Peter Hearn was a total longshot, that nobody thought he was a credible candidate, and that he wasn't making any headway with the public. And they would use polls to show that Rendell would get a sizable chunk of the black vote.

The strategy went beyond simply polling; it meant polling early and often. Rendell himself was under no false illusions that voters were en-thralled by him or that his supporters felt anywhere near the depth of emotion that Frank Rizzo's supporters felt. But he was clearly the best known among the Democratic candidates. Rendell liked to joke about how his son, Jesse, had encouraged him to run, claiming he just knew his dad would win. "Why's that?" asked Rendell, expecting to hear his son loyally recite what a good mayor he would make. But Jesse Rendell, at age nine, was already a political pragmatist. "Because you're the best known," he'd said. And while Rendell would always laugh telling the story, he and Oxman and Cohen knew all too well that being the best known—and generally liked—meant that you would dominate the polls early on. And they knew that those polls would be picked up by all the political reporters in town, particularly Sal Paolantonio, who liked polls and included them in his stories whenever he could. In late November 1990 the reporter had snapped up the results of a Temple University professor's election poll (a poll other reporters in town were quite skeptical of) to proclaim that Rendell had a "sizable lead" in the Democratic race.

The Rendell team was only too delighted with such stories because the people with the deep pockets in Philadelphia paid close attention to which candidate the *Inquirer* said was in the lead. No matter what the *Daily News* had to say, *Inquirer* stories about candidates prompted people to open—or close—their wallets. The more money Rendell received as a result of such coverage, the more he could advertise, which in turn would mean the higher his numbers were likely to be in the next poll, which again would be released to the press. It was a carefully calculated chain of events that Rendell and his advisors were banking on to take the unexciting early favorite into city hall. And it was predicated on the basic hunger, obsession even, of reporters to tell their audiences who was ahead and who was behind.

Knowing what reporters liked and didn't like to cover guided every step of Rendell's media plan. Although his campaign was dedicated to coming up with the most pragmatic and effective approaches to the crushing issues facing Philadelphia in 1991, he didn't believe for a minute that reporters would spend much time or energy writing about either the problems or the solutions. And if they did, those stories would be given little time or newspaper space. He believed instead that journalism was simply about selling newspapers and getting TV ratings. And he and his advisers knew pretty well what journalists thought would sell: color, controversy, and the horse race. If they couldn't deliver on the first and wouldn't deliver on the second, they would be sure to make the third work. They would give reporters the kind of information that would make for good stories and at the same time boost Ed Rendell's chances for victory.

"It's a users' business," Rendell would note after the election. "They use you. You use them."

3 The Right Stuff

February 1991

Sal Paolantonio was well aware of the credo voiced by Ed Rendell, as he embarked on coverage of the hottest election of his career. He knew all too well that both politics and journalism were users' businesses. To him, it was the ultimate "buyer beware" situation with journalists and their political sources. Candidates and their staffs were there to exploit the situation, put their spin on every story, and a journalist had to be aware of that. Particularly if you were writing for the *Inquirer*, people were going to try to use you. Everyone wanted to get their stories in the *Inquirer*, the "paper of record" in town. A story in the *Inquirer* was golden; you could xerox it and send it out to your contributors.

But if Paolantonio was wary of his sources' motives, he thought they had to recognize his, too. It was not the journalist's job to promote candidates and help them win. Reporters were out to "use" the candidates and their campaigns, doing everything they could to get information out of them. Some of that information might be good for the candidate, but much more of it—a lot more, if Paolantonio had his way—would be the kind that made campaign managers grimace. This campaign would be a pivotal moment in Sal Paolantonio's career, and he was not going to go at it like some stenographer sifting through press releases. He'd rather be a lightning bolt than a stenographer any day of the week.

But while Paolantonio would have agreed with Rendell about the symbiosis between reporters and candidates, the two parted ways when it came to what motivated their professions. As much as he loved covering politics, as much as he lived and breathed elections for months at a time,

Paolantonio was almost completely cynical about its practitioners. To him, politics in 1991 was just another form of selling soap. It was about moving a product and doing it with all the latest marketing techniques. He believed that most politicians would say just about anything to voters if their marketing surveys told them the message would get votes.

As for his own profession, and in particular his own brand of political reporting, Paolantonio had a loftier view. He liked to describe himself as somebody who was protecting the consumer by remaining skeptical of every move made in a campaign. Although he knew all the criticisms academics made of news coverage that emphasized strategy over substance, he maintained that strategy was important and valid because all too frequently campaign strategy was based on marketing strategy. To him, if you didn't tell people how a candidate suddenly got religion about health care, then you weren't telling people what they needed to know about this candidate.

But the deeper truth was that he loved campaign strategy in and of itself. He loved figuring out how one candidate would attack and another would block and defend, in the same way that he loved following sports and the U.S. military's game plan against Iraq. All through the campaign, he would sprinkle his stories with sports and military analogies (campaigns would be preparing "smart bombs," candidates would need to "go both ways . . . on offense and defense") because politics, sports, and war all involved some of the same elements for him. It wasn't just winning and losing, either. Like the old cliché, it was how you played the game—how skillfully you plotted out the moves, how bold and daring was your assault. The real winners were those who could pull off the unexpected move and take in the entire pot. Whether in football, a bombing offensive, or a mayor's race, the losers were the guys who didn't have the "right stuff," the candidates who "wimped out."

He himself had no intention of wimping out when it came to covering this election. He wanted to smash the competition, even though he knew the competition would be nothing like what he was up against when he covered the New Jersey governor's race for the *Inquirer,* when he went head to head with the New York media as well as the locals. Here it would be the *Inquirer*'s tabloid stepsister, the *Daily News,* and a few TV stations, if they bothered to take time out from covering all the fires and murders. But even if he didn't think much of the competition, he still wanted to beat them. Once, when asked to define his objective as a reporter, he said it was to make his competitors wake up in the morning, look at his story in the paper, and say, "Oh, shit."

But it was to his own colleagues at the *Inquirer* that he had something to prove this time around. Taking on the plum assignment of covering the Philadelphia mayor's race seemed to him to create a certain amount of resentment. Paolantonio had only been at the *Inquirer* for six years, but he had impressed his editor, Bill Marimow, in his last beat, covering the New Jersey gubernatorial election. When Marimow became city editor, he brought Paolantonio with him to cover city politics, despite the fact that more seasoned reporters might have taken the assignment. In the last mayoral election, H. G. (Buzz) Bissinger had the beat. Bissinger had been a veteran *Inquirer* reporter at the time and had already won a Pulitzer Prize for his reporting on the courts. But Paolantonio was a relative newcomer and was only thirty-three when he took over the beat, starting out covering city legislative races in 1990.

He soon felt that other reporters at the paper were jealous of how much he got into the paper and how often his stories made page 1. And he also felt like the victim of prejudice at the paper because he was Italian. When he first came to the *Inquirer,* a reporter passing by his desk had called out to him: " 'S. A. Paolantonio?' That sounds like it ought to be on the side of a cement truck, not a byline." He had never forgotten that line, and he had never taken it as a joke.

But outside the paper it was different. He thought of himself as a "man's man," a characteristic that served him well in the almost entirely male world of Philadelphia politics in the early 1990s. He was tall and athletically built, the result of long hours spent playing basketball and tennis, and he often used his interest in sports as an icebreaker with political figures. While in his pinstripe shirts, Brooks Brothers ties, and loafers with tassels, he looked like most of his yuppie colleagues at the paper, and although he had grown up not on red gravy but Ragu sauce from a jar, he used his ethnic roots to court many of Philadelphia's street-smart politicians. He used to marvel at the thought of himself as a punk from the suburbs of New York who had wound up covering the inside story of mayoral politics in one of the nation's largest cities.

And part of his success was his ability to connect with sources in a personal way. One of the subtle tools he brought to being a political reporter was using his personality to charm people, to get them to like him, to relate to him, to trust him, so that they would tell him things—and tell him first. It was not that he would out and out mislead his sources by claiming that he was their friend. It was simply that he would act like a friend in the course of doing his job. He'd invite them to a basketball game or take them to lunch, trying to make them feel comfortable enough with him to get them talking in a less guarded way. He would find the subject, even the lingo, of the person he was courting and use it to connect in a

personal way and make them feel he was on their side. Where other reporters adopted an air of formality around their sources, Paolantonio got
up-front and personal.

There were other things that set Paolantonio apart from his colleagues.
Where other reporters wrote their stories and pretty much let their editors
decide where an article would be placed in the paper, Paolantonio was
more a proponent of the hard-sell. Time and again he would make the case
for why his story represented a crucial turning point in the campaign,
encouraging play on page 1 or on the first page of the metro section. He
would succeed because he had an incredible ability to work the angles of a
story, to piece together bits of information to produce drama. Part of his
success in gathering those revealing bits of information had to do with his
prodigious work habits. Some days he'd be on the phone for hours, aggressively massaging his sources, sometimes as many as thirty-five people a
day, digging out the details of this behind-the-scenes meeting or that clandestine phone call. He'd get his information by being everywhere, sometimes starting his day at seven in the morning to catch the Mary Mason
show on the city's black radio station ("required listening," he'd call it)
and ending it at ten at night at a ward leaders' meeting. But the long hours
were just the beginning. If he was really going to show the "right stuff" in
covering this election, it would be because he had the balls to step out on a
limb and interpret what he saw happening. "I love being on the edge," he
would say. "I live for it."

As it turned out, 1991 would prove a good moment at the *Inquirer* for a
reporter who wasn't afraid to put his own interpretation on a story, a
reporter who knew how to take potentially dry and boring material and
transform it into an intriguing saga. The newspaper was in a state of
transition. Its beloved longtime executive editor, Gene Roberts, had just
left the paper after eighteen years. Word in the newsroom was that Roberts had grown tired of the continual battles he had to fight with Miami
(the headquarters of the Knight-Ridder chain, which owned both the *Inquirer* and the *Daily News*), and of trying to maintain the journalistic
quality of the paper under the increasing onslaught of an ever more bottom line–oriented corporation. Maxwell E. P. King, an *Inquirer* veteran of
almost twenty years, had worked his way up through the news ranks to
take Roberts's place. While King had no intention of making wholesale
changes in the in-depth journalism pioneered by his esteemed predecessor,
as a modern-day editor, he could not ignore economic realities. The recession was hurting all the media, and the *Inquirer*'s circulation was relatively
stagnant overall. The paper was losing readers in the city and gaining in
the suburbs, but there was no denying that even in the suburbs circulation

increases were not keeping up with household growth. Clearly, the future of the paper was going to depend on how well it could perform in the outlying areas. A new printing plant was being built out in the western suburbs, far away from the downtown headquarters. It would have the capability to turn out color photos, to more easily zone local news sections, and to get papers out to suburban lawns early in the morning with late sports results. But it was ultimately the news coverage that would keep readers from canceling their subscriptions. A great deal of effort was being invested in designing the paper's zoning strategy for the suburbs and in rethinking the nature of the stories that would make page 1.

The editors would go back and forth over the question of whether a deliberate effort should be made to get more suburban stories on the front page. But one thing was becoming clear: increasingly, for city stories to make page 1, they were going to have to have broad appeal or relevance to the suburban audience. Reporters were also being encouraged to get away from their traditionally dry way of laying out the simple facts about a story and to put more color and flair in their writing. Interpretation was being encouraged as one of any number of strategies to keep people reading newspapers. And so when Sal Paolantonio arrived in Philadelphia to cover the mayor's race, it was in some ways a match made in heaven. The newspaper needed some drama to make a mayor's race more compelling to its entire regional audience and the young, ambitious reporter seemed to have a knack for doing just that. It became clear to him very quickly that something extra was going to be required to get a city politics story on page 1. His story on Rendell's announcement back in October, for instance, had made only the metro section's first page, while in 1987 Rendell's entrance into the primary race to challenge Wilson Goode had been front-page news.

While Paolantonio may have been more out on the edge than his colleagues in the *Inquirer* tower on North Broad Street, in many ways his approach to political reporting was part of the national tide. Where in the sixties journalists covering presidential elections summarized speeches and described platforms, two decades later political reporters saw themselves in a more active role. They knew they had been used over and over again by savvy media consultants to transmit positive messages for candidates. Their response was to place increasing emphasis on campaign strategy itself, as a means of showing voters how the candidates were trying to manipulate images about themselves. It was also, however, a way to make campaign coverage more interesting. If reporters were convinced that the public was bored by the issues, then a focus on campaign game plans could offer a way to make political coverage as compelling as the sports page. By 1991, political reporters throughout the country were starting to regard the issues in a campaign as a mere stopping point on the way to bigger and better analysis pieces on strategy. Now, if an excerpt was picked out of a politician's speech, it was to show how the candidate was exploiting some political opportunity. Advertising campaigns and poll results were getting all the attention, not stands on economic development and health care.

And then there was the new concern with the candidates' private lives. When Paul Taylor, a former *Inquirer* reporter who had gone to the *Washington Post* to cover presidential politics, had staked out Gary Hart's townhouse in Washington in search of proof of marital infidelity, suddenly the personal lives of candidates became fair game for investigative reporting. The Washington press corps would claim that what went on behind closed doors was important in evaluating a candidate's character and judgment, not merely a new way to titillate the audience, and now the rationale was beginning to filter down to the local level. While personal questions had not figured into previous mayoral campaign coverage in Philadelphia, the 1991 mayoral race might be very different.

Sal Paolantonio was determined to be out in front on all of it. In the previous year he had been so bent on covering all the bases in his next assignment that he went about reading everything he could, whether in paper or electronic files, on the people who might be running for mayor. And in his search, personal issues were every bit as important as public ones. In July and August 1990, in a lull in the legislative campaigns he was then covering, he had started digging deeper for background on the possible mayoral candidates. With the help of an assistant, he had searched SEC documents for trade violations and civil dockets for any court cases involving the candidates. And the searches had paid off. He was looking for something new, some transgression by one of the potential mayoral candidates that no one else had found.

And in the court dockets, he hit pay dirt with George Burrell.

4 Feeding the Story

February 1991

✿ While Sal Paolantonio was a reporter who liked to use sports analo-gies to liven up his political stories, George Burrell was a candidate who hoped to use his real-life experience on the playing fields as a metaphor for the grit and determination and teamwork that were needed to run a city. He had played professional football for the Denver Broncos after graduat-ing from the University of Pennsylvania in 1969, and he knew how Ameri-cans revere their sports heros. Being a professional athlete could be particularly helpful to a black politician, who needed to work extra hard in breaking down barriers with white voters.

Although his career in football ended after only one season, George Burrell had enjoyed professional success in other areas. He went to law school at Penn, served as deputy mayor in Bill Green's administration in the early '80s, and had a private law practice in the city. In 1987 he made his first run at public office as an at-large candidate for city council and won with the fundraising support of U.S. Congressman Bill Gray. In coun-cil, Burrell had taken the "good government" positions against the power-ful ruling clique of fellow black councilmen Lucien Blackwell, John Street, and president Joe Coleman. Now he was hoping to draw on the popular dissatisfaction with city council—former Mayor Green had called it the "worst legislative body in the Western World"—to catapult himself into the mayor's office. Like Peter Hearn, Burrell also hoped to be viewed as the "outsider." In Burrell's case, he wanted to be viewed as having been outside the loop of power in city council that had brought the city to the brink of bankruptcy. He was billing himself as the candidate who could best build a multiracial coalition to work for fiscal responsibility without abandoning social concern.

But to have any chance of occupying City Hall, Burrell and the other black candidates were going to have to come to terms with the legacy of W. Wilson Goode, the city's first black mayor. For a city that by 1980 was almost 40 percent black, Philadelphia had come late to electing an African American as its top executive. Los Angeles, where blacks represented only 17 percent of the population, had elected Tom Bradley mayor in 1973 and had kept him in office ever since. But Los Angeles did not have Philadelphia's strong Democratic party machine, which had long stood in the way of black political power in the city.

In the 1960s, machine-backed mayor James H. J. Tate had doled out federal antipoverty funds and patronage jobs to blacks to secure their support at election time, but he had carefully kept blacks out of leadership positions in government. It was part of the Democratic party's plan to assuage the city's white working class, as was Tate's appointment of the charismatic cop from South Philly, Frank Rizzo, as his police commissioner. But when Rizzo ran for mayor himself in 1971—when he campaigned almost exclusively in white neighborhoods, promising to keep housing projects out, to prevent school busing to achieve racial balance, and to get tough on crime—blacks stopped going along with the party's plan. Although Rizzo won the election, this was the first time that black voters, along with liberal whites, abandoned the Democratic party on a massive scale.

Rizzo's eight years in office—particularly his support of the police at a time when most blacks felt there was rampant brutality—only served to increase black political unity in Philadelphia. In 1975, black attorney Charles Bowser ran against Rizzo and won 25 percent of the vote in the three-way race. But the real leap forward in black political power came in 1978, when Rizzo tried to change the city charter to run for a third term and issued a call to "Vote White." A voter registration drive pushed black registration way up, and black turnout jumped from 35 percent in the 1975 mayoral election to 63 percent in the charter reform vote. Rizzo's attempt to change the charter was opposed by 67 percent of the electorate.

Wilson Goode came to political power when Rizzo's successor, former Congressman Bill Green, appointed Goode as his managing director, fulfilling a campaign pledge to hire a black for the position. When Green declined to run for re-election, Goode took his place. Campaigning as a highly educated, hardworking, professional manager, he won 23 percent of the white vote, along with 97 percent of the black vote. But while

Goode started his tenure in City Hall with high hopes and widespread support from both blacks and whites, the MOVE disaster in his second year in office changed all that. A prolonged investigation by a blue-ribbon commission appointed by Goode himself dragged on for a year. He was eventually accused of abandoning his command responsibilities in the emergency. Compounding the problem was the discovery that the construction firm selected by Goode to rebuild the burned-down homes was being investigated for improprieties and cost overruns. Goode's reputation as the hands-on efficient technocrat was forever sullied. When he ran for re-election against newly turned Republican Frank Rizzo in 1987, he won by a mere 17,000 votes. Blacks had continued to support the mayor, turning out at a rate of about 70 percent, with 97 percent voting for Goode and against Rizzo. But his support in the white community had dwindled, and whites had continued to defect to the Republican party. Any black candidate hoping to follow Goode into the mayor's office was going to have to distinguish himself from the image of incompetency that Wilson Goode was carrying out of office.

But in 1991, George Burrell faced a larger hurdle than the legacy of the city's first black mayor. Most people in the city didn't know who he was. Although he had served in city council for three years, he was hardly a media darling. Councilman John Street from poor black North Philadelphia and Councilwoman Joan Krajewski from working-class white Kensington knew how to emerge from a council meeting with the perfect, flamboyant eight-second sound-bite that got them onto the six o'clock news. But Burrell had never displayed the same talent. Although he had often voted against the positions of the politically entrenched majority coalition, he had not figured out how to get much positive media coverage for what he had done. He had the reasonable but naive expectation that maybe reporters ought to be concerned with why a councilman had taken a particular position and not just focus on whether he had won or lost. He thought they shouldn't have to have stories hand-delivered to them, complete with emotional sound-bites and good backdrops, before they would investigate whether a proposal or plan made sense. He thought that reporters should at least sometimes take the initiative in looking for a story. Unfortunately for George Burrell, it didn't really work that way.

In the last year, Burrell had succeeded in getting some headlines for his attempt to secure passage of a bill in council regulating the street vendors who crowded city sidewalks, obstructing pedestrian traffic, and blocking entrances to city stores. But he had little success either in getting the legislation passed or in improving his public image through his efforts. The angry vendors had proved to be shrewder than Burrell in attracting media attention with their vocal demonstrations and in marshaling the political power to block the bill's passage. As a result, news coverage had focused more on the controversy the ordinance had engendered than on the potential benefits of the legislation for the city. Only one of his two vendor bills was approved.

Even when Burrell set out deliberately to attract media attention, his attempts boomeranged. Before leaving council in December to run for mayor, he had held a press conference to lay out his proposal for solving the city's budget crisis. As one element in the plan, he had called for the firing of the city's finance director, Betsy Reveal, who had become something of a household word during the fiscal crisis. Sure enough, the TV stations turned out to cover the story. Assignment editors leaped at any kind of dramatic, emotional dimension that could humanize a city government story.

But to the newspaper reporters who covered Burrell's press conference, the call for firing Betsy Reveal looked like a cheap trick. Although the finance director was often the bearer of bad tidings, they thought, she could hardly be blamed for the impending bankruptcy. Sal Paolantonio, who had covered Burrell's press conference for the *Inquirer,* decided to center his story on criticisms of Burrell's call to fire Reveal that came from other politicians whom the reporter had immediately called for reaction. By the end of the first five paragraphs of Paolantonio's story, Burrell had been attacked by Mayor Goode as being "as much to blame for the city's fiscal quagmire as any other politician in the city" and by an adviser to Lucien Blackwell as "a desperate, desperate guy." Burrell had tried to play the media game but failed. He had gotten some TV coverage for his plan, but he had also produced scathing newspaper coverage.

Now, five months later, the Reveal story long forgotten, George Burrell still had no strong image beyond being "Bill Gray's man." Right after Burrell's announcement in December, the *Inquirer* had run a picture of the two men which showed a smiling Gray with his arm around Burrell's shoulder—and Burrell's back to the camera. The photograph sent a message to readers that the most important thing worth knowing about George Burrell was the fact that Bill Gray supported—some might say anointed—him. It was a suggestion that particularly irked Burrell. He really felt that reporters developed what he called "marketable theories" about the way politics worked and then set out to sustain them. The tale of the seemingly Machiavellian maneuvers of Bill Gray, a local politician who was making his mark in the national arena, seemed to be a better story than the little known city councilman who wanted to put more money into human services.

To Burrell, it was ridiculous to suggest that the only reason he was in this campaign was because Bill Gray had tapped him on the shoulder and said, "You, you're gonna run for mayor." Everybody in the political structure in town understood that Bill Gray's first choice for mayor had been John White, the state welfare secretary. It was only after White had decided not to be a candidate for mayor that Gray decided to support Burrell's candidacy. And for all the time that Gray had been encouraging White to run, Burrell had been out there, trying to drum up support. Everywhere he went, people wanted to know if he would get Gray's support. But when he got it, instead of being regarded as an effective politician, he was suddenly viewed as just a pawn in Bill Gray's attempts to amass further power in Philadelphia. The reporters never even tried to determine whether it was true, he would think; they merely searched for some politician to whom the theory could be attributed. All it took was for one public person to agree to be quoted about something to make one of these "facts" take on a life of its own in the press.

If the articles ever got beyond the plane of pure political intrigue tied to Gray—which wasn't often, in Burrell's opinion—then they made the other simplistic assumption about the candidates: Burrell's for taxes, Blackwell's against taxes. What they didn't report, but what George Burrell believed and was trying to get across in his campaign, was that the city had to do something about human services and homelessness and AIDS. He wasn't calling for more taxes. He wanted to redirect existing resources into places he thought were important, like taking money out of a fund for street alley lighting and putting it into AIDS programs. He knew everybody thought it was the African American position to be for human services as opposed to being a responsible fiscal manager. But Burrell's argument was that the failure to address human services issues in Philadelphia was really as much an economic development issue as a human issue. He believed that the main asset the city had to attract businesses and keep them was the size and quality of the work force. If the city didn't respond to the human services crisis, if they didn't do something about the abused and neglected kids who were dropping out of school at alarming rates, there was going to be more than a big drug and crime problem. There was going to be a work force problem that would further drive businesses out of the city.

But Burrell's ideas for running Philadelphia were not what drew media attention upon his entrance into the race—his ties to the well-known Congressman Gray were—and Burrell knew he remained largely an unknown political commodity. His campaign's plan was to raise enough money to be able to advertise on television and get across his message to Philadelphians—to use money to "define" George Burrell. The strategy was not new in local races, where candidates' television advertising often far outstripped their news coverage and where the size of campaign war chests determined who would win elections, not the images projected on the news. But there were two problems with the strategy in Burrell's case. One was that mayoralty races received a lot of attention in the local media— more than just about any other campaign besides that for the presidency— and Burrell and the other mayoral contenders were liable to get cast in a bad light by their news coverage before their ads had a chance to define them. And then there was the other problem: Burrell's fundraising efforts were moving slowly. Unlike Wilson Goode's campaigns, which had drawn much financial support from the city's movers and shakers, Burrell was having a harder time filling his coffers. Some people in his campaign suspected that the powers that be in the city simply didn't want another black mayor after their experience with Wilson Goode.

There was not even the comfort of being the sole black candidate in the race. If Lucien Blackwell and James White both ran, the black vote would be divided, and victory would be more likely for one of the two white candidates. Burrell's campaign people were hoping, however, that they could keep Blackwell and White out of the race by garnering the endorsements of the key black organizations. The most important was the United Black Clergy of Philadelphia and Vicinity, 450 black clergymen who represented 250,000 church members and who in previous elections had used their church pulpits as rallying points for Wilson Goode. If the group endorsed Burrell at their February 1 meeting, the other two black candidates might stay out of the race. And then Burrell's chances would be much rosier.

As Burrell awaited the outcome of that meeting, he got a boost by landing on the cover of the latest *Philadelphia* magazine. The headline read: "George Burrell. Sam Katz. Who Are They Anyway?" This was a boon for name recognition—the magazine was on display at newsstands throughout the city—but the profile inside was hardly flattering. The author painted a picture of a vain and superficial man who had accomplished little in his pro football career, as deputy mayor, or in his law practice. He was described as twice divorced and barely on speaking terms with his two oldest children. The writer summed up his impression of Burrell near the end of the article: "Through several other interviews Burrell has managed to be talkative without really saying much. Though he is articulate and obviously smart, he has a tendency to speak in platitudes and is constantly bringing the conversation back to his campaign lines."

What *Philadelphia* magazine had failed to uncover in its lengthy profile, but which had not eluded the electronic searches of Sal Paolantonio, was that George Burrell had failed to repay some rather large loans.

In doing his routine search of the court dockets in the summer of 1990, Sal Paolantonio had come across a civil suit by a Herbert Reiss against a George Burrell. It seemed that in 1984 Reiss, a New York garment district worker, had sued Burrell for failing to pay back a $7,125 personal loan. But that was only the beginning of the story. Paolantonio also found out that in 1981, while he was deputy mayor of the city of Philadelphia, Burrell had also defaulted on three school loans from the University of Pennsylvania totaling $9,218 for undergraduate and law school. Four years later, he had also defaulted on a portion of another school loan owed to the Higher Education Assistance Authority in New Jersey. For a reporter looking for an undiscovered personal transgression by one of the candidates, Paolantonio had found his scoop.

The loan default story appeared on January 30, just two days before the black clergy were meeting to endorse a candidate. Under the headline "Burrell Was in Default on $16,755 in Loans," the story listed each loan that Burrell had failed to pay off. For his part, Burrell claimed that the defaults were the result of both his commitment to public service ("I am by choice a public servant who sacrificed a long time ago the ability to make a lot of money") and a "protracted domestic dispute." He also pointed out that he had eventually paid all the loans off. But Paolantonio's story noted that Burrell had paid only when forced to and that in one case the courts had drawn money from his bank account. The reporter also undercut Burrell's defense by quoting the *Philadelphia* article which had Burrell saying that when he first started working at a private law firm he was "making more money than I ever thought existed."

Paolantonio's story, although an investigative coup, was not given great play. It ran on the first page of the metro section, below the fold, with a small one-column headline. The reporter was disappointed with the play and thought the story should have run at least above the fold on 1-B and with a larger headline. But others at the paper had been more cautious, hesitant to overplay a story that had, after all, happened a number of years ago with nothing currently pending. Some of the caution might have reflected increasing concern about being accused of racism. A year ago, almost to the day, the paper had been savagely attacked on those very grounds by Mayor Goode because of a Sunday front-page article about how white voters were being turned off by the Democratic party's image as a "black party." A few months later, a group of black leaders had led a boycott against the *Daily News* because of a front page that gave more prominence to Mike Tyson's knockout than to Nelson Mandela's release from prison after twenty-six years. And then there was the *Inquirer* editorial that had run in December, headlined "Poverty and Norplant: Can Contraception Reduce the Underclass?" The editorial had suggested that the new contraceptive Norplant might be effective in reducing the number of black children living in poverty—an argument that had been attacked as racist by many outraged black (and white) staffers at the paper. Playing up a story about a scandal involving a past personal problem with one of the black candidates just might risk reawakening some of those raw nerves.

But the fact was that the play that an *Inquirer* story got was crucial in determining fallout. Front-page banners meant major scandal, but one-column headlines signaled only passing interest to readers. Even more important, a small headline buried at the bottom of the metro page of the *Inquirer* could easily be ignored by the other media in town. And that's exactly what the *Daily News* did the following day. There was no time for the *News* to duplicate Paolantonio's research, and Burrell wouldn't comment on the story, so their only alternative would have been to credit the *Inquirer* for the story. Despite the fact that the two newspapers were co-owned—or maybe because of it—*Daily News* editors and reporters were intensely competitive with the *Inquirer,* and they would do almost anything to avoid acknowledging one of its scoops.

The TV stations didn't give it much play, either. They were all out covering the campaign that day, reporting on a chamber of commerce candidates forum. But it was hard enough to figure out how to cram the highlights of six candidates' remarks into one minute and forty five seconds, which was all any of them had for the piece, much less add a story about Burrell's loan defaults. Only Vernon Odom of Channel 6 mentioned at the end of his story that night that Burrell's remarks came "amid published reports that he defaulted on five loans for over $16,000, all repaid, stemming from a domestic dispute with his ex-wife."

The coverage of the loans might have died then if Burrell hadn't made a crucial mistake that Saturday, when he was opening his campaign headquarters. Paolantonio was not planning to sacrifice his Saturday morning and his wife's exercise class to George Burrell's empty media event until he got a call at 7:30 that morning from Burrell's press secretary, Harriet Garrett, asking him if he was coming to the press conference. When he said he wasn't planning to, he heard her say, "Well, you'd better come because we're going to attack you and your story"—a threat he could not ignore. As it turned out, however, Paolantonio's name was never even mentioned at the press conference. Flanked by Congressman Bill Gray,

Burrell said, "I've never tried to run away from what my obligations are. I had problems. Everybody has problems. It was difficult." He added, "We didn't seek any ways to get out from under those obligations. We worked with people. We solved it. We settled it. We paid the people what they were owed." It was an eloquent defense, but in the process of making it, Burrell fell into the trap of keeping alive an issue that might have passed out of view as a one-day story. The press conference and Burrell's defense of his actions allowed Paolantonio to write a story for the next day, "Burrell Vows to Overcome Default Issue," in which he told the tale one more time, this time on page 1-B, above the fold, with a much larger headline.

To Paolantonio, Burrell's campaign had made a cataclysmic mistake. They had hand-delivered him a rationale for giving continued attention to his investigative coup. And what was perhaps worse, they had done it on a Saturday, so that Paolantonio's story would run on Sunday, when the paper has its largest circulation, with over two million readers. With one phone call from his press secretary, Burrell had prompted an extremely damaging story that might just sink his fledgling campaign. In the ensuing weeks, Burrell would continue to compound the error by making the small but significant mistakes that invited the *Inquirer* reporter to keep the loan default story alive. At a press conference a few weeks later to unveil a plan for combating drug-related crime in the city, Burrell made what he believed was a perfectly reasonable call for "a campaign about real issues, not focusing on personal issues." But by bringing up "personal issues," he gave Paolantonio an opening to repeat the information about the loan defaults once again. As a result, Burrell's problems with his loans got more attention than his drug plan. Paolantonio wrote:

> Burrell said that as mayor he would enhance special police units, post officers in front of known crack houses, build a 440-bed prison and criminal justice center and put more police on the street by eliminating "sneedless paperwork."

> In the last four weeks, Burrell has been dogged about his past personal finances, including reports that he defaulted on five loans totaling $16,755 from 1981 to 1985, including four from public agencies for his education at the University of Pennsylvania.

While Burrell's campaign staff members were infuriated by the repetition of the loan default story and by the way Burrell's proposals were being given short shrift, to Sal Paolantonio, it was legitimate campaign reporting and his editors backed him up all the way. He wasn't there to serve as a stenographer for all the candidates' proposals about crime and the economy. He was there to chronicle what he viewed as significant events in the campaign. In any press conference he was going to pick out the one or two sentences that he thought defined the campaign. If he had anything to do with it—as he surely did—the story about the loan defaults would become one such defining event, particularly if Burrell mentioned the matter himself. And defining moments warranted repetition.

It was Paolantonio's recapitulation of the loan default story in article after article that encouraged other reporters to pick up the story. Soon, Burrell found himself being identified in the media as the candidate with the personal financial problems, or worse, the deadbeat. The moniker was all the more threatening since it was defining Burrell at a time when he was a little-known quantity to most Philadelphians, before his campaign could pay for ads that would establish a more positive identity. He had been on the doorstep of getting the black clergy's endorsement and Wilson Goode's endorsement, and with that kind of support, Blackwell and White might well have stayed out, leaving Burrell the only black candidate in the race. But the second round of loan default stories, the stories that Burrell in his naïveté handed to Paolantonio, changed all that. They would allow Blackwell and White to get into the race, and they would irrevocably create an image for George Burrell that even the slickest advertising campaign would have difficulty overcoming.

Burrell had made the dangerous move of trying to lead in the dance between reporters and candidates without having sufficiently learned the steps.

5 Sex, Lies, and the Loquacious Candidate

February 1991

❦ In the summer of 1990, when *Philadelphia* magazine writer Lisa DePaulo first approached Sam Katz for a profile, he was not unlike the sophisticated but undiscovered little restaurants *Philadelphia* took pride in unveiling for its readers. Katz was young, wealthy, and articulate, a partner in Public Financial Management—a consulting firm which helped cities finance major capital projects like new sports arenas—and he was trying to parlay his fiscal expertise into a run for the mayor's office. He had started out as a liberal Democrat, working on the campaigns of Congressman Bill Gray and Mayor Bill Green, and later he had been appointed by Green to the school board. But in 1987, Katz had burned his bridges with the Democratic party by unexpectedly backing Democrat-turned-Republican Frank Rizzo in his run against Wilson Goode. Now Katz himself was seeking the Republican nomination to be mayor, but he knew it was not going to be easy. The chances of a wealthy 41-year-old Jewish financial expert getting the nomination for mayor from a party dominated by an aging Irish and Italian Catholic population seemed slim at best.

Katz was trying, nevertheless, because he had simply always wanted to be mayor. Since the time when his parents took him to the home of revered reform mayor Richardson Dilworth when he was only seven (or so went the story he loved to tell reporters), he had dreamed of being mayor of the city in which he was born. His business a success, his lifestyle more than comfortable, he had decided that now was the perfect time to go for it. The city's number one problem was unquestionably the fiscal crisis, and city finances were his strongest suit. What could be a better time to give it a try? And so, like a well-heeled businessman going off to play big-league baseball at a Florida Dream Week, Sam Katz set out to indulge his childhood dream of running for mayor of Philadelphia.

When he got the call from *Philadelphia* magazine about the profile, Katz was delighted. Supremely confident about his ability to handle himself with the media, he agreed without hesitation to talk to DePaulo whenever and for however long she wanted. When she came to his downtown office on the sixteenth floor of Two Logan Square to interview him, he even suggested she come and meet his family and see his home. Months later, Katz's campaign manager, Bob Kutler, would roll his eyes at the thought of this open-arm welcome. Kutler knew from experience that *Philadelphia* articles were rarely an unmixed blessing for their subjects. But when Katz agreed to let DePaulo follow him around, he had no campaign manager or any other handlers who would tell him what to say and what not to say and thus protect him from himself.

Katz had his own agenda when he sat down to talk to DePaulo. He wanted to get out into the open a story that he feared might destroy his political aspirations, if not his whole family. Several years before, a former employee had filed a sexual harassment charge against him, as part of a larger case arguing wrongful dismissal by his firm. The sexual harassment charge had been dropped and the case had been settled out of court, but Katz was still worried about it. Although court records about the case had been sealed, he knew that copies of the documents had been circulating among reporters in town, obtained and leaked, he assumed, by Frank Rizzo's campaign. Katz wanted the opportunity to give his version of the story. He figured that if he told people about the case, they would at least form their judgments about the matter from his facts, not from what they heard elsewhere. Katz was telling reporters and potential contributors alike that he and his firm may have treated the woman badly from a professional point of view. Out of an aggressive need for perfection, he said, they let her go abruptly when her performance didn't measure up to their standards. But he claimed that there had never been any form of sexual harassment, that the charge had been merely a legal strategy on the woman's part.

Katz considered the sexual harassment story to be his line in the sand, an issue that he feared would vaporize not only his campaign but his whole life. He was not prepared to be a candidate in the 1991 race if he thought he could not walk into a restaurant with his wife without being looked at strangely. He would not risk that. He had determined that if he could see in December that the sexual harassment case was going to be a campaign issue, he wasn't going to go past it. It wasn't worth it. He had four young children. His great nightmare was of coming home from work one night and having his ten-year-old daughter, Lauren, ask him, "What's this on television about you and this woman?" He simply wasn't willing to have that happen. And so Katz had methodically gone around explaining his version of the case to reporters—including Sal Paolantonio.

Katz had met Paolantonio earlier in the summer, when the reporter had been scoping out the people he thought might be players in the 1991 mayor's race. Over lunch Katz had discovered an almost instant rapport with the reporter. Katz found he liked Paolantonio, that he related to him unlike any other reporter in town. He thought it was partly born of ethnicity, of the personality traits they brought to being ethnic in WASP professional worlds, Katz a Jew in the investment banking business, Paolantonio an Italian-American in a WASP newspaper. Both of them were young, intensely aggressive, and cutthroat competitive, and they seemed to share the same kind of cocky, "I'm going to show them" attitude toward their work. They had other things in common: both had young children and wives who had put their own careers on hold to care for the family while their husbands worked insane hours. Both men were crazy for sports, especially basketball.

They would take turns with each other in the role of the all-knowing savant about the other's fortunes, Paolantonio the veteran of four political campaigns informing Katz about political realities, Katz offering unsolicited advice to Paolantonio about money making and his journalism career. Katz felt as if he could say anything to Paolantonio. More than once, Katz had goaded Paolantonio about the job of journalist. "What's a smart guy like you doing writing newspaper articles?" he would ask. "Why are you over there observing what's going on? You want to be involved in this stuff. You want to be a player. Why don't you do something where you could make money and take advantage of your talents?" Although the reporter had been offended by these remarks, it was the kind of rough-and-tumble give-and-take that characterized their relationship. And Katz had believed what he'd said to Paolantonio. He always had the sense that the reporter wanted to be a player in the political scene, not an observer, and he had the feeling that, of all the candidates, Paolantonio identified most strongly with him—because they were closer to the same age, because Katz had no paternoster, nobody taking care of him, because he kicked down doors as he believed Paolantonio pictured himself doing.

Early on, Katz invited Paolantonio to a Friday night fundraiser he was hosting at his home for a state senate candidate, as a way of responding to the reporter's overtures. Paolantonio accepted the invitation and arrived at Katz's door in West Mount Airy with a bottle of wine. The present had confused Katz and his wife. They had expected him to come with a pen and a notebook, not a bottle of wine, and they took the gift as a sign that the reporter regarded Katz as something more than just another source. What they hadn't realized that night was that Paolantonio always brought something when invited to someone's house, whether it was the home of a friend or a source. It was just something that his father had taught him at a young age.

What Katz did not realize about Paolantonio in a broader sense was that it was not unusual for him to cultivate his sources in a very personal way. And Sam Katz clearly took the bait, believing that the relationship between Paolantonio and himself was special and that he was not just another source for the reporter. It was not necessarily that he expected to get favorable coverage from Sal. It was more a part of the kick of running for mayor, to be able to enjoy this kind of rapport with a key player in the race. Because Katz was a relative novice to the political game, he didn't have the overarching wariness, paranoia even, that other officials and candidates carried with them when dealing with reporters. He simply didn't think very much about the implications for his mayoral campaign of what he saw as a very intense friendship with Sal Paolantonio.

ʻ In some ways, Paolantonio was responsible for the first big push to Sam Katz's mayoral bid. In the summer of 1990, Katz had organized a conference on the city's fiscal problems. He knew that the future of his mayoral campaign depended on the degree to which fiscal problems became a major political issue. If the voters perceived there to be a serious fiscal problem, then Sam Katz had a mayoral campaign. If there wasn't a fiscal problem, then he didn't have a campaign, pure and simple. And so he set out to attract attention to what he hoped would be viewed as a highly professional and informative conference on the city's financial plight.

But Paolantonio was looking for a good political angle. When he noticed that Katz's program had changed and that the finance director of Cleveland who was supposed to be attending had canceled out, he started making phone calls. One of Paolantonio's marks as a reporter was this ability to fasten onto a small detail that another reporter might miss and build a major controversy around it. And in this case, as in so many others, the digging for controversial reactions paid off. When Paolantonio asked Wilson Goode if he had anything to do with Cleveland's managing director canceling out, Goode lashed out at Katz, calling him a "worm" and an "enemy" of the administration. And suddenly Paolantonio had a story with a large measure of political intrigue. He covered the conference as if it were a major embarrassment to the Goode administration. And as with so many of Paolantonio's stories, the angle carried it to page 1.

Katz had watched with amazement as a story he had thought would make it to a back corner of the metro section, if he was lucky, made the front page of the *Inquirer* on July 4 and was picked up by the *Daily News* and Channel 6 news on July 5. Such was the power of an angle by a reporter for the city's major newspaper. Katz had had no intention of creating any controversy with his conference. He knew if Wilson Goode had called him a "worm," it was not because of any fiscal conference but because Goode was still mad at Katz for a letter he had coauthored linking Goode to Louis Farrakhan in the last mayoral election. Katz had even tried to talk Paolantonio out of writing the "worm story." He didn't want to be a "worm." He wanted to be the "municipal finance expert who moderated a panel."

But Paolantonio had gone ahead with the story. And Sam Katz had found himself the recipient of a great deal of media attention for his fledgling mayoral campaign, directly as a result of Paolantonio's slant. Although Katz never thought the reporter had gotten it right, that the controversy he had created was completely misplaced, he had to admit that it had served him well. It had even given him the opportunity to use what was a pretty minor criticism from the mayor as a learning vehicle for his children about what to do when people call you names. And what's more, it gave Katz a renewed sense of confidence. Yes, he had caused controversy and received criticism in print, but, hey, he thought, I can take this.

In the months that followed, however, Paolantonio's angles on the campaign had gone against Katz. The reporter believed that Frank Rizzo or Ron Castille were far more likely to get the Republican nomination, and so he had focused his stories on them. When Katz announced his entry into the race in November, Paolantonio's story the next day devoted two paragraphs to the announcement before moving on to the question of whether or not Castille would run. It was not until well after the jump— the part of the article that was continued on an inside page—that the reader found out any more about Sam Katz or what he wanted to do for Philadelphia. It was not the kind of story that would spur contributions from the people who searched the *Inquirer* for clues before bankrolling a candidate. Katz hadn't liked the treatment, but he had understood that Paolantonio was always going to give premiere position to the political questions in the campaign.

When Katz had talked to Paolantonio in August about the sexual harassment charges, the reporter had asked him questions but seemed non-committal. Paolantonio had already known about the charges, having been fed the story by a ward leader, and the case had also come up when he did his search of the court dockets. But he and his editor, Bill Marimow, had felt there was really no story. The charges had been dropped, the records had been sealed, the woman was refusing to be interviewed, and Katz wasn't even a candidate for office until November. How would they write a story? "A woman once filed a sexual harassment suit then dropped the charges against the guy who could be running for mayor"? They had decided that, unless the charges became a major campaign issue or were raised by the other media, the *Inquirer* would not cover them.

When Katz was interviewed by Lisa DePaulo for the *Philadelphia* profile, he told her, too, about the sexual harassment story. Getting the charges out in the middle of a profile in *Philadelphia* magazine, where they wouldn't be in a headline and where Katz could have some control over the spin, was his objective, so he took a fair amount of time discussing them with DePaulo. But he was not prepared for one of her questions. Why, she asked, had the *Inquirer* never reported the story, given that the court documents had been leaked to them?

Somewhere in the course of answering that question, Sam Katz was to utter a word that would come back to haunt him throughout the campaign. At some point in the course of his interview with Lisa DePaulo—interviewer and interviewee would later disagree on when it occurred—Sam Katz would note that he and Sal Paolantonio were "friendly." Katz would recall explaining how Sal had said that the *Inquirer* would only report the story if the other media picked it up, or if the story became a major factor in the campaign—and only incidentally mentioning the personal relationship he and the reporter had developed. But Lisa DePaulo would remember it—and write about it—differently. She would remember Katz asking, "Why did the *Inquirer* not pursue it, or why didn't Paolantonio?" explaining that the *Inquirer* was afraid of the possibility of lawsuits, having recently been on the losing end of some sizable libel decisions. But when it came to discussing Paolantonio, Katz talked about the fact that he and the reporter were "friendly," how Sal realized that the charge could kill his campaign and wouldn't write about it unless he felt he had to.

At the time that he discussed the sexual harassment charges with Lisa DePaulo, Katz could not imagine the chain of events that his use of the word *friendly* would set off. He did not foresee that Lisa Depaulo would soon call Sal Paolantonio and ask for his reaction to Sam Katz's claim that he didn't cover the sexual harassment case because he was Katz's friend. He hadn't thought ahead to what Paolantonio's reaction would be to the suggestion that he had withheld information because he had become too cozy with one of his sources—just as he was beginning to take on the full-time responsibility for covering the mayor's race. He hadn't pictured the tirade Paolantonio would inflict on DePaulo before denying the charges and ticking off the reasons why the *Inquirer* had not printed the story. (He never had a friendship with Sam Katz, Paolantonio would tell Lisa DePaulo and anyone else who asked him. He had never socialized with Sam Katz or his family. And he had certainly not withheld a story about sexual harassment because of any personal feelings for Sam Katz, he would say.)

And Sam Katz could not have guessed that, even after denying to the reporter that he had made such claims to the *Philadelphia* reporter, Sal Paolantonio would remain so unconvinced and so furious. Later, Katz would claim that Paolantonio, in his fury, had actually threatened him, saying, "If she writes that I didn't write this story because you said I was your friend, then I have a problem. But you have a bigger one."

Paolantonio would deny he ever said any such thing. And he would always be sure that Katz had lied to him. To Paolantonio, it was Katz's way of bragging to Billy Meehan about how he could operate in the big time, winding this reporter around his little finger. Paolantonio could just imagine Katz thinking he was getting the better of the reporter, sullying Paolantonio's reputation to further his own personal objectives.

What had started out as a great personal rapport between reporter and candidate would, within the span of a single telephone conversation, turn into a great personal rancor, with fallout to both men.

Lisa DePaulo had a different theory to explain why Sam Katz said what he did about Sal Paolantonio. She thought that Katz really believed it. She didn't think Paolantonio withheld the story because he was friendly with Katz, although she believed he created that impression with Katz to gain his confidence. She thought the real reason the story hadn't run was that the *Inquirer* had become deathly afraid of libel suits and that the newspaper was wimping out when it came to investigating the private activities of candidates or potential candidates for office. And in this particular case, the man was not even officially a candidate yet. She also thought that perhaps Paolantonio was saving up the story to use when and if Katz became a serious candidate so that he could break the story when it would create more of a sensation. The more she thought about it, the more she saw Katz as the dupe to Paolantonio's ruthless ambition. And she believed that the reason Katz lied to Paolantonio about what he had said to her was because he was so panic-stricken about how Sal would retaliate against him in his coverage.

But she also had the sense that Katz told her about Paolantonio's holding back on the story as his way of trying to lobby her to downplay the issue in her piece. If a key journalist like the *Inquirer*'s political reporter had held back on the story because of the impact it would have on Katz's campaign, maybe she should, too. And indeed the thought had occurred to her. She herself was quite taken with Katz. She had volunteered to do the profile because she was so fascinated with the man, and in the course of following him around and interviewing him so intensively for the piece, she had come to like him and think highly of his credentials for mayor. (She would later change her registration from Democrat to Republican so she could vote for him in the primary, handing her change-of-registration card personally to Katz's campaign manager at the Palm restaurant on the final day for such switches.) She worried that she was taking advantage of Katz because he was so open, so naive even, when the other candidates were all so well handled. As a result, she debated with herself constantly about how much she should say about the harassment case. In the end, her editor and the magazine's lawyers made the final decision.

As it turned out, the story about Sam Katz and the sexual harassment charges broke neither in *Philadelphia* nor in the *Inquirer*. It appeared in a column in the *Daily News* on December 21. In the midst of dealing with the Sal Paolantonio-Lisa DePaulo furor, Katz received a call from columnist Jill Porter, who asked for his reaction to the charges. From her questions, Katz could sense how the story was going to go, and it was not going to be good. It was going to be the old boys' network versus the old girls' network and he knew he was going to lose. He was literally apoplectic. After all that he had gone through with explaining the charges to Lisa DePaulo, after the emotional falling out with Sal Paolantonio, for it all to blow up in his face in the *Daily News* was unbelievable. But there was one more chance, he thought. He had run into the woman who had brought the charges against him a few weeks earlier at the Pennsylvania Society dinner for Republicans in New York City, and the encounter had been cordial. "This girl is ready for a sit-down," he had said to his wife, Connie, at the time. And now he knew what he had to do. He was on his way to California for business, and the woman, Joan Perry, was now living there. He would make a stab at getting Perry to recant her story.

And after an evening with Katz, recant she did. Perry called Jill Porter, telling the reporter that she dropped the sexual harassment charges "as being unfounded and unwarranted with the settlement of the case" and that her primary concern when she filed suit was to stop Katz's firm from giving her negative references after she left. Perry also accepted an interview from Sal Paolantonio. Katz had called the *Inquirer* to inform Paolantonio that Porter was going to run the story and to suggest that he, too, might want to talk to Perry. Perry told Paolantonio much of what she'd said to Jill Porter, adding that she thought Katz had the technical skills to help Philadelphia solve its fiscal crisis and that if she still lived in Philadelphia, she would vote for him herself.

Porter's column ran on a Thursday. The next day, Katz was interviewed for Channel 6's public affairs show, which would run on Sunday, and Saturday Sal Paolantonio and the *Inquirer* covered the charges as well. With each passing day and each subsequent story, Katz felt better and better, since the coverage was turning out to be fairly benign. The *Inquirer* story ran inside the metro section with the innocuous headline "Katz Accuses Rizzo Campaign of Digging Up Sealed Lawsuit." The lead ran, "Republican mayoral candidate Samuel P. Katz yesterday accused 'representatives' of rival GOP candidate Frank L. Rizzo of trying to undermine his campaign by spreading details of a sealed lawsuit that was dismissed in 1987." The story included Joan Perry's response that she would vote for Katz herself. Katz was relieved not only because the article was relatively undamaging. Equally important was that Sal Paolantonio had gotten to write a story about the sexual harassment charges before Lisa DePaulo had a chance to accuse him in print of not writing about the charges because of a personal relationship between the reporter and the candidate.

And then came the final hurdle, the magazine article itself. Katz got his copy on January 23, right before attending the fundraiser at which his ads were unveiled. He skipped quickly past the opening, which talked about how smart he was and what a good mayor he would make if he could negotiate the Byzantine straits of Philadelphia politics. He flipped past the three-quarters-page color photo of his family, looking terrific sprawled on their living-room floor. Finally, he got to the pages on which the sexual harassment charges were reported, and when he read through them, he breathed a sigh of relief. As far as he could tell, the charges did not seem to amount to anything. There were all kinds of innuendos, he thought, but no smoking gun.

DePaulo did write about the *Inquirer's* coverage of the case: "Sal Paolantonio had documents from the case since last summer. For some reason—Katz thought at first it was their 'friendship'—the reporter had not broken the story. Paolantonio claims that the notion that the two were friends 'is a total figment of Sam Katz's imagination.' Still, many in the Katz camp were 'baffled,' as one close aide put it, about why the story wasn't running. 'It's the $100,000 question around here.' Paolantonio says that though he did, in fact, have knowledge of the suit since last summer he and his editors had decided that the case wasn't newsworthy 'unless it met one of the four criteria,' " which DePaulo then listed.

That night at the fundraiser, Katz ran into Paolantonio.

"Have you seen the magazine?" the reporter asked him.

"Yeh," said Katz noncommittally.

"Not pretty," was Paolantonio's comment.

"It wasn't bad for me, pal," Katz responded.

But in the ensuing weeks, Katz began to wonder if he had spoken too quickly that night. After the article appeared, the lunches and telephone calls between Katz and Paolantonio virtually halted. And then on February 1, an article appeared by Paolantonio. The story was based on the campaign finance reports that had been filed the day before by the candidates, detailing how much money they had raised in the period ending December 31. The story started out fine. "On the Republican side, Katz did surprisingly well for someone who has not run for office before," Paolantonio wrote. But Katz noticed something in the next line that gave him pause. "His political action committee, Philadelphia 2000, raised $209,000, $41,000 less than he boasted he had raised on the night of his first fundraising event." It was hardly a scathing indictment, Paolantonio would later point out, noting that he had praised Katz's fundraising prowess and showed him to be a candidate worth taking seriously.

But, to Katz, that one sentence said something different. To Katz, it said that Paolantonio was calling him a liar. And while it was a minor point in a relatively positive context, it set off warning signals to Katz, who believed that he, not the reporter, was right. Katz knew that Paolantonio had quoted the December 31 report quite accurately. He had filed for a total of $209,234 for the period from November 27 until December 31, 1990. The only problem was that Katz knew he had also filed a report on November 30 for the previous month and that the total listed in that report was almost exactly the sum that Paolantonio had found missing: $42,490. To Katz, it looked as though Paolantonio had simply ignored the November 30 report, which had shown very clearly that he had raised the money he was "boasting about" at his fundraiser on November 27. But more than that oversight, Katz was troubled by the fact that Paolantonio had never even called him to ask about the discrepancy. Although the reporter would point out that he had not called any of the candidates for a reaction to the figures, Sam Katz didn't think that anyone else had been called a liar. It was a small point buried in the middle of an article about all the candidates, but still, it was enough to make Katz begin to worry about the repercussions of his telling the scandal-loving *Philadelphia* magazine that he and the *Inquirer* reporter were "friendly."

Katz had succeeded with his strategy to get out into the media in the most harmless way possible the details of the sexual harassment charge and as a result the charge never became a campaign issue. But as savvy as he had been in handling this issue, his inexperience had led him to stumble elsewhere. He has managed to alienate the journalist who would prove to be the city's most influential chronicler of the primary.

And then there was the matter of the other personal information that Katz, the political novice without a campaign manager or a handler, had not thought terribly much about telling Lisa DePaulo. Katz had chatted freely about how as a college student he had smoked marijuana "fairly regularly" and about how he had gotten suspended after disrupting a faculty meeting during an antiwar protest. And then he told her just as casually about how he had gotten out of the draft and avoided Vietnam because of a medical deferment for an injury that had not stopped him from playing basketball in college. And DePaulo, with the prodding of editors who knew it was the personal stuff that sold magazines, had written up every word.

Sam Katz was to learn the hard way in this campaign that while reporters may look like your friends and talk like your friends, chatting off the cuff with them as you would with your friends can get you into deep trouble. He had instinctively figured out how to deliver one hell of a political sales pitch in this campaign, but he was having a little more trouble learning how to keep his mouth shut.

Dave Davies interviewing Joe Egan (*Northeast Times*/Colleen Boyle)

Barbara Grant

Sal Paolantonio (Dan Z. Johnson)

Tia O'Brien (Courtesy KRON-TV)

Frank Rizzo (left) and Ron Castille (Courtesy WPVI-TV)

Ed Rendell (*Philadelphia Daily News*/Elwood P. Smith)

George Burrell (left) and William Gray (*Philadelphia Daily News*/Bob Laramie)

Ed Rendell (*Philadelphia Daily News*/Michael Mercanti)

Sam Katz (*Philadelphia Daily News*/Michael Mercanti)

Ron Castille (*Philadelphia Daily News*/Bob Laramie)

James White (far left, holding grandson) (*Philadelphia Daily News*/Susan Winters)

Peter Hearn (*Philadelphia Daily News*/G. Loie Grossmann)

Lucien Blackwell (*Philadelphia Daily News*/Bob Laramie)

Vernon Odom (Courtesy WPVI-TV)

6 "If I Am Rejected . . . "

February 7, 1991

❧ It was city council's regular Thursday morning meeting time, but today the ornate chambers were overflowing with spectators. They were Lucien Blackwell supporters, wearing red baseball caps, waving "Blackwell for Mayor" signs, and chanting "Blackwell! Blackwell!" as the city councilman entered the room to make his farewell speech to council. Blackwell, at age 59, was resigning after sixteen years in office in order to enter the campaign for mayor, and he would use his speech, as George Burrell had done last December, to set the tone for his campaign. Almost all the people who crowded into the gallery sections of City Council in a show of support for Blackwell were black, just as almost all the supporters at the Katz fundraiser and the Rizzo announcement party had been white. The political pundits might talk about "multiracial coalitions" forming around the mayoral candidates in this election, but when it came to hard-core loyalists, Philadelphia politics was as segregated as its neighborhoods.

The enthusiasm of Blackwell's supporters was every bit as strong as the ground swell of emotion that was observable at Frank Rizzo's rally back at the roller-skating rink. To many in Philadelphia, Lucien Blackwell possessed just as much charisma as Frank Rizzo. When Blackwell walked the streets of North Philly, people would rush up to him as if he were their savior, much the same way white ethnics in the city regarded each Rizzo appearance with awe. Blackwell and Rizzo succeeded by making sure they helped their constituents deal with the bread-and-butter concerns of their lives. They were both populists, just on different sides of the racial divide.

And today in council, as Blackwell delivered his emotional farewell speech, the crowd roared its approval of the oratory that was so close to the language of the black church. "If I am rejected by the citizens of Philadelphia because I care about the handicapped, the blind, the poor, the homeless, the people walking the streets, then reject me. Reject me." They chuckled in appreciation as he singled out each of his fellow councilmen to express his "love and respect," including Francis Rafferty, with whom he had once come to blows in council chambers. They murmured "Mmmm-hmmm" and "all right" as he talked about his humble beginnings. "I started as a laborer on the waterfront, shoveling iron ore and suffering and working hard. I learned to appreciate the plight of poor people," he said. "God has blessed me to go forward in that mission."

And they nodded their heads in vigorous agreement, chanting, "that's right," as he ticked off his accomplishments: serving as chairman of the Philadelphia Gas Works without having to raise gas rates in three years, gaining city approval for the Gallery downtown shopping malls and the new convention center, and working with Philadelphia business leaders for economic development. (He didn't, however, make much of the fact that he had also served for eighteen years as president of Local 1332 of the International Longshoremen's Association.) Although he sprinkled his speech with humor, Blackwell ended on a serious note. "This is a great city. Some people will have you thinking it's falling apart—but that's for purely political reasons. Purely political reasons. Just take a look at that skyline to see we are doing great things. And now I go with a heavy heart but with a sense of anticipation. Someone once said, 'Don't use the past as a sofa.' We will go now. With God's help, we will prevail."

When he had finished and the cheering of the crowd had died down, his supporter and fellow councilman John Street said a few more words in his behalf. "The people who are now claiming that Lu Blackwell can't work with the business community in this city are hypocrites. When business people wanted something approved by this council, their first stop was always Lu. This man has been the most powerful political influence in this city for the last twenty years." He concluded, "What this city needs is not a novice."

While Lucien Blackwell, like Frank Rizzo, could boast passionate sup-porters, there was one big difference between the two veteran politicians. Rizzo had always been the media darling, the politician who fed journal-ists irresistible quotes, the man the cameras loved. Blackwell, on the other hand, had a different and more complex relationship with the mainstream media in town. It resulted from his race, the way he spoke, and the suspi-cion with which he regarded reporters, particularly at the *Inquirer*. As a result, Rizzo and Blackwell, populist politicians both, came across as starkly different in the news.

Blackwell's farewell to council was a case in point. As powerful and emotional, as warm and humorous as he had appeared that morning in council chambers, on television that night he looked merely angry and inarticulate. While the camera liked to caress Rizzo's larger-than-life features, it seemed to quickly avert its gaze from Lucien Blackwell. Where Rizzo could deliver a fifteen-second sound-bite that made his get-tough message resonate with the polish of a John Wayne, Lucien Blackwell was effective only in the long form, over minutes, not seconds, and in interaction with his audience. His sound-bites, if bites they could be called, were filled with hesitations and halting phrases that made him highly unquotable. There was no question that Lucien Blackwell had been a key player on the political scene in Philadelphia for the past two decades and that he had played a role in transforming the city's skyline. And here today in council, he had conveyed a clear sense of his mission and his strengths. But it was not the stuff that TV reporters could easily condense, and so that night, virtually none of his political accomplishments was mentioned.

But there was more to Lucien Blackwell's news coverage than his lack of quotability and halting speech patterns, and that had to do with the way television news so often stereotyped black politicians. As academics were just beginning to discover, local television news had a tendency to depict black politicians as more demanding than their white counterparts. In 1989, political scientist Robert Entman found that Chicago television news associated black politicians with special-interest politics, portraying them as threatening militants. In contrast, white politicians—even when coming from clear ethnic bases—were presented as if they represented the entire community. That Lucien Blackwell fit in with Entman's characterizations was obvious from his TV coverage that night. His sound-bites were all about fighting for poor people, with no mention of his statements about the skyline, or the Gallery, or the new Convention Center, or for that matter his toeing the line on gas rates—the kind of contributions that could be viewed as benefiting whites as well as blacks, the middle class as well as the poor.

And while television reporters emphasized his popularity with poor people, they made him seem less the charismatic leader and more the conniving politician. Frank Rizzo's announcement a few weeks earlier had been likened by reporters to a rock concert or a Hollywood production. But Blackwell's big day was described as "the moment Lucien Blackwell has been planning, plotting, and dreaming about for months, even years. . . . He packed city council with what he calls the little people, the core of his power." It was a statement that could have as easily been made to describe Rizzo, who had no doubt been plotting and planning for months and years also, and had some hand in packing his hall with his brand of little people. But in this case, as in so many others, the white candidate was regarded differently than the black candidate. And that was particularly true since Frank Rizzo knew how to put on the kind of show for TV cameras that placed a layer of veneer over his most blatantly political machinations. As reporter Harvey Clark had put it, Rizzo's extravaganza was "straight out of Hollywood," and while Hollywood was big on dramatic flair, it had never been known for its plethora of leading roles for black actors.

But there was an even worse type of pigeonholing that Lucien Blackwell found himself subjected to that February night, something that would come to confront George Burrell and James White as well throughout the primary. Because of reporters' preoccupation with the horse race, the most interesting question about the black candidates would prove to be a strategic one: whether one or more of them would withdraw in order to unite behind a single black candidate. Lucien Blackwell barely got an eleven-second sound-bite out of his mouth that night on Channel 6 before the reporter launched into a statement about how prominent black leaders such as Mayor Goode were hoping to narrow the field from five candidates to two. As in other American cities, race would be a fundamental concern of the reporters covering this mayor's election. But it would not be questions of racial inequities in the delivery of city services or how black versus white candidates had served—or would serve—the interests of African Americans and others in the city. The question of race would only enter into coverage in terms of how it would affect each candidate's chances of winning and losing.

In the newspapers, Blackwell's coverage that day was a little different. Cynthia Burton, writing for the *Daily News* with a readership that was almost half black, tried to capture the emotional tenor of Blackwell's farewell speech and to translate his symbolic gestures into policy terms. "The sentiments were sincere," she wrote, describing his praise of fellow council members, "but also sent a campaign message: Blackwell knows how to reach council's diverse members, and the city needs a mayor who can make council follow his agenda. The Rafferty hug shows he plans to reach out to working-class whites as well as blacks." But while Burton's story succeeded in describing Blackwell's appeal and the accomplishments he was touting that day, the photo that accompanied the story sent its own message. It had Blackwell, looking particularly dour in a trenchcoat, entering a ward leaders' meeting that night. For Blackwell, newspaper photographs had been a particular bone of contention over the years. He believed that the newspaper brass had it in for him once he set his eyes on the mayor's office, and one of the ways he thought they tried to do him in was with the photos they ran. You could sue a newspaper for libel and complain about coverage, but there was very little a public official could do about consistently unflattering photographs. Blackwell knew that the pictures of him, looking so angry, or hostile, or demanding, sent a message to newspaper readers who didn't know him in person.

There were other problems Blackwell had with the two newspapers in town. Like other public officials and candidates, Blackwell had his share of bones to pick with the media. He thought the press tended to peg some public officials as good guys and others as bad guys. As a member of city council he had fallen into the latter group. He felt that the newspapers panned council all the time, much of it unfairly. If council refused to raise taxes, they blamed them for the deficit, but if they had voted to raise taxes, Blackwell was sure, they'd have blamed them also. "You can't win with these people," he would say.

To Blackwell, there was a clear reason why the coverage looked this way. The stereotyped images, the unflattering photos, and the failure to get at the reasons why he took one or another stand were not the result of editors trying to sell newspapers or reporters working under time constraints. To Blackwell, it had to do with the people in power—mostly white—trying to stay in power. The media in Philadelphia, Blackwell would say, were exploiting the fiscal crisis so that they'd have more power to pick the next mayor. And the fiscal crisis itself, he would say, was a situation that was totally created by Wall Street. For years, the city had borrowed money from people until the taxes came in and they never missed a payment, he would point out. But this time, they had decided not to let the city have the money. The press could have said, looking at the banks and Wall Street, this is totally unfair. But no, they could only blame Goode and council, Blackwell would say.

Blackwell didn't think all of his press treatment was bad or unfair. He particularly admired the coverage by Dave Davies at the *Daily News,* who he thought was honest and always got it right, and he thought he got very fair coverage in the community newspapers, which were close to home and cared about the work Blackwell did for his constituents, for the neighborhoods he served. And then there was the *Philadelphia Tribune,* the black newspaper in Philadelphia that came out twice a week. Tommie St. Hill, the reporter who covered Blackwell for most of the campaign, gave the candidate very positive treatment.

But when it came to the mainstream media he believed that once you reached a certain level in Philadelphia politics, the big boys on the editorial board directed the coverage. As a city councilman they don't interfere with you, he would say, but when you talk about running for mayor, it's a different story. He had already had some run-ins with Sal Paolantonio at the *Inquirer.* One article in December had particularly irked Blackwell. Paolantonio had used Temple University professor Michael Hooper's poll—a poll whose methodology was greeted with skepticism by other reporters in town—to claim that Rendell would get 23 percent of the vote in the black community, while Blackwell would only get 20 percent. Ridiculous, Blackwell said when he saw it. They're making it look like I can't win. Blackwell's own polls were showing he was leading his closest opponent in the black community 44–4, but Paolantonio wasn't printing that.

Blackwell thought the reporter was very simply working for the other side, for the Republicans, because he thought the *Inquirer* would just as soon have a Republican for mayor. In fact, he would suggest that the *Inquirer* had brought Paolantonio in from New York as an agent to make sure the Republicans got elected. Only not Rizzo, of course. Blackwell thought the newspapers were just as unfair to Rizzo, actually. They used Rizzo, but they were unfair to him. They characterized him as a buffoon, they dismissed him as unelectable. But Blackwell knew that Rizzo was crazy like a fox. You could never underestimate Frank Rizzo.

Like Frank Rizzo, Lucien Blackwell knew a lot about politics in Philadelphia, but unlike the former mayor, the councilman would never be as successful in turning the mainstream media to his bidding. While he recognized all too clearly many of the media's foibles, he failed to see that there was really no conspiracy at all. Sal Paolantonio was not an agent of a power-hungry newspaper hierarchy eager to elect a Republican, just as the city's fiscal problems were not the result of a conspiracy on Wall Street but rather the outcome of deep structural problems. Paolantonio was but one cog in a complex machine in which the quest to come up with good stories—stories compelling enough to appeal to an increasingly disinterested and largely white audience—often reigned supreme. And the stories that television reporters turned out about black politicians, including that night's stories about Lucien Blackwell's announcement speech, had less to do with racial bias than with the need to cover politics as cheap and easy entertainment.

It may not have been a conspiracy that led the media to treat politicians, particularly black politicians, the way they did. But the coverage that resulted from the narrow strictures under which reporters operated often carried pernicious effects, nevertheless, telling the electorate so little of what they needed to know about the candidates and repeatedly tainting the motives of the black, more so than the white, contenders.

7 The Reluctant Warrior

February 13, 1991

❧ It was a major day in the campaign, described by a *Daily News* columnist as "a moment of genuine suspense, a turning point in the mayor's race." The Republican City Committee was set to meet over lunch in the rooftop ballroom of the Wyndham Franklin Plaza Hotel and endorse a candidate for mayor. Although some eighty Republican ward leaders would be attending the meeting to vote on a candidate, the endorsement decision was widely known to rest on one man's opinion: Republican party boss Billy Meehan. The vote that followed the speeches of the candidates and their supporters was always unanimous, and it always followed Meehan's nod. Most of those present owed their jobs to Meehan, and they could be depended upon to go along with the plan.

The suspense typically associated with "Billy Meehan Day" had dissipated this time around, however. Channel 6 had broken the news the night before at eleven. District Attorney Ron Castille, who had spent months publicly going back and forth in his mind over whether he would be willing to accept the nomination, had finally given in to Billy Meehan's advances. At the last possible moment, he had let it be known that he would be a candidate for mayor in 1991. The story of Castille's decision to run had made the front page of this morning's *Inquirer,* one of the few campaign stories to be played so prominently in the paper. And now the story would turn to the ceremony surrounding Castille's endorsement and the question of whether his two very determined opponents, Frank Rizzo and Sam Katz, would step aside.

The Republican City Committee meeting was scheduled for 11:30 A.M., but reporters began to gather in the lobby of the hotel shortly after 11:00. The two well-known black TV reporters, Channel 6's Vernon Odom and Channel 10's Harvey Clark, were early arrivals, chatting together as their cameramen checked out their equipment. Tia O'Brien arrived early also, but headed for the rooftop with her two cameramen to set up for a live story for the noon news. Sal Paolantonio from the *Inquirer* drifted in, and Dave Davies and Cynthia Burton from the *Daily News* arrived soon after. Barbara Grant from Channel 29, the independent station which had started a ten o'clock newscast, was also there along with reporters from the major radio stations and Associated Press.

One reporter set off from the pack was Fred Gusoff from the *Northeast Times,* a neighborhood weekly with a respectable circulation of over 100,000. The citywide press, fairly chummy with each other, seemed to ignore the neighborhood newspaper reporter. But former state senator Joe Rocks, whose base was in the Northeast, warmly greeted Gusoff soon after he arrived and thanked him for a story he had written the week before. Rocks and politicians like him understood just how important courting the neighborhood newspapers could be, knowing that reporters like Gusoff were likely to give him far more attention and less harsh criticism than the citywide press. While the community reporters were regarded by the metropolitan media as being more likely to swallow whatever politicians fed them, it was also true that newspapers like the *Northeast Times* were becoming the place where policies, proposals, and official actions got the most attention. There was a certain irony to the fact that the big-city reporters, in their constant critical scrutiny of campaign strategy, were often losing sight of the bread-and-butter issues that the less sophisticated community newspapers realized neighborhood residents really cared about.

As the other reporters waited for the key figures to arrive, Sal Paolantonio said to Vernon Odom, "I told you he was going to run, Vernon. You owe me money."

"Paolantonio, you waffled on that and you know it. First he was running, then he wasn't running. What do you mean I owe you money?" Odom retorted.

Odom asked Paolantonio if he knew how long Castille could wait before he had to resign as district attorney and about why his successor would probably be a Democrat. Tia O'Brien joined the discussion briefly in a lull, to talk about what Rizzo was likely to do. "Isn't there that sore-loser clause now, so Rizzo can't run as an independent candidate in the general if he loses in the primary?" someone asked. Someone else asked what the latest was on Katz. Was he in or out? Hadn't he said all along that if Castille ran, he'd step aside? The informal banter served to pass the time, but it also worked as a kind of briefing session for the television reporters who were shuffled around from story to story and used these few idle moments to pick up specifics from the beat reporters who followed the details.

The discussion was interrupted as key Republicans began to arrive and the TV reporters and their cameramen went into high gear. Sal Paolantonio listened with half an ear to the interviews. "What a circus," he said, describing the crush of TV and radio reporters. "I'll find out what's really going on on the phone this afternoon." It was Ash Wednesday, and many of the Republican leaders arrived with ash marks on their foreheads. The big game for interviews that day were Meehan and Castille and, to a lesser extent, Katz. Rizzo would have been, as ever, a major draw, but he was known to be boycotting the affair since he knew he was not getting Meehan's endorsement. The TV reporters, who all needed video to go with their pieces, pounced on any relatively known figure who arrived while they waited, such as Councilwoman Joan Specter and former mayoral candidate John Egan.

Tia O'Brien led the questions. She asked Joan Specter "Were you surprised by Castille's announcement? Is Ron Castille a new face?" When Specter answered that, no, Ron had been in city government for twenty years, O'Brien tried again to get the kind of answer that would fit in with what she wanted to get across to viewers. "But is he a new face compared with Rizzo?" she prodded. "New faces" versus "old faces" were to be the buzzwords of this campaign, at least on TV. O'Brien asked Egan whether he thought Frank Rizzo—his opponent in the 1987 primary—would drop out of this primary. While the answers to the questions were not particularly surprising, they were the only sound-bites she'd have in time for the noon news.

Up to the rooftop she rushed to get ready for her piece. In the hallway outside the ballroom where the Republicans were already eating their fruit salads, Tia talked via intercom to the station, telling them which sound-bites she was feeding. "The in cue for Specter is 'Ron will do very well,' the out cue is 'safe streets.' The Egan in cue is 'Castille blah,' out cue, 'appeal to voters.' " After she fed the bites in, she hunched over a table, writing out what she would say in her live shot, heavily crossing out words and rewriting several times. "Find out where we are in the show," she instructed her cameraman. "Page nine, five minutes into the show," he answered shortly after. "Story preceding you is jumbo jet."

After she got the story blocked out in her notebook, she and her cameraman entered the ballroom and, oblivious to the people eating lunch behind them, began setting up for their shot. She rehearsed her lines as the camera focused on her. "Move back, Tia," one of them called. "We need less light on her face," the other noted. "We're about a minute and a half out." She read over her notes and smoothed her flyaway hair again. She had long ago accepted the need to pander to the visual requirements of TV news, including how she herself dressed and looked. God knows, it took her forty-five minutes to get dressed in the morning since she'd gotten into TV news, but she always did it with an air of resignation. Now she practiced her opening line, staring into the camera, stopped, and began again. "Less than a minute." The lights went on.

On her cue, she began, voice raised now for the microphone, "Politics turned very ugly today as Frank Rizzo vowed he wouldn't get out of the primary." As her video and sound-bites ran, she stared down at the floor. "Twenty seconds." Looking up again at the camera, she launched into the close. "The wild card may turn out to be Sam Katz. This primary may turn out to be very bizarre. Back to you." Smile, lights off.

Once the live shot was done, Tia started her reporting again. She was the first one to head after Billy Meehan when he arrived, trying to get an interview. He smiled at her cordially, but declined to be interviewed at that point. "I've got to be fair to the others," he said in an apologetic, grandfatherly way. She moved on to other key Republicans—Joe Rocks, Fred Anton, Dennis O'Brien—while both Harvey Clark and Vernon Odom were focused on the more recognizable faces, like perennial mayoral candidate Thacher Longstreth. As Tia headed for Longstreth, too, her cameraman told her, "Try and get him in the center. It's a hell of a lot easier for my lighting."

"Hello, Thacher. You're looking tall as ever," she greeted the well-known city councilman, who was well over six feet tall. "I try, my dear," he responded, before giving her the stock answers to the questions about Castille's election chances. After a few more interviews, Tia and the other reporters were asked to leave, as the meeting was closed to reporters. The pack of reporters and TV cameramen camped out in the narrow hallway outside the room. Tia instructed her cameraman to keep shooting. "What I'm looking for is people getting off of elevators," she said. Sam Katz and Ron Castille were each scheduled to address the meeting, even though everyone knew that Castille would get the endorsement.

Watching the local media pack in action that day said a lot about campaign reporting in a city like Philadelphia. The newspaper reporters grudgingly attended functions like the Republican City Committee luncheon, knowing that little major news ever came out of such ceremonial events. But for the television reporters, these were the peak events of the campaign. It was the ceremonial occasions that supplied the all-important pictures for their pieces: the highly recognizable political figures massed together in settings other than their visually boring offices. At such moments, the television reporters were often more aggressive than the print reporters in going after interviews, simply because it was the broadcast journalists who were more dependent on getting good pictures and sound-bites in the absence of any real news. But even among TV reporters there were differences. Some seemed to regard the events as the farces that they often were and appeared resigned to having to collect the obligatory components for a serviceable piece. But others, like Tia O'Brien and Barbara Grant, the only two political beat reporters among the TV crews, still seemed to believe they might get something noteworthy out of one of these media events. Grant was seated by the glass doors that led to the meeting, trying to hear the speeches, saying, "Shh!" in an annoyed way to the rest of the pack who were just killing time until Castille and Katz arrived.

And O'Brien was racing between rooftop and lobby, trying to catch the candidates before her competitors. She was successful with Katz, confronting him as he stepped into the lobby elevator on his way to the roof. She asked him how he felt about Castille getting into the race and getting Meehan's endorsement, as if she were trying to get him to say he was angry. "Happy camper, happy camper," he noted as he headed for the elevator. She pushed further. "Then why are you staying in the race?" "Give me a break, Tia," he said as he stepped into the elevator.

A half hour later, Castille emerged from an elevator on the rooftop, arriving for his address to the committee, which was scheduled for around two. As his aides led him into the coat check room and out again, most of the reporters hung back, knowing that he would have a statement after the meeting. But not Tia O'Brien. At first she was bland. "Any thoughts on entering the campaign?' she asked. He hesitated. "I don't think I want to get into that now." "Are you happy to be in?" Again, Castille hesitated, but admitted as to how he was glad to be offering the people of Philadelphia an alternative. Then she pounced. "Why did it take you so long?" Here, his aides interceded. "Give him a break, Tia," they said and ushered him off to a safe spot in the corridor on the other side of the elevators, where he stood with his wife, looking over his speech. Newspaper photographers and cameramen took advantage of the clear view to photograph the man who was clearly the star of the day.

Castille entered the ballroom shortly before Katz finished his remarks. When Katz emerged, he was stopped by the entire pack of reporters in front of the hotel's elevators. Cameras were focused on him, at least eight reporters shoved microphones into his face, while the print reporters listened with their microcassette recorders pointed at him.

"Sam, why are you staying in the race?" one reporter asked.

"I have raised $450,000, I have recruited hundreds of volunteers, people in Philadelphia are encouraging me to run, and I told Ron Castille last night that I intend to be a candidate."

"Sam, are you basically saying that in November you had the impression that he wasn't going to run? You said that you wouldn't run if he decided to run."

"I'm going to run for mayor because I believe I offer the city of Philadelphia the best possible type of leadership to turn this city around. The people of Philadelphia are smart enough to make their own judgments whether that's the case. I recognize that today standing in front of you I am probably not looked at like the favorite. But I have never heard anybody in this city whispering the rumor that it was going to be Katz. So why should I be daunted by that? I am going to go forward, and I believe I can get the job done."

Here Paolantonio asked, "If you're the best candidate, why didn't Billy Meehan pick you?"

"You'll have to ask him. I'm disappointed that he didn't. I did everything he asked me to do. I pursued every step. He said I had name recognition problems, and you're holding a poll in your hand that shows I'm known by 87 percent of all the Republicans. I think after three weeks of television, seven months of speaking out on the issues, the people of Philadelphia know who I am and will have a chance to make the decision of whether they want me for mayor."

Vernon Odom asked, "Do you feel Ron misled you or the other candidates by the way he handled this?"

"I'm not about to get into what Ron did or didn't do. What I can tell you today is that I'm running and Ron Castille had better understand that I intend to be a candidate."

Tia jumped in. "Do you think that Ron Castille wants to be mayor in the gut of his soul?"

"I don't have a clue what Ron Castille wants to be. But I can tell you that I want to be mayor, and I think I'll be a good mayor."

"Do you think you can win?"

"Certainly, I think I can. I'm not a quixotic venturer. I think I have a darned good chance to be the city's next mayor, and the Republican party's nominee and I believe that the voters of Philadelphia are going to make that choice. And I'm prepared to let them do that. I was prepared to have this result, so I'm not disappointed. I never heard at any point in time, I never read in any newspaper story or heard on any insiders' report on television that it was going to be me. You can't believe that I'm surprised that it's not me. And I made the decision to run a long time ago. I pursued the strategy that I thought would be the most prudent, and I continue to do that."

"Even though Ron Castille is in?" one reporter asked.

"Ron Castille's going to have a very difficult time being the next mayor of Philadelphia."

"Why?" (more than one reporter chimed the question.)

"Because I'm going to win the primary. You can't be the mayor of Philadelphia if you don't win the primary."

Odom asked, "Didn't you say you were getting out if he got in?"

"I said to Ron Castille in November that I was going to get out if he got in. And at the end of November I went to see him before he went off to Florida and I told him that was no longer the case. And I was gonna run for mayor."

O'Brien asked, "If your money dries up—"

"I don't expect my money to dry up."

"Well, if your money does—" she tried again.

"You didn't think I could raise a half million dollars. Let me tell you something, Tia. I can raise money. I didn't know, you never know, until you lace up your combat boots, just how good you can be in war. Well, my boots are laced up pretty tight. And I can raise money. And I intend to be there. And don't any of you leave here with an expectation that I'm doing anything but getting myself nominated and getting myself elected because that's what I'm about today."

"Did Castille tell you about this?"

"Mr. Castille called me last night to give me the courtesy of informing me of his decision to run for mayor."

Odom asked, "What'd you say to him?"

"Good luck."

"What'd he say?"

"I'd like you to support me."

"What'd you say?"

"Why?"

"What'd he say?" (The reporters laughed.)

"You want to go back and forth on this?" Katz asked, to more laughter. Katz was clearly enjoying this repartee with the whole pack of reporters, being the center of all this attention. He really felt that he had given the speech of his campaign to the Republican City Committee just now, and even though he couldn't imagine how he could stay in the race and go up against the party, he still couldn't quite leave all this. And he couldn't stop talking.

"I said I had already decided to run for mayor," he continued in a more serious vein. "He knew that. He had to know that. I raised $450,000. I spent money on television. I went out and did the things you need to do to be a candidate. I didn't doubt for a second that there was a possibility that at 11:59 and 59 seconds he would do this."

"What's the difference between you and Ron Castille?" Tia O'Brien asked.

"I don't know Ron Castille well enough to make a judgment about him. I'm telling you that as somebody who's built a business, for someone who's served effectively on the school board, and somebody that's built a campaign organization and raised money and spoken to the issues, I feel I have the credibility and the strength and the determination to be the next mayor of Philadelphia. And as a citizen of this city, as somebody who's wanted this for his entire life, I have the right and responsibility to try to do it. That's what I'm saying. I'm not criticizing anybody else who has a similar right, nor am I criticizing the Republican City Committee or the Republican party, which has a responsibility to endorse a candidate. I am not bitter. That is not me. I'm having the best time of my life, and I intend to keep on doing that."

"And if you accidentally elect Frank Rizzo?" O'Brien asked.

"I expect to be the candidate, Tia. I don't understand why you can't understand that. You know, your lack of confidence is not hurting my feelings" (laughter) "but I think you need to understand I intend to be the candidate. Frank Rizzo will not be the mayor of Philadelphia in 1991, and I will."

"Why not?" she asked.

"Because Philadelphians are sick and tired of what's happening to this city. They are disgusted. They're disgusted about what's going on in there," he pointed to the committee's meeting, "and they're disgusted about what's going on across the street over here," he said, pointing to City Hall. "And I intend to be the candidate that makes change in Philadelphia. And I will have more to say about what I intend to do in this campaign over the next few days. I thank you for your time, and I intend to be leaving."

"What did you mean you're disgusted about what's going on?" she pursued him. She had been fishing all day for some expression from him that he was angry, some emotion to beef up her piece. A politician announcing he was leaving did not stop her from continuing to push to get a response.

And Katz couldn't stop, either. His voice rising, he responded, "I didn't say I was disgusted. I said the voters of Philadelphia. Now, Tia, please don't take . . . " He had had enough of Tia O'Brien's pushing him, and now here she was twisting what he'd just said very clearly. "Please don't take words out of context," he said with an edge to his voice, pointing his finger close to her face. "I said the voters of Philadelphia."

"Please don't put that in my eye," she responded nonchalantly, pushing his hand away from her face. "Why are they disgusted?" she went on with her questions without a pause.

"Is there an elevator in there?" Katz asked, looking for an escape.

When the elevator opened, Katz and his campaign manager stepped in and the door closed, but not before Sal Paolantonio had the chance to quickly step in, leaving the other reporters in the pack. Two days later he would write about Katz's comment to his campaign manager as the doors closed: "Did I do any damage to myself out there?"

When the meeting was over, Castille and Meehan gave their interviews to reporters. O'Brien's questions were still tough on Castille. "Sam Katz says he was set up," she said, waiting for response. "Why didn't you tell him early on there was a strong possibility you'd run? Why after a year of waffling—"

Here Castille interrupted her. "I wasn't waffling. I always said I intended to serve out my four-year term as D.A."

When other reporters asked him questions of what he'd bring to the campaign, he answered, "I hope to bring back honesty, integrity, credibility to city government. We just don't have it. You see what's going on with the bond issues. You see even the governor turning his back on the city of Philadelphia. I'm going to work to get the most talented, the best people we can get in there. I have had promises from industry, from lawyers that I know, just from good people, that they'll come aboard and they'll work really hard to make this a city government we can all be proud of."

After more comments from Castille and Meehan, O'Brien did her stand-up and then checked in with the station to see whether she should head back there or try to get Rizzo's reaction. As she and other TV reporters talked on the pay phones, their cameramen hung out in the hallway. *Inquirer* photographer William Steinmetz passed by Channel 6's cameraman and said, "You missed a great shot in the lobby. There was a great big Valentine set up on a poster for the hotel, and Castille paused in front of it to kiss his wife. That's going to be my shot." The cameraman laughed. "That'll probably be the last she sees of him until November."

Driving back to the station in the truck, Tia O'Brien was cynical about Castille. She felt in his last campaign for D.A. against Walter Phillips he had gotten easily shaken by reporters' questions and Phillips's feeble attacks. How was he going to make it through a campaign in which the scrutiny would be intense and the attacks major league? She talked about how he would sell his military background. "You're going to see lots of shots of the missing leg," she said. (Castille had lost his right leg in Vietnam and had chosen not to wear a prosthesis.) But she was equally cynical about Katz. "Quite a performance back there, wasn't it? It was like his campaign advisors told him that he better come out looking ferocious if he was going to compete against a war veteran and tough guy like Castille. How about that combat boots quote?" She hadn't thought it was very effective. "He came off too strident, kind of mean, like a spoiled child that didn't win the game."

She arrived back at the newsroom, which was located across from Independence Hall in downtown Philadelphia, at 2:50 and began logging her tapes, getting a sense of what sound-bites she had, noting the numbers on the video player's counter where they occurred. Later she would go back with her editor to choose the actual sound-bites, but the numbers would help her locate what she wanted. She sat in front of the VCR, copying down quotes, stopping the picture, freezing the action, jotting down the numbers. She was looking not just for sound-bites but for the shots she had of each key figure in the piece. She needed walk-in shots for each player in her piece, to serve as segue. At Katz's quote about lacing up his combat boots, she stopped several times, to make sure she had it right. As she finished viewing the tapes, she paused a minute to think. "How am I going to do this without any cutaways?" When she got to Castille, she chuckled. "The reluctant warrior," she said.

After viewing the tapes, she went back to her desk and typed into her computer terminal the code to view the story lineup for the evening to see where her story was and how much time she had. The piece was slated for the 5:30 show, at the end of the first block of stories, right after the war news. Tia disagreed with the placement, but thought it futile to argue. "This is a major story," she thought. "It's going to get lost at the end of the first block on the early show. Here they've got a live interview with Castille at six. They should have put my piece before that, to set it up. But they don't see it that way."

She had had a stronger disagreement with her producer the night before. The producer had wanted her to put together a piece to set up the Republican endorsement meeting—a profile of the candidates as if they were appearing on baseball cards, noting their strengths and weaknesses. She enjoyed doing those kinds of pieces, but it involved a lot of work, finding file footage, getting the sports anchor to announce part of it, working with the graphic artist. The problem was she had learned yesterday through her sources that Castille was likely to run. All day long, while doing the baseball cards piece, she had been on the phone trying to confirm the story. When she finally got confirmation and told her producer, he said, "What's that, a VO, a VSOT?" referring to *voice-over* or *voice-over-sound-on-tape,* newsroom terms for stories that show tape and sound-bites, but do not use reporters. She couldn't believe that he was not going to give her another story to report on a major turn of events in the campaign: Castille's entrance into the race. She had decided to use her lead-in to the baseball cards piece to say that sources indicated Castille was going to run, but right before the piece was to air, her producer had decided to edit the statement out of her story. As a result, WPVI's Channel 6 broke the story about Castille at eleven and Tia O'Brien lost another scoop.

The disagreement between O'Brien and the producer over how to cover the breaking news about Castille was evidence of a broader conflict. Tia O'Brien approached her job as political reporter with the same intensity and journalistic values of most print reporters on the same beat, constantly on the lookout for scoops in the campaign. But time and again the station did not find her breaking information interesting enough to run, and her stories never made it to the air—even in some cases where she would have scooped the *Inquirer* and *Daily News*. Unlike most of her television counterparts who were rotated around many beats, she was also keyed into the issues in a campaign, familiar with where candidates stood on positions and how those stands might play with the electorate.

But her producers and news directors believed that their audience included many people who could not care less about the issues in the campaign, many because they did not live or work in the city of Philadelphia. There was a continuing debate between reporters and higher-ups about which stories about Philadelphia politics had widespread interest and which ones were really for insiders. To reporters like Tia O'Brien, the producers' notion of where the switch was flipped between interest and boredom was moving dangerously close to where they were only accepting the pure fluff stories. They were only too happy to see her do pieces like her baseball cards feature, she thought, because they were light, humorous, and entertaining, with good visuals and graphics to please the audience. But in the process of doing these pieces, Tia's one campaign report of the day tended to lose its substance.

Still fuming about last night's piece, Tia sat down to write her story on the Castille endorsement. "Ron Castille came to pick up the endorsement

Republicans have been offering him for months. After months of procrastinating, he now says he's ready to save Philadelphia." She thought about
the sentence for a moment. On the small desk adjacent to her computer
terminal were dozens of tapes tossed haphazardly about, along with a few
newspaper articles and notes from old interviews. Pinned to the back wall
were six or seven snapshots of her ten-month-old baby, Kaley. Kaley on
her father's shoulders, asleep, Kaley being held by a slightly disheveled
Mommy, who looked very different from the tough and aggressive political reporter.

She changed the line a bit. "But for months he's been procrastinating,
and now he says he's ready to help save Philadelphia." After each bit of
text, she typed in a space for a sound-bite, or for "nat sound" (such as
cheering for candidate). In the third paragraph she wrote, "Republicans
are convinced Castille, the popular district attorney, former Vietnam vet,
the only Republican in recent history to win citywide . . . that Castille can
win back city hall after forty years of Democratic control."

From there she decided to use Rizzo's reaction. The station had sent a
field producer to get Rizzo's statements. She had checked with O'Brien
first before she left, and the reporter had suggested the kind of questions
she wanted and had asked her to phone the station if Rizzo said anything
surprising. When the field producer returned, O'Brien called out to her,
"Can you get me a five-second sound-bite that says 'I'm in this race to
stay?' "

"Sure. He said it a couple of times."

"Get me the most ferocious."

"Well, he really wasn't very ferocious. He was kind of subdued when he
said it. He seemed tired. Every reporter in town had been in there to get
his statement. He was going on a lot about a deal that Castille made with
the law firm before he decided to run."

O'Brien continued to type into her computer. Leaving room for the
Rizzo sound-bite, which she would identify later in the editing booth, she
typed, "Across town, Castille's arch rival Frank Rizzo vowed a bloody
primary . . . then suggested Castille is getting a high-priced law firm job
. . . in return for running." She called the field producer over. "Is this
right?"

" 'Suggested?' I don't know. It was more he raised the question."

O'Brien changed the wording: " . . . then questioned if Castille is getting a high-priced law firm job." Here she left room for another Rizzo
sound-bite where he would attack Castille for the law firm deal.

From there she moved to Sam Katz's reaction. Leaving a space for video
of Katz's entrance, she wrote, "Back at the Republican meeting, more trou-

ble was brewing. Businessman Sam Katz emerged to say that he also would be in the race to stay." There she left room for the combat boots sound-bite. "Republican leaders made it clear that both Rizzo and Katz will be under pressure to drop out. . . . Rizzo and Katz have until March to drop out. If they don't, there's no guarantee who will be the Republican winner." As Tia O'Brien wrote, she was aware of the need to get her information across in the form of a mini-drama. She sometimes used the term *soap opera* to describe how she made city politics stories interesting to an audience that she knew was not inherently fascinated with the topic. She tried to package the news into stories with clear plot lines, using words like *arch rival* or phrases like *trouble was brewing* to liven up the tale.

When it was done, the story was all of six short paragraphs, written in a half hour. At 4:40 her producer asked to see the copy and made few changes. At 4:50 she was back in a tiny editing room with sliding glass doors, working with an editor to cut the piece. Standing up, she read the voice-overs for her story into a microphone. "On the count of one, two, three, Ron Castille came to pick up the endorsement—let me do that again, on the count of one two three . . . " After the voice-overs were recorded, she and her editor went through the tapes to pick out the video and sound-bites. "We've got to race, I'm on the 5:30," O'Brien said. They looked for shots that fit her sentences and that lasted long enough to get to the end of the thought. When they got to shots of Ron Castille going into the meeting, they found that people passed in front of the camera, obscuring the shot after a few seconds. "Let's try something else. I have him shaking hands at 45:40," the reporter said, looking for a longer shot.

They got to the tape of the Katz interview. "Ooh, gang bang, eh?" the editor joked, watching the pack of reporters surround Katz and barrage him with questions. When they searched for video to match "the popular district attorney, former Vietnam vet," Tia pointed to shots of Castille against the window rehearsing his speech. "Good, we have a shot with the leg missing to show the Vietnam vet. Do we want to show a wide shot? O.K., now maybe we can go back to schmoozing at the press conference. It's all got to last this whole time." The editor kept going. "Channel 6's mike is in that shot, and so is Harvey Clark. Do you want that?" she asked. "No," Tia answered.

As they continued to go through the sound-bites, O'Brien listened to some of the statements the candidates made. "There's so much in here," she said, "I just can't get all the nuances in, like Sam Katz being a fiscal expert, or Castille talking about his credibility." The sound-bites that she used fairly jumped off the screen. Sam Katz's combat boots went in, although Tia debated with herself whether she wanted the last phrase of the bite, "I can raise money." At first she thought not, it was crisper without it, but finally she let it stay. Frank Rizzo's sound-bites required almost no selection. After a few desultory comments to the field producer, Rizzo had looked straight into the camera, raised his voice, and said, as if he had rehearsed it, "What's the deal, Castille? What's in it for you? What's in it for the law firm? What's in it for the people of this city, Castille? Tell the truth." Two days later, the same sound-bite, read this time offscreen by an announcer, would run virtually unchanged in Rizzo's first campaign ads against Castille.

As they chose what they wanted, the editor played with the buttons and dials to get the bit onto the final piece. Two screens were before her, one with the final piece, one with the raw tape. At 5:30, minutes from when the piece was to air, they were still looking to see if they had file tape that had cleaner shots of Castille. "If it's going to jeopardize the piece, let's not do it," said Tia.

They finished at 5:32, with O'Brien herself walking the tape of the piece down to the first floor to the control room, handing it to the producer of the show. She read over the intro. "Why doesn't it say I'm the political editor?" she asked the producer, who dutifully spoke into his microphone. "Keith, can you change the script to 'As Channel 3's political editor Tia O'Brien reports'?" With her piece finished, she returned to the newsroom to help with the six o'clock piece, briefed anchor Steve Bell on questions for his live interview with Castille, and then stopped by the news director's office. "Well, Tia, at least you got a political story tonight," joked Scott Herman, the news director. "At least it wasn't measles." The station had been using her increasingly as a general assignment reporter, and the last few days she had been assigned to report on the city's growing measles epidemic. She responded by telling the news director about how her producer had cut the Castille story the night before and how they had lost out on the exclusive because of it.

Then she was done. She sat at her desk looking tired but relaxed, after a day of high-pitched intensity, waiting for the call that her husband and baby had arrived to pick her up. Every night they came for her, so she wouldn't have to pay the eight-dollar parking fees around Independence Hall and also so her husband, who was a free-lance writer, could keep the car at home. When her husband and baby girl arrived, she cooed at the baby and turned to ask her husband, "How did she do from the shot?" After her story was done, Tia O'Brien stopped worrying about city politics and turned her attention to the feverish side-effects of her own baby's measles shot.

In the *Inquirer* and *Daily News* the next day, the story of Castille's endorsement ran on the front page, as had the story the day before that he had decided to run. All the other announcements of candidates—all eight others—had run inside both papers. Even Frank Rizzo, the man who had been known for years to sell newspapers, the man who had managed to get his picture, not Wilson Goode's, on the front page of the *Daily News* the day he lost the last mayoral election to Goode, even Rizzo's announcement had run in the *Inquirer's* Metro section. But Ron Castille had made page 1 two days in a row. And alongside the stories in both the *Inquirer* and the *Daily News* there appeared the virtually identical photo of Castille—taken as he stood away from the reporters rehearsing his speech, with his wife, Judy, next to him—shots which clearly showed his missing leg.

Sal Paolantonio had attended the Republican City Committee meeting with the rest of the reporters, but he was, as ever, determined to set himself off from the pack. That day he had managed not just to step into the elevator with Katz after the candidate's impromptu press conference, but also to walk Billy Meehan back to his law office and to talk to some other Republican ward leaders later in the day. He knew the immediate news that day would be Castille's anointment and he, like everybody else, would write up the story of Castille's official entry into the race. But he wanted to write something beyond what every other reporter was doing, another piece taking off from the meeting, one more story about Sam Katz before his candidacy ended. And he would use the details he picked up that day at the Wyndham Franklin Plaza to do it.

Two days later, on Friday, February 15, Paolantonio's story ran, at the top of the metro page of the *Inquirer,* which was the best play a story could get short of the front page. The headline read, "Katz's Conduct Killed Chances, GOP Leaders Say." In it, Paolantonio picked up the combat boots quote that all the TV reporters had used as their sound-bite and turned it around as the TV reporters hadn't. He wrote:

"After losing his quest for the Republican mayoral endorsement, municipal finance consultant Sam Katz emerged from the GOP policy committee luncheon Wednesday afternoon with—as he put it—his "combat boots laced up."

"He wasn't kidding. After about 15 minutes in the glare of television lights, Katz apparently heard one too many questions, turned to KYW-TV (Channel 3) reporter Tia O'Brien and lashed out at her." Paolantonio recounted the interchange between O'Brien and Katz, when she misquoted him and he pointed his finger at her. And then he made his point.

"The reason given by city GOP boss William A. Meehan for Katz's not getting the party's endorsement is that, in his opinion, Katz was not well known enough to beat former Mayor, Frank L. Rizzo.

"But top Republicans said yesterday that Katz's sometimes irascible conduct—so clearly demonstrated in his exchange with O'Brien—and several incidents disclosed about his past turned off GOP ward leaders, making his selection as the party's nominee virtually impossible."

For Paolantonio, Sam Katz's interchange with Tia O'Brien had been one of those nice epiphanies he liked to write about—a neat little anecdote that could serve as a great start for a story and make a point as well. Here was a guy who wanted to be mayor. How was he going to react on a street corner if a gang leader was having a confrontation with him? Was he going to point a finger at his face and start screaming and yelling? He blew up at Tia O'Brien in a situation where you don't blow up at reporters. Everybody goes through the feeding frenzy. It's the rite of passage. Nobody likes it, it shouldn't be that way, but that's often the way reporters are, he would say. Tia happened to be a very aggressive reporter, and she got under Katz's skin. But to Paolantonio, if you wanted to be mayor of Philadelphia and you let a TV reporter get under your skin—if you laced up your combat boots to attack a five-foot woman with a microphone in her hand—then it was worth telling people about.

Paolantonio also used the story as a place to describe the revelations of the *Philadelphia* article: that Katz smoked marijuana while in college in the 1960s, that he'd been suspended once for participating in an antiwar protest, and that he had gotten a medical deferment from the draft even though he had played for the Hopkins basketball team. It was all the information that Katz had volunteered to Lisa DePaulo without urging, and here it was repeated in the *Inquirer* before the jump. But Paolantonio also mentioned one item about Katz that DePaulo had not noted, which had never before made it into the *Inquirer*. He wrote that Katz had been accused of a conflict of interest when he had invested in real estate around the city's proposed convention center, at a time when his firm was acting as a city consultant on the project. It was not a new story—it had been covered in both the *Daily News* and the *Inquirer* at the time that it had been uncovered—and it was easily retrievable from the electronic files. But the fact that it had never been covered in this campaign, up until now, showed how ad hoc were a newspaper's decisions on when to bring up old controversies and remind the public of an old story that just might make a candidate look bad. For whatever reasons, Paolantonio and his editors had decided that this was the moment to bring up Sam Katz's conflict-of-interest story. Just about the only thing that was missing from this negative story about Sam Katz was mention of the sexual harassment case.

For Katz himself, angrily reading the article, the omission was hardly reassuring. More retaliation by Paolantonio for the *Philadelphia* article, he thought. What bull that I didn't get the nomination because of my temper. I didn't get the nomination because Ron Castille, whom Billy Meehan had wanted all along, decided to run. Pure and simple. And to use unnamed sources, referring to them as "top Republicans" to savage his reputation, he found reprehensible.

As for the combat boots quote, it had a curious origin. Katz had not been coached about what to say that day, and he had not had it in his mind to come out sounding like a "warrior," as Tia O'Brien had assumed. But neither was he, as a guy who had successfully evaded the draft in the late sixties, a person to whom military terms came naturally. Rather, Katz owed the combat boots quote indirectly to someone who did often use the vocabulary of war, ex-navy man Sal Paolantonio. All through 1990, in their private conversations, Paolantonio would say to Katz, whenever something controversial or contentious would come up in the campaign, "Lace up your combat boots, dude." And so when Tia O'Brien asked Katz what would happen when his money dried up, he had looked at her and used the line that had so amused him whenever Paolantonio had laid it on him. And even with the intensity of responding to the pack's questions, he couldn't help but notice that Sal Paolantonio smiled when he heard the line.

And so it was that Paolantonio unwittingly fed Katz what was to be one of his most memorable television sound-bites of the campaign—and that Paolantonio used that very same sound-bite to skewer Sam Katz on one fine February day.

8 "Marijuana Smoking? Peace Activist?"

February 19, 1991

❦ Tia O'Brien herself had not felt that Sam Katz's pointing his finger at her was all that significant. Like other reporters present at the Franklin Plaza that day, she was surprised by the story Paolantonio wrote two days later, which made it seem as if Katz had exploded in anger at her. Beyond her reaction that Katz was a bit "strident," she hadn't thought much about the encounter, particularly regarding her own role in it, and she felt that Sal had overplayed the story.

But it was O'Brien who was to put one final nail in Katz's coffin in a piece that she had never meant to do. Today she was sent to cover a photo shoot of the Republican candidates that *Philadelphia* magazine was doing about the new political gathering spot, the Palm restaurant in the Bellevue Stratford Hotel on South Broad Street. Tia O'Brien had been in television news long enough to know these photo opportunities could provide her with the all-important video she needed for each and every political story, but she was still always looking for some real political news to go with the pictures. On this day, she had been gathering information about Sam Katz's campaign, and was hoping to do a story about the surprising strength of his finance committee, even after Castille's endorsement by the Republican committee. Once Castille was in the race, the conventional political wisdom held that financial support for other candidates would dry up. But O'Brien had heard that Katz's financial backers were sticking with him—at least for awhile.

When Katz arrived for the photo shoot, O'Brien interviewed him about his finance committee and whether they remained committed to him. At the end of the interview, however, she threw in a few more controversial questions, remembering something Ron Castille had said to her last Friday. It had been a long interview, her first in-depth session with Castille since he'd decided to run. She had started out probing about the law firm deal and Rizzo's allegations that the job was a trade for city business should Castille become mayor. Next, she asked him whether he would use negative campaigning in retaliation against Rizzo. And then she had turned the topic to Sam Katz.

"If Sam Katz had looked like a stronger candidate, would you perhaps have stayed out of this race?"

"I perhaps would have, because of my love for this office," Castille had responded. "I mean, literally, this has been my life for the past twenty years. I'm a lawyer. This is a lawyer's job. Were there a stronger candidate for us to put up in the fall, I think I might have just stepped aside and continued in the important work of this office. But it didn't work out that way."

"What were the concerns that you saw surrounding a Katz candidacy?" O'Brien asked.

"He's an expert. He's the kind of person I'd like to attract to me to be an adviser. The guy's a financial expert. But this is probably his first attempt at a major campaign. I've been through two major campaigns already, actually four total elections if we count the primaries. Things just didn't work out for him. I've talked to Sam, and I've asked him for his support, and I've asked him to help me learn some of the things he knows and give me some of the knowledge he has so that I could step over into that job in City Hall."

"Do you think it's a mistake for him to stay in this primary?" she continued.

"He's run a good race up till now. He's got name recognition, he's raised a lot of money, he's positioned himself very well. I think if you look at the polls and believe in polling, if he stayed in the race it would be as a spoiler. He still thinks he can win, but I don't think so. The polls show that I have a lead over everyone, that even in a three-way race, I should still win."

"And the *Philadelphia* magazine article has raised some doubts in your mind when you were reading that?" Tia asked.

"It raised some doubts about Sam's ability to win the race. And that's what we're headed for. We're in it to win. He perhaps could overcome some of the issues that were raised or were placed in there, but I think that the overall tone of it—"

"Marijuana smoking? Peace activist?" She was pushing Castille to be concrete.

"Yes. I don't think that appeals much to the Republican hard-core voter. You know, you do things as a kid, these are childish type things, but some people can't overlook that, you know."

Remembering the interview, Tia threw out another question for Katz. "Castille said in an interview last week that he was close to backing you for the nomination when he read the article in *Philadelphia* magazine about your smoking marijuana and avoiding the draft in Vietnam. What's your reaction?" To Katz, the question sounded like a direct affront from Castille. The guy wants him to get out of the race and support his candidacy and this is how he goes about doing it? Calling him a draft dodger on television? On camera, Katz shrugged off the question and answered O'Brien dispassionately, giving his stock answer about how Philadelphians cared about the future of their city, not the personal backgrounds of the candidates. But later that afternoon he got on the phone to Republican leaders and lashed out in fury. "I hardly regard bad-mouthing me to a TV reporter as a way to get me on the team," he lectured them, as they tried to smooth his ruffled feathers. Eventually, Katz had gotten a call from Castille denying that he had ever said any such things to the reporter.

But Katz couldn't let the matter drop after Castille's call. He told his campaign manager, Bob Kutler, about what Castille had said, prompting Kutler to pick up the phone and call O'Brien. He told O'Brien that he wanted to come down to the station to view the raw tapes of her interview because Castille said he never made any such claims against Katz. It was not the first time that O'Brien had been subject to these kinds of demands from political figures. She rarely paid any attention to them, though, beyond thinking how ridiculous some of these requests were—to even think that a television station would let them view raw tapes of an interview. But she didn't say any of that on the phone. Instead, she followed protocol and referred Kutler to her news director, Scott Herman, who in turn denied Kutler's requests outright.

The campaign manager's indignant phone call did not exactly go unheeded, however. As Kutler went on and on to Scott Herman about what Castille did or did not say to Tia O'Brien about Sam Katz being a draft dodger, he sparked Herman's interest in what had been a fairly dead story. Herman had come out of a news background, working in news radio before coming to television. But once in the role of news director at a major market television station, he was forced into the position of making sure the news produced ratings, which in turn produced profits for the station. In 1991, many television news directors were not even coming from journalistic backgrounds. Most worked their way up from the business side, because increasingly their jobs involved less journalism and more marketing. News directors like Scott Herman spent more and more time trying to figure out what the audience wanted in the way of news and less on what it was important for them to learn. And what many news directors believed the audience wanted in the way of political coverage was soap opera.

Bob Kutler's phone call to Scott Herman that afternoon suggested just such a soap opera: the war hero facing off against the draft dodger. O'Brien had been striking out with her producer in her attempts to get the Katz finance committee story on the air because it held no such emotional elements. A story about the potential viability of a candidate in a campaign was deemed just too much for "insiders." But the personal clash between Katz and Castille over matters like drugs and military service, now that was another story. Suddenly Tia O'Brien got the go-ahead for the story—only now with a different slant. The angle was now to be that behind the friendly facade exhibited at the Palm that day "a political war is raging." In the story, the reporter said that Katz was accusing Castille of not really wanting the mayor's job. And then she launched into the intrigue.

"In fact, in this interview last week, Castille revealed that he considered backing Katz for mayor instead of running himself. But then he read this *Philadelphia* magazine article. [The video moved to a shot of *Philadelphia* with Katz and Burrell on the cover.] In it, Katz confesses to smoking pot back in the sixties and getting thrown out of college for anti-Vietnam war protests. [The camera now showed a photograph of Katz and his wife, Connie, both with long hair in the sixties, which had run with the magazine article.] The war Castille, a Marine, lost a leg in."

Castille: "It raised some doubts about Sam's ability to win the race."

O'Brien: "Marijuana smoking? Peace activist?"

Castille: "I don't think that appeals too much to the Republican hard-core voters."

O'Brien ended the piece by saying, "Katz doesn't apologize for his anti-Vietnam war activities, and he doesn't think voters will hold it against him. Meanwhile front-runner Castille believes funding for his opponents will soon dry up."

The positive story she had been about to do about the tenacity of Katz's finance committee and his determination to continue the primary fight without party support had been abandoned. In its place was a negative story for Katz, one which reinforced Castille's image as the war hero. As cynical as Tia O'Brien was about Ron Castille, her piece clearly worked in his favor. She was being led along, and she well knew it, by a combination of her newsroom's values—which favored sexy personality conflicts over issues or even campaign viability—and the machinations of sources, both clever and stumbling. Because of the kind of simplistic personality-dominated story her higher-ups demanded, the reporter had been led to suggest that Castille, the war veteran who had lost a leg in Vietnam, was personally affronted by a man who had escaped being drafted in that very same war. But even more important, because of the requisites of television news, Tia O'Brien never got to tell the story of how Sam Katz had an excellent chance to stay in the race and raise enough money to mount a viable campaign that would challenge both Castille and Rizzo. She was the single reporter in town who recognized the potential strength of the Katz candidacy, and by the end of the campaign she would be proved exactly right in her instincts. But, being a television reporter, she never got to tell the story.

9 Saving Philadelphia

February 1991

❧ As Sam Katz was taking his lumps in the media, Ron Castille was sitting back in his chair in the district attorney's office, enjoying a very different kind of coverage and a very different set of political expectations. As he had been told many times in the last year by Republican leaders urging him to run, he had an excellent chance of being the first Republican elected mayor in forty years. He was a war hero in a year when the United States had gone to war, and he had shown himself capable of winning a citywide election in a Democratic town.

And then there was the other advantage he took into this election: an excellent media image, particularly on TV. Since taking office five years ago, Ron Castille had enjoyed the kind of benign treatment accorded to many district attorneys across the country. In the never-ending quest for stories about sensational crimes, TV news reporters had a habit of lionizing the prosecutors who were putting the bad guys away, without looking too closely at dry subjects like conviction rates and office management. The simplistically positive television coverage that resulted allowed many of these officials to make the leap from prosecuting criminals to running governments.

And Castille had been no different. Among the print reporters who had long covered city government in Philadelphia, Castille's record as district attorney was viewed as mixed. He was known to insiders as a relatively low energy but competent prosecutor who liked to delegate much of the administrative work of his office to his deputies. But on television his image was quite different. Local television reporters didn't have the time to investigate any public official's performance, and they knew their producers and news directors wouldn't want the results even if they did. What the higher-ups liked in the newscast in the way of local government coverage was personalities and emotion and drama. They were particularly enamored of good guys and bad guys, local heroes and villains. The more simplistic the image, the better.

While Sam Katz had in his short time in politics managed to lock up the role of "fiscal expert," Ron Castille had long ago been tagged as the clean, honest war hero who was fighting to lock up criminals. This television image was one of the main reasons Castille had a chance to win in November. TV had made him a candidate who was known and liked by Democrats as well as Republicans throughout the city of Philadelphia and in the surrounding region. And if his media image had been good as D.A., after his endorsement for the nomination for mayor it got even better. Castille was now portrayed as the modest hero, the noble altruist who had been wooed to the idea that only he could come to the aid of his city. Before he entered the race, reporters like Tia O'Brien had been cynical about Castille's behavior. In her "baseball cards" piece about Castille the night before his endorsement she had referred to him as Ron "the Waffler" Castille, and even when she wrote her first opening to her story on the party's endorsement, she had used sarcasm to describe him: "After months of procrastinating, Ron Castille says he's now ready to save Philadelphia." She was not alone in her characterization, either. Other reporters privately viewed it as a sign of weakness and lack of desire for the grueling job that it was taking Castille so long to make up his mind.

But once he jumped into the race, all that was forgiven and forgotten by the media. "The Waffler" was transformed into "the Soul-Searcher and City Savior." On Channel 10, on the day of the endorsement, anchor Larry Kane had done a personal interview with Castille. "Tonight in a quieter moment, away from the roar of the crowd, I talked to Ron and Judy Castille in their home about their fateful decision, one that was a long time in coming," Kane said. The piece then moved to Castille, looking relaxed as he sat on his sofa. "We were approaching the filing date," he said quietly, "and, you know, I really thought long and hard about this thing. Literally, it's been on my mind for over a year, and I've discussed it with probably over a thousand people. And it just came to the decision time. When push came to shove, I thought that I was the person best able to try and turn this mess around in the city of Philadelphia."

That Sunday, two pieces about Castille appeared in the *Inquirer*, both on the first page of the metro section, both written by Sal Paolantonio. The first article, headlined "Castille Seen as Hero, Villain in Republican

Drama," was an attempt to reconstruct the actions that led up to Castille's last-minute decision to run. But the word *drama* in the headline said it all. Whether unwittingly or quite deliberately, Castille had managed to create suspense about his decision, making it into bigger news than if he had simply planned to run all along. It also reinforced his image as the local hero. Like the good guy in an old silent movie untying the hapless female on the tracks seconds before the train came barreling along, Castille had rushed in at the last minute to save Philadelphia—or so his news coverage made it seem.

Although the headline of the *Inquirer's* story suggested that Castille was viewed as both the hero and villain of the drama, there was relatively little villainy in evidence. The story chronicled Castille's "courtship" by Republican leaders, noting how "deliberate and cool under fire is the man who may be Philadelphia's next mayor." There was no mention of the insider talk that Castille's decision resulted from fear that his political career would be over if he declined Meehan's advances. (Tia O'Brien had tried to do a story with this theme—that Meehan was basically holding a gun to Castille's head, that if he ever wanted to be state attorney general, he'd better do this for the party—but she'd been vetoed by higher-ups because they couldn't imagine how she could make that visual.)

Here in Paolantonio's article, Castille's wife, Judy, explained the candidate's motives, attributing the decision to her husband's "overwhelming desire to pay back the city that took him in twenty-three years ago after he lost a leg in Vietnam." "He loves Philadelphia," Judy told Paolantonio. "And when it came down to crunch time, he said to me, 'I'm a citizen of this city and I've got to help any way I can.' " Paolantonio also quoted supporters who traced Castille's indecision to love of being a prosecutor and said they encouraged him to run because "with the Republican in the White House he could turn Philadelphia around" and because "he can shape a real vision for the city into the twenty-first century."

Letting a candidate, his wife, and his supporters be quoted at length about the candidate's sense of duty might have been perfectly natural in another era of political reporting, but in 1991, it was downright noteworthy. In all the other cases when candidates had jumped into the race, they had barely gotten out a single quote before their chances for victory were assessed and their critics' voices injected. In all the other cases—even Rizzo's—announcement speeches were explicated for the carefully tailored "messages" they were sending to potential voters, not for what they were actually saying about why the candidate wanted to be mayor, and certainly not because the candidate wanted to do good. But Castille's treatment was different. Castille was being singled out from all the other candidates, portrayed as a politician who wasn't really a politician at all, but rather an altruistic public servant.

There was no small irony in the fact that the same mythology had been laid upon the man whose record Castille would now be running against. When Wilson Goode had first run for office, he was portrayed as the Ivy-League educated technocrat, the black candidate who was different from all those angry, militant, separatist black leaders who were making demands for their people. Back then, Wilson Goode had been the politician who wasn't really a politician, the man who had dedicated his life to public service, who worked night and day, weekday and weekend to help the people of the city—not cutting backroom deals for jobs and contracts like the typical political hacks. His race had been significant only in that it would help him work to overcome racial divisions, to fight for the good of the city, black and white.

The story of the hardworking, highly skilled manager who had lifted himself up by his bootstraps, the sharecropper's son who had fought prejudice and low expectations to reach the pinnacle of responsibility in city government, had made for inspiring reading. The only trouble was that it had not been a very good predictor of what kind of mayor Goode would make. The so-called brilliant manager had for months avoided dealing with the code violations and disturbances of a radical back-to-nature group called MOVE, before finally stumbling into a deadly confrontation. The man who had seemed so noble and unsullied by backroom politics was unable to make the kind of deals with city council that would get a badly needed trash-to-steam plant built or win concessions from labor unions in new contracts. And the man who would be mayor of all the people seemed to invest more time working for minority set-asides than protecting the city's bond rating. But the media never seemed to look back at how well a mayor's performance jibed with the expectations set forth in his campaign coverage. Instead, they simply moved on to new leading men and new mythologies.

And now it was Ron Castille's turn. The era of the "moderate black hardworking technocrat" was giving way to the ascendance of the "moderate Republican war hero crime-buster." It was not that reporters or editors or news directors all met in a room and decided to anoint a candidate like Ron Castille, and then, like Madison Avenue gurus, set out to create an appealing image for him. It was more that they all recognized instinctively what and who made a good story. And what often made the best story was the tale of the politician who wasn't really a politician. That was why "outsiders" were so appealing and often got such a big push in the initial news coverage of campaigns. It was not just that they were fresh goods in a profession programmed to track what was new and discard what was old. It was also that as "outsiders" they could be portrayed as pure and untainted protagonists going up against the dirty and corrupt power structure. It was a fairly unrealistic view of politics, ignoring the importance of being able to forge compromise and to secure cooperation from the diverse and often warring interests that existed in a big city. But as with any fantasy, the appeal of the image had little to do with the cold glare of reality.

In this election, Ron Castille was hardly an "outsider" or nonpolitician. He had run in four political campaigns, and in 1991 he was the man who had been selected by the party boss. But he was being singled out, nevertheless, for the same reasons Wilson Goode had been in 1983, because of the appeal of his simplistic media image. And it happened as a result of a series of small piecemeal decisions about who should be covered, and how, and where the stories should be played in the paper or on the newscast. In the *Inquirer*'s case, it was Sal Paolantonio's editors who told him to set up a Saturday morning one-on-one interview with Castille after the endorsement. After all the focus on the political intrigue, they told the reporter, we owe the guy a chance to spell out his views. But if the editors had stopped to think about it, they might have realized that all the candidates were being covered largely for their political intrigue, and they were all probably owed a chance to lay out their views. Something else was going on in their decision to allow Castille the luxury of spelling out his views. And that something else, even though it may have been quite unconscious on the part of the editors, was that the clean-cut white Republican war hero made a better story than any of the other candidates in the race.

For the reporter who would actually go out and interview Castille and write up the story, there were other considerations that might have figured in. In the days following the Republican party endorsement, Paolantonio considered Ron Castille the easy favorite to win the primary and challenge the Democratic candidate in the fall general election. For some time now, he had been courting the key people in the Castille campaign, as he had been doing with all the campaigns, to get them to talk about what their candidate was up to. The trouble was he had found them a pretty closed bunch, a tight-knit group that didn't deal with the press that much. A relatively uncritical piece might encourage them to open up in the coming months, and he would need that to write the kind of inside strategy pieces he thought were crucial to political coverage. There would be plenty of time later on to be critical.

The story that resulted from Paolantonio's interview was called "Candidate's Vision: Good Government." It summed up Castille's plans for the city this way: "Restore reliable city services. And restore credibility in city government." Castille's plans included no new taxes and no cuts in services. He was not targeting the city's municipal unions or offering privatization to save money, as some of the other candidates had been discussing. Rather, he talked about building bridges to Republicans in the suburbs, where he would "parlay his party ties into help for Philadelphia." In what form that help might come was not spelled out, nor did the reporter press him when he claimed he could get more money from Harrisburg at a time when the state was facing billion-dollar deficits itself. Castille's philosophy was summarized in a quote presented in the last paragraph of the story. "I want to get in there and have an honest government," he said. "We're going to get good people in City Hall, back them up, make the government credible again." Even the caption on the photo of Castille in his home, sipping coffee in his tastefully decorated dining room, had a positive spin to it: "A year's worth of soul-searching about the mayor's race ended last week when Castille said the magic words: 'I'll go for it.'" Where Tia O'Brien had used *procrastinating* and Channel 6's Vernon Odom had used *wavering* and *indecision* before the endorsement, in this postendorsement piece, the *Inquirer* caption-writer had chosen *soul-searching*.

It was noteworthy that no similar Saturday morning interview at home over coffee had been scheduled by these same editors and rushed into print in the same way about Ed Rendell, the front-runner in the Democratic primary. In fact, Paolantonio had been trying to get a profile of Rendell's campaign into print for weeks, but had not succeeded. It was pushed out, he assumed, by all the war news. But it was also true that Ed Rendell, in 1991, just didn't have the same kind of audience appeal as Ron Castille, the war hero. While Rendell thought of himself as a man with strong leadership qualities, good political instincts, and solid ideas about tackling the city's problems, in the media he was merely the political has-been, the retread. And so while Paolantonio had chopped up his Rendell profile and included pieces in other campaign stories, he had followed his editors' suggestions that Castille be given a more leisurely platform for his ideas.

Even after the drama of Castille's surprise announcement had faded, the positive coverage continued. On television, Castille basked in coverage for even the most routine activities of the D.A.'s office, from which he planned not to resign until the last legal day. One day he would be seen on Channel 6 talking about how "long overdue" was a newly passed Pennsylvania law for restitution and damages for suffering for crime victims. Another day, he would make it onto a story about the city's measles epidemic, talking about what the city might do about the children of a church group that did not believe in medical treatment. And the following week, when a downtown high-rise office building burned, causing the death of three fire fighters, Castille was there again on all three newscasts, arriving at the scene of the fire to see if there was any criminal negligence. Although he wasn't performing any noteworthy public action—he was hardly central to the city's action to force parents to immunize their children, and the problems of high-rise buildings without sprinkler systems were not his to solve—still, there he was. And unlike his competitors, both Republican and Democrat, who were shown only in their roles as politicians, Castille was appearing as a concerned, in-charge public servant.

In the ensuing days, as other candidates espoused more of their positions on the city's issues, they did not get the same kind of lengthy, unchallenged forum as Ron Castille had been given to put forward his "vision" for the city. When, a few days later, Ed Rendell called a press conference to announce a plan to cut municipal labor costs by changing work rules, reducing benefits, and privatizing trash collection, the story made page 3-B of the *Inquirer,* with the headline "Rendell's Plan to Save Money Earns Him Unions' Wrath." After sketching the bare details of the plan in the first paragraph, Paolantonio moved immediately to an attack on Rendell by a city municipal union leader who called him a "scab candidate." Similarly, when George Burrell called a press conference to lay out his plan to curb drug-related crime, Paolantonio accorded it a scant paragraph in the middle of a larger article about all the Democratic candidates. It was the same on television. Only one station had even bothered to cover the Rendell and Burrell press conferences, and in both cases the reports had been a mere forty-five seconds in length. Clearly, Ron Castille was getting the chance to ruminate about his vision for the city when most of the other candidates could barely get a sound-bite.

Even when Frank Rizzo began to attack him in a series of political ads, Castille's image protected him on the news. In the week after Castille jumped into the race, Rizzo began his first negative ad of the campaign with the slogan "What's the Deal, Castille?" This was the same line he had used on reporters the day Castille was endorsed by the GOP. "A big law firm with clients doing business with the city has offered to give Ron Castille a job if he runs for mayor," the ad began. "What's the deal, Castille? What are you getting? What's the law firm getting? And what will their clients get if you get elected? Are you running for office or just selling it? What's the deal Castille?"

Although the ad was highly critical, when it was picked up by reporters and turned into news stories, the spin was decidedly in Castille's favor. The *Daily News* "ad watch" pointed out that Castille had done nothing illegal or even unethical in accepting the law job, and an *Inquirer* editorial, "Flag That Ad! Rizzo's Anti-Castille Spot Draws a Penalty," noted, "Hard as it may be for Mr. Rizzo to understand, with his multiple pensions and his big recent earnings as a radio talk show host, some people still actually have to earn a living." Channel 6's story featured a Temple political science professor suggesting that Rizzo had "misstepped" with the ads, while Channel 10 gave equal time to Castille, who responded, "It's just Frank being silly. I'm a lawyer. I'm not independently wealthy, and I need a job. If I took a job digging ditches, Frank would say I'm in the corner of organized labor." The reporter noted that insiders in the Castille campaign claimed that the ads would backfire.

In only one corner was Castille's golden image in the news tarnished. It came in a story in the *Daily News* by Dave Davies, "Bashfulness Cost Castille . . . Late Start Lost Contributors." Davies, a former city hall bureau reporter for radio, had focused on Castille's qualifications, not his inspiring image. "As he begins his quest for the city's highest office, he is a candidate with few ideas for governing, not much cash, and little of what politicians call fire in the belly," he wrote. Davies quoted Castille as saying, "As we got closer and closer to the decision date, it looked to me like I was going to have to run." Unlike the television stations, which had run similar quotes unquestioningly, Davies countered this statement with "*Have to run*? Is that enough desire to endure a bruising nine-month campaign and then run a city that's broke?" There were other less than flattering references in the article. Davies described Castille's desk as "cluttered with studies and reports on the city's complex financial problems. . . . Like a man studying for finals, Castille is cramming." He noted that the district attorney managed some 520 employees and a $21 million budget and did not set tax rates or negotiate union contracts. In contrast, he said that the mayor "has 50 times as many employees and 100 times the budget and must also worry about a $1.1 billion a year school system. He must bargain with four municipal unions, develop tax policy, and wrestle with City Council."

But the *Daily News* story was clearly the minor discordant note in the local media chorus. For both the *Inquirer* and the TV stations with their diverse regional audiences, the nitty-gritty details about the city's problems and the qualifications of people to solve them were not taking center stage. Here it would require simple, appealing themes and larger-than-life personalities to draw people in, and for now that equation was working in Ron Castille's favor.

10 The Candidates on *Hollywood Squares*

February 27, 1991

❦ It was starting out to be a quiet week for Philadelphia mayoral politics, overshadowed by other major news stories at home and abroad. After a miraculously brief and successful ground campaign in the Iraqi war, Kuwait had been liberated and Saddam Hussein's troops were poised to surrender. At the beginning of the week, the only mayoral candidate visible on the local media scene was Ron Castille, who made a tour of the Meridian building fire and was interviewed by all three local television stations about possible criminal investigations in the fire fighters' deaths. But then on Tuesday an item appeared in the *Inquirer's* television gossip column. Gail Shister reported that Tia O'Brien, "Channel 3's ace political reporter," was leaving KYW, having accepted a more lucrative offer from KRON in San Francisco. With the uncertainty floating around the station in the past months and the possibility of major staff cutbacks looming, O'Brien had put out feelers to other stations and had gotten an attractive offer from the San Francisco station to cover business. She had given KYW time to match it and would have stayed had they been able to meet the other station's terms. But as the San Francisco station kept sweetening the offer, KYW couldn't keep up. Westinghouse simply wasn't giving them the leeway to make her a competitive offer.

But there was more to it than money. O'Brien found it frustrating to be working in a news environment in which there seemed to be so much confusion over what the product should be. She had watched the news director and his assistants spending much of their time in the past few months developing new "prototypes" for the news shows, and talk was that every time the prototypes were tested with audience research, they bombed and sent the honchos back to the drawing board. With all their attention focused on radical changes in the show, there was less of an eye on the day-to-day running of the operation and the basic journalistic mission. It was hard working in a shop where there wasn't a clear sense of what management was looking for in reporters' packages.

There was also uncertainty about budget cuts. A memo circulated to staff by the station's general manager, Jonathan Klein, emphasized that KYW would be looking to cut costs in the future. The memo talked about the need to produce good shows "with the right people at the right price" and for the 11 P.M. newscast to be a "differentiated show that appeals to a majority of the viewers and costs less to produce." The memo had appeared as an evil omen to reporters in the newsroom, who wondered just how far Klein would go. While news director Scott Herman, who was in charge of the entire news operation, seemed to value Tia highly and agree with her news judgment, the executive producer, who directed the evening newscast, frequently disagreed with her on everything from what was a big story to what kind of details to include. Just the week before, she had done a story about Councilman Jimmy Tayoun being investigated by the IRS and FBI and how that would affect his chances for re-election. In the piece, she had put in a line about how, years ago, these same voters had elected a dead man to city office. Her producer wanted to take the line out, but Tia fought to keep it in, claiming it was important to understanding how this neighborhood behaved. The next day, Herman told her the line had made the piece.

What she sensed from her producer was that he was unsure of what his higher-ups wanted in the news product and terrified of not giving them what they wanted. Because of hypersensitivity to ratings, there was inconsistency over what KYW's news product should be. She was tired of working in an environment in which people did not seem to know what they wanted in their news. And she was sick of getting stories first, only to see them not run, as when she had a potentially exclusive confirmation that Castille was running and it was edited out of her piece. Even when she did break stories and get exclusives, there were no obvious rewards because there was no place for her scoops to be heralded. If the *Inquirer* or the *Daily News* had an actual media critic, she would think, maybe she would get a few kudos for all the hard-news stories and exclusives she broke compared to the other stations. That might be the kind of very visible attention that would make KYW take notice. But the only kind of reporting the papers did about TV news was Gail Shister's gossip column. And so while *Inquirer* readers had been extremely well informed about the progress of Tia O'Brien's pregnancy last year, they had little idea that she was one of the best television reporters in the city. As a result, she got very little leeway from her station to do hard-news reporting, and now she was choosing to move on, hopefully to a station that would value her journalistic skills more highly.

O'Brien was still going to be covering the mayoral campaign for a few more months, however, and this Wednesday night she had convinced the station to send her out to cover a candidates' forum sponsored by the Philadelphia Board of Realtors at the Wyndham Franklin Plaza Hotel. Chatting with *Daily News* reporter Dave Davies, with whom she had worked at the public radio station years before, she was the recipient of joking and homages as people came up to talk to her during the wine and cheese hour preceding the forum. When someone mentioned all the attention she was getting in the media, she told Davies that Stu Bykofsky had mentioned her in his column in the *Daily News* that morning. "Stu seems to have some criticisms of my reporting style," she said drily. Bykofsky had claimed that many of Philadelphia's politicians would be delighted to see her go because she was "too aggressive for her own good."

Sam Katz made his way over to her, starting to shake her hand, but stopping to theatrically throw his hands up in the air and hide them behind his back, playing on the story Paolantonio had written about his pointing his finger near her eye after the Republican endorsement luncheon. "You know," he said, smiling, "I was looked at as a dull guy before that incident. But with one sweep of the hand, one pointed finger, I became . . . " he tried to remember how Paolantonio had described him in the article. "Irascible," an onlooker supplied the word. "That's it," he said, still smiling. "Irascible."

As the time for the forum neared, O'Brien and Davies talked about how Lucien Blackwell had canceled out at the last minute. "Has anybody seen Lucien since he announced at city council?" asked O'Brien.

"I haven't," said Davies.

"You know, he told us at council that he was going to have this big fundraiser the next Friday to announce formally, and then we tried to cover it, but we couldn't even find out where his campaign headquarters are," O'Brien said.

"I think it might be time that we do the 'Where's Blackwell?' story, don't you?" said Davies. "We went after Castille this week. I think it's about time we beat up on the Democrats."

The WWDB reporter piped up. "If it's 'What's the deal, Castille?' then how about 'Haven't got a clue, Lu'?"

Sal Paolantonio had also been having a problem getting in touch with

Blackwell. The candidate and his people weren't responding to his phone calls and were almost totally inaccessible. Paolantonio had found it unbelievable that a candidate running for mayor was not talking to the largest newspaper in town. But at the same time, he recognized that the black candidates had other ways of getting their message out: through the black radio stations, the *Tribune*, the clergy, and people on the street.

Two other candidates wouldn't be attending that night, either: Ron Castille, because he was not yet an announced candidate, and Frank Rizzo, who rarely appeared at such forums, according to O'Brien, because he liked to maintain an image of "being above it all."

When the forum started, O'Brien took her seat in the front row of the ballroom, along with Davies, Paolantonio, and Kevin Boyle from talk radio station WWDB. The media "pack" was much reduced from the Republican endorsement luncheon; O'Brien was the only television reporter whose station had thought this forum was interesting or important enough to cover. And it was doubtful whether even she would get a piece on. As she sat down in her seat, Ed Rendell leaned down from his seat on the podium. "I got interviewed about you today," he called to her. "I've been waiting a decade to do that. Answer questions about you, not from you." At that moment, a photographer from the *Daily News* began snapping shots of O'Brien for a profile the paper was doing on her.

The forum itself was intended to get the candidates to clarify their positions on issues of concern to the local real-estate industry. The candidates were each allotted four minutes in which to discuss restructuring taxes to attract business to the city, developing more affordable housing, and working toward regional cooperation. It was a lot to fit into four minutes, and the candidates seemed to have different strategies for trying to impress the group—and to get media attention in the process.

James White, Wilson Goode's former managing director and the third black candidate to enter the Democratic campaign, spoke first, attempting to answer the questions in his methodical, almost plodding, manner. "One of my top priorities as mayor will be to ensure the ultimate success of the economic recovery that the city has pursued since 1980," he said. He talked about the economic development projects that had been begun in the last decade. "As mayor, I will exert the leadership in this process by guaranteeing timely completions of these projects in the public domain, while supporting private sector growth in jobs and businesses." He summarized city policies to encourage development and said he would continue them. "I've been told to stop. Thank you very much."

Sam Katz was second, and his style was dramatically different from White's. As people clapped for him, he said jokingly, "You're running into my time, please," to which he gained appreciative laughter. He then went on to argue forcefully that the success of the real-estate industry in the city was tied to the quality and performance of the public education system. "Tonight I would like to propose a substantive reform in public education in Philadelphia. I would like to endorse the concept and practical implementation of choice in education." While providing few details of his proposal, he struck the chord that public education, as much as other parts of city government, needed to be run as a business with free-market competition. And he suggested that he, as a former member of the Philadelphia School Board, was the one candidate who could tackle the issue effectively and come up with new initiatives.

Peter Hearn followed. (As he got up to stand at the lectern, O'Brien instructed her cameraman to get a shot of him walking up. Hearn was still carrying the attractive image of the "outsider," which might make him more interesting to feature in her piece than the rest of the candidates.) His speech offered no new proposals or even strategies. Rather, he stressed the importance of image—the need to improve the city's, and the value of his own as an "independent." He began, "I am not Charles de Gaulle, but I believe that politics is too important to be left to politicians. That's why I'm running. I am different. I am different by background. I have never run for political office before. I am not part of the partisan political system that has brought us to the brink. I am known as somebody who will shake this system to its roots. I am known as a person who accomplishes things."

When Hearn had finished, O'Brien whispered, "Well, he didn't answer one of the questions, but he made the best presentation." As each of the speakers took his turn at the lectern, the cameraman waited for his cue from the reporter about when to shoot and when to cut. As Hearn was speaking, he turned to her, making a hand gesture across his neck to ask, "Cut him off?" She shook her head. "I'm waiting for him to make his point," she whispered. Even for a relatively short debate, there was a need to be economical and not tape the entire forum. The cameraman traveled with battery packs that ran out quickly, and the television reporter simply didn't have the time to log lengthy tapes when it came to choosing sound-bites back at the station. As a result, in these situations television reporters were forced to predict when a crucial sound-bite was approaching, and often they were too late in getting their cameramen to capture something that they realized, after it was said, was important.

Ed Rendell addressed the crowd with his trademark informality. (For much of the debate, he had leaned to the right or left to chat with Hearn or White.) "Hello, everyone. Let me start by apologizing because, unfortunately, I'll have to leave the forum a little early. Tonight conflicts with

Philadelphia Legal Secretaries Association dinner, which is honoring my wife, who, as many of you know, is a lawyer. She has been chosen Boss of the Year. And as Boss of the Year she has ordered me to attend for at least a little while." He then got into a substantive response to the questions. "Peter is absolutely correct that all of the things that you care about so very much are tied to the overall image of the city." He laid out what he claimed were Philadelphia's three options. "One is raising taxes, and that is unacceptable," he said. He suggested that once the city's immediate fiscal problems were "under control," which he argued he could accomplish in the first year in office, the city should actually experiment with lowering the wage tax as a "prod to development."

"Second, people are hoping that the federal government or Harrisburg is going to bail us out." (Castille had suggested in his *Inquirer* interview that better relations with Washington and the state government would solve Philadelphia's problems without the need to raise taxes or cut services.) "Not going to happen. The federal government is going to bail nobody out. The state government will help us partially. Partially," he stressed. "But they are not going to help us until they can see that we can lead, make tough political decisions, and manage this government.

"What we have to do is take this government and shake it up. We need a new mayor and a new city council. We need to cut the cost of the operating budget by 10 to 15 percent. Through privatization of trash collection, through capping overtime." Rendell had come the closest to addressing not simply the realtors' questions but the major problems of the city, and he had taken a clear-cut position on how to do so. But it would never be captured by a sound-bite. Over the years, his advisers had tried to get Rendell to speak in sound-bites, but it was something he had always resisted as intellectually dishonest. In this campaign, however, it might not matter that much. Rendell was already way ahead of the other candidates in fundraising, and chances were that he could get his message out quite nicely through his advertising, as election day neared. Unlike his competitors, who were actively courting the news media, Rendell had to avoid controversy and try not to offend any key constituencies.

George Burrell was next, reading from a prepared speech as White had, making no jokes or informal comments, as some of the other candidates had. He argued that the city could not afford to raise taxes or cut services and that the answers to the problems should come through stimulating economic growth. He noted that Philadelphia was a center of great health care, research, and educational institutions, all of which should be tapped in order to stimulate growth in high-technology industry and attract federal contracts to help build small businesses. This task, he argued, "requires a mayor who knows how to get things done not just in city hall but down in Washington and out in the neighborhoods." He was reminding the audience of his strong ties to Congressman Bill Gray and how those ties might help the city. He also noted that he was a strong supporter of affordable housing and of replacing high-rise public housing with low-rises. As he spoke, the Channel 3 cameraman turned to Tia, making a gesture with his hands that asked, "Keep shooting?" He rolled his eyes as if he were bored. She nodded, almost apologetically. George Burrell had made some important points in his speech, but there was nothing that held the simple television appeal of Peter Hearn's "I am different."

Dennis Morrison Wesley, the black Republican accountant, was the "clean-up hitter," as he put it. As mayor, he said, he would reduce the wage tax by 2 percent, he would not raise real-estate taxes, and he would cut the number of city government employees in a big way. "We can cut three thousand people," he said. While extremely concrete, Wesley was obviously promising more than anyone could hope to deliver as mayor.

Midway though the forum, O'Brien was beeped. When she called into the station, she learned that President Bush was going on television at nine o'clock to declare a cease-fire with Iraq, so she would probably not have a package that night. Depending on what was happening the next day, she might put together a package then. The forum was the kind of thing that didn't age too quickly. She was playing with an idea for a piece laying out the candidates' stands on the issues, where the candidates would be shown as if they were playing the TV game show *Hollywood Squares*. She was thinking how she could use video from the evening's forum for the piece and about how humorous it would be to have the candidates put in the little squares answering their questions about the issues. She knew that was the kind of package her executive producer and her news director would love and that they would put it on the air even if, on the same day, someone like Ron Castille dropped out of the race.

When each candidate had spoken and answered questions from the audience, the forum was concluded. The candidates waded out into the auditorium to chat with members of the audience and to answer questions from the few reporters in attendance. Tia O'Brien did not hesitate for a moment in deciding what line of questioning to pursue. After listening to the candidates describe their many proposals for stimulating business in Philadelphia, she headed straight to George Burrell.

"Councilman Burrell, can I ask you what you think about the fact that Lucien Blackwell's not here tonight?" Like Paolantonio, O'Brien didn't think of herself as a stenographer. She prided herself every bit as much as he did on finding and creating the story, not getting it hand-delivered to her. And working at a television station, she had long ago learned that a piece that focused on what candidates said at a forum wouldn't have a snowball's chance in hell of making it to the air.

Burrell demurred. "You'll have to ask Councilman Blackwell or members of his staff about the direction of his campaign strategy."

"Well, do you think it's important for a candidate to be out here answering these types of questions?"

"I think it's important for candidates to offer their views to every constituency in the city, as I have done over the last several weeks, whether in Northeast Philadelphia, South Philadelphia, North Philadelphia, West Philadelphia . . . " Burrell answered.

"Do you think his failure to show up indicates he is not as willing as others to answer these questions?"

"I can't speak for Councilman Blackwell. Whether he's got a different strategy, whether he's got a different group of people he's talking to, I don't know. I think it's important to reach out to people, that we be available to different kinds of constituencies. It is inconvenient for all of the candidates to come to this kind of event, to give a large block of time, but I think it's important." She then asked him what was happening with the endorsements from black clergy and ward leaders. Again he deflected her question, saying she would have to speak with them.

Next, she went to Peter Hearn to ask the same question about Blackwell's absence. "Would that concern you as a voter?" she asked.

"I think it would," Hearn answered. "It's my job, it's his job, it's everybody's job, to get out there before the people and tell them what they stand for and let them decide. And the only way to do that is to show up."

"Do you feel that he is trying not to put himself in a forum like this?"

"Tia, I just don't know. I know why I'm here and why I think it's important to be here, but I really can't speculate why he's not here."

The candidates' forum did not make it onto KYW news, but in the newspapers Paolantonio and Davies both made a stab at summarizing what the candidates had put forward that evening. The blandness of their stories pointed up a fundamental problem with much traditional campaign coverage. While forums provided an opportunity for Philadelphians to hear the candidates talk about issues and, over the course of two hours, get a feel for the way the contenders thought on their feet, they were hard to summarize for a short newspaper piece or television story. The problem for reporters was that it was very hard to take the bits and snatches of proposals on widely different issues and tie them together in a story that would be interesting or informative. What Paolantonio and Davies wound up doing was all that any reporter could expect to do, given the nature of the assignment: give each candidate one paragraph, then move on to the latest on campaign strategy, culled from an afternoon on the phone with sources in the campaigns. The play for the two stories testified to what the editors thought about this approach: Paolantonio's story was played on 4-B, Davies's on page 19. If Tia O'Brien had gotten a package, she would have taken the same approach to covering such forums: giving a brief nod to substance before proceeding to strategy, i.e., the question of why Lucien Blackwell wasn't coming to the forums.

The real problem was with the conventional definition of campaign reporting. To the assigning editors back in the newsroom, the campaign was to be covered on two tracks. First, there were the day-to-day "events" of the campaigns, the forums and public appearances by the candidates, the announcement speeches and endorsements. Second, there was the daily assessment of the horse race, gotten by working the phones to get scoops on each campaign's constantly evolving strategy. But neither was likely to generate the kind of information voters needed to choose between candidates. That kind of information required a form of journalism that was less focused on events and strategy. It required that the candidates' speeches at forums and other public appearances be the starting point, not the ending point, of the reporting process. If voters were to make any sense out of Sam Katz's proposal for School Choice, they needed to know what it was and what it cost and whether Katz had any chance of implementing it. If they were to evaluate George Burrell's claim that the city didn't need to raise taxes or cut services, that it just needed to grow the economy, then they needed to know if this was a realistic proposal and whether economic growth could happen quickly enough to wipe out the impending deficit. The trouble was that the reporters covering the campaign were not being given the time or space to explore these questions or many others that would really provide voters with meaningful information about their choices.

And even if Tia O'Brien were not leaving Philadelphia, it was unlikely that she would get the chance to do that kind of reporting, either. It was going to take more than putting the candidates on *Hollywood Squares* to help voters make informed choices in this or any other election.

11 Waiting for Wilson

March 8, 1991

As the primary campaigns moved into the first week in March, all eight declared candidates fanned out across the city to attend forums and other public appearances, trying to get media attention in the process. Lucien Blackwell finally came out of hiding (or so it seemed to reporters like Tia O'Brien and Dave Davies). He held a rare press conference outside Olney High School, in one of the city's outer ring neighborhoods, to propose a new scholarship program for public high school students. Where a school district facing a huge pending deficit was going to find money for such a worthy cause was not at all clear, but the story did win the candidate thirty seconds on local TV news, as did George Burrell's walk through a public housing project that week where he talked about drugs and his proposals for getting more police on the streets.

But more and more, the black candidates running for the Democratic nomination were finding that they could not capture the imagination of the local media with their press conferences and media events. What the media wanted to cover about Lucien Blackwell, George Burrell, and James White was not their proposals for establishing scholarship funds or fighting drugs, but rather the paramount political struggle each faced to win the nomination. There was no question that it would make victory harder for any one of them if all three stayed in the campaign and the black vote was split. And that was the story all the reporters wanted to cover.

What the media were watching ever so carefully were endorsements, which would be important in bolstering one black candidate's fortunes and encouraging the others to drop out. The most crucial was the endorsement of the black clergy, a group viewed as having a major influence in Philadelphia's black community. After a series of delays, twelve leaders of the group had held a press conference the previous week to announce that they would endorse George Burrell. But the vote for Burrell had not been unanimous. Blackwell and White supporters had stormed out of the meeting and contended that the clergy were not united behind Burrell. And both Blackwell and White vowed to stay in the race.

With the clergy divided and all three men committed to running, reporters might have been expected to turn finally to the question of what each man stood for. At this point in the campaign, Philadelphians relying on the media knew little more about the three black candidates than that Blackwell was the "poor people's candidate," that Burrell was "Bill Gray's man," and that White was well liked and backed by the municipal unions. Beyond that, coverage of the black candidates' positions or plans or skills was meager. One TV station caught a glimpse of James White's anger as he campaigned in a Latino neighborhood and was interviewed about whether he would consider dropping out. "I didn't come here to talk about that," he said testily. "I came here to talk about what we need to do for the people of this community—" But the station never let him finish. They had their simple theme for the three black candidates, and it had nothing to do with what any one of them was going to say about the Latino or any other community.

And so it was not surprising that on March 8, the hottest issue for both the newspapers and television newscasts was the question of which of the three black candidates would receive the endorsement of Mayor Wilson Goode. Goode had been postponing his announcement for weeks. Some campaign reporters saw the delay as one last evidence of Goode's indecisiveness, while others traced it to the embarrassing position that the mayor had found himself in because he had promised to support at least two and possibly all three of the black candidates at some time in the past year. (James White had served as Goode's own managing director in the aftermath of MOVE, resigning just seven months before to take a job at a local bank.) For the past week the mayor had been tantalizing reporters with interviews in which he led them to believe he had selected a candidate but would not reveal it. He had told many reporters that he would definitely have an endorsement by the close of the business day on Friday.

On Friday morning there was still no news. At ten-thirty in the morning, Dave Davies and Tia O'Brien were in Room 138 of City Hall waiting for a press conference scheduled by James White, as he formally filed his petition for mayor. As O'Brien and Davies waited for White to arrive, they discussed Goode's endorsement.

"Do you really think it's worth anything?" O'Brien asked Davies. Her tone revealed that she didn't think so. Sal Paolantonio had written three stories that week about Goode's endorsement, stressing its importance, but Tia O'Brien knew that the mayor had endorsed people before and it hadn't meant much. "I think it's worth something," answered Davies. "I think his choice means something to some people in the city." She asked him what he'd heard about the endorsement, what the word was on the street.

"The word is he's still praying."

"Praying?"

"Praying." Davies added that Lucien Blackwell was meeting with a group of ward leaders at his headquarters at that very minute, and O'Brien immediately found herself torn about which direction to go in.

She was hardly excited about covering Jim White's media event, but she needed the shots of him for any piece she would put together. That was the tough part about being a television reporter. You didn't just have to report the news like a newspaper reporter. You had to run around finding video to go with each and every word you said. For any piece she might do on Goode's endorsement—no matter who he picked—she was going to need pictures of Burrell, Blackwell, and White. And the problem was she had virtually no video of Blackwell. The councilman had held a major campaign event March 7, an early morning prayer breakfast where eighty black ministers endorsed him. But KYW had missed it because O'Brien had been out with laryngitis for three days, and without her, the station had not realized what an important political event the breakfast was. She was embarrassed that her station hadn't covered the event and frustrated that she hadn't gotten video or an interview with Blackwell since he'd left City Council. So while his meeting with ward leaders was unlikely to yield any new information, she wanted to cover it to make up for the previous day's gaffe. Also, if Goode did endorse someone, she'd need sound-bites from the candidates commenting on the endorsement, even if it was before the fact. Who knew whether she would be able to catch them later on, before her piece had to be on the air.

At the same time, she didn't wanted to miss Goode. She had originally planned to go up to Goode's office after White filed to check out the endorsement. She called up to the mayor's press secretary. "Karen, what's the word on the mayor's announcement? Is he gonna do it today?" The press secretary told her that Goode had invited reporters to attend the farewell party for Finance Director Betsy Reveal, suggesting that might be when he made his announcement. ("Isn't that typical of Wilson," one of the reporters later said, "not even letting Betsy have the satisfaction of having reporters cover just her?") She looked impatiently for White and asked his aide, "You think he's going to be early?" Her cameraman mentioned that Harvey Clark was upstairs with the mayor, but she answered, "Harvey's the least of my problems."

Finally, she decided to call the station to get another camera crew to cover Betsy Reveal's farewell and any statement the mayor might give and announced she would cover White and Blackwell. "They're probably cursing you at the station for calling another crew," commented Davies. White soon arrived, and with him came more of the reporters from other TV and radio stations. Soon what had been a quiet, dingy City Hall office with two journalists conversing listlessly was transformed into the crush of a media pack surrounded by klieg lights, all bearing down on a man with a file of papers saying, "Can I turn this in here?" A bit belatedly, White, a no-nonsense career army officer who was new to the world of media events, borrowed his one-year-old grandson to hold for the camera's sake. "This is James White II," he said, more like a grandfather than a candidate. O'Brien asked genially, "A future mayor?" "A future president," White shot back indignantly, to good-natured laughter. He turned to O'Brien and said, "When was your child born, Tia?" "March 30," she answered. "March 30. He was born on February the sixth." To which the baby added, "Dada." "He likes his father," said White honestly, as the baby struggled to get back to that parent.

Soon the microphones were pointed at White, and the interviewing began. Most of the questions concerned the mayor's endorsement—what White had heard, what he would do if he didn't get it. He was not asked why he thought he could do a better job as mayor than his opponents, nor were any of the city's problems addressed.

Tia O'Brien, as usual, began the questions. "What's the word, Mr. White? Think you can get the mayor's endorsement?"

"That is the mayor's decision. I can't speculate on that. I'm hopeful of getting all endorsements, but there's really no way that I can guess about that."

"Well, you had a sit-down with the mayor the other night," she continued. "What was the message that you tried to convey to the mayor that you're trying to convey this morning?"

"What I'm doing this morning has nothing to do with anything other than the next step that's necessary in our campaign. I think you would all say that my policy as managing director was and continues to be that I don't discuss publicly my discussions with the mayor."

"Did you get into this race with the expectation that Wilson Goode would help you out . . . would support you?" O'Brien continued to press the issue.

"I don't think today—which is a very important step for me—I want to concentrate on what I'm doing today and what I'm doing in the future. . . . There is no controversy, no conflict. We have a clear sense of anticipation, of victory. I am very optimistic, and I want to focus on the future of our campaign, not on things that happened in the past."

"If you don't get the mayor's endorsement, do you plan to stay in the race?" O'Brien would not give up.

"We're going to win, and that is our goal, and in all clarity we've made that statement. . . . Not only are we in the race, but we're in it to win. All of us in the campaign are very optimistic about that. And what I'm receiving in terms of vibes, yesterday on 52nd street, it was just an enthusiastic response . . . "

Dave Davies asked, "Why file early? The deadline isn't until Tuesday. Most of the candidates wait until the last minute. Why be here now?"

"I have a very aggressive committee. They work real hard, they've organized a superb field organization, and we're rewarding them for their hard work. There's no need to wait. It's an important day for me, a day I've looked forward to since I entered the race." There were a few more questions, but none focused on what White stood for or why he was different from the other Democratic candidates.

When White's little media event ended, the reporters and cameramen drifted out to the corridors of City Hall, where they ran into Henry Nicholas, president of the predominantly black hospital workers' union in Philadelphia and a major White supporter. O'Brien stopped to ask him for his comment on White's entry into the race. He answered by taking a shot at two of the other Democratic candidates. "I believe that the strategy in the Rendell camp is show Burrell, elect Rendell," said Nicholas. O'Brien knew what he was talking about. She had heard that the slogan "Show Burrell, run Rendell" had been making the rounds on the streets of the city's black neighborhoods. The talk was that Blackwell's people were behind it, a way to discredit his two toughest opponents, by suggesting that Burrell's candidacy was simply a front for Ed Rendell, a way to keep the city's black community divided and assure Rendell's victory. O'Brien asked Nicholas a few questions about White's chances before heading off for Blackwell's center-city campaign headquarters five blocks south of City Hall.

In the station car inching down 13th Street, she discussed with her cameraman the latest run-in with her producer, how he had written a story for Thursday night's news to cover the fact that they'd missed the Blackwell breakfast. (She had been assigned to cover the traffic problems around City Hall as a result of the Meridian fire.) She said Burrell had been described as "the Democratic front-runner" until she had corrected the copy. It was distressing to her, to say the least, that the person who controlled so much of what went into the newscast didn't know who the Democratic front-runner was. She and her cameraman talked about who they thought might stay when all the tumult at the station resolved itself. (Just that week anchor Jerry Penacoli and Linda Gianella, who did the weather, had been let go.) "Anything can happen," he said. "I wouldn't be surprised if they asked me to do the weather in a bikini."

At Blackwell's campaign headquarters, they left the car in a no-parking zone and unloaded their equipment. O'Brien instructed her cameraman to get a wide range of shots of the headquarters itself and Blackwell talking to reporters. Dave Davies, who had walked down to Blackwell's head-quarters from City Hall, set in on questioning Blackwell. First, he asked him about Goode's endorsement and whether he had heard anything, to which Blackwell demurred. Then Davies asked, "At all the candidates forums we've been to, you haven't been there. Why?"

"I intentionally did that. I was one of the last to resign a few weeks ago, and we have had a few things that we had to do. We're going to wage a full-scale campaign. . . . I was not boycotting. There just wasn't time for it. Today everybody has a forum, panel discussions. Today you have about thirty or forty already scheduled, so if you miss one, you'll pick it up on the other side."

O'Brien joined the questioning. "This morning, the mayor was expected to make an endorsement. Have you had any word?"

"No, I don't think he's made it. I don't know whether he intends to make it today or not. There are some indications that he might not make it today. I don't know."

"Did some people that you've been talking to say that the mayor has agreed to delay this?" she continued.

"No. But it's possible that he would modify what he's been thinking. Yesterday, Tia, I had over one hundred ministers at a breakfast that we called rather hastily. I have to admit that I didn't expect so many to show up, but they did. I'm sure the mayor knows about that, and that would be one of the considerations that he would use to decide who to support. Maybe that would have some bearing on what he does today."

"If you fail to get the mayor's endorsement, will you drop out?" She seemed to be trying to get a sound-bite out of him saying something like, "No, I'm in this race to stay," which she could use if Goode endorsed Burrell.

"No, I will not drop out. I'm my own person, and I want every endorsement that I can get. It would puzzle me if I did not get it, but it would not concern me enough that I would stop doing what I'm doing."

"Why would it puzzle you?" she asked.

"Well, because I've been very close to the mayor, and the mayor said at one time that he was going to support me and I expect him to do that. People have the right to change their minds, even the mayor, and I respect that. But I still think there's a chance I might get it."

"If you fail to get it, how much of a blow would it be to you?" Again, she was pressing for a sound-bite.

"No blow at all," Blackwell answered.

"But you want it?"

"Absolutely. Sure, I would like to get Channel 3, Channel 6, Channel 10, Jim Gardner, Tia O'Brien, Dave Davies. I'd like to get it all, but we're all big boys. I did not get in pending on any one endorsement. So we're gonna keep on going, and we're gonna win."

Davies jumped back in. "Can I ask what you think of this very notion of getting a consensus black candidate?"

"I've said before that I'm not interested in that. I think some people are turned off by that. When you say that you've got Peter Hearn and Ed Rendell who are running who are Caucasian, and you turn around and say we're trying to come up with a consensus candidate who happens to be African American, you're going to turn off the people who would ordinarily vote for you. So I've said all along they can stay in. I'm not asking anybody to get out. I'm not getting out."

"Apart from the question of turning off people who might support you," Davies continued, "is it wrong to . . . there are some people who say when the mayor says we need one black candidate, what he's saying is the priority is to have a mayor of a particular color. Do you think, apart from the fact that it might turn people off, is it the wrong approach?"

"Yes, I think the person who becomes the mayor of Philadelphia should be the person who is the most qualified, that the people want, regardless of his race, creed, or color. I think we're going to have to get away from that. It's sort of gotten out of hand . . . but I don't think the mayor's saying that. You know, for years we've had other than black mayors, and now we've had one and it feels good and we'd like to do it again."

O'Brien joined them to ask a question. "Yesterday at your event there was a chant: 'Show Burrell, run Rendell.' "

"And I have nothing to do with that. I do not mention any of my opponents."

"Do you believe, though, that there is something afoot here?"

"I'm not going to get into that. I've said to my people I don't want them doing that. . . . But I cannot control what our people say."

"Well, do you find it odd that Jerry Mondeshire [Bill Gray's aide and an advisor to George Burrell] is spending time once a week with Ed Rendell?" she pressed.

"Well, he has every right to do that. I think people are accusing him of what you just asked me about. I, for one, could care less about Jerry Mondeshire."

The interview was over and, as with James White, it had focused almost completely on campaign strategy.

Goode never made his endorsement that day, though the reporters had continued to trail him. He waited until Sunday to hastily call reporters to his office, and when they arrived, he announced, using notes written on a few sheets of a yellow legal pad, that he was going along with the black clergy's endorsement of George Burrell.

But, as with the black clergy's endorsement, the decision by Goode to back a candidate did not put an end to the media focus on the horse race. The black candidates would continue to be dogged by one question and one question only: whether or not they would consider dropping out for the sake of black unity. Although time and again they would try to take control of their news coverage, each time they would fail. Following the textbook formulas for getting a message across in the media was just not going to cut it in 1991. Whether holding up a grandson for the cameras or calling a press conference in front of a local high school, the old tried-and-true techniques were not going to dissuade reporters from going with the script that was tying up the Democratic primary in a nice, tidy package.

The three black candidates may have had considerable experience in making laws and deals and managing city services. And they may have had any number of divergent ideas about how Philadelphia could emerge from its fiscal and social crises. But none of the reporters assigned to the campaign were delving very deeply into any of those subjects. There had not been a single question to Jim White or Lucien Blackwell that forced them to confront the issue of why they would make a better mayor than their opponents or why they were any more likely to solve the city's fiscal problems or find a way to reduce the problems of the underclass.

For some of the candidates in the race, the media's failure to focus on the issues and the tough choices facing the city would prove an advantage. It would create a vacuum into which a hero's image or a slick advertising strategy could be pushed instead, without having to get into all those messy decisions that a mayor would inevitably have to face, decisions that would alienate one or another constituency. But for James White, George Burrell, and Lucien Blackwell, the story that would fill the vacuum would not be one of their own choosing. They would never succeed in sending through the media the kind of simple messages that, while doing little to genuinely inform the electorate, help win elections. In that department in this campaign, the Republican candidates were proving to be the real masters of the trade.

12 Defining the Enemy

March 12, 1991

From the day Ron Castille decided to run, Frank Rizzo had been attacking him, both in interviews with reporters and in his television ads. Rizzo's latest ad, called "the shocker," announced: "First Ron Castille said he didn't want to run for mayor. Then he tries to cut a deal. Now the *Daily News* says, 'He is a candidate with few ideas for governing.' And here's the shocker: Ron Castille praising Wilson Goode's top people, his police commissioner, his streets commissioner, his managing director." The screen showed pictures of the officials with words Castille had used to describe them. "Castille isn't running against the Wilson Goode team. He's running with it. C'mon, Philadelphia. Frank Rizzo for Mayor."

The Rizzo campaign was also suspected of leaking damaging information about Castille to Chuck Stone, the *Daily News*'s veteran black columnist. Stone's column recounted claims that in two instances Castille had improperly drawn his gun in public. The first occurred in 1983 when Castille was an assistant D.A. He got into an argument at a restaurant with an attorney who was wearing a good conduct ribbon in his lapel. Castille allegedly told the attorney to take the ribbon off, since he had not earned it (it had belonged to the man's father), and when the attorney refused, Castille supposedly laid down a gun on the bar and demanded, "Now, what are you going to do?" The second incident had occurred in 1978 at a birthday party for another assistant D.A., at which Castille was said to have pulled out his gun when someone had raised the issue of how the candles should be extinguished. Stone noted that Castille claimed that both incidents were done "in jest and endangered no one."

A few days later, the *Daily News* ran an editorial called "Some Joke, Ron," in which they wrote, "Many people have wanted to be mayor over the years. Some have been nuts. This one, alas, is currently the city's top prosecutor. . . . If a guy's this irresponsible with a weapon, you have to wonder not just whether he should be mayor, but also whether he's too far gone to be a district attorney or even a salad bar sneeze shield adjuster. It's not good enough to say he was joking. Having a .45, a weapon that fires a bullet big enough to cause damage if it were merely thrown at you, pointed at your face is no joke. . . . Let's leave aside why a lawyer needs to carry a cannon. The issue here is whether anyone who waves guns at people has too many loose screws to be a public official."

The following Tuesday, the day Castille was to resign from his office and formally enter the race, Sal Paolantonio reviewed the gun incidents for the *Inquirer's* audience. The story, "Castille Has Allowed Foes to Get the First Shot, Strategists Say," was a far cry from the interview in Castille's living room a month before. Paolantonio pulled out his heaviest artillery of military analogies to describe Castille now as "the political equivalent of Iraq's Republican Guard . . . a stationary target for relentless pounding by a coalition of opponents."

Using unnamed "political strategists" as sources, he described how Castille had allowed Rizzo to "cast the first impression" of his opponent. He summarized the major blows to Castille's character: Rizzo's television ads on the law firm deal and the Goode cabinet, Sam Katz's characterizations of Castille as a "reluctant candidate who knows little about the city's number one problem: fiscal policy," and the latest, revelations that Castille drew his gun "in a way that legal experts considered inappropriate and in violation of Philadelphia Police Department directives about the use of firearms." Both the *Daily News* and the *Inquirer* stories showed that Frank Rizzo was beginning to systematically cut nicks in Castille's heroic media image. Frank Rizzo, not Ron Castille, was setting the media stage for Castille's entry into the mayoral campaign.

Castille's formal announcement was set for today, March 12, the day he had to resign his office as district attorney in order to file his papers to appear on the May ballot. Castille's campaign had planned the day's schedule carefully, designed to send the right messages via the media, particularly television, to the city's electorate. The first event, scheduled for 2:30, was an outdoor public rally at which Castille would announce his candidacy on the steps of the district attorney's office building at 1421 Arch Street. Up to the very last minute, Castille would use the symbolism of his powerful office as the backdrop for his coverage. After his announcement, he would then walk the block to City Hall to file his petition.

This walk was a brilliant piece of staging for the television cameras. While other candidates—like James White—would merely have pictures of themselves standing in front of a metal counter holding papers, Castille would be shot in a symbolic march to City Hall.

At 2:20 P.M., the "public rally" at the D.A.'s office was exclusively a gathering of the media. Standing in the cold on the sidewalk bundled in overcoats were reporters Harvey Clark of Channel 10 and Rick Williams from Channel 6, along with their cameramen. Tia O'Brien was on vacation in Florida, and Channel 3, on their own, had decided to send only a cameraman to cover the event. Barbara Grant and a cameraman from Channel 29 were also there, along with Cynthia Burton from the *Daily News,* Sal Paolantonio and Bill Miller from the *Inquirer,* and a few radio reporters. Five minutes before Castille was to speak, twenty to thirty assistant district attorneys filed out of the building and, along with a few curious onlookers, became the public rally.

On cue, Castille appeared, accompanied by his wife, Judy, and announced that he had formally resigned his position that day. "So I am now a full-fledged candidate . . . so let the fun and games begin," he said, which drew laughter from the crowd. Then in his characteristically low-key manner, he recited his speech, speaking a little too quickly and with little pause for emphasis. "As mayor, I will restore the essential elements of good government that are required for the survival of this city. Good government is no longer a luxury; it is a necessity." Since credibility and honesty were the hallmarks of his media image, Castille was going to push the idea that the way out of the city's dire problems involved these two character traits.

When he finished his prepared remarks, he took questions from reporters. Barbara Grant started off. Besides Tia O'Brien, Grant was the only other political beat reporter at a local television station in Philadelphia, and like O'Brien, she took her job seriously. She was not content to merely collect pictures and sound-bites, but jumped in aggressively to question the candidate. "Do you think it was a mistake for you to wait so long to announce your candidacy and that one of your opponents, Frank Rizzo, has had a couple of weeks to define you in front of the voters' eyes as someone who may have made a deal with a private law firm?" The question picked up on the point Sal Paolantonio had made in his story that morning.

Castille responded, "No, those were just negative commercials. We want to run an aggressive campaign, one that talks about the issues and doesn't come up with silly commercials like those that have been on TV. The citizens know what I've done for five years as D.A. They know my record. My ratings are extremely high. But they also know my dedicated service, fifteen years as a prosecutor, two years in the U.S. Marine Corps, where I almost died in combat for my country. So the citizens know that. And that nasty stuff, that negative stuff, that's not what campaigns should be about. And I'm going to take the high road. I'm going to talk about the issues."

Cynthia Burton asked whether he did have a job with a law firm. Castille said he was negotiating with several and would announce his decision soon. The next question was how much he'd spent thus far. "Not much."

"Do you think that the African American vote will make a difference in the election?" asked a reporter from WDAS, a black radio station in the city. "I've always had good support in the African American community," Castille answered. "In my first go-around I think I had something like 13 percent of the African American vote, and last time I did also. The issues are there for all of the citizens, and I'll be there in all the communities of this city seeking their support, and I hope to get a significant part of that community also."

The WWDB reporter asked, "Can you tell us how you size up the race, the other candidates, and how you're going to fare against them?"

"It looks like there will be a primary fight, but we're ready to do that. We think the Republican organization will be very strong in this race. The Republicans are excited about this because the polls that we've seen . . . all of the polls have been very favorable, and we're in a position that Republicans haven't been in in a very long time, with running a candidate who can win. So they're excited, and we think we can take that excitement all the way through the primary and into the general election."

Sal Paolantonio, who had been biding his time through the press conference, finally asked a question. "You characterized the commercials as silly. Was the leak about the gun incident by the Rizzo people also silly, in your opinion?" Castille had been unavailable for personal comment on the issue since the incident had been reported.

"No, that was more like dirty."

"Can you characterize that for us?"

"Dirty."

"Is it something that you are going to refrain from doing?" Paolantonio asked.

"Uh, yes, I'm going to refrain from doing it. The one incident was eight years, the other incident was thirteen years ago," he answered with an embarrassed smile.

"No, I meant leaking dirty information about other candidates."

"No, we won't be doing that. We won't be having any dirty information squad or people bringing us dirty information. We're going to talk about the issues. That's what we want, to talk about the issues in the campaign."

"What do you see as the major issues in the campaign, besides the financial crisis?" asked one of the radio reporters.

"Well, the financial crisis. The other most obvious issue is crime in the city of Philadelphia and the effects drugs are having on our society. And I have over twenty years' experience in that area," he said, as if fending off criticisms of his lack of experience in the other area. "I'm going to bring that experience to making crime and the fight against crime one of our most important priorities along with the financial situation."

"How are you going to rebuild neighborhoods?" asked Burton.

"We're going to . . . uh . . . we'll have position papers along the line as we address those issues more in-depth. We've issued a position paper today on what we will do to return Philadelphia's economy back to a . . . or rather its government back to a functioning government, without this tremendous debt that's really killing all of us." The questions about the city's issues did not play to Castille's strengths as a candidate. He was running his campaign on a simple image, an image that played particularly well on TV. While he was more than willing to expound on that image—to talk about good government and his war experiences—he did not seem prepared to speak about issues.

A few reporters protested that they didn't have time to read the whole position paper now.

"Well, I'll be available to talk about it tomorrow or later on."

Paolantonio asked a specific question about finances. "Well, the mayor's going to have to submit a budget in a couple of weeks and most likely raise some kind of taxes or ask some kind of tax increase. At this point, how do feel about tax hikes?"

"Well, I think tax hikes, in the wage and property tax, are going to be killers for Philadelphia. I can't see how under any circumstances we can raise those taxes and still maintain the viability of this city. There may be other ways to get revenue . . . we will be pushing for those. The only tax that would be appear to be a viable tax right now would be a one-cent increase in the sales tax."

Burton asked, "Would that be a sales tax for Philadelphia or a sales tax for the region?"

"Philadelphia, if we can get it. If we can get it for the region, to help finance SEPTA, and some of the areas where it's needed, great. But most critical is for Philadelphia, right now, if they cannot cover the gap in the budget with some of the things that we have suggested in here." He pointed to the position paper. "You know, I get these things all the time from the city controller's office, audits that tell you where you save 7 million, 2 million, 3 million dollars. We can use cash conservation measures such as those, which I've hardly ever seen implemented. We get them from the controller's office, and I look at them very closely so that we can follow what they say. I mean, they're the auditors."

Paolantonio pursued the tax question. "You said you can't see raising wage or property taxes. Does that mean that wage or property taxes proposed by city council you would veto it as mayor, no matter what?"

"Absolutely. I think it's dangerous for the city. It's bad for our economy. It just exacerbates the city's problems."

Burton asked "What would you cut out of government?"

"If you read in here," again, he pointed to his position paper, "you'll see that we want to audit every department, consolidate activities, see where you can even nonfund activities . . . you're going to have to see where you can eliminate the bloat in city government. We're going to take a hard look at that and make the tough decisions. I'm going to need a council with me if I'm elected mayor."

"Ron, can you sum up your feelings on your last day as D.A.? How does it feel to be leaving?" one of the radio reporters asked. While the print reporters had focused on some of the substantive issues, the broadcast journalist gravitated to the personal and emotional side of the day's events, serving to stoke Castille's image even more.

"It's been a great twenty years. When I first came to Philadelphia, to the navy hospital where I spent a good deal of my time, nine months to be exact, I'd never been in Philadelphia in my life. I thought it was a great city. The people were great. It had great culture, sports, you name it. It even had Thacher Longstreth. But the citizens of Philadelphia were great to me back then. And I chose to come here after law school, starting out in the D.A.'s office in 1971, because it was a place that I thought was great. It looks like it's my time to get in there and go for it. And I'm going to do it. I'm looking forward to the campaign. I'm looking forward to getting in there, trying to sort out that mess. I know it's not going to be easy. I've never thought that that was an easy job over there. I want a good government in a good city, but we're right near the edge."

As his press secretary motioned for him to head to City Hall, he said, "So let me go over there and file my petitions and thank you very much." The television cameras had long since stopped shooting him at the podium, knowing their stations had little interest in what Castille had to say about taxes and housing. They were all in position across the street, waiting to shoot his one-block walk to City Hall.

Throughout his talk, Castille had sounded like a man coached to have certain buzzwords and themes to respond to reporters' questions. He would be the "good government" candidate, characterizing Rizzo's charges as either "silly" or "dirty," claiming he was taking the "high road" and wanted to talk about the issues. However, every time the reporters asked him about the issues, he either referred them to his position paper or said that the campaign would issue position papers on other topics later. Again and again, he returned to his war experience—even when the questions had nothing to do with personal background—in order to deflect questions about running the city. More time had been devoted to carefully setting the stage for pictures—both still and moving—than to thinking through campaign issues. Every full-body shot of the candidate reminded viewers that he was a war veteran and a hero and that he had struggled with adversity and won. As Castille walked off to City Hall, all the cameras were focused on him.

But the best laid plans of media advisers are hardly foolproof, particularly in a city where murderers, rapists, and other candidates and their foes are all vying for media attention on any given day. Castille's big day was overshadowed by an even more appealing media event. When George Burrell had gone to file his papers at City Hall that day, he had been greeted by militant protesters blocking his way. The Black Vendors Association, which had opposed Burrell's bills limiting vendors' locations in center city, forcibly blocked Burrell's way and caused a scuffle in which two campaign aides were injured. And in the midst of the chaos many had repeated the "Show Burrell, Run Rendell" line. Although Lucien Blackwell would deny he personally had anything to do with either incident, it seemed that Blackwell supporters were just as capable as Frank Rizzo's of defining their opponent in the media.

And so, on the all-important six o'clock Action News on Channel 6 that night, Castille's leaving the D.A.'s office was accorded twenty-five seconds, while the Burrell incident got a package that was almost two minutes in length. And in the *Inquirer* the next day, the large photo that made the front page was of a hapless George Burrell marching down the street to chanting protesters. The front page of the tabloid *Daily News* also featured a stoic Burrell, with fingers pointing at him. In the battle of media events, it was evident that the black street vendors had beat out Ron Castille, but it was hardly clear who had won and what information had been provided to voters.

While Castille's announcement got pushed down in priority, his carefully planned photo opportunity did yield some payoffs. Accompanying Sal Paolantonio's story on the first page of the *Inquirer's* metro section ran two pictures: one a three-by-three-inch photo of Lucien Blackwell filing his petition papers, the other a ten-by-four-inch shot of candidate Ron Castille marching toward City Hall. Paolantonio's article did report the results of a poll he claimed "showed that Castille's four weeks of silence might have hurt him," and he did present, late in the article, criticisms of Castille's proposal for a one-cent sales tax increase. But the photo sent a far more powerful message than those few sentences buried deep in the story.

Two days later, Paolantonio expanded his look at Castille's sales-tax proposal in an article headlined "Castille Criticized for Suggesting City Sales-Tax Hike." It was a major substantive piece that outlined the opposition to the tax by many parties, including Castille's opponents in the primary as well as academic experts, and it was just the kind of story that provided useful information to voters trying to evaluate Castille's candidacy. But as with Paolantonio's other issue-based stories (a piece he did on where the candidates stood on women's issues had only made 6-B), the article did not get great play. Buried on the inside of a second metro section on 12-B, lost behind pages of full-page department store ads, it was unlikely to change many minds about Ron Castille. And it was equally unlikely to encourage Sal Paolantonio to invest the same energy in many more such stories in the primary.

13 The Defensive Witness

March 22, 1991

❦ On Tuesday, March 19, another volley was tossed at the Castille mayoral campaign. A lawsuit was filed in Common Pleas court by a private citizen who was widely assumed to be allied with the Rizzo campaign. The suit claimed that Castille had violated the city charter by effectively running for mayor while still district attorney. The charter stated that "No officer or employee of the city, except elected officers running for re-election, shall be a candidate for nomination or election to any public office unless he shall have first resigned from his then office or employment." If Castille lost the suit, he would be barred from running for office in Philadelphia for a year.

The case was set to be heard on Friday, March 22, by Judge Leon Katz. The night before, yet another bombshell had been dropped by the Rizzo campaign. On Channel 6's six o'clock news, Rizzo had accused Castille of having a drinking problem. The charge came in an interview with reporter Vernon Odom. Earlier in the day, Odom had covered the American Bar Association's forum, which was attended by eight candidates with one conspicuous absence: Frank Rizzo. Even Lucien Blackwell, who had assiduously avoided such forums, had put in an appearance, making Rizzo's absence all the more glaring. Castille and Sam Katz had jumped at the opportunity to make Rizzo's no-show the media issue of the day. "He just doesn't want to come out and talk about the ideas," Castille said to reporters. "It seems like he has to be in a structured situation. His campaign so far has been, as far as I can tell, one-liners, innuendoes, and malicious prosecutions." Castille went on with his criticisms of Rizzo, as the cameras rolled. This, after all, was the good stuff, not what any of the candidates said at the forum.

Odom, like the rest of his colleagues at Channel 6, was a general assignment reporter who might one day be covering a warehouse fire, the next a suburban murder trial. But he was a veteran reporter who had followed Philadelphia politics for over a decade—particularly black politics—and he was often assigned to campaign stories. After the Bar Association forum, he went to get Rizzo's response, playing a tape of some of the things Castille had said about Rizzo. Rizzo listened to the tape and responded offhandedly, "He must have been drunk when he said that." By the time the six o'clock news went on, Odom had a piece about Rizzo's charging Castille with a drinking problem. Odom described Rizzo as launching into "numerous but unsubstantiated allegations":

Rizzo: "He does have a drinking problem, yes, he does. Do we want to elect a mayor that drinks excessively every night or almost every night of the week?"

Odom: "Are you saying that he does that?"

Rizzo: "Yes."

Odom: "Now?"

Rizzo: "I don't know about now, today, but I know what his conduct was and I'll give you the names and the places, proof. I have all kinds of proof . . . people who will stand up. You know if I've said anything that he don't believe is true, he's a lawyer, he oughta know what to do with that."

Odom continued his report. "But despite my repeated requests for the time and places, Rizzo refused to produce anything in the way of documentation."

That evening, Rizzo attended a Fraternal Order of Police function, and by then other reporters had gotten wind of what he told Odom at six. Rizzo was only too happy to embroider on the charges to any reporter who put a microphone to his face. The charge was aired on each eleven o'clock newscast, and on Channel 6, the allegation was Jim Gardner's "big story" at the top of the news program. Now Rizzo was claiming he had more instances of Castille mishandling his gun. "This guy's not wrapped tight," Rizzo claimed in the report, adding, "If he wasn't drinking when he was wavin' them guns, then he's got a bigger problem, he's got a mental problem."

Rizzo's latest charges were very much in the minds of those gathered for the court proceedings the next morning on the seventh floor of One East Penn Square. Before the hearing began, a few journalists gathered outside the courtroom, discussing Rizzo's charges. Cynthia Burton, who was covering the hearing for the *Daily News,* said Rizzo had repeated his charge to her that night. She had covered it, but was glad that Channel 6 had aired the charge first, so that the *Daily News* hadn't had to be in the position of breaking the story of an allegation that seemed to be totally unsubstantiated. Reporters in Philadelphia, as in other cities, had heard a lot of rumors about the personal lives of their public officials—everything from wife beating to skirt chasing. While there had been talk about Ron Castille's liking to drink, reporters were personally skeptical about Rizzo's leap that the man had a "drinking problem." No one had ever seen him falling-down drunk in a public setting, and for a man who led a fairly public life that included open bars at official dinners, that was saying something. But even though they doubted there was any truth to Rizzo's allegations, they all felt obliged to report them. If a candidate for mayor publicly claimed that an opponent had a drinking problem, then the media felt they had a duty to tell people about it.

There was a discussion among those gathered about whether Rizzo had planned to make the charge, or whether he had been goaded into it by Castille's attacks about why he hadn't attended the forum. Some people felt that Rizzo's attacks against Castille had been relatively effective so far, but this one was going to backfire and make him seem wild and irresponsible. But others disagreed, saying Rizzo never shot from the hip, that he carefully calculated each move and each charge he made in the campaign. Indeed, longtime Rizzo watchers would observe that while the ex-mayor may not have planned at what precise moment and in what exact words he would unleash an attack, the general contours of the assault would have been carefully discussed beforehand. Rizzo was known to get out his negatives on an enemy in a very particular way: first, through private conversations with reporters, suggesting they follow up this or that lead, and then later through leaking potentially damaging materials that the reporter was advised to pursue. If that too failed, eventually he was known to go on the record, slipping a seemingly offhanded remark to an individual reporter—never at a press conference, where the scrutiny would be more intense—and then adding a new dimension to the story with each new interview, so that every reporter would leave with a scoop.

The reporters broke off their discussions, as the hearing began. In the courtroom, the chairs were filled mainly by attorneys and journalists. Sal Paolantonio and Dave Davies had both been subpoenaed, as lead political reporters for the *Inquirer* and *Daily News,* but the lawyer for Philadelphia Newspaper Inc. (which owned both newspapers) had obtained an agreement that neither one would have to testify unless there was a prior agreement. Paolantonio, against the advice of PNI's lawyer, was in the

courtroom, unable to resist the temptation to witness the spectacle. However, because of his own involvement in the case, he would not cover it.
Instead, Henry Goldman, who had for several years covered the courts in
Philadelphia, would write the story. Barbara Grant from Channel 29 was
there, along with John Rawlins of Channel 6 and Harvey Clark from
Channel 10. With Tia O'Brien still on vacation, Channel 3 again sent only
a cameraman. The reporters covering the hearing sat in the jury's box,
which was fitting since they would be the people who would decide the
outcome of what would turn out to be a purely media event.

In an unusual move Judge Katz allowed a television camera into the
courtroom to record the proceedings. (Cameras are banned from Pennsylvania criminal and jury trials, but judges may allow a camera into nonjury
civil cases.) Channel 6's camera was allowed in, and the courtroom tapes
would be pooled by the other stations; other photographers would park
outside waiting to shoot interviews with people as they left the courtroom.
When the proceedings began, the judge noted that rarely had he been so
deluged with motions to quash subpoenas to testify, most notably from
Ron Castille and Billy Meehan, who were not in the courtroom.

After hearing arguments from Castille's attorney, Louis Fryman, the
judge ruled that Castille and Meehan would have to testify but only to
those matters which had relevance to the question of whether Castille had
publicly announced his candidacy prior to filing his petition. He said that
he would allow no testimony by subpoenaed witnesses on the question of
Castille's negotiations with the law firm for employment. "That may be
the proper source of a TV commercial, but I won't have it here," the judge
said. Fryman was instructed to produce Castille. With this ruling, Paolantonio and Harvey Clark rushed from the courtroom to call their offices
and let them know of the development. Shortly thereafter, Channel 3 reporter Walt Hunter arrived to cover the proceedings. Hunter was one of
the city's premiere police reporters and rarely covered politics, but KYW
didn't seem to care much about reporter specialties at this point.

Shortly after Castille arrived, he was called to the witness stand and
asked to state his name and address. "Ronald D. Castille. Home address?
I'd rather not state that. 1740 Penn Center."

The judge interjected, "That might very well be your home address on
certain days."

"Absolutely," Castille responded good-naturedly.

The attorney for the complainant, Arthur Shuman, began his questioning. "Mr. Castille, when did you first make the decision to run for mayor?
Or, excuse me, when did you first make the decision to seek the nomination of the Republican party for the office of mayor?"

"Did I make it in my own mind? It was something that I had been toying with . . . "

"Assuming that you made it at all," said the judge.

"I eventually did, Judge. I think that was a bone of contention and still appears to be."

"Well, when did you make the decision in your own mind that you would like to seek the mayoralty?" asked the judge.

"I probably became convinced of it when I was flying back from the West. I read an article in *Philadelphia* magazine describing the two candidates, Mr. Burrell and Mr. Katz. . . . But I never made any oral or public decision."

Shuman asked Castille about a meeting he had with Billy Meehan on the afternoon of February 12. "Mr. Castille, at that meeting, did you state to Mr. Meehan that you would 'go for it,' that you would seek the nomination?"

"I informed Mr. Meehan that if the Republican party wanted to have me as their candidate, then I could be available in the future."

"Did you say, 'I will go for it'?"

"I don't recall those specific words, Counselor."

"Then are you saying you didn't say, 'I'll go for it'?"

"I don't recall those specific words one way or the other. There's no transcription of the meeting. There were no reporters at the meeting. It was a private meeting."

"Do you remember granting an interview to a reporter named Sal Paolantonio of the *Philadelphia Inquirer* on February 16, 1991?"

"I've talked to Mr. Paolantonio for well over a year, so I don't recall that specific date."

"Do you recall meeting with him on a Saturday in your home?"

Castille confirmed this. The judge claimed there was little legal significance to whether Castille had said he would accept the nomination or he would go for it. "It's a matter of phraseology," Katz said. "Again, the *Inquirer* is not the source of my opinion in this case." He paused. "I guess they'll print that tomorrow." (Laughter filled the courtroom.)

Castille jumped in. "You can bet on it, Judge. And Frank Rizzo might have a commercial against you the next day," he said sarcastically, but realizing the judge might take offense at this levity, added, "Sorry."

"If he wants to waste his money on me, he's entitled to do that."

"Mr. Castille, do you recall the events of February 13, 1991?" Shuman continued.

"You mean like world events, things like that, Persian Gulf?" Castille asked sarcastically, making the lawyer work to get his answers.

Shuman asked Castille what he had told the Republican policy committee, which had met that day at the Wyndam Franklin Plaza Hotel.

"I told them I would be available for their nomination. "

The lawyer probed for more. "Tell us what you said to that committee."

"I didn't record it or transcribe it, Mr. Shuman. I told them that if they
were so willing, that I would be willing in the future to accept their nomination for mayor of the Republican party. And I recounted my background in the DA's office, I recounted how in 1985 when no one thought
we could win the race and the Democrats put up their equivalent, in the
words of Mr. Fumo, of Rin-Tin-Tin, how . . . I went into the record of
what my office has done, raised the conviction rate from 85 . . . uh, 84
percent in 1985 to 93 percent in 1980, uh, 1990, I went into the legislation that I have rammed through Harrisburg, forfeiture laws, the manda-
tory sentences for drug dealers, my office wrote that particular act. And I
described the leadership I provided the city of Philadelphia and the world
of criminal justice for the last five years. And I even described my entire
twenty years of public service to this city. And I described how I first came
to this city after my being severely wounded in combat while rescuing
marines from a rice paddy who were caught in combat and how I was
wounded and ended up in the navy hospital and how I came to Philadelphia, and how I knew no one, I had no friends whatsoever in the city of
Philadelphia, and how I was delivered on the steps of the navy hospital,
and I described to them how wonderful the people of the city of Philadelphia were to me, to the other wounded marines and other navy individuals
who were in the navy hospital . . . they took us to the Phillies games . . .
something along those lines, Mr. Shuman."

"Did you ask for their endorsement?" Shuman probed.

"I told them I would be available."

Shuman tried again and again to get Castille to say he had made a
public pronouncement of his candidacy before March 12, but came up
with nothing. At noon, the judge recessed for lunch.

The reporters gathered in the hallway in front of the elevators, waiting
for Castille to emerge for questions. "Any reaction?" he was asked when
he came out. "It was grueling," he replied, to their laughter. "It was a
waste of time, though, and really, while it's pending before the judge, that's
all I want to say, a waste of time."

"Who's buying all of this?" asked Harvey Clark.

"Well, we'll have a comment on all of that after the judge rules, but the
judge has already thrown out significant portions of it as being inappropriate for this court. And it's a waste of court time. That's all I'll say right
now."

"Frank Rizzo have something to do with it, Ron?" again from Clark.

"I'll comment later."

After lunch, Bob Kutler, Sam Katz's campaign manager, was called to the stand and asked about a February 12 meeting with Castille and Katz. "Mr. Castille said that he had asked us there as a matter of courtesy to indicate that he is going to run for mayor."

"Mr. Castille related for us two meetings he had that day, the second of which was about 4 P.M., at which time he said after wrestling very difficultly and longly he decided he will accept the nomination and he is going to run for mayor, and he asked Sam Katz to get out of the campaign and support him, and he indicated clearly that he is a candidate and Sam Katz should not be because he was."

He was asked if those were Castille's exact words.

"As best as I can recall during two different parts of the discussion, which was a difficult discussion at best, Mr. Castille said at one point, 'I am running for mayor and I think you should support me,' to Sam Katz. At another time, in answer to a question, he said, 'I have only made this decision in the last three hours. I have only been running for three hours. I can't know the answer to all kinds of questions that people are starting to ask.' "

On cross-examination, Castille's lawyer asked Kutler whether he had worked for Frank Rizzo in the past. He said he had. Kutler was an old friend of Rizzo's campaign manager, Marty Weinberg. Weinberg had been Kutler's camp counselor back when they were both teenagers. Kutler was asked when he first learned about this lawsuit, and he said, "I knew that people were, in fact, drafting such a suit because I caused such a draft to be done on behalf of our campaign, but decided not to file it."

A few minutes later, Fryman asked Kutler, "Wasn't it the purpose of this lawsuit to make political hay, to embarrass the Castille committee?"

"Not to my knowledge. The purpose, to my knowledge, is to prove legally and only legally that Mr. Castille does not, in fact, belong on the ballot. And it is a legal attempt to remove him, from my perspective, so that Sam Katz can be the mayor of Philadelphia."

Later, Republican party boss Billy Meehan was called to testify. He was asked to recount what Castille had said to him when they met on February 12. Meehan said that Castille told him he would make himself available to be a candidate if he received the nomination of the Republican party.

"You were looking for a candidate, weren't you?" the lawyer asked.

"I certainly was. And the candidates were looking for me," he said to much laughter.

"It has been your practice, has it not, Mr. Meehan, to recommend yourself to the committee a candidate?"

"I always do."

"Never been an election when you didn't do it, has there?"

"And there never will be."

"Let me ask you something. Was there ever one where your recommendation wasn't followed?"

"I don't recall. Usually I have the best candidate," he said with another devilish smile.

"Has there ever been an incident when you recommended a candidate in advance without knowing if that candidate was going to accept the nomination?"

"No."

Shuman asked then if Meehan knew that Castille would accept that endorsement.

"That he would make himself available at the proper time." Meehan said that those were Castille's exact words.

Shuman tried again. "After February 13, at Palumbo's you stopped looking for candidates, didn't you?"

"They didn't stop looking for me." Laughter again greeted his statement.

"You had your candidate, didn't you?"

"I was convinced that Mr. Castille's word that he would make himself available, that he would be a man of his word, that he would make himself available. And he did."

Raw tapes had been subpoenaed from Channel 6, to see what clips had been run of Castille the night of the Republican committee meeting, and video tape equipment was brought into court. The tapes did not include entire news packages of the days in questions, but rather sound-bites of the key figures. At one point, Sam Katz's sound-bite saying he could raise money, that you don't know until you lace your combat boots how good you can be in war, was played. In the gallery, Castille laughed derisively at the quote and leaned over to make a comment about it to his neighbor. Altogether, the tapes showed nothing that looked like a public pronouncement of candidacy. As the video equipment was being removed from the courtroom, Castille stood up and walked back the two rows to where Paolantonio was sitting. Castille leaned over to tell Paolantonio something and the reporter nodded, then smiled appreciatively. Paolantonio was very much aware of being courted by this kind of attention from the candidates, even when there were other reporters in the room. He felt that the candidates often singled him out, in part to get their information out to the public, but in part, just to keep the influential reporter on their side.

Castille's side conversation with Paolantonio was not lost on Sam Katz, who had entered the courtroom after lunch, having also received a subpoena to testify. Watching them talk together smiling, Katz couldn't help but wonder whether there wasn't some camaraderie between the two based on their common background in the military. Shortly after, Katz was called to the stand. As he took his oath, Paolantonio whispered, "This has got to be a political first in Philadelphia, one candidate in court testifying against another."

Katz was asked to recount his February 12 meeting with Castille at the Ritz Carlton Hotel. "Tell us what statements, if any, Mr. Castille made to you or in your presence during the course of that meeting as to his candidacy?" Shuman asked.

"Mr Castille said to me that he had decided to become a candidate for mayor. He said that he had made the decision at the very last minute. In fact, he said he made the decision at 4 p.m. that day. He said that he wished that I would support him. He said that he'd spent a long time thinking about it and that he'd only come to the conclusion that he would run at the very final hour. In fact, he told me that he had called Mr. Meehan at twelve o'clock and he had told Mr. Meehan at twelve o'clock that he had decided not to run. And that in the intervening period he changed his mind and decided to run."

Katz was asked once again what Castille had told him concerning his candidacy at the February 12 meeting.

"He told me he was running, and he asked me for my support."

"Running for what?"

"Running for mayor."

When the proceedings were finished around four-thirty, the reporters massed outside the courtroom once again. Barbara Grant requested a comment from Castille.

"We're anxiously awaiting the judge's decision. As I said before, I think the proceedings are meritless, but we did find out that it was really at the instigation of Frank Rizzo and Marty Weinberg and James Baumbach, their campaign manager. So all Frank Rizzo ought to do is be a man, quit hiding behind his lawyer's skirts. That's it."

"Do you think it's a valid campaign issue?" she asked.

"No, it's not. It's frivolous. It's a waste of the court's time. You know, we sat in here, and there were some pretty high powered lawyers who were dragged in here really to sit there all day to clog up this courtroom that ought to be used for real cases."

John Rawlins from Channel 6 jumped in. "Do you think that the plain-tiff drew anything out that will be damaging in any way to your cause?"

"No, we'll wait and see what the judge rules. He'll make a factual decision, but that's totally up to Judge Katz."

Rawlins continued. "I mean, even the images of putting you on the stand . . . just seeing the images, is that damaging in some way to your campaign? Does that hurt your image?"

Castille dismissed the notion.

"Are you going to countersue Frank Rizzo for his remarks on the air last night?" a radio reporter asked.

"Well, we have to watch the tapes first."

"Do you think Rizzo's statements might stick with some of the voters?" the reporter continued.

"That's really up to the voters. I'll take my record to the voters, five years in the district attorney's office, one of the best offices in the nation. My personal integrity I think will go beyond baseless claims and allega-tions made by Frank Rizzo for which he has no foundation whatsoever. What Frank Rizzo did yesterday was probably in my experience bringing campaigning to an all-time record low."

"Do you think that filing this kind of suit is in that same vein?"

"It's just part of Frank Rizzo's general way of running a campaign: innuendo, character assassination, meritless law suits, now groundless, baseless assaults on my personal integrity."

"Is he reaching for straws?"

"He is desperate, there's no doubt about that. He can't seem to talk about any of the issues. The only issue I've known for him to discuss was rounding up all of the homeless and putting them in trailer camps out in Montgomery County. But he was sensitive because he wasn't going to let the police do it. He was going to give people red crosses and white shirts and let them round them up. So I can see why he doesn't want to discuss the issues and why he wants to resort to this level of campaigning. OK, thank you," he said and left.

The hearings got little play on the evening news. (The big story turned out to be another court case—the trial of a New England teacher accused of seducing one of her students into killing her husband.) But what did make it on TV could not help but damage Castille's image: video of Ron Castille on the witness stand, accused of wrongdoing, on the defensive. Frank Rizzo, the former two-term mayor of Philadelphia, the veteran of some five major campaigns, knew you didn't make headway in news cov-erage by going to nickel-and-dime forums and traipsing through housing projects. You had to work with the very simplest of images, and you had to make inroads on your opponent where he was strongest. Although this suit was eventually thrown out, Rizzo would succeed in the court of public opinion, as molded by the media, and that would count for far more. Bit by bit, he was replacing Castille's good-guy image with another less flattering one. And although neither image had much to do with the real Ron Castille and the question of how he would govern Philadelphia, the media were only too willing to put the spectacle on display.

14 Eight Weeks Out

When Neil Oxman arrived at his home in the Main Line suburb of Merion after work, the first thing he would always do was turn on the local news. Oxman was Ed Rendell's media consultant, the ad man. He was the guy who put together the video and still images, who decided when to go on television and when to stay off, whether to place an ad adjacent to a newscast or go with *Jeopardy* and soap operas. It was his masterful ad conjuring up the very worst memories of Frank Rizzo's time as mayor that helped elect Wilson Goode the first black mayor of Philadelphia. Another equally powerful spot by Oxman on the MOVE disaster almost helped Ed Rendell defeat Goode in the 1987 primary. But in the 1991 campaign, Oxman was concerned with more than just ads. Part of his job was to follow how the campaign was being covered in the "free media"—that being the pragmatic way media consultants referred to the news. To the people paid to manipulate the images of the candidates and their opponents, the news was "free" not in the sense of being unhampered or uncensored but as in media exposure you don't have to pay for.

Whereas in his downtown office at 16th and Locust, Oxman had at his disposal all the latest in video technology, at home he didn't own a VCR. Oxman was a movie buff. He would see between 150 and 200 movies a year. He even had a contest going with a friend to see who could take in the most movies, and he was afraid if he owned a VCR he'd never get out to a real theater. So if he was going to catch the news, he'd have to catch it live. And mostly he would turn to Channel 6. He knew the numbers. Channel 6 had more viewers than 3 and 10 put together. And with Tia

O'Brien soon leaving Channel 3, there was almost no one covering politics in Philadelphia except Vernon Odom and Marc Howard at Channel 6. If Ed or any of the candidates were going to be covered that day, it would most likely air on Channel 6.

On this Tuesday evening, if Neil Oxman had gotten home in time to catch Channel 6's 5:30 newscast, he would have smiled. For the media consultant, this wasn't March 26. It was eight weeks out from election day. And at eight weeks out, the picture couldn't be better. The campaign's own internal polls showed that Ed Rendell's numbers were all moving in the right direction. When they asked people who they would vote for if the election were held today, Ed was in the forties, Blackwell and Burrell were in the twenties, Hearn was at ten. Even more important to Oxman was the favorable/unfavorable ratio, the measure of how many people had a good opinion of your candidate, how many a negative one. Ed had started out back in the fall with a 50/30, which was not great. A lot of people remembered him as a two-time loser and the man who had supposedly broken his promise to the black clergy about not running against Wilson Goode for mayor. But that's where advertising came in. Oxman put together a sixty-second biographical ad about the candidate, where Rendell was painted as an independent who had cleaned up the district's attorney office and a courageous man of vision who had warned about the city's financial problems when challenging Wilson Goode. The spot had run when no one else was on the air, and sure enough, Ed's negatives started to turn around. At this point, his favorable/unfavorable had shifted to 65/13.

And then there was the other number that Oxman was really focused on: not how many people would vote for Ed on election day but how many people thought he was going to win. One of the chief aims of the campaign was to use news coverage to make it seem as if Ed Rendell couldn't lose, that he was a fait accompli, that his momentum was building through the campaign and never letting up. Oxman never expected that to be an easy task, because he understood all too well where the reporters would be coming from in this campaign. This was not some small town where the reporters took your press releases and changed a few words and threw it into the paper. Philadelphia was the fourth largest media market in the country, and the *Inquirer* and *Daily News* were two of the nation's best papers. In a town like Philadelphia, the reporters were going to be out looking for their own stories, and they were going to be searching for stories that had an edge. Oxman knew that if there was one thing political reporters hated, it was a campaign that was done before it began. They were not going to be led easily to the party line that no one but Ed Rendell could win this thing.

Oxman had seen it in Sal Paolantonio right away. In the beginning, he had seen Sal thinking, "I'm going to bring these guys down; I'm going to make Hearn a player." To Oxman, the whole Hearn thing was only a Sal story. Hearn would have been nothing without the stories Sal wrote about him in 1990. And then there was Sal at every meeting of the black ministers, doing everything he could to cover anything that would have made the dynamic change for the Rendell campaign. He didn't have a quarrel with what Sal was doing or with the coverage of any of the other reporters. Sal was a smart guy; Cindy Burton was a smart woman. These were real reporters, not flaks. Oxman understood that.

But for a campaign that was prepared for anything and aimed to be the best at everything—the best on issues, the best in the field, the best at getting every editorial endorsement—they knew they had to be prepared for the sophisticated political reporters they would confront in the Philadelphia media. In fact, those eight or nine reporters—Sal Paolantonio from the *Inquirer,* Cindy Burton and Dave Davies from the *Daily News,* Dale Wilcox from KYW Newsradio, maybe Kevin Boyle from WDDB talk radio news, and of course Vernon Odom and Marc Howard from Channel 6, Tia O'Brien from Channel 3, and Barbara Grant from Channel 29—they were the audience the Rendell campaign was playing to in the early weeks of the campaign.

And Oxman knew exactly what that particular audience of reporters cared about: the horse race. Back in the fall of 1990, the campaign had succeeded in getting coverage for Rendell's early lead in Temple University's Hooper poll, which had helped them raise money. Money was important to the campaign at that point, but not for the reason many people would have figured, not for what it could buy. The real reason it counted now was that the political reporters were going to make a big story out of how much money each campaign raised. Your war chest was just one more measure of the horse race in the media calculus. The Rendell campaign managers knew that and were determined to be ahead there as everywhere else. They knew the reporters were just looking for a reason to knock the king off the hill.

And so they pushed themselves through the fall of 1990 and through January 1991 to make sure that, when the January 31 filing date for campaign finance reports rolled around, they were ahead. Not only did they release their reports for calendar year 1990 on that day, but they also put in the quarter of a million dollars they had knocked themselves out collecting in January. And so when Peter Hearn and George Burrell all sort of strutted into the city commissioners' office, the Rendell camp was one step ahead of them. They had put out a press release with their numbers bumped up by the extra quarter million dollars, and they had made sure they hadn't spent much of the money so that they could claim they had a lot in the bank, knowing Hearn had just dropped $490,000 in advertising. Oxman had a lot of respect for Hearn's media consultant, Saul Schorr— Schorr had clearly succeeded in pitching his story to Paolantonio last year—but to Oxman it hadn't made a lot of sense to put Hearn's ads on in November and December. In those two months, ad rates were at their highest because of Christmas demand. And then, of course, they depleted their war chest at just the moment the reporters would be measuring it.

Sure enough, just as Oxman had hoped, there was the *Inquirer* story on February 1, with the headline "Rendell Grabs Fundraising Lead; Hearn, Katz Do Surprisingly Well." Paolantonio's lead ran, "Democrat Edward G. Rendell, who has a long history of prodigious fundraising, turned up the big winner in the first round of the 1991 money race for mayor of Philadelphia." After a few words about the Republicans, he continued: "Rendell, by far the best-known Democrat in the race and leading the field in all polls, raised $702,000 for the May 21 primary, the first finance reports of the campaign showed yesterday. Spending $97,000 in the early going, Rendell has $605,000 in the bank—more than double any candidate for mayor, Democrat or Republican."

"Another Democratic candidate," the article continued, "Peter Hearn, the former Philadelphia Bar Association chancellor, raised more— $831,000, a remarkable sum considering he has never run for public office before. But Hearn spent $490,000 on television ads late last year to give his campaign respectability. Hearn has $290,000 in the bank." To the casual reader, those few sentences would look fairly innocuous. But Oxman knew how much Sal's spin on the numbers counted. It was the lead sentence that mattered, not the numbers themselves. Another reporter might have led with the fact that Peter Hearn had raised more money than any other candidate, but Sal had selected the measure of money in the bank—as Oxman had expected—and here Ed came out the winner. Even though the story only made 3-B, that didn't matter. It was not the general electorate the campaign was trying to reach with these stories saying Rendell was in the lead. It was the fundraisers they were after, the people who were going to commit a couple million in the primary. That was their target: $2 million in the primary and $3 million in the general.

Getting that kind of money depended on convincing a small cadre of wealthy people that Ed was in the lead and maintaining it. And the way to do that was to make sure that every poll that was taken and released to the press showed Rendell ahead. And in turn, the way to do that, in the Oxman plan, was to stay on TV with ads. To Oxman, it was a pretty simple equation and it applied to just about any candidate: you went on TV, your numbers in the polls went up. You went off, they went down. Now, in a normal campaign where you were ahead and the election wasn't for sixteen weeks—and in a world where there was no free press clambering to cover each and every poll—Oxman would not have spent money on ads until the last four to six weeks. People had short memories. What you told them in January didn't have much to do with how they'd vote in May.

No, it wasn't to convince people to be for Rendell on election day that led Oxman to go on TV in January and not get off. It was to anticipate the polls. They wanted to make sure that Rendell was ahead, so the stories in the papers would send the right signal to contributors. The political reporters were scrambling to make a race out of this, and Oxman knew the only way to stop that was to maintain the lead in the polls. And it was working. In his story about Rendell's finance reports, Paolantonio had picked it up in his third paragraph. It was no longer "Ed Rendell, who hasn't won an election in nine years," it was "Ed Rendell, who is leading the field in all polls." It was those qualifying clauses that political reporters took pride in being able to make astutely, and finally the clauses were working in Rendell's favor. It became a wonderful circle. Oxman and company put out the fact that they had the most money and got free press, which let them raise more money. Then they took this money to stay on TV and stay ahead in the polls, which got more press and let them raise more money.

Of course, there were other elements that fell into place, the places where Ed got lucky. Having more than one black candidate in the race was a big break, no question. That helped them raise money, too, because the gossip in political circles was that if there was more than one black candidate, Rendell was going to win. And then the fact that there were three black candidates in the race was dominating news coverage of the primary. Whenever reporters did a story about the black candidates staying in, Oxman couldn't believe how it was playing right into the Rendell campaign's agenda, because they always made it seem as if Rendell had to win. With each story, Rendell's inevitability increased.

Then, Oxman watched Hearn start to get desperate. Eight, nine weeks out, in mid-March, he does these negative ads knocking Rendell as just another politician. "Ed Rendell promises to make government more efficient. But for six years as district attorney Ed Rendell gave employees double pay for holidays—without even making them work," Hearn announced in one spot. "Is that what Rendell means by efficiency? Look, if we really want to change things, we've got to throw the politicians out." But Oxman had been ready for negatives. David Cohen quickly got together some materials on the incident, lobbied the *Inquirer* to write an editorial about the ad, and it worked. A week later, the paper came out with an editorial called "A Penalty for Hearn," claiming Rendell was not at fault in the labor practice.

Then Oxman took the editorial and turned it into a rebuttal ad. "The *Philadelphia Inquirer* says 'a penalty for Peter Hearn' . . . 'it's as easy to see Mr. Rendell as hero rather than villain,' " the ad announced, quoting from the newspaper. That did it. After Hearn did his negative ads, and Oxman did his rebuttal, Hearn's numbers went down and Rendell enjoyed his widest lead of the campaign. It all helped Rendell seem unbeatable. By March 15, the number of people who thought Rendell was going to win was actually higher than his lead. And that was a number Oxman cared about. It was fantastic. The reporters were doing the campaign's job. They were making it seem as if there was no one else besides Rendell.

And now something even better was happening. The Republicans were having a fight. Oxman knew that there were only a certain number of reporters, a certain number of television crews, and here was Mr. On-Top-of-the-World Ron Castille, who's ahead in the polls with 45 percent, here's Frank Rizzo in the twenties, and an unknown Sam Katz who has ten—and this really great dynamic is happening on the Republican side. You had Castille playing Hamlet for a long time and Meehan finally getting him in, and then the guy doesn't resign for four weeks. And you have Rizzo going crazy and finally coming up with the trumped-up stuff, and you have this incredible fight between the two of them. And all of sudden, where people thought the real battle was going to be the Democrats—because, of course, there were so many more Democrats than Republicans in the city—all of a sudden the Republican race becomes more fun to cover than the Democratic race.

And it was all there on Channel 6 that night, eight weeks out from election day. The longest story was about Ron Castille—how he was filing charges with the Fellowship Commission claiming Rizzo was spreading malicious lies about him and how the suit against him was being thrown out. (There was that video again of Castille on the witness stand, defending himself against Rizzo-originated attacks.) The second story was a press conference Peter Hearn held to charge Rendell with "shoddy bookkeeping" in previous campaigns, with Ed getting a bite saying, "This is the worst type of gutter politics." And finally, the last story that day was about Ed's endorsement by black state senator Hardy Williams ("It's the first major black endorsement of any white candidate in the Democratic primary," noted anchor Marc Howard.) Bingo. Rizzo and Castille were fighting, Peter Hearn was getting more desperate, and Ed was looking like

Mr. Substantive, picking up endorsements that helped build the momentum and make it seem like everybody was for Rendell.

Yes, if you were Neil Oxman, you certainly might say the reporters were doing the campaign's work for you. And at eight weeks out, everything was going Ed Rendell's way.

15 The Lethal Blow

March 27, 1991

❧ When Sam Katz woke up on Wednesday, March 27, he gave little thought to the fact that in a few hours he would be appearing on live television, sitting next to his two opponents in the Republican primary. Even though his scheduled appearance on AM *Philadelphia* would be the first opportunity of his campaign to address hundreds of thousands of Philadelphians without the filter of the media getting in his way, his mind was focused elsewhere that morning. March 27 was the last day for candidates to withdraw, and by five o'clock he would have to make a choice about whether or not to stay in the race.

As he thought about his predicament, he went out to pick up his morning *Inquirer*. When he unfolded it, he was surprised to see he had made the front page for the first time since the "worm stories" from the previous summer. The headline stopped him in his tracks: "Katz Dealt Lethal Blow in Race," with the subhead, "Top Fundraisers Defect to Castille." He read on to see what Sal Paolantonio had to say about him this time. "The long-shot Republican mayoral campaign of Samuel P. Katz all but ended yesterday when his two finance chairmen jumped to rival Ronald D. Castille. The defections raised speculation that Katz will withdraw from the May 21 primary by today's 5 P.M. deadline." The article described the loss of David Girard DiCarlo and Fred Anton, while noting that Katz received another "serious setback" that day when Judge Leon Katz threw out the suit against Castille's candidacy. It quoted Republican party sources as saying that, although Katz had run "a surprisingly effective campaign," without money he would be unable to advertise on television or marshal a street organization that would be comparable to the party's organization.

Katz reread the story, his eyes focusing again and again on the words *lethal blow* and *all but ended,* which were writing him out of the 1991 primary campaign for mayor. He was all too well aware that the loss of David Girard DiCarlo was a serious blow, but Fred Anton had not just jumped ship the day before, as the article had suggested. He had been gone since the day Castille got the Republican endorsement, even if he had chosen not to go on the record with his decision. But when Katz got to the point in the article that said he was expected to withdraw by 5 P.M. that day, he really got incensed. He himself had never said he was getting out, and he had certainly not told Paolantonio he was calling it a day.

Katz had run into the reporter the day before on the street outside the Liberty Place tower. Katz had been talking to someone when he noticed Paolantonio at one of the sidewalk vendor's stands, lingering as if lying in wait for him. At first Katz tried to avoid him since he had an idea of what Sal would want to talk about on the final day before the withdrawal deadline. But the reporter came up to Katz before he could get away. "I've been looking for you," he said.

"You've been walking along the street looking for me?"

"Yeh. I've got to buy a tennis racket. Walk with me."

As they walked along Chestnut Street, heading for Everyone's Racquet Shop at 17th Street, they touched on one of their favorite subjects, basketball, lightly discussing the chances of Katz ever becoming commissioner of the National Basketball Association. When they got to the shop, Paolantonio introduced Katz to the owners, whom Paolantonio, the avid tennis player, knew well from frequenting the shop. After he bought the racket, the two went to Rittenhouse Square and sat down on a bench, where Paolantonio brought up politics and the campaign for the first time. "Girard DiCarlo is bailing out," he said. Katz knew that DiCarlo had abandoned him, but he didn't want to reveal it publicly yet. Not a good liar, particularly to Sal, he said lamely, "I haven't heard that."

"Well, what are you going to do now?"

"You know, I don't know. I'm going to go home and think about it. I have one more day to think about it."

"It sounds to me like it's already been done. It's a done deal," said Paolantonio, referring to DiCarlo's defection. But Katz thought he was talking about his decision to go on with the campaign.

"I don't know, Sal. I'm being honest with you. I'm going to go home and think about it. I'm going to think about it real hard. I don't have to decide until five minutes of five tomorrow. That's what I'm going to do."

"But how can you win?"

"I don't know how I can win. But I didn't stay in on February 13 convinced that I could win."

When Katz went home that night, he did seriously consider getting out of the race. He was sitting at his kitchen table with his wife, Connie, trying to decide, when he got a call from Ron Castille, saying they should talk. Katz invited Castille to come up to his Mount Airy home, which was about ten minutes from where Castille lived in East Falls, but Castille said he was tired and suggested they do it in the morning. Though Katz readily agreed to talk to Castille after their *A.M. Philadelphia* appearance, he marvelled that Castille was unwilling to make the fifteen-minute ride, to stay up a little late, to get Sam Katz out of the race. Just such a move probably would have done it.

All along Katz had doubts about how far he could go in his race for mayor, and all along he had considered getting out. But nobody ever offered him the very intangible thing he wanted to get out. Meehan had offered him a spot on city council, and he felt sure that Castille would have offered him a position as finance director. But he didn't want any of those things. He was financially well off with a successful business, and all he wanted was to be mayor. Or if not to be mayor, he wanted to be included in a very personal sense in the campaign of the man who had a good chance of becoming mayor. Katz had felt that if Castille had come up to his house that night and brought his wife, and if it had been Ron and Judy and Sam and Connie, and they had said, "Look, guys, we're only interested in doing this thing for four years, Ron wants to run for something else, you'd be the bright young star then, Sam, let's wipe this Rizzo guy out, the four of us will be together in this," that would have appealed to Katz.

The mistake of the Republican party and Castille was that they had tried to make a deal with Katz. They wanted to get him out of the way. But Katz didn't want to be out of the way—not after the excitement, the exhilaration of the past nine months, not after seeing himself develop as a candidate, and the time seeming so right, what with the city's fiscal crisis coming to a head and his being so firmly established as the "fiscal expert." He wanted to be precisely in the way. And he was never going to step aside simply because Sal Paolantonio decided to declare his campaign prematurely dead. "Oh, yeah?" was the way he had always reacted to being told he was dead professionally, that he just couldn't do something. "Well, just watch me." And so he felt a certain belligerence as he got dressed and headed off for the morning's fundraising breakfast, to be followed by his appearance on *AM Philadelphia*.

Being on television was no big deal for Katz. He had gone on all the Sunday morning public affairs shows for months. He didn't know much about *AM Philadelphia*. He thought of it as just an innocuous little talk show that he had never watched himself. The show was, however, more than that. It was the only locally produced television talk show in the region and one of a disappearing breed nationally. As local broadcast stations across the country faced increasing competition from cable and tried to cut costs to stay profitable, they were finding that syndicated programs were a much better deal than producing local shows. But in the process, their audiences were losing many of the last remaining television outlets they had to learn about local issues in any depth. Although *AM Philadelphia* on any given day was as likely to run exclusive interviews with convicted murderers or shows about medical students working their way through school by stripping, it was also the only television program in Philadelphia where a relatively unfettered debate could take place between local political candidates.

Katz had given little thought to the platform the show offered, and he had done absolutely nothing to prepare for his appearance. He was, as a result, thrown off balance when he arrived at the studio with his wife only to be confronted by the entire media pack, including TV cameras. Of course, the pack was not there to cover Sam Katz and whether or not he would drop out of the race and certainly not to hear what the candidates had to say about the issues facing the city. They were there to cover the growing feud between Ron Castille and Frank Rizzo. Rizzo had kept up his charges that Castille had a drinking problem and was unfit to be mayor because of the way he had brandished a loaded gun before groups of people. And the television stations were covering the charges, almost to the exclusion of anything else about the campaign, including what any of the Democratic candidates were doing.

Tia O'Brien had done a piece on the charges a few nights previous in which she had Rizzo claiming he had himself seen Castille drunk. When O'Brien asked him how he knew Castille was drunk, he answered, "The way his hair fell in his eyes, the way he was walking . . . I knew he was intoxicated." She shot back, "But the man's on crutches!" "You can be on crutches and still be intoxicated," Rizzo answered. O'Brien noted that Rizzo had yet to produce any hard evidence for his charges; nevertheless, she continued to report those charges as all her competitors were doing. This morning, all the TV reporters were out to cover what they clearly expected might be another chapter in the verbal "slugfest."

The unexpected presence of the pack was unnerving to Sam Katz, as he sat being made up for the show, thinking for the first time about what was going to happen. He was going to go on TV with Ron Castille, in what was to be Castille's first public appearance since formally announcing, and he was going to be sitting on the same TV set as Frank Rizzo, a veritable political legend in Philadelphia, a man who was the notorious police commissioner when Sam Katz was at Central High School, a man Katz had fought against. The man who had carefully avoided appearing at the cut-and-dry forums that Katz had been attending day in and day out.

When he walked onto the set taking his last sip from his can of soda, he appeared unruffled. He shook hands with Rizzo and Castille. "Gentlemen," he greeted them, before noticing that the only seat left for him—at five minutes before ten—was the one in between his two opponents. At first, he balked at being the man in the middle. But host Wally Kennedy, with three minutes to go, looked him in the eye and said, "Mr. Katz, either you sit in that chair, or we don't do the show." The *AM Philadelphia* staff had been prepared for the possibility that one of the three candidates might not show up, or might walk out before the show started, and they were resolved that they wouldn't do it unless all three were present. They had a tape all cued in the control room, should one of the men back out. While all the political candidates were looking for media exposure, they were sometimes a little nervous about a format like this where the candidates could freely confront one another. Not Frank Rizzo, however. He had showed up early at the studio, put his arm around Kennedy's shoulder, and said, "Wally, you know this whole election revolves around credibility. I guarantee you, you ask me about credibility, you won't be disappointed." He patted his chest pocket with a knowing smile.

Sam Katz gave in and agreed to stay, taking his seat between Rizzo and Castille. And the first question Kennedy asked, when the show began, was directed to him. "According to the morning paper," Kennedy asked, "as of 5:05 today you will not be a Republican candidate for mayor. Is that true?"

In the few seconds that it took Kennedy to ask the question, Katz found himself wildly wondering how to answer it. Of course, he should have seen it coming, but he simply had not. He thought to himself, even as Kennedy was talking, "I gave Ron Castille the clear indication last night that I was going to talk to him. If I say I'm in, I'm going to piss off Castille because I haven't even given him the chance to talk to me. But if I say I might not be in, everything else I say on the show will be ridiculous and they might even ask me to leave." All this flashed into his mind, before he launched into his answer.

"I've learned in this election that reading the newspapers can be a very dangerous sport," Katz said, almost on automatic pilot. "And I have also learned that the press is not always accurate in its reporting of the facts. I intend to be a candidate in this election until May 21."

With that matter out of the way, Kennedy launched into questions for the other two candidates. "Mr. Castille, the last week has seen you going to court to defend your candidacy because a supposed Rizzo supporter has filed suit against you claiming that you were campaigning before you left your job. There is the allegation of heavy drinking. There were the number of times that you supposedly brandished a loaded pistol in front of other people. There is a political impression, created by the man who now sits seven or eight feet away from you, that you, sir, are a loaded gun." Frank Rizzo couldn't have said it better himself if he'd had the chance to write Kennedy's lines.

Castille denied the charges and offered his sound-bite of the day. "Mayor Rizzo's campaign . . . he's trying to lead the city from the gutter," he said.

"Well, that sounds nice," responded Rizzo, not unfamiliar with the world of the ten-second sound-bite himself, "but this election is about credibility, judgment, integrity." He repeated versions of the Castille "gun-toting" incidents, and then went one step further. For the past two days, since he had restated his drinking allegations against Castille on Channel 6's Sunday morning interview show, Rizzo had been hearing from places like the *Daily News* editorial page that he had better "put up or shut up," putting pressure on him to produce some evidence of Castille's supposed drinking problem. And while Sam Katz hadn't given much thought to appearing on the show, Frank Rizzo had understood its importance perfectly. He had carefully planned to use his *AM Philadelphia* appearance that morning to produce what he claimed was a sworn affidavit from a retired police officer. The affidavit stated that the officer had been called to Castille's home in March 1989, where he found that Castille had been drinking excessively and was "twirling" a gun around his finger. Rizzo was recounting the story, telling how the police officer went to Castille's home sometime between 1:30 and 3:30 A.M., when Castille interrupted him:

"Between 1:30 and 3:30? Can't he get the facts straight?"

"No, we'll get the facts—" Rizzo said.

"This is just another—"

"Wait'll you hear the whole story, then you'll get your chance to sue me—"

"You got another one of your flunkies to come forward and tell some lies—"

"Flunkies? They're not flunkies, they're telling the truth—"

"Your whole campaign has been nothing but lies—"

"Now, look, I shut up while you were talking, let me talk—"

"Nothing but lies—" Castille repeated.

Rizzo continued to tell his story about how the officer found "a heavy odor of booze" on Castille's breath, how there were "empty liquor bottles all over the place," and how Castille began to "twirl" his guns. When asked to respond, Castille denied the story and claimed that such lies on Rizzo's part made him unfit to be mayor.

Seated between Castille and Rizzo, Katz watched, as if from on high, as the two men attacked each other. When Kennedy eventually turned to him for comment, he looked straight into the camera and said, "Wally, Philadelphia is ninety-five days away from default. I think that people have to understand that when a city defaults on its bonds, the potholes will get to be the size of Iraqi potholes, people will not be able to improve public schools, we will not have a city that can borrow money and pay its bills. While all this is interesting and entertaining, this election has to be about the future of Philadelphia and saving the city, and I am someone who has helped cities all over the country solve their financial problems, their human problems. I'm not running for mayor because I care about personalities. I care about the city I grew up in, I care about this place, I love this place, and I think that's what Philadelphians care about. They're not interested in this petty personal politics."

When Kennedy asked him how his campaign could tackle the "gargantuan task" of winning the nomination without the support of the Republican machine, he answered, "The gargantuan task I face in this election pales beside the gargantuan task this city faces in recovering its future."

Kennedy turned the questions back to Castille and asked him how he felt about being the candidate of "the machine." Castille denied that enjoying party support reflected "machine politics." He seemed to realize that he had been completely on the defensive for the course of the show, so he tried to turn the discussion in another direction. "Sam is absolutely right, Sam is absolutely right, we ought to discuss the issues just as he said. I could not agree with him more." Both Rizzo and Castille began to speak kindly of Katz as a way of softening the blows to each other. Rizzo said he would support Katz if he won the nomination, but not Castille, and claimed he would like to have Katz as his finance director.

But Katz did not let the kind words stand unchallenged. When Rizzo tried to say that he was as skilled at finances as Katz, claiming he had an A-bond rating when he was mayor, Katz interjected, "When you were mayor of Philadelphia, the bond rating came down. You had the largest deficit in the history of the city, the largest deficit, the largest tax increases in the history of the city." Although he had not rehearsed for the program and had completely failed to foresee its importance, he knew instinctively that Rizzo had fed him the perfect line to lead into his strengths. All through the campaign, Katz shot from the hip in front of reporters, and in many cases it had hurt him. But here today, in a forum that was playing to his strengths, it would help. Katz had managed to turn the freewheeling discussion back to serious issues, the platform on which he looked best and Castille and Rizzo worst.

Rizzo responded, "Sam, I'm pro-union, and I'm proud of that, so you'll know—"

"So I am," said Castille.

"No, you're not," shot back Rizzo.

"—but you can't give away the store," finished Castille.

When the issue of privatization was raised and the question of how each man would deal with municipal unions "who will fight you every step of the way," Katz was the first to respond. "Well, they may not fight me every step of the way. I think the unions need to understand that they just finished a four-month period in which they did not know if they were going to get paid on Friday. They do not know if their pension benefits will be there. And they certainly don't know if they will match the health and welfare benefits as it was. What I'm trying to say is not privatization, competition. Philadelphia city government has a monopoly on trash collection, vehicle maintenance, data processing, and a number of other services that cities like Los Angeles, Phoenix, Indianapolis, and Newark have put out to competitive bid and have given their unions the opportunity to competitively bid."

Rizzo came next and was against privatization, repeating again that he was pro-labor. Castille could only come in third. Shifting uncomfortably in his seat, he said, "Well, I come from a union family also, Wally. My family were all plumbers," trying again to match Rizzo on his claim this time that he came from labor roots. "I respect the unions . . . but we have to bring in economies . . . by competition. We just can't have the bureaucracies we have now and continue to pay high wages for inefficient work. And the unions will be allowed to see if they can answer the competitive bids of private industry." Once again, he seemed to be weakly agreeing to what Katz had already said.

Rizzo used a pause in Castille's answer about union wages to jump back to his personal attack. "Wally, we talk about high wages. This is a man who was making $79,000 as D.A. He made a deal, went into a law firm—and he denied that for a long time—and they gave him $130,000 a year—."

"Let's talk about your—" began Castille.

"—$130,000," continued Rizzo.

"Let's talk about your $160,000 with the Gas Works after you supported—" Castille pushed to say.

"What $160,000?" asked Rizzo.

"—after you supported Mayor Goode. You made a good deal."

"No, he had nothin' to do with that. So you'll know, this is an issue of integrity and character—"

"You can't lead the city from the gutter," Castille tried again.

"He was making $79,000 as D.A. and they gave him a sweetheart deal with the law firm where Boss Meehan works . . . where Boss Meehan works—" Rizzo went on.

After a few more counterattacks, Katz reentered the conversation. "I think the voters of Philadelphia want something different than is being offered by either of these two gentlemen. Let's talk about where the city is going to be in the twenty-first century, whether we're put there with machine politics, which has brought the city to where it is today, Democratic machine politics and Republican machine politics. Philadelphians are smart people, and they'll look at what Mr. Rizzo and Mr. Castille are saying and what Mr. Katz is saying, and I think they'll choose Mr. Katz."

Kennedy closed the show by asking the three men to respond to their "weaknesses." To Rizzo he said, "The rap on you is that you're unelectable," to which Rizzo responded that he was proud of the fact that he lost by only 17,000 votes to an incumbent mayor in 1987. When asked if he regretted the personal attacks on Castille, he said no and launched into them again. To Castille, Kennedy said, "The rap on you is the trip to court last week, the gun incidents, the allegations of alcoholism . . . or heavy drug use . . . or rather heavy alcohol use . . have politically taken you from the heir apparent to the Republican party to a fighter on the ropes." Castille responded again that that was "just gutter politics." He said he hoped the voters knew his record, of "twenty years in public service, plus two years in the U.S. Marine Corps, where I was seriously wounded in Vietnam . . . "

It was Castille's old campaign mantra to mention his injury in Vietnam fighting for his country, but Rizzo could not let it pass. He was one of the few individuals willing to call Castille on it. "Frank Rizzo served the city of Philadelphia, and I fought on the streets of this town. Maybe I'm not as brave as Ron Castille, but I got seriously injured twice in my career as a police officer. I respect you," he said to Castille, almost spitting out the words, "for your injury in the war, but that has nothing to do with running this town."

Kennedy gave Katz the final say. "Why not the best? Why settle for something someone else has told you you should do?" It was his argument for fighting the party-backed candidate. "Think about the future of the city." As he spoke these words, he felt how good he had been, how buoyed he had become in the process of taking on Rizzo and Castille and coming out the man who talked issues.

After the debate wrapped up, the cameras moved to an adjacent set where three local analysts were sitting with the show's co-host, Liz Starr, waiting to tell the audience who had won and lost the debate. Temple University political scientist Sandra Featherman did not hesitate a moment. "Sam Katz was a big winner, because he talked about the issues, he urged voters to support him, he talked about his ability to straighten out the city's financial problems. If there was a loser, Ron Castille was not adequately prepared to talk about what he could do. He spent too much time defending himself against Frank Rizzo's charges."

Paul Bennett, editor of the *Philadelphia Tribune,* the black newspaper in town, also lauded Katz for "taking the high road through this whole thing, . . . through it all he remained focused, statesmanlike." Rizzo was described as "kind of retro, kind of a nostalgia thing for Philadelphia." When Liz Starr wrapped it up, she said, "Well, this was a morning when it looked like Sam Katz was out of it, but he certainly changed that around."

That afternoon, Katz held a hastily called press conference outside the city's Municipal Services Building across from City Hall. Cynthia Burton of the *Daily News* was one of the first reporters to arrive. Bob Kutler, Katz's campaign manager, arrived next and walked up to her.

"Mrs. Burton," he said genially, "how are you today?"

"I'd be a lot better if you had let me know about DiCarlo yesterday." When the *Inquirer* played a story on page 1, the *Daily News* editors put the heat on their reporters for not getting it, too.

"Sorry," Kutler apologized sheepishly. "He started returning calls. I didn't know. What can I say? I'm sorry."

Sal Paolantonio arrived soon after, along with Dave Davies from the *Daily News,* Dave Wilcox from KYW-Newsradio, and a few other radio reporters. While all the TV stations had sent cameras, the only TV reporter who came was Jacqueline Boulden, a general assignment reporter from Channel 29. March 27 was also the day that Mayor Wilson Goode was set to reveal his last budget—with big tax increases expected—and most of the major TV reporters, like Tia O'Brien, were covering the budget story. Katz had probably only gotten so many cameramen because the TV stations, taking their cues from the morning *Inquirer,* had expected him to pull out of the campaign that day. Instead, he read a prepared speech in which he said he would defy "party bosses" and "conventional wisdom" and stay in. He tried once again to tie his candidacy directly to the fiscal crisis that the mayor would be addressing that night.

"Philadelphia is ninety-five days from default. Last August I stood here and proposed that the city support the creation of a financial control board. I said our financial situation was out of control. I said our leaders had lost their way. Tonight a bankrupt administration will unveil a bankrupt budget for a city on the verge of bankruptcy."

When he finished, the reporters threw questions at him. How much money did he have left in his campaign fund? In the six figures, he answered, noting that he'd had a successful fundraising breakfast and luncheon that day. While saying kind words about his two ex-finance chairmen, he claimed that he was the one who had raised most of the money in his campaign and that he would continue to do so. "I stand on my own two feet," he said. He was asked if he was under a lot of pressure to pull out and he made a joke of it, turning to his wife, standing at his side in a bright red dress, to ask her if she was pressuring him. "Absolutely not," she said, laughing.

"What did they offer you to pull out?" Burton asked. Earlier she had talked with Wilcox about how there was little they could offer to a man who was making something like $300,000 in his own business. City contracts maybe, but it was hardly much of an enticement. To her question, Katz answered, "Nothing."

Paolantonio asked, "When did you decide to stay in?"

"It was always an issue of whether to pull out. And I decided that to pull out would not be true to myself, and it really wasn't true to the purpose I started out this campaign with, to turn this city around . . . "

Burton asked "How do you win this election, Sam?"

"I believe I win this election in an environment in which two candidates engage in the kind of personal politics that has characterized this campaign for the last two weeks. I believe I win this election in the face of the worst financial disaster confronting any American city in modern history, and I win this election because people decide that I am urging them to consider, why not the best?"

Dave Davies, who was assigned to cover the mayor's budget announcement, said, "The man across the street there is going to propose a $50 million wage tax increase tonight. How do you convince people that you can do it better?"

"The man across the street has never talked seriously about a long-term solution. Every solution that has been on the table for the last three months has been about this year's budget. Last year it was about last year's budget. Philadelphia faces a cumulative gap in the neighborhood of $2 billion in the next five years. I think that the way to go about that gap very simply from a strategic point of view is to use the capacity of a control board or intergovernmental cooperation body which has the power to borrow between $900 million and $1 billion over a five-year period.

"And every time that authority goes to the bond market, it borrows money to cover over the next five years a portion of Philadelphia's deficit. They do so conditioned upon the taking of actions by Philadelphia City Council and the mayor that reduces the size of this government, that reforms the relationship between union and management." He repeated that Goode had no strategy for solving the fiscal problems. "Ninety-five days to default, ninety-five days to default," he reiterated, pointing out that when New York had been facing bankruptcy, its leadership had been sitting down for months with the unions to discuss a solution.

"Is the wage tax wrong, Sam?" Paolantonio asked.

"Yes, the wage tax is a disaster for Philadelphia."

"Can you be more specific?"

"You can't have a wage tax increase. Everybody in this city that's not involved in a long-term lease . . . when those leases expire, will be looking to leave. The wage tax is the single greatest contribution to the demise of Philadelphia's economy."

"Do you think the candidate endorsed by Wilson Goode is going to have to disavow the wage tax?" Paolantonio asked.

"The candidate endorsed by Wilson Goode supported the wage tax last year; he supported the budget of Mayor Goode. He supported not a decrease in the operating budget of the city to reduce the deficit, he proposed an increase. He proposed to increase taxes and increase spending. If we had done what George Burrell proposed, we would still have a $230 million deficit today. This is a government which pulled a note issue on September 8 for a $400 million bond sale so that they could develop a long-term solution. They don't have a long-term solution."

As the press conference dwindled down to the print reporters, the television cameras having shut down long ago after getting their pictures, Dave Davies asked a question about how he would get his message out. Katz claimed that polls had shown back in November, before he did any advertising, that he had significant name recognition from his conferences on the fiscal crisis. "And I believe it is incumbent on those who cover this race on a daily basis to cover issues. And you know and Sal knows and Cindy knows that I have consistently talked about issues. I'm not going to argue that issues are the only things that matter. There's the element of personality and character. But I think I have personality, I think I have character, and I also have something else going for me that nobody else in the Republican primary has—an idea about how to fix the problem."

After the press conference, when most of the reporters had left, Katz wandered over to Dave Davies. Drinking a can of ginger ale, he asked Davies, "What's he saying tonight?" referring to Mayor Goode. As they stood and talked on the street corner, Davies explaining the various tax increases, a homeless man approached Katz, Davies, and Kutler and asked for a quarter. All three said no and then went back to discussing the budget.

As Dave Davies strolled back to City Hall, where he would await the next press briefing about the budget, he went over the press conference in his mind. He was glad that Katz was staying in the race because he thought Katz was a substantive candidate who talked about the issues. He personally thought Castille was an overrated public figure. When he had read Castille's position paper on the city's fiscal problems, handed out to reporters the day Castille formally announced, he had found it really thin.

But Davies thought Katz was going to have a problem with what he had just referred to: getting his message out. He wouldn't have enough money to advertise, and if he kept calling press conferences like this, saying the same things, people would stop coming, Davies knew. He thought Katz would have a particularly hard time getting television news to cover him if he were to simply talk about the issues. The news coverage for the past few weeks bore out his point. Television news about the campaign had been dominated by Rizzo's charges against Castille.

It was even hard for Katz to get covered on television that very night, despite the fact that reporters had been following him for much of the day. Despite the way he had shined in comparison to Castille and Rizzo in his performance on *AM Philadelphia* that morning, despite the number of stations that had been present at the afternoon press conference, despite Katz's attempts to link his campaign to Goode's budget message that night, still he was stiffed by television news. The Channel 6 piece was typical. It started with a Sam Katz sound-bite ("Let's talk about where this city is going to be in the twenty-first century") but quickly moved to the Rizzo-Castille battle.

"Sam Katz, adamant that he's in the race to stay, tried to look to the future, but this TV face-to-face degenerated into something resembling a nineteenth-century street brawl." The rest of the piece focused on Rizzo's police affidavit about going to Castille's house and finding him drunk and twirling guns. It had Judy Castille near tears saying, "The whole thing is absolutely despicable. . . . Nobody had any liquor with them. Ron was not twirling a gun." Katz's point about the city sitting down with the unions to work out concessions couldn't hold a candle to Judy Castille's crying on camera. (While the TV stations loved catching Castille's wife at her most emotional, they would miss the more dispassionate detail that those "empty liquor bottles" Rizzo's police officer had claimed were "all over the place" were actually a collection of antique whiskey bottles, each meticulously placed on shelves in the Castille kitchen.)

Sam Katz's coverage was similar in the next day's *Inquirer*. Although he did make the front page once again with the headline "Katz Defies GOP, Stays in the Race," the subhead was "Rizzo Accuses Castille again," and it was that theme which dominated the article. Frank Rizzo was just too much for the media to resist.

In this one case, however, being relegated to the back pages of an *Inquirer* story did not spell the final word for Sam Katz's campaign, because here another strain in the local media chorus chimed in. Newspaper columnists had always enjoyed a loyal following in Philadelphia, interpreting the news from their own unique vantage points, often appealing to one or another ethnic group in the city. They might not have the impact of a front-page headline or a piece on the evening news, but there was no question that they represented a strong voice in Philadelphia politics. And the columnists, particularly those at the *Daily News,* decided to weigh in for Sam Katz. They had been watching *AM Philadelphia* that morning and the spectacle had not been lost on them. Gossip columnist Stu Bykofsky wrote a piece entitled "Man in the Middle/ Katz Shined in Not-So-Great Debate," in which he talked about how on *AM Philadelphia* Katz had come to "play the role of the Responsible Adult to the testy exchanges between the former mayor and the former D.A." Veteran black columnist Chuck Stone wrote a column saying that the show "boldly revealed that Sam Katz was the GOP's *thinking* person's candidate. No way could he have pulled out after his brilliant performance."

On the following page, still another *Daily News* columnist, Dan Geringer, devoted his entire column, "Amid Brays, Whines, Katz Meow Is Mellow," to singing Katz's praises. Describing the *AM Philadelphia* show in great detail—emphasizing Katz's substantive answers as compared with Rizzo and Castille's personal attacks—he wrote, "Katz should party with these guys on TV as often as possible. Rizzo attacked Castille. Castille whined. And underdog Katz came out looking like the Republican party's best and brightest hope." Later on he wrote that Katz "acted like a guy who can stay focused on Philadelphia's desperate needs while the air around him is filled with the noise of hissing and dissing and whining and bad attitude. . . . I like the sound of the Katz meow."

Katz had said nothing on *AM Philadelphia* that he hadn't been saying throughout his campaign at forums and to the handful of reporters who were covering the election. But because of the requirements of the news business, little of it had gotten out to the public before. Katz had the good fortune this one time to triumph over his two better-known and better-covered opponents not on the campaign trail but on camera—in one of the few remaining local television forums that allowed candidates to go beyond eight-second sound-bites and get their message across directly to the voters. This one time Sam Katz managed to escape the stranglehold of silence reporters had imposed on him throughout the campaign because they didn't think he could win. But only time would tell whether it would be enough.

16 The Slugfest

April 2, 1991

❦ When Frank Rizzo walked into his first mayoral forum of the 1991 campaign at the Howard Johnson's Motor Inn on Roosevelt Boulevard, he was confronted with television crews from every news station in town. Although TV newscasts were increasingly turning off to the day in/day out forums where candidates were peppered with questions about the city's problems, today they were all out in force, and it was probably not much of a surprise to Frank Rizzo.

As police commissioner, then mayor, then political candidate, Rizzo had two decades of experience watching how the media worked and using that information to his own ends. It was no secret to veterans like Rizzo that assignment editors took their cues from the morning newspapers, and on this particular spring morning, Rizzo was well aware that another bombshell had been dropped in the press, in a column by Chuck Stone in the *Daily News*. The column reported on an affidavit by an anonymous city police officer, who claimed that in 1974 he had handcuffed Assistant District Attorney Ron Castille after a parking dispute and that Castille had been drinking and driving. Stone's column presented Castille's vehement denial of the incidents, but the bulk of the piece focused on the charges. Not much attention was paid to the fact that the sworn affidavit was anonymous.

The column had succeeded in drawing forth reporters and cameras from all of the television stations to this morning's Northeast Chamber of Commerce candidates' forum. And that was no easy feat. Increasingly disdainful of the issues, the TV stations were demanding more and more that there be a guarantee of drama and barbed exchanges before they were willing to commit cameras—much less one of their ever-dwindling stable of reporters—to cover a campaign event. And as the primary campaign moved into its last six weeks, there was one more thing that seemed to be needed to get local television crews out. The story had to fit into one of the two simple themes that TV stations had come up with to describe each primary.

It was the sad fact of life in local television news that increasingly the job of the reporter was not to seek out information about the candidates—whether qualifications or performance or proposals and plans—but rather to figure out how to fold each day's media events into a couple of ultrasimplified story lines. Simple themes were important to the television stations because if the primaries could be viewed as minidramas or ongoing soap operas, then people might be more likely to stay tuned for the latest chapter. But there was more to it than just attracting an audience. The larger truth was that pouring the complexities of a big city's problems and policies into a few simple plots made the TV reporter's job that much easier. And in a business where cutbacks were routine, where reporters were being asked to do more and more in less and less time, where political or city hall beats were disappearing and in their place general assignment reporters were being asked to merely put pictures on newspaper stories, the easiness factor was increasingly becoming decisive. Since most of the TV reporters covered the campaign only intermittently and all were under pressure to produce pieces with good video and sound-bites in a matter of a few hours, reducing campaigns and government stories to the simplest of themes was the only way to get the job done.

And so it was that in 1991 the two Philadelphia primary campaigns with their nine different candidates—many with substantial records, most proposing a range of solutions to the city's problems—had by April 2 been reduced to two of the simplest possible themes. On the Democratic side, it was the question of whether one of the black candidates would drop out of the election. On the Republican side, it was the fight between Frank Rizzo and Ron Castille, or what was being referred to, with obvious relish by the newscasters, as the "war of words" or "slugfest." But there could be no denying that one theme was far more fun to cover than the other. And so it was not surprising that the Republican candidates were dominating television coverage and that all the newscasts had suddenly decided to cover this morning's campaign forum.

While the Democratic candidates could barely get a single camera out to cover their forums or press conferences, Frank Rizzo, with his promise of a new chapter in the slugfest, was having no trouble at all. He was leading television reporters along like well-trained house dogs on leashes, and they seemed only too content to follow, even if they wound up fouling Ron Castille with unsubstantiated charges in the process. The stories were just too delicious to turn their backs on, the kind that took the yawn out of city politics and made assignment editors sit up and take notice. Rizzo knew precisely what TV reporters needed for a good story and precisely what he needed to win the primary. The newscasts wanted fireworks, not issues, personality clashes, not differences in positions. And that was just fine for Frank Rizzo because what he needed was to cast major doubts on Ron Castille, not as a government official, but as a man. At the same time he had to make the third contender in the race, Sam Katz, look just good enough to cut into Castille's share of the uncommitted voters, since Rizzo's core support of white ethnics was not enough to win the primary.

When Rizzo had first called Castille a drunk in his interview with Vernon Odom on Channel 6, there had been speculation that the Big Bambino had finally gone over the edge, that the carefully crafted accusations had turned into a wild man's ravings. But as Rizzo repeated the charge, embellishing it each time for the TV cameras, he seemed less and less like a man who had lost control of his arsenal. Rizzo and his campaign manager, Marty Weinberg, were no political novices. They understood perfectly that only through drastic measures could they hope to win. And in the first week in April, it was time for drastic measures. Polls showed that Castille still had the lead, with an estimated support of 42 percent of Republican voters, as compared to Rizzo's 27 percent and Katz's 18 percent.

When he walked into the breakfast campaign forum, Rizzo was well prepared to step up the attacks before all the television cameras. In a way, it was Rizzo who had orchestrated the television crews into attending in the first place, since it was likely that his campaign had been involved with the release of the anonymous affidavit to Chuck Stone. And the bait had worked. Here was reporter John Rawlins from Channel 6, the ratings leader in town. And while Tia O'Brien was absent, using up more and more of her vacation time before leaving the station, Channel 3 had sent reporter Marge Pala to cover the event. Even Channel 10, the station that was increasingly pulling back from election reports to cover more crime and health news, had sent a crew, virtually proving that expectations for something juicy were running high.

Rizzo waited patiently through the introductory remarks before getting up to make his latest attack on Castille. "This is a guy who doubled his budget as D.A. after MOVE because he got a payoff from Wilson Goode for not bringing any indictments," he said.

"You don't have the facts, Mayor Rizzo," Castille shot back.

"Oh, I know the facts," Rizzo retorted.

A few moments later, he got to the real meat of his attack, bringing up the charges that had been described in the Stone column that morning. For dramatic effect, he even held up the column, positioning it perfectly so that the TV cameras could get in close. "This election's about character, about judgment, about integrity," he said, in his most earnest voice. "And I say you don't mix guns and alcohol." It was his stock campaign line, the perfect simple, short sound-bite, but every time Frank Rizzo uttered the words, they sounded as if he'd just thought of them.

When Ron Castille got his turn at the podium, he was on the offensive himself. "There's only one certifiable liar on this stage today, and that's Frank Rizzo. And he told a couple of big lies." As if on cue, Castille hoisted up his own neat visual for the cameras. It was a copy of the front page of the *Daily News,* dated August 14, 1973, with the front-page headline "Rizzo Lied, Tests Showed," and it was a piece of infamous political lore in Philadelphia. Back when he was mayor, Rizzo had agreed to a suggestion by *Daily News* reporter Zack Stalberg (now the paper's editor) that he take a polygraph test to settle a political dispute. Rizzo was trying to prove that he was telling the truth when he claimed that he had not pressured the head of the city's Democratic party to back a certain candidate for district attorney. With all the local media looking on, Rizzo flunked the test. And now Castille was trying to conjure up the memory of the debacle, not for the one hundred or so neighborhood businessmen at the forum, but for the wider audience that the television cameras would reach. Even when he took his seat, he continued to hold up the newspaper headline whenever he was attacked by Rizzo.

As was so often the case in the video-politics of the 1990s, the quest for the perfect visual—by both candidates and television reporters—seemed to dwarf any concern with actual issues facing the city. And indeed, the pose of Ron Castille holding up his newspaper as if showing cue cards to a game show audience, was a carefully calculated strategic move designed to change the course of his campaign. He had started out in the "Rose Garden" mode, staying in his office as D.A., ignoring Rizzo's charges or making light of them, all the while trying to look like an effective public official. But when Rizzo started calling him a "drunk" and a "mental case," Castille's inner circle of advisers knew it was time to change direction. They had debated their options. Castille could go on ignoring Rizzo's charges, trying to stay above it all, talking about issues, not responding to the charges. But these new charges were just too serious to ignore, campaign strategists thought. If Castille said nothing, voters might assume his silence was an admission of guilt, and the political reporters would cast the candidate as passive, not fighting back. People in the campaign also had little hope that talking about issues was going to get a candidate much coverage in this or any election.

A second option was to aggressively deny the charges, which Castille had tried to do. He had called press conferences where he categorically denied that he ever had a drinking problem and where he accused Rizzo of engaging in "gutter politics." At one press conference, Castille had announced that he was submitting a complaint about Rizzo to the city's Fellowship Commission, charging that Rizzo had violated campaign fairness standards. The trouble was that every time Castille called one of these press conferences, it became an occasion for reporters to repeat Rizzo's charges that Castille was a "gun-toting drunk" and a "mental case." At one point, Castille had even unwittingly pronounced the charges himself. Looking directly into the television camera, he said of Rizzo, "He has said, to quote, I have a drinking problem. He has said, to quote, I am a mental case." Rizzo's attacks were so personal that when Castille responded he could not help looking personally defensive. It was not his stands or even his performance that he was being called upon to defend. It was his very character.

Aware that denial was not working, Castille shifted to the offensive. Starting with the breakfast forum, the strategy was to attack Rizzo right back. He would argue that Rizzo was a liar and that Rizzo had a long history of being a liar, so that anything he said about Castille should not be considered credible. At the Northeast breakfast forum, he tried to make the point that Rizzo had lied to the people of Philadelphia when he had claimed before re-election as mayor in 1975 that he would not raise taxes. He was trying to suggest that Rizzo wouldn't hesitate to lie to defame an opponent and that he just might lie to the voters about how he intended to get the city out of the fiscal crisis. It was an argument that had a certain amount of logic to it and that could be said to bring the slugfest back to the real problems of the city. Even more important, it reminded the citizens of Philadelphia that Castille was the one who had a personal reputation for credibility, not Rizzo.

But the argument was lost on the media, since the reporters chose to interpret Castille's new strategy in a different way. The TV stations had their simple, appealing theme, and Castille's new charges fed into it. Castille's counterattack was not about to send the newscasts scurrying to reconsider Rizzo's record as mayor and what he did and did not promise to the citizens of Philadelphia. It was merely going to be lapped up enthusiastically as one more round in the slugfest. The message of the day was easy as pie: Castille was finally stooping to Rizzo's level. Coming up against the irresistible slugfest theme, Castille failed in his attempt to link Rizzo's baseless attacks on him to the ex-mayor's raising the city's taxes after he had promised not to. He failed to get the campaign debate to focus on Rizzo's actions when he was mayor of the city. Instead, he just got accused of name-calling himself.

The same thing happened when Castille went on television that week with his first ad, put together by media consultant Chris Mottola. In the first half of the ad, run in black and white with ominous death bells tolling in the background, the announcer talked about Frank Rizzo: "A disgraceful record of runaway spending . . . higher taxes . . . and lies. Frank Rizzo's personal attacks on Ron Castille have been called a 'new low' " [shot of *Inquirer* editorial] "even for Rizzo." [the name almost spat out] "What's his problem?" [change to upbeat music and color video] "He can't compete with the Castille record. Combat hero, hard-nosed prosecutor, a no-nonsense administrator who's led the D.A.'s office in hard times. A tough, tested leader for Philadelphia. Ron Castille for Mayor."

By classic conventions, the ad was doing everything right. It took Castille away from doing his own negatives, using an announcer to conjure up the things about Rizzo that voters would dislike, and it employed a piece of video of Rizzo from 1975 that would trigger a reminder of what the ex-mayor's reign had been like. The negatives it discussed about Rizzo were hardly petty or personal: runaway spending and tax increases by a former mayor were perfectly legitimate election issues. And the upbeat part of the ad was merely trying to reawaken all the positive images Castille had enjoyed before entering the mayor's race. The only problem with the ad was that it too became fodder for the slugfest theme, particularly since Rizzo was on TV with his new ad criticizing Castille for drawing his gun at inappropriate times.

KYW had jumped at the opportunity to connect the two ad campaigns, using the slugfest theme. Reporter Marge Pala began her piece, "Experts say negative ads are the most potent weapon in any political arsenal. Analysts say that negative ads can also be the most dangerous. If the public believes the message is either irrelevant or unfair, the mudslinging can boomerang."

And then, instead of analyzing the truthfulness of the claims made in the ads—which might have actually required some time and research—in typical local TV news fashion she punted to man-on-the-street interviews. Such interviews were a staple of local newscasts because they were so cheap and easy to carry out. No need to even take the time to schedule an interview with someone who might actually possess some expertise. With man-on-the-street interviews, or MOS's, as they were called, you could literally stop your van anywhere and find the faces and voices you needed to "humanize" a political story and at the same time give the impression that you were assessing public opinion. Of course, the idea that the three or four interviews obtained in this fashion said anything about public opinion was fairly ludicrous. But that didn't keep MOS's from being used as the quick-and-dirty method for TV reporters to make their preconceived points, with the conventional wisdom coming out of somebody else's mouth.

In this case, Pala invited people on a downtown street to watch the ads on monitors inside the Channel 3 van, then asked for their reactions. "Most of them thought both ads were losers," she announced as convincingly as if she'd actually taken a poll rather than interviewed a handful of center-city office workers on the street.

One of the men she had interviewed produced the pat sound-bite of the day: "The city is in terrific trouble. And neither of the guys is saying anything that has anything to say about the city's difficulties in any way. And they're blowing smoke at each other. I don't think it's constructive. And I think they both ought to be ashamed of themselves."

Pala closed the piece with the kind of denouement that producers love: "You might have just heard the sound of a boomerang."

What she did not report, however, was that her man-on-the-street was mistaken when he said that "neither of the guys is saying anything that has anything to say about the city's difficulties in any way." Both Rizzo and Castille had, by this date, issued a number of position papers and had made statements at their public appearances that addressed many of the city's "difficulties." The problem was that almost none of it had been covered on television by reporters like Pala. Position papers were being ignored and the candidates' forums were being covered by television only for their soundless pictures. But city voters could not know that. They assumed that what they were seeing on television news was all the candidates were saying in their campaigns. And all they were seeing on television was the Castille-Rizzo slugfest.

While the slugfest theme was killing Castille, it was giving Sam Katz his only crack at being covered on television news. From February 13, the day of Castille's endorsement, until March 27 and his appearance on the local talk show *AM Philadelphia,* Sam Katz's campaign had been invisible on TV news. The *Inquirer*'s Paolantonio had written Katz off, and the TV stations had been only too happy to follow, since what Katz was saying about substantive issues was too difficult to work into the slugfest theme anyway.

But after *AM Philadelphia,* after Katz provided them with the perfect visual of himself sitting in the middle of Rizzo and Castille talking issues while they traded accusations, after the *Daily News* poured forth with its columns lauding Katz's performance, the TV reporters finally got the message. There was a way to keep the slugfest theme alive and give it a new twist, and old themes with new twists are just about all you could ask for in TV news. They would start to cover Sam Katz as the man who was "above the fray," the guy who was talking about "the issues." Never mind that the TV stations never quite got around to telling viewers what exactly Katz was saying about the issues, much less whether any of it made any more sense than what the other candidates were saying in their position papers and public appearances. In the simplistic nomenclature of TV news, Katz had gone from being the "municipal finance expert" to something even better: the "issues candidate."

Now it was becoming Sam Katz who would wear the mantle of the mythical "nonpolitician's politician," the man who was in the race not for his ego or for petty politics but to save his beloved city. It was Sam Katz who was becoming the clean, honest candidate with integrity, who stood for change, fighting against the politicians who were wedded to the past. It was the identical message that Castille had claimed upon his entrance into the race, but now a month later Sam Katz was beginning to own it and the Castille campaign watched helplessly as it happened.

The night of the Northeast Chamber of Commerce breakfast forum it became frighteningly clear to the Castille campaign staff what was happening to their candidate, the former media darling. They watched as John Rawlins, reporting for the all-important Channel 6, focused his reports from the Northeast breakfast forum on Sam Katz. Rawlins gave prominent play to Rizzo holding up the Chuck Stone column and Castille holding up the *Daily News* "Rizzo Lied" headline, but he used both as a foil for interviews with businessmen about how much they had liked Sam Katz. He even noted that Frank Rizzo attacked Katz that day, saying Katz had gotten too many sweetheart contracts from Mayor Bill Green. But he gave Katz a great sound-bite to retort: "The first city that we ever got hired by, the very first city, was Philadelphia in 1978. And the mayor of that city was . . . Frank Rizzo." (The bite even included the amused laughter of the crowd in response to Katz's quip.)

The Castille campaign watched at eleven as the city's most important television station summarized Rawlins's earlier report: "Once again Rizzo and Castille traded character attacks while Sam Katz tried to stay above the fray." They watched as Stephanie Stahl at Channel 10 used special effects to portray the forum as a prize fight, ringing a bell in between each accusation, making Castille seem no better than Rizzo even though the former was attacking a documented record of policy while the latter was making loosely substantiated character attacks. Only Sam Katz was shown in a favorable light, saying, "These two guys are engaged in sandbox politics. The people don't want children running the city of Philadelphia."

The *Daily News* provided supporting evidence for the new theme. Cynthia Burton led her story about the forum with the statement that "Sam Katz won a three-way slugfest with Frank Rizzo and Ronald Castille yesterday in the increasingly volatile Republican mayoral primary." She went on, "Several people attending the Republican mayoral forum . . . gave the victory to Katz, who they said came off as level-headed and well grounded in the issues. 'We knew very little of Sam Katz coming in this morning,' Chamber board member Bill Logan said. 'We're impressed.' " Although the rest of the article detailed Rizzo's and Castille's charges against each other, the impression that Sam Katz was the issues man got prominent play, even if, once again, not one of Katz's statements about "the issues" was actually included.

Only the *Inquirer* refused to jump on the Katz bandwagon in their coverage, continuing to downplay Katz's campaign. The paper was beginning to pull in additional reporters to cover the day-to-day events of the campaign as the primaries heated up, keeping Sal Paolantonio in the lead position to follow campaign strategy and political developments. Reporter Bill Miller had been assigned to cover Republican public appearances, and he wrote a story on the Northeast forum headlined "Castille Lashes Back at Rizzo," which did not mention Katz until the fifth paragraph. Katz "attempted to concentrate discussion on the fact that the city is courting financial disaster. . . . Katz talked about saving the city. Rizzo and Castille talked about the issues, too, but their most colorful remarks were their comments about each other." Like his broadcast counterparts, the *Inquirer* reporter chose to focus his story on the "colorful" discussion rather than Katz's or Castille's or even Rizzo's discussion of any issues. The paper, which prided itself on its searing coverage of issues, which had won seventeen Pulitzer prizes in the past two decades, could still cover a local campaign forum where the city's problems and opportunities were being debated, yet mention nothing but personal allegations in the resulting article.

If Katz's campaign was still being ignored by the *Inquirer,* he was clearly on a roll with the other media. His biggest coup that week was winning the *Daily News* endorsement. Newspaper editorials counted for a lot, not just because they influenced readers but because they got added mileage when the television stations picked them up and when media consultants

later turned the endorsement into political ads. The *Daily News* editorial
was particularly glowing. "Sam Katz—young, tough, and independent—is
precisely the kind of person the party should elect as its standard-bearer
for the general election," it read, noting his expertise in municipal financial
management and his service on the school board. It talked about his
stands on education and the management of the school budget. Though
the editorial called some of his ideas overly optimistic, it added, "But Sam
Katz has a plan and the will to carry it out. His vision for Philadelphia is
thought-out and convincing . . . his positions are derived from solid experience and backed by considerable intelligence."

With all this new attention in the aftermath of his *AM Philadelphia*
appearance, it seemed as if Sam Katz's campaign was on an upswing. It
certainly appeared that way to people in Castille's campaign, who viewed
with alarm the results of the campaign's own polls showing Katz with a
favorable rating of 51 percent as compared to an unfavorable rating of
9–10 percent. Katz had started building those favorable ratings early on,
with his ad campaign saying he could solve Philadelphia's fiscal crisis,
which had reached so unexpectedly many viewers because of the war with
Iraq. During that same time, he had managed to secure an image as the
"new face" and the "fiscal expert," and he had managed to appear on TV
news when most of the other candidates could not. Even his early inability
to speak in sound-bites had strangely helped him. The television reporters
couldn't seem to figure out where to stop his quotes on financial strategies,
so they tended to let him talk longer than his competitors. Viewers seemed
to find something reassuring about a man who knew so much about the
city's finances that you could barely understand him.

And though he had dropped from view for almost two months, he was
not forgotten when he reemerged as the hero of *AM Philadelphia*. Voters
were ready for something other than Ron Castille and Frank Rizzo trading
charges, and with Sam Katz they thought they were getting it. Castille's
campaign strategists could see it with frightening clarity. Katz's latest
favorable/unfavorable ratings could just carry him to win the election,
particularly seeing as how he owned the number one problem in the city,
the fiscal crisis. They were worried, no question about it, not simply that
they would lose, but that Sam Katz would win. But it was a fear they never
aired publicly. Publicly Castille was saying, "A vote for Sam Katz is a vote
for Frank Rizzo," using as his most effective weapon the idea that Sam
Katz could never win.

And they were aided in this strategy by two forces. The first was that Sal
Paolantonio and the other *Inquirer* reporters who came to cover the campaign consistently downplayed Katz's ability to win. They never wrote

about Katz's favorable/unfavorable ratings, which were carefully guarded by the Castille campaign, and they never even suggested Katz had a chance. A sentence here, a quote there, usually buried in the depths of articles with headlines about other matters, might suggest that Katz was coming closer to challenging Castille and Rizzo as the election neared. But there was nothing with the kind of prominence or play to encourage Democrats to change their registration to Republican to vote for Katz. Although the *Inquirer* was to editorially endorse Sam Katz in the strongest possible terms, the Katz campaign was still finding it almost impossible to get covered in *Inquirer* news stories.

The other problem was that while Sam Katz found it easier to get covered once he became part of the slugfest theme, he had just as hard a time making it into the news when his two sidekicks weren't doing their routine. He was only a story if Rizzo and Castille were feuding and he was staying above the fray. When he called a press conference to simply discuss a position, as on the day when he released a major position paper on a plan to solve the city's fiscal crisis, only one television station, Channel 6, bothered to cover it. And even there the plan was covered only as a story read by the anchor, lasting a mere fifteen seconds.

It wasn't much better in the newspapers, either. Katz's press conference got covered by the *Inquirer* on page 7-B with a one-column head, "Katz Offers Finance Plan for the City." It ran below another campaign story, this one with a much larger headline that ran across the entire page: "Rizzo softens his manner, but he's still on the attack." A story about Rizzo's latest ads was always going to get more play than a story about a candidate's plan, even if that plan concerned the most pressing problem facing the city that year.

Page 7-B of the *Inquirer* that day said a great deal about what Sam Katz was up against at this point in the campaign. Going substantive was not going to win him much coverage, either in the newspapers or on TV. His plans, whether good or bad, were not going to attract the attention of the news media and the voting public, no matter how visual the backdrop or how many sound-bites he threw out. Only his responses to Rizzo's and Castille's charges and countercharges were going to be covered. He could only be painted as "above the fray" if Rizzo continued to attack Castille and Castille continued to countercharge. But as Sal Paolantonio's article on Rizzo's ads had correctly picked up, Rizzo was about to change his media strategy. He had succeeded in his expert orchestration of the media coverage of the election, making Castille look mean and petty and Sam Katz just credible enough. And so, after one or two more encounters with his chief opponent, he was about to stop the fray.

17 The Third-Base Coach

April 16, 1991

❦ Frank Rizzo's final blow to Ron Castille took place away from the television cameras and microphones. It was at an off-the-record meeting that the KYW editorial board held with the Republican candidates at the studios on Independence Mall. The meeting was the brainchild of Charlie Thomson, editorial director for both KYW-TV and KYW Newsradio. For all its internal turmoil, KYW was the only television station in the market that regularly broadcast editorials. The station had a long history of strong editorial involvement in the city, the result of a corporate requirement enacted back in the sixties by Group W that each of its stations do regular editorials. They had even insisted that each station's general manager read the editorials on air, to give them more clout.

KYW had suffered through a succession of general managers for whom on-air appearances were not always easy. But then Pat Pollilo had arrived. He had worked as a news director in other stations and was known as a flamboyant troubleshooter, a guy who would come into a station and shake it up. When Pollilo arrived at KYW, he thought up a new high-profile concept for his editorials. He wasn't going to sit in some boring TV studio with a row of bookcases behind him, intoning about charter reform. No, he had the idea that he'd be out on the streets in every editorial, with an image that was half consumer reporter fighting on your side, half the investigative reporter uncovering corruption in government. This was the time when KYW had its "I-team" of former newspaper reporters doing serious investigative reporting, and Pollilo wanted to build on that image. One day he'd be walking down the streets of a poor neighborhood bouncing a basketball to talk about city workers playing ball on the city's dime when they were supposed to be weatherizing poor people's houses. Another day he'd be riding in a tugboat on the Delaware talking about what the city needed to do about the port. A lot of people at the station and at Group W in New York had thought the guy was a joke, but they stopped laughing when market research showed that Pollilo was better known than the station's anchors. He helped encourage people to tune in, and even back in those days, news ratings were mightily important.

While it was Pollilo who had all the visibility, the person who was writing all the editorials—as he had done for previous general managers— was Charles F. Thomson. He had come to KYW in 1979 from the *Philadelphia Bulletin*, the venerable afternoon newspaper that died in 1982. Thomson had liked the Pollilo era at KYW, because it was nice to have people really pay attention to his editorials. And the pieces actually seemed to have some clout. Pollilo had this gimmick where he would tell viewers to send him postcards with their responses to the editorial, and then the station would pass the postcards on to government officials. And people did write, and the letters did matter—not as much as Pollilo liked to claim on the air, but the station did get some response.

After Pollilo left, the on-location editorials continued for a short while, with black veteran reporter Malcolm Poindexter delivering them, but the station didn't air the editorials as much, or promote them, and eventually the format had returned to the studio, with successive GM's returning to the delivery of editorials with the old blank wall behind them. Thomson continued writing editorials for both the radio station, which was number one in the market, and the television station, where ratings continued to lag behind the competition.

Thomson had not convened this meeting with the Republican candidates for the purpose of endorsements, since neither the television or radio station endorsed political candidates, by directive from Group W. The policy against endorsing may have reflected an unwillingness to go that extra step in alienating a segment of the audience (probably the reason why most other stations didn't editorialize at all) or concern about meeting FCC regulations about the timing of statements and responses and rebuttals, which made political endorsements trickier for broadcast stations than for newspapers.

While Charlie Thomson would have liked KYW to endorse candidates in Philadelphia's 1991 mayor's race, he had to content himself with these meetings instead. He thought that this election was so important that he wanted the managers at the station, particularly the general managers, to get a sense of the candidates and their programs for the city. And so he invited Jonathan Klein, general manager of the television station, and Roy Shapiro, general manager of the radio station, news directors Scott Herman and Mark Helms, assistant TV news director Paul Gluck, and some reporters, like Tia O'Brien and Marge Pala from TV and Dale Wilcox from radio. They would have another session for all five Democratic candidates, but this morning it was the Republicans' turn.

The meeting was held in the third-floor television conference room, with windows overlooking Independence Mall and the Liberty Bell. Castille arrived first, with his press secretary, Laura Linton. Thomson chatted with them briefly before they walked the few steps back from the door to admire the view outside the windows. A few minutes later, Frank Rizzo arrived with two campaign aides in tow. KYW had specified that each candidate bring only one aide, so as not to have any one person offset the balance, but Frank Rizzo had ignored the instructions. Thomson watched as Rizzo spied Castille out of the corner of his eye, refused to acknowledge him, and immediately turned his back to Castille to leisurely circle the large oval conference table in the room until he stopped just short of where Castille was standing. No hello to his opponent, no handshake.

Watching Rizzo circle the room reminded Thomson of a scene from almost twenty years before that was etched in his memory. Back when Thomson was a reporter for the *Bulletin* he had covered Frank Rizzo's first term as mayor. In fact, Rizzo had stopped talking to him as a result of several stories he had written about the mayor. There was one story in particular that would come to haunt Rizzo for years to come. It was Thomson whose investigation had turned up the story that ten thousand people had waited for hours in the rain to apply on a supposedly first come/first served basis for 280 city jobs that had already been doled out to Rizzo supporters. It was a story that Neil Oxman would later turn into a very effective political ad for Wilson Goode's campaign.

Back then Thomson remembered that it was a deliberate tactic of Rizzo's to freeze out a city hall reporter who was doing critical stories. Thomson saw Rizzo use the same tactics as mayor that he had used as police chief. Rizzo forced reporters to take a stand. You were either for him or against him. To Thomson, Rizzo was a monumental force; very smart, very shrewd, very quick, and with no scruples about how he would use his talents. City hall press conferences were amazing because the mayor's staff would pack them with people from South Philly who would jeer at and shout down any reporters' questions that were difficult. After Thomson wrote some of his more critical articles, Rizzo had said to the reporter, "I'm going to dry you up and I'm never going to talk to you again. You're never going to get a story out of city hall again. You're going to walk down the halls and nobody's going to talk to you." Thomson even remembered a day he was supposed to be on Channel 10's Sunday morning current affairs show with the mayor. When Rizzo heard Thomson was going to be on the show, he said, "It's either me or him," and Thomson was unceremoniously dumped.

By 1991, with Thomson long gone from the *Bulletin* and now writing editorials for the influential KYW Newsradio and KYW-TV, Frank Rizzo was once again talking to him. But as Thomson watched him circle the KYW conference room, ostentatiously avoiding eye contact with Castille, he couldn't forget another Rizzo appearance he had covered back in 1974. It was the Jefferson-Jackson Day dinner, a Democratic party function held each year at the Philadelphia Civic Center in West Philadelphia. Pete Camiel, the party chief with whom Rizzo was feuding at the time, was running the dinner and, as a snub, had not invited Rizzo to sit at the head table. Reporters had flooded the Civic Center that night, curious about what Rizzo would do in response to the slight by Camiel.

Thomson still remembered the scene vividly. The doors to the Civic Center's main hall opened, and Rizzo came in with a phalanx of supporters from the building and trades industries. And then, with his bodyguards surrounding him, Rizzo circled the huge room, stopping at tables where his supporters sat. During that time, scuffles broke out as the union men picked fights with people—occupying tables where seats had been bought by others, starting fistfights with people who tried to take their seats. Plates and glasses were smashed and faces bloodied. For reporters like Thomson who were not used to this display of brute power, it was quite a sight. Thomson realized that this was a man who lent himself to metaphors and analogy, who was brilliant at creating symbols. No one was going to put him down, and he was more than happy to display that message at the Jefferson-Jackson Day dinner. But later in Rizzo's tenure, Thomson had witnessed something else interesting. After Rizzo flunked the lie-detector test, his aides seemed to put something of a muzzle on the mayor and to advise him to go underground. No more daily press conferences, and no more quite so blatant displays of bullying tactics. Until this election, of course. Thomson's agenda in scheduling this meeting today was, in part, to let the influential people at the station get to know Frank Rizzo and perhaps glimpse the sides of the man he had observed back in his city hall days.

Today, Thomson had the three candidates sit next to one another, first Rizzo, then Sam Katz, then Castille, and he let them each talk for five or ten minutes before opening up to questions. Through the opening statements, the discussion stayed pretty calm. But as the meeting began to get into questions, it happened, just as Thomson suspected it would: Rizzo went on the attack, interrupting Castille, taunting Castille, making it difficult for the man to get out a full sentence. And all the while, Sam Katz sat silently by, not criticizing Rizzo, not trying to draw the line against the personal harangues, making Thomson think for the first time that maybe Rizzo and Katz were in league. When Rizzo brought up the guns, Castille did not respond, but when a few minutes later Rizzo made a reference to Castille's drinking too much, Castille finally had had it. "I'm not going to put up with this," he had said, getting up to leave. "This is not what this is supposed to be about."

Thomson leaped up, too, and talked the candidate into staying, promising to control the session more tightly. But Thomson was not at all disturbed by what had occurred. He had wanted the younger reporters and the editors to get a sense of what Rizzo was like personally, the tactics of a bully that he used, the vindictiveness and virulence of his personal attacks. It was the Rizzo that Thomson remembered from the seventies, not the Rizzo who had tried to remake his image in the following decade to challenge the very controlled, the very well educated Wilson Goode. In 1983 and 1987, Rizzo was trying to dispel the old image, but Thomson had not forgotten any of it—the unsubstantiated charges that he threw out when he was feuding with someone, the way he had always progressively escalated his attacks. His style, Thomson knew, was to try out some charges and see how they flew in the press. He would develop and modify and moderate his attacks, and with his tremendous wit and ability to think and talk on his feet, it had a certain spontaneous feel to it. To Thomson, Rizzo was like a pit bull: you knew what direction he was going in, but you never knew how hard he was going to hit or exactly what he was going to do. In 1991, Thomson saw that the pit bull was going after Castille. If today's retreat by Castille were any indication, it was certainly effective.

The next day Castille announced that he would no longer go one-on-one with Rizzo in debates. He was canceling his appearance with Rizzo and Sam Katz on a live debate on KYW Newsradio scheduled for the following morning. The radio station had set up a "Breakfast with the Candidates" forum that would air from eight to nine—prime drive-time in Philadelphia—but Castille would not be there. In the *Inquirer* article that appeared the next morning, Castille said he was tired of subjecting himself to Frank Rizzo's personal attacks whenever he appeared with him, adding that it was impossible to discuss the issues with Rizzo in the room. "I'm not going to get in there with Rizzo . . . He doesn't want to talk about the issues. . . . We're just not going to go in the same situation with Frank

Rizzo being less than a gentleman." Castille added that, although it was not a debate, the reporters would "try to instigate name-calling because they'd fear a fair and impartial examination of the issues puts people to sleep."

The reaction from his opponents came later in the article. From Frank Rizzo: "It's a tough job being mayor, pal. If every time somebody says something he doesn't like, he's going to hide, I don't know what's going to happen to Philadelphia." From Sam Katz: "The problems confronting Philadelphia make the problems confronting the Castille campaign seem modest. . . . He should be there." The *Daily News* article by Dave Davies that same day introduced another possible motive for Castille's decision not to debate that had not been mentioned in the *Inquirer*: any confrontation between Rizzo and Castille would help the rising fortunes of Sam Katz. Tia O'Brien read both articles and decided to focus her story for KYW's six o'clock newscast on Castille's decision not to debate Rizzo and Katz. She was biding her time before she left Philadelphia for San Francisco, gradually disengaging from the local political scene before she made her break. The Rizzo/Castille "slugfest" was turning out to be an easy sell to all the TV stations and today she would simply follow the pack and turn out a serviceable product. There wasn't much mystery about what she'd get from Frank Rizzo.

She and her cameraman set off first for Castille's campaign office to get his explanation for his decision, and the candidate was more than obliging. He repeated what he had told the newspaper reporters the day before: "We're not going to go into those kind of situations with Frank Rizzo and be subjected to those kinds of accusations. Frank Rizzo . . . he's nothing but a thug . . . a bully." It was great stuff for TV. These guys usually danced around what they were trying to say, and here was Castille saying it in the bluntest terms. "Did you get that?" she turned to ask her cameraman, but unfortunately he hadn't set the camera running when she asked the question. "Mr. Castille, can I possibly ask you to say that again for the camera? What do you think of Frank Rizzo?" Castille obliged. "It's in his psyche to be that way . . . a bully and a thug." At this point he didn't seem to care what people heard him call Frank Rizzo.

From Castille's headquarters, O'Brien, her cameraman, and her student intern headed the few blocks to Rizzo's campaign office to get his reaction. Local TV stations like KYW relied heavily on college students working as unpaid interns to take up the slack that resulted from their small staff sizes. Tia O'Brien particularly liked to work with interns and used them extensively to "log" the tapes of her interviews—writing down where on the tape each comment occurred—so that she could go back quickly and find the video and sound-bites she wanted when it was time to put together her piece. But in return for doing the scut work, the reporter liked to give her students interesting jobs, sometimes sending them to interview politicians, asking their opinions, using their input on the story. The timid students were put off by her no-nonsense, even gruff manner. But the aggressive, bright ones who managed to earn Tia's respect felt as if they were themselves ace TV reporters for a few months and loved it. O'Brien's intern this day, Tereza Nemessanyi from the University of Pennsylvania, was one such student.

Nemessanyi was excited to be out with Tia that day interviewing Frank Rizzo, of all people, in his office. As Tia took her seat across from Frank's desk, and the KYW cameraman set up for the shot of the two of them speaking, the student unobtrusively sat down in the back of the room across from one of Rizzo's campaign aides. The reporter had asked Tereza to take notes on the interview, to make it even easier to log later on. As she sat listening to the interview, she became fascinated by what Rizzo's aide was doing. Out of the reporter's view, the aide was making hand motions to guide Rizzo through the interview. It struck Nemessanyi that the hand motions were similar to the kind of signals a third-base coach might give a batter at the plate, and, for fun, she jotted them down in her notes. Tia would get a kick out of seeing them later, she thought.

All told, she watched five distinct gestures used to coach Rizzo through the interview. The first one was a downward press of the hands as if to indicate "calm down" or "tone it down." The second was like a windshield wiper, indicating that Rizzo should get off the subject. The third was a wave goodbye, telling the candidate not to answer the question. The fourth was a thumbs up, as if to say "fantastic" when Rizzo had hit the mark exactly with the answer, and the fifth was a nod, to indicate "that's great, keep going."

She listened carefully as Tia began the interview. "Mayor, after you had your little meeting with Channel 3 last week, Ron Castille has decided not to go head-to-head with you except in engagements that they've already accepted. What do you think about that?"

"I think that's wrong, Tia," Rizzo responded. "I think that, first of all, he says 'the issues.' I talk the issues every place I go, every night. I even have a slide presentation that I use, and it's about issues—where our town is headed, what we have to do to correct it. So the issues—we talk about. But getting back to Ron Castille, it would seem to me that, if he's that thin-skinned . . . in my life, I've had a lot of things said about me that I didn't like, I didn't agree with. Some of them were true, most of them were not. But I didn't hide. I'm back the next day to take my lumps if I deserve them. This is what this city's all about. It's a tough town. You can't run and hide because people are critical of you."

"What he's saying," O'Brien continued, "is he doesn't mind criticism, but haranguing, interruptions, mudslinging, name-calling—"

"They're adjectives that are easy to use," Rizzo answered, "Mudslinging? Everything that was said was reported by the media. Three out of four. I didn't say it. A newspaper columnist said it."

"Respectfully, Mayor, last week, at Channel 3, however, you did interrupt Mr. Castille and make it difficult for him to talk," O'Brien said.

"No, that's not true," Rizzo said, getting more excited. (His aide made a hand-press motion.) "I interrupted a couple of times because what he was saying wasn't true. So, but even then, it don't mean . . . any . . . uh, you know" (another hand-press motion to calm down). "The issues here are very . . . and . . . you know . . . And I challenge Ron Castille, Tia, before—you're leaving town, and I'm gonna be sorry to see you go, dear. But let me tell you . . . I challenge Ron Castille to debate me on the issues any place, any time."

"Well, he says he can't get a word in edgewise even if he tried."

"Well, Tia, why don't you, before you leave, call Mr. Castille and tell him that he and I will sit down and talk the issues—all about issues. I would think the issue here is, are we thin-skinned? Because someone says something about you, do you want to run and hide? Are we ready to talk about issues—lead this city, make it a great city with an agenda that's gonna make it great? He hasn't said anything that impresses me or a lot of other people. In fact, a lot of people are disappointed that he has decided to go hide because he doesn't like some of the things I'm saying. I didn't say anything. It was the media that said it all."

"Today, he described you as being a bully, a thug, and inconsiderate," Tia said to get his reaction.

"Well that speaks for itself—that he's thin-skinned because the newspaper reported some things about him that he don't like—that he doesn't like to hear." (Another hand-press motion.) "Now what would I . . now I'm gonna go hide. He called me a thug. I'm gonna go in that room and lock the door. I'm not comin' out for a week. This is not what it's about, Tia. He can call me a thief. In fact, he called me a horse thief. Nobody ever picked that up in the press." (The aide imitated a windshield wiper.) "A thug—now, you know that I'm not a thug. I was a police officer all my life and a mayor. Never a thug."

"Well, he—" Tia began.

"Helped people all my life," Rizzo went on. "Went to the rescue of people. No, a thug I'm not."

"A bully?" she pressed. This was just the kind of visceral reaction on Rizzo's part that her producers ate up.

"I'm not a bully, either." (Here, another windshield wiper came, to get Rizzo off the subject.) "I never—the only—I used to go out of my way to help people that were being pushed around by bullies."

"Well, he's claiming that your tactics these days should remind people of what Frank Rizzo was like in the 70s," she said.

"Tia, Frank Rizzo in the 70s?" Rizzo was incredulous. "In the 60s, I was police commissioner. Every other city burned. Philadelphia didn't burn. Nobody died, either police or civilian. No, I'll stand by my record in the 70s." (The aide gave thumbs up.) "It's a great record."

Tia took another tack. "What do you think about the fact that Ron Castille, the man who touts his record in Vietnam, doesn't want to sit down next to you at a joint appearance?" (The aide waved good-bye.)

"I wouldn't even want to discuss that. You'd have to ask him why," Rizzo answered, to a thumbs-up motion from his aide. "I'm—I'll be anywhere, anytime that I have to be."

Tia moved on to another subject. "He said today he had promised he would support whoever wins the Republican primary, but he is now retracting that promise, and if it's you, he refuses to support you."

Rizzo got a windshield wiper motion, but ignored it. "I have no problem with that one, either, Tia. It doesn't bother me. I'm not gonna lose any sleep over that one, Tia."

"Would you support Ron Castille if he wins this primary?," she continued. (The aide waved.)

"I've said it. I'll have to wait and make a decision further down the road."

O'Brien pressed on. "Do you feel that you want to endorse this guy that you call a drunk and liar?" (The aide motioned not to answer.)

"When I called him that," Rizzo answered, "I only reported what the press said about him, not what I said."

"Well, I don't think anybody in the press said he was a drunk," she countered. (The aide motioned not to answer.)

"Well, you know, I'm not going to talk about—what his condition was. I will just say that I am willing and able to talk about Castille no matter where he wants to talk about issues. So again, Tia, you've been around a long time. You're a political reporter. Do you think a candidate—I'll ask you the question—should go hide because Frank Rizzo said something he doesn't like? I think that shortchanges the people. They want to see Mr. Castille. They want to hear from him. They want to hear about the issues. You can't go in and lock your door because your opponent says something you don't like. That's not American politics."

The reporter tried one last time to get an answer to her earlier question. "Are you a little surprised that Ron Castille, the 'war hero,' is doing this?"

Rizzo got a wave. "Tia, you'll have to ask him the questions why he's not doing something. I can't speak for Ron Castille."

"No, I'm just saying, you know, he touts his record, how he is so brave," Tia continued.

"And I'm sure he is," Rizzo responded with a smile, ending the interview, but not before he got a last thumbs-up from his aide.

O'Brien returned to the station with her intern and cameraman to put together a story that required very little thought. She knew the story would run and, what's more, that it would probably make more than one newscast, not because it had any particular news value but because of Frank Rizzo. Over the sixteen years that she had been in Philadelphia, she had learned that all Frank Rizzo had to do was open his mouth and the TV stations would run it. Didn't matter that what he said today was not very much different from what he'd said sixteen years ago and that it didn't have a whole lot to do with Philadelphia's fiscal crisis. O'Brien knew it would meet the station's definition of news. And she was right. Her package ran at 5:30, with major segments repeated at 6 and 11. It would be Tia O'Brien's last campaign story at KYW, and it would run this way:

Introduction from the anchor: "The mayoral race may be getting too hot for one of the candidates. Republican Ron Castille says that he's boycotting future face-to-face campaign appearances with his opponent, Frank Rizzo. Channel 3's political editor, Tia O'Brien, reports on Castille's spitting venom on what's being called gutter politics."

Castille: "It's probably the rudest, most boorish display I've ever seen."

O'Brien: "That's how Ron Castille sums up Frank Rizzo's behavior during joint appearances like this one [video of AM Philadelphia appearance] when Castille was trying to fight off Rizzo's attacks. Last week, during an off-the-record meeting here at Channel 3, Castille threatened to walk out after Rizzo kept haranguing him. Now Castille is refusing most invitations to appear with his arch rival."

Castille: "Frank Rizzo has shown, even in your editorial board, that he can't talk about the issues. All he wants to do is sling dirt."

O'Brien: "As we talked with Castille, the former district attorney used the harshest language to date to describe Frank Rizzo."

Castille: "It's in his psyche to be that way . . . to be a bully and a thug."
(Cut to Rizzo.)

Rizzo: "Now I'm going to go hide. He called me a thug. I'm going to go into that room and lock the door. I'm not coming out for a week."

O'Brien: "Frank Rizzo is reveling in the controversy over his campaign tactics. Rizzo has no plans to halt the attacks on Castille."

Rizzo: "This is a tough town. You can't run and hide because people are critical of you."

O'Brien: "Is this growing feud between Rizzo and Castille helping or hurting the candidates? Voters we talked to here in center city had strong opinions."

O'Brien to Man-On-Street: "What do you think of Frank Rizzo's tactics?"

MOS: "I think of Rizzo as more Gestapo than anything."

MOS: "If you can't take on Rizzo, you know, there's a lot tougher problems he's got to deal with."

MOS: "I think both of them at this point have made the mayor's race kind of hard for the public to deal with."

O'Brien: "Castille had this parting shot: He told Channel 3 he's retracting his promise to support Rizzo if Rizzo wins the Republican primary."

Rizzo, chuckling: "I'm not gonna lose any sleep over that one, Tia, really."

O'Brien: "Voters should brace themselves. This is only April 16."

With a little help from his third-base coach, Rizzo had gotten just the kind of coverage he wanted. The aide had kept Rizzo from straying into dangerous waters or from getting too angry and excited. He had gently guided Rizzo into his most sardonic mode—making fun of Castille—and those were the sound-bites Tia O'Brien chose to pick out from the interview to use in her piece.

So it was that, with the help of an obliging media, Rizzo had accomplished the final stroke in his attack. He had not simply gotten Castille to call him names back, he had maneuvered Castille into a position where he looked as if he had nothing to say on the issues, as if he were even afraid to confront his opponents in the election. Rizzo had used the media as the weapon with which to drive Ron Castille into retreat. And now, from this point in the campaign until election day, he would no longer call Castille a drunk or a mental case. He would become a kinder, gentler Rizzo. He would begin to talk about the issues and wonder why Mr. Castille was avoiding forums in which those issues were discussed. He would claim he had never really attacked Mr. Castille, he had merely repeated what the

newspapers had said. And he would do all this through the careful orchestration of campaign aides who, like third-base coaches, carefully guided
his moves—even if the audience at home never got to see any of the hand
signals.

And no matter how hard Ron Castille tried to turn it around by talking
about the issues, he could make no dent in the irrevocable image that
Rizzo had created for him. Castille would talk to a TV reporter for forty
minutes about court reform, but then the reporter would ask him offhandedly what about the latest salvo from Rizzo. And whatever he answered
about Rizzo would get on the air, not the forty minutes of issues. Or he
would carefully orchestrate a press conference at an illegal dump site in
Juniata Park to talk about his trash plan, to find that only one station,
Channel 6, had shown up to cover it. Even with Castille offering forceful
words for reform and kicking around a few illegally dumped tires for good
measure, the piece ran as only a twenty-second voice-over with no sound-
bite from Castille.

The television stations had made a decision somewhere along the line in
the last six weeks of the primary campaign that Ron Castille would only
be allowed to speak to the voters of Philadelphia if he talked about Frank
Rizzo.

On Tuesday, April 23, with Ron Castille absent, Frank Rizzo and Sam
Katz sat side by side in the KYW studios, on the radio station's *Breakfast
with the Candidates*. For one hour, with only brief pauses for traffic and
weather checks, Katz and Rizzo discussed the options the city faced in
sanitation, the police and fire departments, and the public transportation
authority. They talked about how they would go about attracting federal
aid for education and how they would approach social services and problems like child abuse in a city that faced dire financial circumstances.

As they answered each question, clear differences emerged between the
two candidates. Some of the differences lay in specific policy alternatives:
Katz was in favor of privatization and competition to city unions; Rizzo
was against it. Rizzo advocated hiring 1,500 new police officers; Katz said
Philadelphia couldn't afford it. But other differences were more subtle,
although equally important in revealing how each man would approach
the mayor's job. Time and again in responding to the panelists' questions,
Rizzo looked to a nostalgic past and the tried-and-true approaches he had
used while mayor in the seventies, while Katz turned to the future to
propose courses for the nineties that were as yet unexplored.

One question focused on how the candidates would get suburban officials to force the collection of taxes from the paychecks of city residents

working in the suburbs, a sum that was estimated to be between $8 and $16 million a year. Katz responded first:

"The word *regionalism* is very important in this campaign. But I think that when most people in the suburbs hear the word *regionalism* from a Philadelphia politician, they understand that what we mean is you give us your money so we can give you our problems. I don't think there's any trust between the suburbs and the city. I think that the key to the city's long-term economic future, obviously, is the tax reform issue. But you can't start with the most difficult problem, you've got to start with some things that build trust.

"I think we can build trust around the issue of regionalizing the airport. I think we can build trust around the issues of waste management and transit and transportation. You know, a lot of people move to the suburbs to improve the quality of life, but how good is the quality of life when you spend forty-five minutes on Route 202 going to work in the morning? So I think that Philadelphia can begin to demonstrate that through leadership we understand the difficulties of suburban living and we're prepared to provide votes from the legislature for highway aid, we're prepared to work out long-term contracts for delivery of waste for their plants, we're prepared to work cooperatively on a system of regional airports, and then, when we prove that we can be good partners, hopefully we can get some help on the issue that is so critical to Philadelphia, which is tax reform."

When Rizzo was asked the same question, he responded:

"Jay, I've heard all this conversation before. Politicians are great at telling people what they're going to do. What we have to do is restore confidence in this city. And there is no way, absolutely no way except leadership ability to run a deal with politicians . . . to make them deliver. When you talk of regionalism with the suburbs, forget it. They want no part of it. I've been there, and I know because I've been there. When we talk about our problems in Philadelphia, why people are fleeing, the wage tax is one of the problems. But there's other reasons, too. Crime. People are not going to live in a city that's not safe. When you call 911, you wait three days for a police car or an officer to respond. When you talk about community policing—we'll hold hands and sing and that's gonna stop crime—"

The reporter interrupted to ask Rizzo about the uncollected wage taxes from suburban employers.

"Jay, the lost tax revenues, we're losing them, we're losing people, we're losing our tax base, they're running out of this town. And I believe the media when I read it. We've lost 100,000 people in the last ten years. I remember when the suburbs were open fields when I was a young man.

Now there's cities outside. Why did these people leave? I'll tell you why they left. They left because of the tax structure, the highest tax structure in the United States, Philadelphia. Then we look at crime. You believe me, nobody but nobody's gonna live in a city where it's not safe. The only reason they'll stay, if they're politically beholden to the administration or politicians for a job. They are running out of this town, and crime is the issue. The dirty, filthy streets, the lack of heart, the lack of compassion in city hall, that's part of it."

Where Katz talked about specific solutions that raised new ideas on how to approach the city's problems—like working with suburban officials on projects of concern to them in return for cooperation—Rizzo talked about the good old days when he was mayor and the city worked. He dismissed new ideas like regional cooperation, saying they would never work, but he did so based on his experience as mayor twenty years ago. He took most of the questions asked of him and turned them around to how the city was dirty and crime-ridden, and only he had the leadership qualities, the charisma, the compassion to turn them around.

And when it came to talking about the complex problem of the city's financial situation, Rizzo couldn't even talk in Katz's league. It had been a long time since Frank Rizzo ran a city. Back then, federal funds had been pouring into Philadelphia, and still Rizzo had been forced to ask for a massive tax increase barely a year into his second term. Unlike Sam Katz, who spelled out his approach clearly that morning, how Frank Rizzo would attack the number one issue facing Philadelphia in 1991 was still a mystery. When the reporters pressed him again and again about how he would pay for the new 1,500 police officers and the new 300 firefighters he was claiming he would hire, he simply said he would find "the monies." When they suggested that those "monies" might have to come from recreation centers or social services—the very expenditures that play a role in keeping kids from committing crimes to begin with—he denied their claim. Leadership, he claimed, could solve everything, dismissing with one small word the tough choices the city would have to face.

But when the debate came to be covered by other reporters, it was not Katz's and Rizzo's differences that attracted attention, nor the unrealistic promises that Rizzo made that he could hire more police officers without making other cuts or raising taxes. No, what attracted all the attention from reporters was Ron Castille's absence from the debate. Vernon Odom's report on Channel 6 that night used video of the empty chair where Ron Castille would have sat had he attended the debate and showed file tape of the *AM Philadelphia* show to explain why Castille did not want to be portrayed as "a whiskey-guzzling gun nut." He noted that "without Castille to kick around, Katz and Rizzo spent the hour lightly sparring on issues like taxes, crime, and minority set-aside programs." But the reporter used only a short sound-bite on the set-aside programs to highlight the "sparring." (As a prominent black reporter on Philadelphia television, Odom made it a point to touch on issues of concern to an African American audience whenever he could.) Odom ended the piece with the suggestion raised by Castille that the Katz and Rizzo campaigns were in secret collusion, including a sound-bite from Castille. "A vote for Katz is a vote for Rizzo," said Castille in an almost singsong voice.

In the *Inquirer* the next day, it was the same story. A large picture from the debate—focusing on Castille's empty chair—ran on the front page of the metro section; the story ran a few pages back. The headline read, "Rizzo, Katz Talk, as Castille Balks." The story by Bill Miller and Sal Paolantonio began, "Republican mayoral candidates Sam Katz and Frank L. Rizzo disagreed on just about every subject during a one-hour radio program yesterday, but they were in complete accord on one thing: Opponent Ronald D. Castille is a lightweight." The story was relatively long— twenty inches—but only one paragraph dealt with the issues. It read "For fifty-seven minutes, Katz and Rizzo answered thirty-two questions on some of the major problems confronting the city. Then, as the hour wound up, they took turns blasting Castille as someone who lacked the guts and ability to lead the city."

The story did point out that some 850,000 people could have been listening to the KYW radio debate that morning but that the overwhelming majority of those listeners were no doubt suburbanites driving to work, not the city residents who would be voting in the Republican primary. Unfortunately, the *Inquirer* and the TV stations were not doing much to tell those people what Frank Rizzo and Sam Katz had said that morning about the "major problems facing the city" or to help them sort out the differences between the two candidates. While there would be continuing talk about "collusion" between the Katz and Rizzo campaigns—that they were pulling their punches against each other in order to focus attacks on Castille—the real complicity could be said to exist among the reporters in their unspoken agreement to ignore substance. Sam Katz and Frank Rizzo did not mask their differences that morning on the radio. Their sharp distinctions on questions of substance were abundantly on display for anyone who was listening. The problem was that the reporters were not really listening.

18 One Floor Up

April 29, 1991

As election day drew nearer, the *Philadelphia Inquirer* prepared to make its endorsements. For the campaigns, newspaper endorsements were just about the best "free press" they could get. Endorsements not only swayed the newspaper's readers but, when carefully excerpted and photographed, could be turned into television ads capable of reaching a broader audience with the clout of the newspaper's legitimacy. As important as newspaper endorsements were to a candidate's fortunes, the process that a newspaper went through to make its choices was little understood by readers. To many, even the largest metropolitan newspapers such as the *Inquirer* seemed like monolithic institutions that spoke with one voice. In reality, they were nothing of the kind, and nowhere was this fact clearer than on the editorial page. Readers may have assumed that the people who wrote the editorials were the same ones who reported—or at least assigned and edited—the news stories, but it was a mistaken impression. The editorial board of a major metropolitan newspaper was quite separate from the news staff and often acted with minimal input from the reporters covering an issue.

At the *Inquirer* the editorial offices were located on the sixth floor of the white tower on North Broad Street, a floor above the city newsroom. The editorial board had for many years been headed by editorial page editor Edwin Guthman, a Kennedy liberal who had kept the paper's positions definitely left of center. When Guthman retired, he was replaced by David Boldt, editor of the Sunday magazine, who was known as a conservative and libertarian. Boldt's stint as editorial page editor had already stirred considerable controversy, particularly after the appearance of the editorial linking the contraceptive Norplant to reducing the number of black children living in poverty. The editorial had been written by Boldt's deputy, Donald Kimmelman, and both men had suffered the wrath of *Inquirer* staffers who were incensed by its implications.

The rest of the editorial staff was composed of editorial writers (generally former reporters who now did their own research for editorials), editorial page columnists, and commentary page editors. In total, the board numbered twelve. While editorial writers had specialty areas and found their own sources for stories, the board convened regularly as a group to decide which issues to focus on and which stands to take on major issues. It was their regular practice to invite public officials and community leaders to speak to the group about current issues, and political endorsements were carried out in much the same way. Candidates were invited into David Boldt's expansive office and asked questions about their positions. Since the board wanted to endorse mayoral candidates early, they had begun interviewing the candidates back in February.

The differences between the editorial board and the news staff did not stop with the way they gathered their information. It extended to the objectives behind what they wrote. Where reporters would swear they had no intent in swaying the electorate toward one candidate or another, editorial boards did intend to influence readers. For reporters covering a campaign, the premium was on stories that chronicled the horse race: who was ahead and by how much and for how long? Who had raised the most money? Who would get the key endorsements? But to editorial boards, such questions were almost beyond the point. Issues, positions, and qualifications reigned supreme. As a result, editorial endorsements in elections were often directly at odds with news reporting. That didn't mean that editorial board members were without their biases. It just meant that their biases tended to be different from those of the reporters. Where political reporters tilted away from candidates who didn't seem to them—and to their hard-core political sources—to have a chance and downplayed the chances of ho-hum front-runners, editorial writers had their own reasons for favoring one candidate over another.

And so it was that on April 28, three weeks before the election, the *Inquirer* endorsed Democrat Ed Rendell, a man portrayed in news stories as the unexciting, albeit front-running, retread, and Republican Sam Katz, a candidate who had been written off by the paper's reporters back in February. In the Rendell endorsement, they wrote, "In a strong Democratic mayoral field, he has the skill—and pizzazz—to make it all work," adding a quote from Rendell himself: " 'I'm going to get City Hall smelling, if not like roses, at least like Lysol." In their editorial on "the Katz phenomenon," they wrote, "Once a long shot in the GOP mayoral race, he's coming on strong and deserves to win," and "Eager and informed, he's shown a potent combination of damn-the-torpedoes grit and gut-level interest in the job."

On Monday, April 29, four members of the editorial board sat in their offices, each reflecting on their impressions and the thinking that led up to the endorsements that appeared the day before.

David Boldt, editorial editor:

"Since the beginning of last year, we knew that this was going to be perhaps the most important election in the city's history, and we were looking for a way that we could affect the agenda of the campaign and ultimately try to get somebody elected and get Philadelphia out of this mess. So we decided to endorse early and told Max King, the editor of the paper, about it, and we told Bob Hall [the publisher]. They both sat in on most of the endorsement interviews, which was kind of a different practice from the past, where it had been left pretty much to the editorial board.

"After the interviews, on the Republican side, there was no one for anybody but Katz. A couple of people had thought Castille might be good, that he could be very effective. He could deal with the Republicans in the suburbs. He does have national exposure. He was heading some committee for Bush; he does have entree in Washington; he'd be a Vietnam veteran with a missing leg. He'd be somebody that the Republicans in Harrisburg and the Republicans in Washington might want to help, like Richard Lugar, the mayor of Indianapolis who was said to be Richard Nixon's favorite mayor. That would have worked as a dynamic.

"But after he was in here, nobody would stick up for him. Castille was hapless. He doesn't want the job. We'd do him a favor if we let him off the hook. I said to him, 'People say not only do you only like being a prosecutor, you don't even like the administrative parts of being D.A.' And he went off on this one- to two-minute reverie—a fairly long answer—where he talked about how much he loved being a prosecutor. He just kind of proved it was all true.

"Did Rizzo's attacks on Castille influence the editorial board? Nope, none of that bothered me. The law firm deal, even though we thought it was a pretty low blow from Rizzo, that kind of sat with us. But I don't think anybody thought he was a drunk or a crazy man with a gun. So, no, I don't think the Rizzo charges against Castille made much difference. It was his performance in his interview here. He didn't know shit. You'd think in the three weeks since he'd become a candidate, someone would have given him a little primer on what to say.

"Nobody ever thought we could veer so far as to endorse Rizzo. In point of fact, at the end of his interview with us, Rizzo said, 'I know I have about as much chance of getting your endorsement as I do of becoming a nun.' And that was actually fairly realistic. There was just so much history with Rizzo. So many people on the board have something against him from the past. I'll never forgive him for blowing the Bicentennial. With Rick Nichols it was the episodes involving the police, the unbelievable excesses. He had a vintage performance in here, though. Partly because no one interrupted him, they just let him run. The old Rizzo we knew and loved, a phenomenon. Someone said to him, 'I take it you really do want to knock Castille out of this.' He said 'I'm gonna snip his balls off.'

"Katz was very strong in here. His only weakness from my point of view was that he didn't really have a vision for the future of the city.

"On the Democratic side, the performances were more mixed. Burrell was very impressive on the issues, he made himself look credible in the endorsement process. He was really good. It got to the point where people didn't have to be embarrassed to be for him. You know, he'd got this reputation as a do-nothing deputy mayor and a do-nothing city councilman, a hack or a drone or the willing dupe of Bill Gray. But he showed us in here he knows what was going on. So that probably helped him.

"Rendell, I remember, as he was leaving, he said this thing about cleaning city hall if he got to be mayor, how he was going to enlist the city's people to help him clean it up, and immediately there were two snide comments. I said something like, 'I bet there's a lot of kids we can get to come down there and bring their own paint, their own spray cans.' And Rendell said, 'That's just the kind of thinking we have to campaign against.' Rendell solidified his support when he came in. There was always a certain inevitability about Rendell.

"Hearn was good in here. Max King had never heard him before and thought he was impressive. And he is. I would sleep better with Peter Hearn as my mayor, but then . . . the next mayor's going to have to take care of business down there at city hall and somehow I couldn't see Hearn sitting down with [Councilman] John Street for a rapprochement. Hearn, if he could have really turned things around in here, might have done better. We wished Hearn had been better.

"Blackwell was awful, just awful. Rambling, sometimes incoherent, he came in with a claque of six people and he wouldn't or he couldn't answer things directly. People started to doze. He would have had us believe that the city's financial problems were basically a conspiracy of the bankers. He seems not to know that revenue collections have kind of gone south as compared to projections. He thinks that the bond rating agencies are just doing this to be mean to Philadelphia. It was sad. And afterwards people were embarrassed for him. He was worse than Castille.

"Someone had a comment about James White after he left. He said, 'I'm actually for Jim White, because he'd put the whole city to sleep for four years and that might be the best thing.' Everybody went around afterwards and said, 'God, what a snore.' So decent, so well meaning, incapable of giving a short answer to a short question. There was a little bit of a difference of opinion about his performance as managing director. Some people said good things, but somebody else said they'd heard one insider call him the worst managing director in the city's history, who couldn't get anything done and never realized what the revenue problems of the city were. He had fairly good answers, but people were nodding off.

"And then we came in that Tuesday morning, a week and a half before the endorsements, and we went around the room on what I call the 'first ballot,' though it was the only ballot, as it turned out. It was 8 to 4 for Rendell. Max King, if he had been given a vote, would have made it 9 to 4. Hearn did not get any votes. I might have made a pitch for him if he had had any kind of support. I guess I myself was for Rendell. Rendell was the only guy that got me pumped up. He was exciting. He does have a little bit of magic to him. I said, 'Since we were split 8 to 4, it's not a consensus. Do we still want to go ahead and do it early? Does anybody want to throw their body across the tracks?' It was my way of letting the people who were for Burrell ask for a delay, but they didn't.

"Burrell or Rendell were everybody's one-two choice except one person. It was Acel Moore [a black columnist] who injected the racial issue. He made a strong pitch that we shouldn't be against a black candidate just because of Wilson Goode. We went around the room and people spoke, some at length, about what they thought about Burrell's student loans. Don Kimmelman thought the loans were a big deal. Acel did not. Don says, 'Here's a guy, they give him full scholarships to bring him into the middle class, then his Ivy League alma mater has to sue him to get the money back when he's making more money than he's ever seen before in his life.'

"When he was in here, he said, 'Well, has anyone in here ever had trouble with student loans?' And I piped up, 'I certainly had trouble with student loans. I didn't pay them off till I was 35, but I found that if you sent them a check for anything, they'd shut up.' I think he is personally very irresponsible. We all recognized that these were flawed candidates in a flawed city in a flawed country. But several people made the point that we were lucky to have a good number of good choices. I think we had at least three people on the Democratic side and one real strong Republican.

"In the end, the decisions were made here. Bob Hall came down and listened to most of the interviews. That was different from the past. Neither [former editor] Gene Roberts or [former publisher] Sam McKeel ever came to endorsement meetings, they were not involved at all. Max saw the editorials, Bob probably did not. I told him what the probable outcome was, gave him a chance to stick in his two cents. We figured it was Max's job to tell Bob. Did Knight-Ridder tell us who to endorse? No, it was almost the opposite. Knight-Ridder, for better or worse, couldn't care less. Some people had apprehension that Bob Hall was playing a greater role. We'd be in much better shape if people thought the *Inquirer* as an institution, including its business operation, were behind what we said on the editorial page than we are now where we're using what Don refers to as the 'Wizard of Oz effect.' We try to speak with assurance and pretend that what we say is terribly important.

"The outcome was pretty much by vote. I'm not sure what we would have done had it come out 7 to 5, or within a vote. Editorial boards are consensus-seeking machines, which is one of the reasons why so many editorials are just so much crap. At the end we asked, 'Is everybody comfortable with this?' And they said, 'What do you mean, comfortable?' And I said, 'Are you ready to face your neighbors in the supermarket?' Well, they said, 'We all lived through Norplant. We can live through this.' "

Don Kimmelman, deputy editorial editor:

"My main contribution was to push for an earlier endorsement. We arrived at the magic number of three weeks and two days. Give the impressions time to sink in, and the candidates we endorsed could use it in their ads. They could get maximum use out of it.

"What we wanted was to have as much influence as we could manage on the outcome of the race because this was a particularly important race. The thing that was in my mind was a situation that happened in Maryland back in 1978 when I was working for the *Baltimore Sun* and there was a governor's race. Marvin Mandel had been convicted and gone to jail, and there was disarray in state politics, something like what is going on in city politics with the bankruptcy and the complete discrediting of Wilson Goode. It was very much of an open game, and there was the feeling that voters might do something completely unexpected if you led, or helped lead, them in the right way.

"In that race, the *Sun* also endorsed three weeks early and put the endorsement on the front page of the newspaper. The candidate they endorsed was running a weak third in the Democratic primary, with 7 percent in the polls, but the endorsement helped him to a surprise victory. It was because people were so undecided and so uncertain that, by giving this guy credibility, he just took off and became a phenomenon. I learned two lessons from that. One was how much power the newspaper has to do that. I was political reporter then, and the insiders were all saying, 'Well, now the newspaper's the boss in the state, we're not anymore.'

"At the same time, the guy that they endorsed and pushed to victory turned out to be a rather mediocre governor—for reasons that the political writers understood better than the editorial writers. He had a rather weak, disorganized campaign, and that was probably reflective of how his administration would be. So I learned that (a) we can have influence but (b) that we have to be careful about going with any outsider just because that person represents change.

"I went into the process with a very open mind. I realized that Katz was more our kind of guy and we have to be careful about that because we're not Republicans running in a Republican primary. Katz is glib and articulate and Johns Hopkins educated, probably moves in similar social circles, so you have to be careful to distance yourself from that. Ron Castille was more appealing to the typical Republican. And I thought that for a city like Philadelphia at this time to elect a Republican D.A., a decorated Vietnam war veteran, would so change the image of the city in the minds of outsiders.

"I thought he would immediately become the president's favorite mayor. Republicans would seize on this as an enormous friend in their favor. And the same thing would happen in the suburbs. He's the kind of guy who would have tremendous appeal—more so than Katz, since Katz seems kind of urban, Jewish, and liberal. Castille would have a kind of tough-on-crime, more conservative, prosecutorial type image. It'd be like one of them running the city. That would sort of get over that aversion that suburbanites have to giving us anything. We're an alien culture.

"But when Castille came in here, everyone was struck by how weak a mayoral candidate he was. We had known him as a D.A. candidate, of course, and he was never very impressive in an editorial board setting. But being D.A., prosecuting criminals, that was a job he'd done basically most of his adult life. He could talk crime with a certain confidence. And as D.A., he had a record to fall back on which was mixed but nothing terrible and some good things. And he certainly has been someone who's been able to appeal to voters, in terms of his personality and background.

"Our concern about Castille all along was, does this guy really want to be mayor? Or is he being talked into it by Billy Meehan, or by his wife, or by people whispering into his ear, 'Ron, you'll be famous.' But it's such a tough job you don't want to have someone in there who really never wanted it that much to begin with. And what was clear when he came to see us—this was already some weeks after he had gotten into the race—was that he had done almost nothing to prepare himself for what he would have to know to run for mayor.

"There was one scene where we were trying to get him talking about the city's finances and he pulled out his position paper and throws it down on the desk. And Dave said, 'Well, we know you have a position paper, but tell us what you know.' And he said, 'Well, it's right in here.' And he starts looking in it, and we say, 'Hey, no cheating. You have to be able to tell us off the top of your head.' And he couldn't do it. All he could do was talk about cutting fat, you know, just all the clichés. He could just express his desire to be mayor in sort of general terms, that he liked the city, that he believed in the city, felt he could help. Which is fine, but they could all say that. We wanted to see something more, and we just didn't see it.

"Rizzo had his innings as mayor, and we were not at all enamored of the job he did in the seventies, and we just didn't think he'd do any better in the nineties. And it would also send a terrible signal that Philadelphia is absolutely in a rut, they cannot come up with anything resembling new leadership. With Rizzo, he had such a history as a racially divisive candidate. His protestations to the contrary, he galvanized the black vote in a way that few black candidates can. We had a sense that we don't want that kind of mayor.

"His answers to our questions were all kind of Rizzo-an answers. He didn't talk details, he'd talk about leadership. 'You need a strong leader. When I was mayor, I was a strong leader. I could get things through Council, and I'll be able to do it now. Enough of this nonsense, we've got to make the city safer.' You know, those kind of things. In terms of the fiscal realities of the city, it's fine to say we need more cops, but how was he going to pull it off? And where was he going to cut? And where was he going to add? He just hadn't thought to that level.

"With Katz, we had a sense that here was a guy who without our help had made a lot of things happen in this campaign. He had been a good candidate. He had taken advantage of opportunity, creating a certain excitement, moving up in the polls on his own. I'd had lunch with him months before the campaign, which was part of his strategy. For him to have a successful campaign, he needed editorial endorsements, so he'd been kind of lobbying us for some time. I was impressed by his forums on the fiscal crisis, how he had seized the opportunity to put his name across, but in a very constructive way. He had brought good people in and got people to say what they had to say. So I knew he was a strong, assertive, knowledgeable, smart guy. What I didn't know was whether he'd be a good candidate or not. He seemed a little stiff to me, and I think that's probably still a bit of a problem for him.

"If his campaign has not been that visible in the newspapers, I think it's because political reporters can get in trouble because they're always around politicians and ward leaders and people like that so that they become purveyors of conventional wisdom. And so someone like Katz was essentially written off after the endorsement of Castille. We effectively wrote him off twice, you know, once with the Tia O'Brien article, the other we said that when Girard DiCarlo left, it was a lethal blow. And, oops, he's still alive, coming up in the polls. So I guess we in our editorials try to be a countervailing weight.

"It does seem that Sal has had a change of mind about Sam. Sal, there's a lot of emotion behind what he does. He went very cold on Sam, and now he's sort of warmed up to him. There was a story in the paper on the Sunday before last, it looked like an editorial it was so positive. It was a day in the life of Katz. Talked about how wonderful and personable he is, the exact opposite of Katz's biting off Tia O'Brien's head and being testy and negative and how he blew the Republican endorsement. But you know, Paolantonio, there was some bad blood there because Sam, in the *Philadelphia* magazine article, referred to Sal as a friend, and Sal felt compromised in some ways, so there was a little blow-up between them over that.

"It was a hard choice on the Democratic side. I spent the whole weekend before the endorsement following the candidates around, trying to make up my mind. But I was very uncertain. I spent some time with Hearn. I've been quite impressed with him as a human being. We wanted Hearn to have a chance. We wanted him to get the credibility and the attention of the business groups that were trying to give out money. But Hearn was not a particularly effective type of campaigner, and he wasn't particularly effective in his endorsement interview.

"Rendell, what I liked about him is that he's an effective politician, and he basically has good instincts, wants to do the right thing, and he's able to win political support without prostituting himself in the process. He's not part of any kind of machine. He's run as an outsider most of his political life, even if now some of the insiders are hopping on board because he's the front-runner. But it didn't seem like he had to sell a piece of himself to anybody to get their support.

"In the endorsement interview, he had a certain kind of infectious energy about him and people said afterwards, he's almost like a happy warrior. We need that. We need someone who can kind of pick up the spirit, someone who can sort of understand the symbolism of the job as well as

do the kind of burdensome chores that have to be performed. I think he'd
be good at that. He could create some excitement.

"Burrell was very articulate, well briefed on the issues, good at presenting himself. I think with Burrell the problem is, what's he ever done? I
remember Rendell was telling me that his advice to Burrell when he got
into council was, 'You're never gonna get anything done there; you're
clearly not part of the ruling group. So be the conscience of the council.
You should be out there blowing the whistle on everything they do wrong.
There's a way to play Burrell's role if you're elected to council, and you
want to be mayor, saying, "This is wrong," and standing up, being a
battler.' But he wasn't. He was basically invisible in council. And, you
know, George Burrell without Bill Gray is nowhere.

"We were divided on whether his defaulting on his loans was the kind of
thing that raised serious questions about character. I thought so, some
didn't. If you get to the point where they're garnishing your wages when
you're a lawyer in a major firm . . . in a high government official, it's
simply not acceptable. I don't know quite what all led up to it, but there is
something wrong there that I just felt uncomfortable with. For someone
who didn't have a lot of assets to weigh against it, in my mind, that was a
major liability.

"Blackwell, somebody said he's a good councilman, a West Philly guy,
fierce at defending his constituents' interests. But it's hard to imagine him
as mayor. And again it would send the wrong signal for Philadelphia . . . a
not particularly well educated labor leader elected mayor of a city in terrible financial trouble. And you know, during the budget stuff, he was finance committee chairman of the council, and he was virtually invisible.
Basically John Street was running the show. There was never really serious
consideration of either Blackwell or White."

Acel Moore, columnist:

"I argued that George Burrell expressed his views in a very clear, very
thoughtful way on a range of issues involving fiscal responsibility and
fiscal matters that would get the city out of its current malaise and also out
of its current what I call 'feelings of self-deprivation.' I thought that the
support of Congressman Gray was a plus, not a negative. I thought Burrell
was a progressive who could work well with various groups of the community. I thought Burrell was a better leader than Rendell. Rendell was
good, but I thought the case for Burrell was stronger.

"I thought the criticism of Burrell as a weak deputy mayor was a non-
issue. He wasn't the mayor. The deputy mayor is not ever very powerful.
You'd have had to do an analysis of what the other deputy mayors did to
say whether Burrell was any better or worse. City council was something

different now. The city council is unlike any other legislative body. Philadelphia City Council, compared to the legislative body in Harrisburg and
the U.S. Congress, does not play by a set of rules that the others do. It is
run by a troika with an iron hand in a dictatorial way. It doesn't abide by
any rules, so the fact that he was in the wrong political camp kept him
from accomplishing much. It was hard to prove yourself on this council. It
was difficult for anyone to exert any leadership in the city council.

"The loan default issue I think was a false issue. He was an African
American, first-generation middle class. I think that he's the first person in
his family to go to college. He was earning $48,000, but he was only three
paychecks away from being poor again. I don't really think that says much
about his character. I think that that's something that people who go to
work for a living feel every day. If your grandfather was not able to leave
you life insurance policies, because anybody in his grandfather's generation couldn't buy life insurance past $5,000— So black people lack the
financial legacy that white people have and are behind even though they
are maybe middle class. Probably he is the only one of his generation and
the only one of any generation of Burrells who have reached middle-class
status, so there was nothing to fall back on other than the salary he
earned.

"And if you run into any problems, whether there's a financial problem
that anybody else would run into or a divorce or anything, then what do
you do? I think that middle-class status on the part of black people is
partly an attitude. And black people support a wider range of people in
their family. But the loans were paid off, and it was ten years ago, and he
had problems paying them off. I believe him. I believe that he had problems paying them off. I don't think it was an issue that showed that he did
not have the character to be mayor.

"Lucien Blackwell's candidacy I don't think is as strong as Burrell's or
Rendell's or Hearn's for that matter. I think you get problems on what he
really knows about the issues. I think he clearly understands the government, the political process, better than any of the candidates. I think he
clearly understands how to operate on city council, but I think he didn't
have a clear vision of what the city should be and how he could lead the
city into the future. I think that you could not forget that he was an
integral part of city council, and that city council, because of the obstruc-
tionist view, is responsible for the demise of the city on the financial markets. A man who was a leader of that body has to take responsibility for
what it did.

"James White I think is a very honorable man. Of all the candidates, he
probably understands the nuts and bolts of the operation of the city best. I

think that, under the best of circumstances, Jim White would not be a charismatic, dynamic political campaigner. He has a very dry personality. Hearn was someone who felt he was right and who cares about the city, who has some good ideas. But the city, with the problems it has today, needs somebody with skills in dealing with the political process.

"With the Democrats, I was concerned that there's a phenomenon, an element, a feeling, an undercurrent that was something like this: the first African American mayor, W. Wilson Goode, failed miserably for a lot of reasons. Some of them [are] external, and some of them are the direct result of his lack of leadership and his inability to show character and strength at a time when it was needed. He was at the helm when all these problems came down on this city and other cities in the country. He has to take the blame for that.

"But I think there is an undercurrent in this city of 'Never again will we vote for another black.' It's interesting that all the talk of racial voting has focused on blacks. Race is a major factor in how people vote, but I think it's more of a factor with whites than blacks. No black candidate can get more than 22 percent of the white vote, even if he could urinate in a thimble or splash in a drum wearing the Red, White, and Blue. But white candidates have always gotten votes from black voters. Even Frank Rizzo got double-digit percentages of the black vote when he was running."

Rick Nichols, editorial writer:

"I covered the school board years ago when Bill Green was trying to wipe out the last vestiges of the Rizzo school board. He was doing a housecleaning, trying to get 'em out of there before their terms were up. That's when Sam Katz came in, after that brouhaha, a sort of reform candidate, with an aura of being a fresh new breeze. I didn't have that much connection with him except that I knew he was one of Green's people, a sort of technocrat, good government kind of guy. And I think he was probably a generally positive influence there.

"Once I'd come up here to write editorials, however, a couple of things happened that gave me a slightly sour taste about Sam Katz. One had to do with a contract his financial consulting firm had through the Green administration to do some consulting work on the convention center. He'd invested in land around the proposed center. Goode's people had said, 'Look, one or the other. You can be a real-estate speculator, or you can have a city contract.' Katz said, 'Heck, I'll go for the dough, and I'll give up my contract.'

"And then he came in here and raised holy hell about how the Goode administration was playing hardball with him, was cutting his cojones off. There was a big trash-to-steam contract, and he was going to lose that, too. And he was hopping mad and tried to present it as a bona fide issue about Goode. They're reneging on their deal, Wilson is a liar, etc. And you know, Wilson's got problems, but I just found it a bit of a self-interested crusade. So a little bit of his luster from his school board days started peeling off.

"But then he jumped ship and became Rizzo's finance chairman in the next campaign. He'll tell you that that has to do with Goode's performance. You know, Wilson had an awful lot of black marks against him by that time. He'd had MOVE. But if you want my personal feeling, I think an awful lot of it goes to his grudge against Goode about the contracts. If you're really public spirited, it seems to me, it's not so much that you have to stick with Wilson because, like I say, the guy was carrying a lot of baggage. But it wasn't Wilson against somebody else who was better than him, it was Wilson, in my view, against the only guy who was worse than him. But Sam went with Frank. He knows that he is a bozo. He knows in his heart—he had to know—that Frank was not a good, positive influence for Philadelphia. So from all of this I had a little bit of a taste in my mouth that Sam was not particularly looking out for the best interests of the city.

"However, I eventually came around to him in this sense. He was seriously trying to convene people to discuss what I consider a fundamental issue, the fiscal problems, and doing so in a way that I thought was not only showcasing his own expertise, but trying to draw on other people who had some kind of knowledge or experience about those kinds of things, and to me that's the kind of thing that a chief executive has to be able to do. That was one thing that started me taking a look at him afresh. And he's grown up a little bit. Some of these greenhorn, raw, kind of crass political false starts that I was looking at maybe half a dozen years ago . . . maybe the guy has mellowed a little bit, gotten off some of his personalized politicking.

"But to tell you the truth, I guess my main route in getting to Sam Katz is through Frank Rizzo and Ron Castille. I mean, I'm not going to go on about Rizzo. Rizzo's a charming rogue of a guy, tells funny stories. But to me he personifies what is wrong with Philadelphia. That willingness to be bluff and bluster and not be serious about government and be just that South Philly macho stand-up guy that leaves the place sort of crippled. Like I was asking about the latest polls on Ron Castille, how Castille was coming up, and he says, 'I'm gonna cut Castille's balls off.' That's exactly where he's coming from. That's exactly what he'd do.

"Frank, in my opinion, is not serious about putting together a governing operation for Philadelphia. Frank Rizzo is a personality, a celebrity, a guy who's in love with his own persona and just wants to run for mayor. I'm sure he'd like to be mayor, but he's not to me a serious candidate. That's leaving aside all of the problems about how he polarized the town and, in fact, ran fiscal problems into the ground last time he was here, giving away the union contracts and so forth.

"So that leaves me with two candidates, Castille and Katz. And to tell you the truth, I was keeping an open mind on Castille. I don't think he's been a great D.A. I don't think he has a lot upstairs. I think he's kind of a lightweight, but that I don't think precludes one from being mayor necessarily. If you have other skills that compensate, the ability to make coalitions, the ability to draw on expert advice, the ability to create excitement that somehow attracts talent, the ability to go to the community and to rally people behind programs. Those are all political skills, and you don't have to be a Harvard school of politics type guy to have 'em. So I was sort of neutral on the guy.

"He comes in here just like everybody else. He's been in here a half a dozen times for one thing or another. But every time I've asked him about higher office, he's always said that he's a career prosecutor, if anything, he'd want to be attorney general of Pennsylvania or something like that. I almost got the feeling that maybe he was already living out a little bit of a Peter Principle being D.A. He was Rendell's assistant, sought the Democratic nomination, is not really considered one of the stars of the department, didn't get the nomination of the Democratic side, jumped to the Republican side at the time when the Democrats put up a weak candidate. He'd always tell us he'd never seek that kind of office, repeatedly never showed any interest in broader public life beyond the judicial system and law enforcement. I think he has a relatively low energy level.

"Nevertheless, I didn't have any gut feeling of disgust for the man like I did with Rizzo. So it was sort of his game to lose. And he came in here and had zip to say about what he would do regarding the fiscal crisis. He would say things like, 'I'm on a learning curve,' with a little smile, a little smirk. I would ask him about education. 'Well you know,' he says, 'the mayor doesn't handle education.' I would ask him about anything that was outside the law enforcement world, and his understanding or interest level—and that's even more important to me, because he can learn—just wasn't there. It was as if Billy Meehan had called him in and said, 'Goddamn it, Ron, look at these polls. You're our best chance, you know. You're the only guy who can go citywide. You're a war hero, we just had a war, this is yours. This will be good for all of us. We'll make it easy for you. We'll raise the goddamn money, we'll buy the TV time, we'll get you a law job. It's a no-risk, win-win situation for you, Ron.'

"He was the absolutely logical choice for Billy Meehan for the Republicans, but it was up to him to prove that he was a logical choice for Philadelphia. And he failed to demonstrate that to me. I'm not looking for a high IQ or sophisticated answers. I want a guy that shows that he grasps that this is an important job, that we are in dire straits, that he has the capacity to bring in the kinds of people with talent and expertise and outside help and resources that we need to grapple with the problems. That he's got a little bit of pizzazz or pixie dust or whatever that Schaeffer had down in Baltimore, something to kind of get us to shake the apple tree a little bit to get the city shaken. I don't want a guy who's a power freak, but I want a guy who wants to be mayor.

"He doesn't want to be mayor, I don't think. I think he was dragooned into it, and I don't think he's gonna do the kind of hard-core political work we need. Wilson Goode didn't understand it, either. He didn't go down and work with the councilmen and cut deals with them. I don't mean illegal deals. I mean political deals. And when they disappointed him and went against him, he never put up guys to punish them. He basically created his own sense of powerlessness and impotence, and now we've got a guy who has no ability to make things move or happen. It's a very sad story to me. We sure don't need another one.

"The Democratic side? To me, Peter Hearn was a neophyte dilettante egghead guy who should be running the grassroots, common-cause appendage of somebody's campaign; he's not the candidate. He's a pleasant guy, he's a smart guy, and there's a million of 'em like him running around. Nothin' wrong with him. Just nothin' right with him, in my opinion. I just didn't see him as a political candidate. People say, 'Peter Hearn is right on civil rights and gave up a partnership in a law firm.' And I say, 'That's just great, so put a plaque in his little church or something.'

"Ed Rendell versus George Burrell, that to me is a lot more subjective. George Burrell I have found very, very thin, very, very superficial, very, very without any independent or personal agenda or plans or those intangible qualities of leadership and . . . and rallying. Ed Rendell, for all of his failures and flaws, has run the D.A.'s office, has expressed an interest in government plans, stands at least on paper for what I'd consider enlightened, appealing, realistic coalition-style government in Philadelphia. You started seeing Rendell pulling in some nice endorsements. He had an ability to make inroads in the black community which I found interesting. From Bobby O'Donnell in Harrisburg, just the kind of person that you have to be able to work with, to try to set a pro-Philadelphia pro-region agenda in Harrisburg. He also has energy. He has interest in the job. He also knows Philadelphia, knows politics. I think he would get down and dirty with the guys, roll up his sleeves, and find out where to make common ground with council people.

"Lucien Blackwell I think is hyperactive to the point of needing Ritilin. He is a motor-mouth. He takes wild swings at targets of convenience, be it the banks one week or big business or . . . or whites or what have you . . . that he might later make peace with. But I think that you can't go banging around as mayor of a big city alienating key constituencies or whole racial groups or what have you, and expect to have some kind of a harmonious city. He probably could deal fairly well with city council, but what would come out of that process scares me.

"When I assess them all, a lot of what I'm looking at is not where they stand on issues necessarily. It's character, energy, ability to draw people together, ability to attract brains and energy to government, as a calling worthy of getting involved in, the ability to have an image of credibility with external political powers and resources. Somebody told me that FDR, when he ran the first time, had a platform that was so nebulous and so vague, like a chicken in every pot. But he had this quality of attracting good people to his administration, of being able to set an agenda and rally people in support of it."

A few days later, four of the city's political reporters were asked to give their assessment of the campaign on a local public radio show.

Dave Davies of the *Daily News* said, "It's been very difficult for the voters to sort out eight candidates. It's a little bit harder to build the kind of head-to-head controversies that you're used to seeing in political campaigns."

Kevin Boyle of WWDB radio said, "I'm inclined to agree with Dave. It gets to the point where you need a program even if you're sitting at home just seeing who the candidates are. Everybody's talking the same lines."

Sal Paolantonio said, "Voters came into this election already very disenchanted and angry. They came into this race looking for something compelling or dynamic and they really haven't gotten it yet. On the Democratic side, particularly, the candidates don't really stand for anything different from one another, so it's hard to draw any kind of distinction among the candidates, so I think that's why the voters are confused."

And Dale Wilcox of KYW Newsradio said, "On the Democratic side, since so many of them agree with each other, the real question for voters is which one of the five is going to be able to pull the political muscle together to deliver on what seems like the common agenda with a few exceptions, and whether the apathy we saw going into this election has turned into atrophy."

The reporters were not inaccurate in their assessments. It was hard for the voters to make sense of these candidates, to differentiate one from another. And the electorate did seem to be disenchanted and apathetic, even though their city faced serious problems, and they had any number of choices for leadership before them. But what the reporters did not stop to reflect on that morning on public radio was how much the news coverage of the campaign was to blame for the apathy and confusion. If voters could not tell the candidates apart, wasn't that an indictment of the news coverage? If apathy was turning into atrophy, didn't that say something was terribly wrong with the way the media portrayed the questions that were before the electorate?

To members of the *Inquirer*'s editorial board, who had the chance to study the candidates' records and interview each one at length about his plans for the city, there were clear differences, particularly in terms of the candidates' records in past positions and the qualities of leadership they exhibited. To the editorial board, it would have seemed ludicrous to claim that there was little difference between a candidate who traced the city's financial problems to a bank conspiracy and one who thought privatization of some city services was necessary to cut the costs of running city government. But it was also true that for voters who were hearing nothing more than ten-second sound-bites that were mostly about the slugfest and reading little more than assessments of strategy, it would be difficult to draw out these obvious distinctions among the candidates.

The irony was that all four journalists, if asked to assess the leadership qualities and approaches of the mayoral candidates, probably could have answered with as much detail and insight as the members of the *Inquirer*'s editorial board. But that was the problem in a nutshell: those were not the questions their news organizations were asking that they address in their reporting. Unlike the editorial board members, the political reporters were not expected to focus their stories on who would make the best mayor. Rather, time and again, they were asked for the horse race. Even on public radio, they all understood what was being demanded of them: not a discussion of the issues that had so absorbed the newspaper's editorial board, but rather one more assessment of the question that was penultimate in the realm of political reporting: who was most likely to win the election.

19 The Trap Door

May 1, 1991

🎄 The dais was set up with a long table and name plates for yet another candidates' forum. They had been so numerous that the press had begun writing about the forums themselves—debating their value (assumed to be minimal, since they gave the candidates so little time to express complex positions on issues) and discussing the fact that all the candidates were saying the same things at them, particularly on the Democratic side. Either they'd all heard one another's ideas for so long they'd begun to cannibalize them, the reporters surmised, or else they didn't want to offend anyone else's constituencies.

Today's forum was on minority issues, cosponsored by the Philadelphia Urban League and a coalition of black media outlets. The forum was held in the brand-new headquarters of the African Methodist Episcopal Church at 38th and Market Streets in West Philadelphia, a few blocks from the University of Pennsylvania campus. It had been the site of many black clergy meetings about candidate endorsements and the place where only a few weeks before a dissenting group of black clergy had endorsed Lucien Blackwell. Inside the plaza on the third floor where the forum was to be held, a group of predominantly black middle-class professionals slowly gathered before noon.

Before the forum began, as the audience was eating lunch, Sal Paolantonio wandered from table to table, interviewing people about their preferences in the primary. He would use the comments for his "two weeks before the election" piece, which he would write for that Sunday's *Inquirer*. He was approaching people, politely introducing himself, and then asking them how they felt about the election. People generally seemed flattered by the attention. "I'm looking for somebody who really knows what he is doing, who can clean this city up," said one older black woman, a community leader from North Philadelphia. "We've got to do the little things, like stop people from dumping trash in our neighborhood." He wrote down his name and phone number, in case she wanted to tell him anything else. She was hardly a key political figure, but you never knew where information might come from, and part of his success as a reporter was his ability to cultivate sources throughout the political spectrum.

Vernon Odom, the veteran black reporter from Channel 6 news, also chatted with participants, but he did so while eating lunch at one of the tables, more like a member of the audience than a distanced reporter feeling out the mood of the electorate. The two other reporters present, Dale Wilcox, a white reporter from KYW Newsradio, and Tracy Matisak, a black reporter from Channel 29, sat in the back of the room in chairs reserved for the press, keeping their distance from the crowd. Wilcox was telling Matisak about the latest Peter Hearn radio ad, in which an announcer in a mythical Philadelphia future tells the audience that Hearn was just elected mayor and that sources on Wall Street announced the immediate improvement of the city's bond rating.

"How naive can you get?" asked Wilcox. "It's going to take six years to improve the image of this city on the bond market." He talked about the Democratic candidates' debate at KYW radio the day before. Although most of the reporters had described the candidates as being in complete agreement, Wilcox, one of the panelists, had found some significant differences. He was surprised that two of the candidates had strong reservations about whether the city should provide its annual funding for SEPTA, the region's ailing transit system. But it was a difference few reporters had picked up on. It was little wonder that voters were having difficulty drawing distinctions between the candidates, when reporters seemed to take so little note of where the contenders took divergent stands.

When the forum got under way, the cameramen for the two TV stations set up to shoot a line-up that was familiar. Lucien Blackwell's chair was empty. He would arrive late for this forum on his own home turf. George Burrell, looking comfortably at ease with the audience, sat back in his seat and stared into the distance as the introductions were made. Ron Castille was next to him, elbows on the table, chin resting in his hands. Then came Peter Hearn, staring forthrightly down at the audience from behind his aviator glasses. Sam Katz's chair was also empty, another late arrival, this not being a group he, as a Republican, was likely to get much help from in the primary. Ed Rendell was next, a study in fidgets and perpetual motion, changing positions constantly, leaning over to whisper comments to his neighbors. Last was James White, the third black candidate, looking like a military commander surveying the field. Only Frank Rizzo chose to turn down the invitation.

Robert Sorrell, the president of the Urban League, introduced the program. "While the League is not oblivious to the political realities of the campaign, we would remind you that we are here today to discuss the issues that are important to the black community." He talked about the social and economic problems facing the African American community: the poor housing, the lack of employment, the run-down neighborhoods. "With all this coverage of the political side of the campaign," he noted pointedly, "we have been concerned that there has been very little discussion about those and other issues."

Each candidate was asked to make an opening statement addressing the concerns of the black community. George Burrell led off by suggesting that perhaps too much focus in the campaign had been on how to solve the fiscal crisis and provide basic services, like trash collection.

"If we solve the fiscal crisis of this city without solving the human crisis," he said passionately, "without responding to the abused and neglected children, without responding to the drugs and crime that run rampant in our neighborhoods, creating equal access and equal opportunities for minorities and women to participate in the government as contractors as well as people holding individual jobs, by the end of this decade, by the end of the second term of the next mayor, we will not have a city that any of us will want to live in or have our children grow up and live in." He had a point. There was no question that the city had to come to terms with its near-bankruptcy, but there had been relatively little discussion in this campaign of a question that was almost as fundamental: how was Philadelphia or any other city going to make any headway in solving the problems associated with poverty? Although Burrell had raised the question, his time was up before he could offer any answers, particularly given the fiscal constraints of the city budget.

Ron Castille was next. He launched into his background, leading up to how he had been severely wounded and shipped to the Philadelphia hospital where he got to know the city. He told the group how as district attorney he had "done more with less," how he had raised the conviction rate while giving back "almost five million dollars to the taxpayers of this city." He talked about the need to not raise taxes, about how he would "introduce competition into union contracts," about selling city assets. Castille talked about using the relationships he had established in Washington and Harrisburg to bring new sources of state and federal funds to

Philadelphia. He ended by talking about how "inclusive" he had been as D.A., hiring and promoting women and minorities to high positions. His talk offered solid proposals about the city's financial problems and reflected a commitment to affirmative action, but he had more or less ignored Burrell's plea for more attention to the "human crisis." It wasn't clear what the ex-district attorney might be able to do to help poor minority kids stay in school and off drugs and get decent jobs if they finished.

Then it was Peter Hearn's turn. The silver-haired candidate who lived in Society Hill, one of the city's toniest neighborhoods, had been mistakenly introduced as "Peter Hearn, Republican candidate for mayor." He responded to the mistake. "I may look like a Republican, but I don't think like one and I don't act like one." Hearn talked about his active involvement in the civil rights movement in Mississippi in the 1960s and about how, in the Rizzo years, he brought civil rights cases against the police department for abuses. He talked about how he had raised funds for scholarships for African Americans, about his involvement in getting African Americans appointed as judges, and about how he had worked to create drug-abuse programs in minority communities. His speech sent a strong message to the group about his solid record on civil rights. Unfortunately, the problems facing blacks in the central cities in the 1990s were increasingly more the result of abandonment than discrimination. Americans—both black and white—who could afford to leave cities were doing just that, turning their backs on the problems of the people left behind. More than ever, cities were turning into warehouses for the poor, and nobody was even talking about how it could ever be turned around.

Ed Rendell spoke next. Rather than start with his credentials, he talked about what the candidates were hearing as they traveled around the city, how there was a "real similarity of concerns" across neighborhoods. He described the city as being "abandoned by the federal government and, to a lesser extent, abandoned by the state government." He talked about how the United States had spent an enormous amount of money liberating and rebuilding Kuwait and how an equal commitment was needed to rebuild American cities. He said cities like Philadelphia had to get out of the "trap of hopelessness" that the poor and minority communities fell into, by prioritizing two areas: education and employment. For education, he proposed choice of schools within regions and school-based management involving councils of parents, administrators, and community groups. He ran out of time before he could talk about strengthening economic opportunity for blacks, but he had managed to hit on some crucial points. There needed to be more discussion in a city like Philadelphia of the "trap of hopelessness" and of how schools and jobs might be used to fight it.

When it was James White's turn, he moved into a compassionate talk about how city government should not forget its neediest citizens in the attempt to solve the fiscal crisis. He talked about the importance of the city as a "provider of last resort" and as a "facilitator and coordinator" for the various programs to help poor populations. His priorities were to restore peace to the city's neighborhoods, he said. But he was for doing so with compassion for "those people who have historically been the victims of police abuse of power," promising that as mayor he would prohibit the use of excessive force. Where Rendell had chosen to focus on the concerns shared by both black and white citizens of the city, black candidate White had zeroed in on an issue that tended to divide the two communities. While blacks in Philadelphia were as alarmed as whites about the rising crime rate—and the fact that, as blacks, they were more likely to be the victims—they also remembered all too well the routine practices of the police department when Frank Rizzo was police commissioner and mayor.

Lucien Blackwell had entered the room late and was now given a chance to speak. He said he believed he had more experience in running government than any of the other candidates. He talked about keeping rates down as gas commissioner, how he had spoken out about deficit financing, how the city was being bilked by those people who were getting interest from the city for the loans. "If we keep borrowing money, we will never take care of those social problems that we have in the neighborhoods," he remarked. Blackwell complained that people had criticized city council for passing budgets that produced deficits when so many states and cities around the country were suffering from similar problems as a result of cutbacks in federal funding. City council's bad reputation was being perpetrated, he suggested, by the people who held the real power in the city. In a sense, Blackwell was the voice of the status quo this afternoon. If he were elected mayor, he implied, he would keep on taking care of business down at City Hall just as he had as a district councilman.

When the opening statements were completed, questions from the panelists began. How would the candidates change the image of Philadelphia nationwide, so that when the new convention center opened, people would be drawn to it? What would the candidates do to improve the abandoned and run-down housing in the city? What about health care for poor children and the problem of child abuse? The questions were serious, but the candidates were given so little time to respond that their answers seemed glib and shallow. Programs were thrown out for every problem raised, as if it were perfectly simple and straightforward to solve each deep social and economic problem, with no winners or losers in the process. The problem of housing the poor? Simple, two of the candidates answered, both supporting a plan to phase out high-rise public housing in favor of renovating scatter-site dwellings. What they failed to mention, however, was how very difficult it would be for any mayor to bring about change in the face of the many layers of entrenched interests at the city's public housing authority, where graft and corruption were almost routine.

When it was time for a question from Georgie Woods, the long-time host of a talk show on WHAT, the focus changed from the problems of the city back to the political sphere. Woods asked George Burrell and James White, "For the sake of black political empowerment, at this late date, if a solution could be worked out where you two could leave the race and save face and put your egos and agendas aside, for the sake of black political empowerment, if we could find a solution to that, would you be prepared to step aside to give one fellow the chance to get this thing over with?" The candidates seemed prepared for the question. Burrell argued that it was a sign of strength that there were three black candidates and that the African American community had the opportunity to "consolidate their votes" behind one candidate. White, on the other hand, said that he was open to discussion on the matter if it were in a context of "honesty, integrity and fairness," which he said he hadn't seen thus far. But, he added, "I remain open to do anything that will unite a divided community."

The questions then returned to issues, not politics. How would the candidates ease the tensions between African Americans and Asian Americans? Would the candidates support the city's black police commissioner, Willie Williams, in the face of the controversy that had arisen over his promotion of police inspectors outside the civil service system? How could the city get more funding from the state to aid abused children? What about the high rates of infant mortality in Philadelphia's poor neighborhoods, and what about the fight to stem sexually transmitted diseases?

As the candidates answered these questions, it was clear that they were trying to avoid mentioning the kind of pain that would be caused when the next mayor tried to address the deficit. In the short run there would have to be spending cuts or tax increases, but none of the candidates, for obvious reasons, wanted to focus the group's attention on those troubling alternatives. Instead, they talked about increasing efficiency of city government and stimulating economic growth. It was nice for audiences to hear that the city could put more police on the streets, build more low-income housing, and reduce infant mortality, all without raising taxes. But it was hardly realistic.

As the forum neared its end, Sal Paolantonio sat wondering what he was going to write, what angle he could take on the forum. He knew he wasn't going to just describe what people had said. He'd started out the primary campaign doing those kind of stories about forums, where each candidate got a paragraph or two to expound a position. But that had proved fairly boring. No, he wasn't going to do that kind of story today. The alternative was what so many campaign journalists had come up with as they traveled the campaign trail. With no time to dig deeper into any of the proposals—to offer readers a meaningful report on the concept of scatter-site public housing or choice in education—the reporters all too often returned to the realm in which they felt more comfortable making assessments: the horse race. It may not have been any more informative to voters than picking out fragments of stump speeches, but it was a hell of a lot more interesting.

And so, when the forum was over, Paolantonio leaped from his seat to head to the dais to interview Georgie Woods. "Do you think it's likely," he asked, "that one of the African American candidates will step aside?" When he had gotten the answer, he moved quickly to Lucien Blackwell. "Should one of the African American candidates step aside?" he asked. "I'm not asking any of them to get out," said Blackwell. "In fact, I'm asking them to stay in. I'm going to beat all of them. Watch Lucien Blackwell on election day."

Paolantonio moved briskly to George Burrell. "Was that a fair question for Woods to ask, about one of the African American candidates stepping aside?" Burrell downplayed the question and turned his answer to the white candidates. "Would Ed Rendell like to figure a way to get Peter Hearn out of the race? I'm sure he would. Is that going to happen? I suspect it's not. Would the African American candidates in this race like to try to figure a way to get other African American candidates out of this race? Sure they would. It strengthens their ability to win." Jim White had left immediately after the forum. But Paolantonio did interview Urban League president Robert Sorrell, who said there was genuine concern about the black vote being split by three candidates. "The African American community made some gains through affirmative action under Wilson Goode, and they don't want to lose that."

Although White and Hearn had left immediately for their next campaign engagements, the other candidates lingered on, stopping to talk to participants and shake hands. Although they appeared to be working the crowd, there was another purpose in lingering: to leave time for the reporters to reach them for interviews. In a campaign in which it was relatively difficult to get attention in the media, any opportunity to get your message across to reporters was valued. Sam Katz eventually approached Paolantonio as the reporter was interviewing one of the black candidates. "Hello, Sal," he said, extending his hand. The reporter appeared not to see him. Katz tried again, more forcefully. "Hello, Sal," he said a little louder, still keeping his hand outstretched. This time, Paolantonio saw him, shook the extended hand, but went back to his interview. A few minutes later, Ron Castille also approached Paolantonio. "Why wasn't Rizzo here?" he asked, hoping to get the question posed in the next day's *Inquirer*. But Paolantonio quickly turned away from him as he had from Katz. There was nothing Castille or Katz had to contribute to the theme he was exploring today about the horse race between the three black Democratic candidates. He had his spin on the Urban League forum, and nothing the candidates could say could change his mind.

When he had finished interviewing Sorrell, Paolantonio was beckoned over by Channel 6's Vernon Odom, who was holding a microphone, in between interviews himself. "How do you like that?" Odom said. "We've both got flowered ties on today."

"Mine's from Brooks Brothers," said Paolantonio, smoothing down his tie with its small blue, pink, and yellow flowers discreetly mingling. Odom's was a much bolder, splashier print of greens and oranges, with a handkerchief to match tucked into the pocket of his suit jacket. "Mine's from Today's Man. I can't afford Brooks Brothers."

"What are you talking about?" Paolantonio retorted. "You make twice the salary I do."

Then Odom got serious. "What do you see happening? Was Jim White sending a message?" Odom was obviously pursuing the same question as Paolantonio in his coverage of the Urban League forum: would one or more of the black candidates leave the race? It was a theme that he had used many times in his coverage. Just two days before, at a candidates' forum in the white Republican enclave of the Union League, Odom had talked about how Blackwell and Burrell were in a dead heat for second place and how efforts had been intensified by movers and shakers in the black community to get two of the three black candidates to step aside.

But while Odom didn't need Paolantonio to supply him with a theme, he did seem to want to consult with the newspaper reporter about how he was interpreting what had happened that day. Newspaper reporters were often interviewed by television reporters like this, probed on what they saw happening. TV reporters were usually so busy lining up on-camera interviews and collecting video that they didn't have the time to follow a subject as closely as a newspaper beat reporter did. And the newspaper reporters, who didn't view TV as serious competition, didn't really mind offering their assessments. In the process, however, newspaper reporters began to hold a monopoly over interpreting events for the local audience.

Paolantonio replied, "Sounded like he was looking for a trap door."

"You think he was looking for a trap door?"

"Maybe."

"Would it make any difference if he got out?" asked Odom.

"In a tight race, it might," answered Paolantonio.

While the reporters were talking, Ed Rendell kicked the back of a chair aimlessly as he waited for them to get to him. Finally Odom and Paolantonio made their way over for an interview. Paolantonio had been worried before the forum that Rendell was ignoring him, that he might be angry about his Sunday profile in which the reporter had suggested that enthusiasm for Rendell's campaign at the grass roots was minimal. "Are you mad at me about that article?" Paolantonio asked bluntly. "Mad? Nah, it was OK. The picture could have been better." (The *Inquirer* photographer had shot Rendell and his wife, Midge, in a particularly unflattering pose, squinting into the sun as they watched their son Jesse play softball.) Rendell, a veteran at dealing with the media, would never freeze out a reporter after what he considered a bad story. If anything, he would do the opposite, go out of his way to act normally at the next press conference, the next interview. Any public official who responded to a negative story by freezing out the reporter who wrote it, Rendell thought, was just about signing his death warrant. At the Urban League forum, he was surprised by Paolantonio's question. For a guy that's a little bit of a ballbuster, he would later observe, Sal was certainly sensitive.

He was not surprised, however, by Paolantonio's asking for his reaction to Woods's question. All through the primary he had been trying to talk about issues of substance, and all through the primary he had been covered largely for political intrigue. In particular, he was viewed in the media as the candidate who was benefiting the most from the multiple black candidates in the Democratic primary. Time and again, Rendell and his campaign manager, David Cohen, had tried to get Paolantonio and the other reporters to cover the substantive issues more or to see that some of their notions—like the racial polarization theme—were simplistic. Rendell had been claiming all through the campaign that he would get a double-digit percentage of votes in the black community, but still the coverage had emphasized that whites would vote white and blacks would vote black.

So, that day Rendell knew that he, unlike Castille and Katz, would be interviewed because he was a piece of the day's story theme. None of his answers to questions about minority issues in Philadelphia would make it into either Paolantonio's or Odom's stories about the forum. Only his opinion on running against three black candidates and his reaction to the notion of one of them dropping out was of interest to them.

At six o'clock, the Channel 6 newscast opened with the heart-wrenching story of the latest development in the story of Tyler Olson, the 16-month old boy whose arm had been ripped off by a part-wolf, part-dog. It followed with a report, based on "informed sources," that former mayor Bill Green was likely to be Governor Casey's pick to replace Senator John Heinz, killed in a plane crash a few weeks before. After a few more stories including a police shooting and two murders, at nine minutes into the newscast, Vernon Odom's piece on the mayor's race ran. His angle was revealed by his lead-in: "With five liberals vying for the nomination and polls showing Democratic voters clinging to candidates of their own race, the most intriguing question, who'll step aside to foster racial unity?" And then he used a sound-bite from Georgie Woods, asking his question at the forum, followed by a bite from Burrell in response. Then Odom jumped back in:

"James White, who is being pressed from many sides to pack it in, at times sends out signals that he is looking for a trap door," he said, borrowing Sal Paolantonio's line before using the sound-bite from White where he suggested he was open to further talks.

"Sources tell me that a clandestine meeting last night with key supporters of all three black candidates ended with them taking an oath not to discuss their unification efforts with reporters." He then turned to Ed Rendell, saying the candidate was prepared for any "May surprises, knowing he needs a high white turnout even if all three blacks stay in the race."

"Whatever happens, we'll be ready for them," Rendell said in his two-second sound-bite. All told, participants in the forum got four sound-bites, not one of them touching on any of the substantive minority concerns raised at the forum.

The next day in the *Inquirer,* Paolantonio presented his version of the theme, which made the front page of the metro section. The headline was "Pressure to Withdraw Builds in Mayoral Race." His lead ran:

"It is the big question remaining in the five-man Democratic mayoral primary, and it was asked live on radio yesterday during the campaign's only minority issues forum.

"George Woods, WHAT-AM radio personality, cut through the thinly veiled decorum and got right to the heart of the matter. Which of the three black Democrats running for mayor would step aside to preserve black political empowerment?

"It is a question that has entangled the black community for two years, and with twenty days remaining until the May 21 primary, it was a question that had taken on increased urgency."

Paolantonio's article, like Odom's story the night before, reported nothing that any of the candidates had said at the minority forum about improving public housing, about getting more money from the state to help abused children, about infant mortality or police brutality.

Neither the reporters nor their news organizations seemed to realize the depth of the disservice they were doing to their audience, black and white, by such reporting. They didn't seem to perceive that even if the candidates hadn't offered any earth-shattering solutions to the questions that day, it was still important for the questions to be posed—if only so that the public did not forget about them. The decision to edit out all substance from the coverage of the Urban League forum also sent a misleading message about the concerns of the minority community and of the black candidates. Judging from the coverage of the forum, the black candidates cared only about getting one of their competitors out of the race so that they could win. The only concern of black voters, it would seem from the reports, was that they succeed in getting an African American into the mayor's job once again, the only major black "problem" or "issue" in unifying a divided electorate.

While some would claim it was racism in the newsroom that led to such coverage, one had only to look back at the coverage accorded to Wilson Goode eight years before to see that it was not so much racism as the need for good story lines. Eight years before, it had made a good story that a black Ivy League-educated technocrat had pulled himself up by his bootstraps to distinguish himself as a devoted public servant to black and white communities alike. Eight years before, the story line had worked to the benefit of the black candidate. But in this election, the drama had evolved along different lines, and unfortunately for the black candidates, the roles left open for them were not very appealing.

But in a city that already operated across a considerable racial divide, the coverage would only widen the chasm. Ed Rendell's observation about a "real similarity of concerns" across Philadelphia's neighborhoods would not be picked up by the media that day or any other. Instead, one more story would reinforce the notion that it was every group for itself—that whites would vote white and blacks would vote black. And by so doing, the news coverage would only help make all the predictions come true.

20 Magic Tricks

May 6, 1991

❦ A torrential May rainstorm had forced Peter Hearn's press conference on finances to move indoors to his campaign office. Hearn's campaign had clearly lost its momentum weeks earlier, in both the polls and
the media. When the *Daily News* commissioned a Gallup poll of registered
Democrats for the last week in April, it had shown Ed Rendell pulling in
31 percent of the vote and Hearn trailing behind Burrell and Blackwell
with only 10 percent. And in a crowded primary, with the Republican
candidates serving up much sexier stories, Hearn was finding that his
campaign was not getting much coverage.

But Hearn's staff was not giving up. Today, they had come up with an
idea that may have seemed guaranteed to draw media attention. A magician was hired to perform tricks to symbolize what Hearn was calling the
other candidates' "sleight of hands" in producing fiscal recovery plans.
The magician would succeed in pulling out reporter Cynthia Burton and a
photographer from the *Daily News,* Dale Wilcox, the city hall reporter
from KYW Newsradio, and Laurie Hollman from the *Inquirer.* Hollman
was one of eight reporters from the paper who were now assigned to
follow the individual candidates in the last two weeks of the campaign.
The television stations would all pass on Hearn's press conference, however; their reporters were busy getting local medical experts to explain
President Bush's irregular heartbeat and following up on a car crash that
had seriously injured Phillies baseball players Lenny Dykstra and Darren
Daulton. Peter Hearn's press conference on fiscal plans, even with a magician in attendance, was not going to sell to television that day.

Wilcox was the first to arrive, looking tired from dragging himself to too many political events of late. "I hope it's a good magician," he said glumly, putting down the shoulder bag in which he carried the tape recorder he used to put together his radio pieces. When Hollman and the *Daily News* photographer arrived, aides ushered them all back to Hearn's office, where the candidate greeted them, making a particular fuss over "Laurie," who was to write the *Inquirer* preelection profile of him. At the candidate's side was the magician, a 60-year-old artist by day, dressed in a tuxedo and patent leather shoes, wearing aviator glasses. Hearn, a prominent attorney and veteran of many liberal causes, looked somewhat uncomfortable standing next to a magician in the corporate setting of a South Broad Street office suite.

There were a few awkward moments as the tall, lanky candidate perched on his desk and the reporters sat on the facing sofa, waiting for Burton to arrive so the press conference could begin. "Is that OK with you two, to wait a few minutes for Cindy?" Hearn asked Wilcox and Hollman uncertainly. They nodded, and the magician decided to fill the time doing a few tricks. He pulled out three red ropes of different sizes and, with a few sleights of hand, produced three ropes of the same size.

"Presto," said Laurie Hollman. "And now you're going to put it around our necks, right?"

Wilcox added, "Have you ever been employed by the Goode administration?"

Finally Burton arrived, and they got started. The difference between a press conference with the television stations in attendance and one where they were all absent was stark. When the TV crews were there, their massive cameras and blazing klieg lights gave a press conference an aura of importance and drama, even if there were only a handful of reporters in the room. But without them, the scene was pallid, like a children's birthday party where the most popular kids had decided not to show up and the ones who did show felt like maybe they had made a mistake. Here today, there was a particularly awkward sense in the room, since the magician had clearly been a ploy to attract television cameras, and none of them had deigned to attend.

Hearn began. "Why I've called you all here today is to say that all this talk about 'plans' to solve the city's fiscal crisis on the part of the other candidates is sleight of hand. You cannot do anything other in the way of a plan than to have a process where we will be required to have balanced budgets in the city of Philadelphia. Beyond that, the best you can do is identify targets, identify priorities, and use the best information available to assign values to them. But the idea that you can set up a plan with a spreadsheet . . . is the kind of sleight of hand that the voters in this city do not need."

He criticized George Burrell for balancing his budget by assuming an additional $150 million from Harrisburg, and he disparaged Ed Rendell for claiming he could save $250 million "without cutting back on services one iota." Hearn pointed to a poster reading "Office of Voodoo and Management," which he said was equivalent to Rendell's proposed Office of Management and Productivity.

"These candidates irresponsibly refer to their budgetary fairy tales as 'plans' and talk about them as if they have some real usefulness other than just being a list of goals and ideas. And for the most part, the press simply accepts the contention that these candidates have plans and fail to look any further."

This last comment was probably a reference to stories that had appeared in both the *Daily News* and the *Inquirer* comparing the candidates' fiscal plans. In the last few weeks before the primary, the newspapers were finally devoting more attention to where the candidates stood on the issues. But it was a little late in the game, after the candidates' images had been so well set by all the coverage of the horse race and personal attacks. And it seemed to be coming in such torrents that it was difficult for the reader to digest all at once. In this case, veteran reporter Bob Warner of the *Daily News*, who had often distinguished himself with his coverage of technical financial issues, had written a long analysis of the candidates' fiscal plans. He had noted, "Hearn has taken strong positions for contracting out trash collection and other city services, and reducing paid benefits for city employees. Both ideas have the potential to save money and they've been embraced by several mayoral contenders. He also proposes specific reforms in the budget-making process, to reduce the potential for phony revenue estimates. But he hasn't yet developed an overall plan to balance city spending against revenues." Presumably this press conference was a response to the conclusion. Hearn was trying to make the point that it was unrealistic for any candidate to come up with a plan to balance the budget when there were too many unknown factors to project accurate estimates.

Hearn said of Burrell's assumption of an additional $150 million from Harrisburg, "That's some plan. The only problem is that the mayor of Philadelphia doesn't decide how much state aid Philadelphia gets. Either Mr. Burrell thinks he's running for governor, or his budget plan for Philadelphia included hiring a hypnotist to go on up to Harrisburg to put the governor and legislature into some kind of a trance."

About Rendell, he talked about numbers being pulled from the sky for cost-savings estimates. He also criticized Rendell for claiming he would cut overtime. "To have a guy who was cited three times by the city controller for excessive overtime while he was D.A. tell us he's going to help balance the budget by cutting overtime is incredible."

"What we need is someone who simply has the guts to cut and keep cutting until the budget is balanced. . . . I don't have real numbers, and neither does anyone else. But the difference is I'm not going to tell you I do." He said he would leave police and fire untouched but that any other department was open to cuts.

He pushed his own ideas of having an independent board estimate revenues for the city. He claimed that in past years city council had always taken the mayor's revenue estimates and raised them; they would make unrealistic assumptions about revenue streams, which allowed them to add expenses to the budget, which resulted in the deficit. He also recommended changing the city charter to give the mayor an amendatory veto, so that he or she could prevent city council from reallocating funds and undermining the administration's budgetary priorities. What he didn't mention, however, was just how hard it was to change the city charter.

He concluded: "Walking around with magic plans seems to have impressed some editorial boards. But what we really need is a leader who can lead through changing and uncertain times . . . someone who is not part of the problem and hasn't let us down in the past."

Burton began asking questions. Would the city accept a strike under his administration? "Yes," Hearn answered. "People are willing to put up with a strike. They want these costs to be reduced, rather than suffer another increase in these critical taxes, the wage tax, the real estate tax." Wilcox asked what Hearn thought about the fact that the last three city controllers had stated that if Rendell's proposals had been adopted in 1987, the city would have saved millions. Hearn responded that this was 1991, not 1987. When asked by Hollman why reporters shouldn't be equally doubtful of Hearn's projected estimates for savings from privatization of trash, he answered that he had given estimates only for the savings from privatizing half of trash collection for which good estimates were available because of bids solicited in 1988. In response to Burton's question, "Do you have a concept of what services the city can do without?" he suggested, proprietary services, like running parking garages. "We can do better by selling assets."

When the questions petered out, the magician did one more trick—he "printed money" on the floor in front of the reporters—and then the press conference was over and the reporters slowly drifted out. Laurie Hollman made a face when asked what she'd thought of the press conference.

"That's what I mean about him. Here he is the 'outsider,' but whenever he steps in, he steps in it."

Wilcox was also skeptical. "There wasn't anything new there. Everybody makes projections for revenues and expenditures. Three controllers who I think are pretty credible claimed Rendell's projections for 1987 were correct. That's something a mayor has to do, and as far as I can see, Rendell's were accurate." He wasn't sure if he'd do a report on the press conference. It depended on what other things were happening. "Maybe something on the magician." He was about to head on to Burrell's press conference for an endorsement by black women in business. But when he heard the location of the conference had been changed from outside City Hall to inside Burrell's ninth floor office at 15th and Walnut, he decided to skip it. Hearing businesswomen endorse Burrell was not worth going that far out of his way.

Cynthia Burton was headed back to the *Daily News*, where she was researching a long piece on leadership in the Democratic candidates for Friday. She was going back over each candidate's career in public office to write about the relevant events that might have displayed their leadership. It was a long and laborious job, since Rendell's and Blackwell's careers had begun before the *Daily News* had computerized their back stories on a data base, and she needed to search actual clippings files. She'd already done Burrell. "He was easy," she said with a smile. "He's done so little." She expected to be working until 3 A.M. "Dave Davies says it's like we've been on a roller coaster all this time. For most of the campaign we've been going up, but now we're coming down. Fast."

She hadn't thought much of the Hearn press conference. She respected Hearn for talking about substantive issues, and she thought his point about Burrell's invented money from Harrisburg was valid. But the points about Rendell were weak, she thought. She did wind up writing about the press conference the next day, however. "Democratic mayoral candidate Peter Hearn paid a magician $150 yesterday to do magic tricks while he told reporters that his rivals' plans for the fiscal future are mere sleight of hand," she wrote in a short item for the "Campaign Notebook."

The magician had succeeded in getting Hearn five and a half inches on page 16 of the *Daily News*. But Hearn had failed once again to get the television cameras out, and he had failed to impress the newspaper reporters who had come. What Hearn did not realize was that he could never make headway in the media by debating the fine points of city policy. His early success in the news had come from casting himself in the ultrasimple role of the "outsider," and for awhile that had been enough. But the plot had largely passed him by. The story of the Democratic primary had moved from a tale of insiders and outsiders to a plot involving the leading white candidate and the three black candidates. To the very end of the primary Hearn would continue to mouth his lines about being different, about being outside the political game, but it was as if he were an actor who had stumbled into the wrong play. It was going to take more than quibbling over revenue estimates to change the script so that Peter Hearn could once again appear in a leading role—and more than magic tricks to resurrect the candidate's media image in the remaining week of the campaign.

21 Fold Up the Podium

 It was an unseasonably hot and humid afternoon for mid-May, and the pavement outside the District Health Center in South Philadelphia seemed to radiate heat and the sour metallic odor of the subway underneath. In a ritual known only in South Philly, the Italian section of town which had always been a Frank Rizzo stronghold, cars were haphazardly parked along the median strip on Broad Street. It was against the law, but here they were never ticketed or towed. Along the curb, parking meter poles sat lifelessly with their heads carved off.

Frank Rizzo had scheduled a press conference for this afternoon to talk about health issues in the city. It should have been a good day for Rizzo, since the *Daily News* had run the results of their second Gallup poll and he appeared to be narrowing Castille's lead. The Gallup poll had cost the *Daily News* big money, but it was a chance to make some important waves in the city. Sold on the newsstand every day, the *News* lived and died by the kind of daily splash it made, by its ability to entice commuters to lay down their fifty cents for that day's issue. And what could be more exciting than heralding the results of your own exclusive poll on the mayor's race, while also describing the issues that Philadelphians were found to really care about. (Sal Paolantonio had actually tried to get the results of the first Gallup poll so that he could break them before the *Daily News* could. What a coup that would be, he had thought, oblivious to the improbability that his editors would actually pirate poll results purchased by their sister paper.)

Today the giant headline was "UP AND DOWN." The poll showed that

Rendell's lead over his challengers was widening (he was now at 35 percent, while Burrell was down 6 percent and Blackwell was unchanged). Castille's lead was shown to be shrinking, down to 35 percent, while Rizzo had made some small gains to 26 percent and Sam Katz stood at 23 percent, with 16 percent undecided. Rizzo's strategy to deflate Castille seemed to be working, as was Blackwell's attempt to topple Burrell, although Castille still held a considerable lead. And though the *Daily News* didn't choose to showcase the fact, the numbers also showed that Sam Katz was becoming a credible opponent to both Castille and Rizzo. What the *Daily News* also didn't mention was a point Sal Paolantonio was well aware of: many of the candidates knew when the pollsters would be in the field, and had run television ad spots all weekend to bump their numbers up. Neil Oxman and some of his shrewder colleagues—those with money, at least—knew the importance of being on television when anybody was polling.

This afternoon's scheduled press conference with Frank Rizzo was not, however, crowded with reporters clamoring for Rizzo's reaction to the poll or, for that matter, eager to hear Frank Rizzo talk about public health. It was not the kind of issue that Rizzo was thought to care about, but there was no question that it was important to Philadelphia. In 1991, public health issues in the city had never been more demanding or complex. Whether it was the number of people with AIDS, or the growing prison population suffering from a resurgence of tuberculosis, or the need to immunize poor children and get young mothers to obtain prenatal care, health problems seemed to demand more and more money that the city didn't have. Here today, accompanied by Dr. Michael Phillips from the prestigious Hospital of the University of Pennsylvania, Rizzo was going to talk about federal programs that were going unused and matching dollars that were unexploited.

At three o'clock, when the session was set to begin, a portable podium was set up on the sidewalk outside the health center with a "Frank '91" sign on the front of it. Next to the podium were several charts. While there were any number of Rizzo press aides and advance people, the television cameras were noticeably absent. In fact, at 3 P.M. there was not a single reporter in attendance. Frank Rizzo was there, to be sure, arriving promptly, as was his habit. He pulled his huge body out of the back seat of his maroon Chevy, wearing a short-sleeve shirt and navy pants, rumpled from the heat of the day. As he got out, he carefully put on his suit jacket and then began to walk along the sidewalk, shaking hands with the curious passers-by who had heard he would be speaking there. He walked up to one older man, seated on a half-wall in front of the center, and very deliberately asked him how he'd been. "Do you remember me, Frank?" the man asked enthusiastically, reminding the ex-mayor of where they'd met before. "Of course, I remember you. That's why I come over. How you been?" The man produced a wallet photo of himself and the ex-mayor. Rizzo peered at the photo, as if he had all the time in the world. "You had more hair then," he said with a smile. The man beamed.

Rizzo slowly made his way along the sidewalk, shaking hands, stopping to chat, looking even the most casual bystander in the eye with a regard of warm recognition. He appeared not in the least uncomfortable with either the heat or the fact that no reporters had shown up. As he milled, the people on the sidewalk regarded him with awe. "Anybody don't vote for him's gotta be crazy," said one man in an undershirt. "He's a good man, all right, but his problem is his mouth," said a woman in a housedress, standing next to him. "He don't know when to stop shooting off from it." The man wasn't going to be stopped. "You need a big mouth in this city."

If Rizzo carried himself with grace, his staff was heard to be grumbling about the media. "In '87, they'd have been out for this. We got covered in '87," one press aide said to another aide. "You know what they'll cover tonight? The debate, the committee meeting, that's it." It was not an idle observation. A major shift in the media had occurred in just four years. TV stations, competing with cable and forced to pay more and more attention to their bottom line, were redefining what they considered news. Increasingly, stories about city politics and government were being downplayed, particularly if they focused on dry issues like health. "It's like Marty says. When you do these things, you take a risk," the aide replied.

Frank Rizzo had gotten a remarkable amount of coverage in this primary election campaign, there was no question about it. He had gotten more sound-bites on television than just about any other candidate, with the exception of Ron Castille, who was shown constantly defending himself against each new Rizzo allegation. But Rizzo was having just as hard a time as the other candidates in attracting the attention of television news when he talked about issues. Although Rizzo was more likely to get reporters out for his press conferences and position papers—because assignment editors would always gamble that Big Frank would say something colorful that could be used in a sound-bite—it was no longer automatic for him to draw reporters at the drop of a press release. In fact, Rizzo got a bigger turnout at a press conference if he didn't say it was going to be about health or crime or fiscal issues, because then there was a chance he'd be out on a personal attack.

Rizzo walked over to the doctor and talked to him apologetically, as he instructed his aides to fold up the charts and podium. "Get it out of here quickly," he said, with an edge to his voice. He took off his suit jacket and folded himself into the car again. He was seventy years old, but he followed the same kind of campaign schedule as did the other candidates who were in their forties and fifties. By this point in the campaign, they were all spending long days and nights, including weekends, making appearances before hundreds of small groups throughout the city, appearances that never got any news coverage at all.

The campaign aides who remained were instructed to fax the speech to all of the media. Unlike that day in early January when hundreds of adoring fans and all of the city's media had filled the roller-skating rink to watch Frank say he was back, today the press conference had been canceled, the podium quickly folded up because not a single reporter arrived in time for Frank Rizzo to talk about health care in the city of Philadelphia.

Five minutes later, Murry Dubin from the *Inquirer* arrived at the health center. He was the reporter who had been trailing Rizzo for the last week of the campaign, but he had gotten caught up in a meeting at the paper, and so was late to the press conference. He was given the written copy of the speech. He sat down to read it, then asked the press aide a few questions. He did not seem terribly impressed with her answers. "That's a drop in the bucket," he said when she told him how much money could be gotten from enrolling people in a particular federal program. "Well," she said, "that's just two of our examples."

Although none of the TV stations covered Rizzo's plan, it would be covered by the two newspapers the next day. The *Inquirer* would run a story on page 4-B about the Republican candidates' activities of the day, leading, as usual, with the political side of the campaign, a fundraising event for the GOP that had been held the night before. Rizzo's press conference on health would make the tenth paragraph. The section read:

"Rizzo, meanwhile, stood outside a district health center in South Philadelphia in the warm afternoon, and called for 'sweeping changes' in the city Health Department.

" 'Do you realize that the number of babies needlessly dying in neighborhoods like this one is higher than in some Third World countries? That prenatal care for pregnant mothers is almost nonexistent? That 50,000 children are going without necessary shots?' Rizzo said.

"He spoke of a reorganized Health Department with three major divisions: epidemiology and strategic planning, management and resource coordination, and preventive medicine and health services.

"Rizzo called for a study of health care needs, a more coordinated effort to get state and federal dollars, and improved community outreach and involvement. Dr. Michael Phillips, an immunology specialist at the Hospital of the University of Pennsylvania who designed the revamped Health Department plan, joined the candidate outside the health center, at Broad and Morris Streets."

Dubin, having arrived late, apparently hadn't realized that the press conference had never happened, that the tents had been folded when no reporters showed up. He wrote the story the next day as if the press conference had occurred and Rizzo had said all the things listed in his press release. When Daniel Boorstin coined the term *pseudo-event* to describe activities staged solely for the benefit of the press, little did he know that one day the events themselves did not even have to occur as long as there were adequate press releases to make it sound as if they had happened in some particularly appropriate locale.

Boorstin also could not have foreseen that, by 1991, pseudo-events were not going to be enough to attract the attention of the news media for more than a blink of the eye, if at all. As Peter Hearn had discovered the week before, gimmicks like magicians were hardly going to be enough to entice cameras to a press conference where you were going to talk about budget calculations. But the lack of coverage of Frank Rizzo's press conference signaled a more disturbing trend. Rizzo was no unschooled novice putting together an embarrassingly cheap photo opportunity. And the issues surrounding public health in Philadelphia were not some hairsplitting matter of how one candidate chose his revenue estimates. There were real questions involved in how the health department was run and hard decisions surrounding the politically charged issue of how much money should be spent to improve the health of poor residents. They were questions that received all too little coverage in between elections, and they had barely been addressed by any of the candidates—or the media—in this campaign. But it was going to take much more than a candidate's press release to address the solutions. It was going to take time and resources and the commitment to substance, not horse race or personal scandal—commodities in short supply in the 1991 primary campaign.

22 Nobody Landed a Blow

With only one week to go before the election, the League of Women Voters had scheduled for this warm spring evening the only Democratic debate in the primary campaign. While that morning's *Daily News* had shown Ed Rendell with a wide margin over his opponents, it had also shown that 28 percent of those polled were still undecided. If there were no big surprises in the last week of the campaign, it looked as though Rendell would be the winner. But because live debates sometimes produced just those kinds of surprises, reporters would be watching the evening's events closely.

The *Inquirer* assigned a team of five reporters to the televised debate. Doreen Carvajal, a city desk reporter who had been brought in to cover the late stages of the campaign, was set to write the lead story. She would be assisted by Amy Rosenberg and Laurie Hollman, city reporters who were following Democratic candidates down the stretch. Sal Paolantonio was writing the analysis piece. The fifth city reporter on the team, Terrence Samuel, was to do the "color piece," and was the only one of the five reporters to actually go to the debate at the KYW studios. Samuel would feed information to the reporters back in the newsroom as well as write his own piece on what it felt like to be in the room with the candidates and what they were doing when the camera wasn't on them.

At 6:50, Carvajal and Paolantonio prepared to watch the debate from a twelve-inch television set on Paolantonio's small metal desk in the *Inquirer*'s fifth-floor newsroom. The old-fashioned set seemed emblematic of the fact that newspaper reporters were only grudgingly beginning to admit that they needed to follow what was happening on television. On makeshift bookshelves set up on the pillar behind his desk were a few books: among them, *The Making of the President, Conversations with Kennedy*, and *Fame and Obscurity*. There was a picture of his three daughters, aged seven, six, and two, and a homemade card with a child's giant scrawl: "Dear Daddie, I love you, Zoe."

Paolantonio and Carvajal were seated at computer terminals on either side of the television set, ready to type in highlights. Both reporters had set up their microcassette recorders next to the TV. There were no videotape recorders in the newsroom. Shortly before seven, the two reporters were joined by metro editor Steve Seplow, city editor Bill Marimow, assistant city editor Will Sutton, and editorial writer Rick Nichols, who all pulled up chairs in front of the small TV.

Before the debate, the numbers in the Pennsylvania lottery were announced on Channel 6. Seplow fished a set of tickets out of his pocket and checked his numbers. "Remember a couple of years ago when the jackpot was three million dollars?" he said. "I missed by one number. I almost had a heart attack."

"I've never bought a lottery ticket in my whole life," said Paolantonio.

"Terrible odds," added Carvajal, as she began typing.

The debate opened with a shot of the four candidates standing at podiums with colored fronts. Behind them in the KYW studio hung colorful grids, a backdrop for the lighter fare that the studio was usually used for. Carvajal shook her head in amazement. "It looks like a game show. It really does." Charles Pizzi, the head of the chamber of commerce, which was cosponsoring the debate with the League of Women Voters, began to speak, but no sound came through the television. When his words began, they were out of sync with his lip movements, and the reporters started to laugh and talk about what an auspicious beginning it was.

Then the candidates were introduced. Lucien Blackwell was grim-faced when the camera panned to him, but then he put on a little smile and glanced to his left, as if to see if anyone was coming at him when he wasn't on his guard. While the Gallup poll that day had shown him trailing behind Rendell (Rendell was shown with 35 percent of the vote to Blackwell's 16 percent), there was a chance that Blackwell could further erode Burrell's base and pick up some of the undecided to win. But even if he couldn't beat Rendell, there was another prize: leadership of Philadelphia's black community.

Rendell looked nervous and shook his head in a little bow when his name was read, giving a small smile. He was the candidate who had to be particularly careful tonight. He had to present himself effectively to voters in what was one of the few chances they had to see him unfiltered by the media and uncontrolled by his own ad campaign. But he also had to be careful not to offend the voting bases of his opponents. It would be particularly important not to be viewed as criticizing the black candidates, since Rendell needed black votes to win.

Peter Hearn looked directly into the camera in a forthright demeanor when he was introduced. The Gallup poll showed Hearn going nowhere, locked at 10 percent of the vote, unchanged from the month before. It would be his mission tonight to discredit Rendell at every opportunity.

George Burrell didn't smile, either. He simply nodded his head in a confidant manner like someone who knew what was coming and was ready. He had been coming under fire over personal issues in the last month, and tonight he needed to get out from under the cloud that seemed to be following him. James White was absent. He had finally acknowledged the futility of his campaign and responded to pressure from black leaders by dropping out of the race four days earlier.

The panel of questioners, moderated that night by Malcolm Poindexter from Channel 3, was packed with electronic journalists, as the Republican debate had been. It included Vernon Odom from Channel 6, Terry Ruggles from Channel 10, Doug Schlatter from public station WHYY, and Stephen Collins from black radio station WDAS. Cynthia Burton from the *Daily News* was the only print reporter on the panel. The predominance of TV and radio reporters was a result of a deal that had been struck with the League. The TV stations would only agree to preempt programming to air the debates if each station was awarded a spot on the panel of every debate. As a result, the four or five newspaper reporters who had most closely followed the campaign would not be asking the bulk of the questions in the only televised forum. TV reporters, some of whom like Ruggles had never even covered the campaign, would get that opportunity.

Cindy Burton did, however, get to ask the first question. "Good evening, Mr. Burrell. As a gesture of openness, candidates for years have been releasing their federal income tax returns to the press. You released yours only a few days ago. But there are some questions. In 1989, you earned $132,000 and declared $66,000 in business deductions. Could you please explain why those business deductions appear to be so high and if you were not reimbursed for them by your employer."

"Whoa," said one of the *Inquirer* journalists watching on TV. "Go get 'em, Cindy."

The issue of Burrell's tax returns was only the latest in the negative stories concerning his personal finances. Paolantonio, Burton, and Davies had been on Burrell for months to release his tax returns, but he had delayed. On May 3, Paolantonio had written a story that made the front page of the *Inquirer*, analyzing the returns of all the candidates—except Burrell, who less than three weeks before the election had still refused to release them. Paolantonio wrote that the IRS had filed a tax lien against Burrell because he failed to pay back income taxes totaling $3,718. He added that, when questioned about the matter, Burrell had referred questions to his personal attorney, but that the attorney had never been made available. Paolantonio had wanted to make the revelations about Burrell's income taxes the lead of the story, but he had been blocked by his editors. Instead, the lead became how four of the eight candidates for mayor had each reported more than $250,000 in income last year. But Burrell's failure to pay his income taxes had still made it to the front page, before the jump.

The next week, Burrell released his tax returns from 1987 to 1989, and both papers reported that he had claimed unusually high deductions. One year he paid only thirty-two dollars in federal income taxes. Two years he reported his salary as lower than the $40,000 he received as a city councilman. Even more troubling to the reporters was the fact that Burrell had failed to answer any questions about the returns. Once again his campaign had said that they would make Burrell's attorney available to answer questions, but once again the attorney had not been accessible. The strategy had kept the story off television news, but Burton was not going to let Burrell off the hook tonight.

Burrell was prepared for the question. He launched into a carefully planned answer. "I haven't been reimbursed for any of my business expenses by my employer, either the law firm that I am employed by or by the city of Philadelphia. I am a practicing attorney. I do attempt to get clients. I do incur expenses to do that, which are not reimbursed. I've been doing that for a number of years. But the important issue is that all of my tax returns have been filed, all of my taxes have been paid. It is not an issue. They're not subject to discussion.

"The issues in this campaign—" he began, but then interrupted himself, as if remembering a part of his rehearsed response that he had temporarily forgotten. "And every candidate in this race has had problems in the past. Mr. Rendell has had problems with parking tickets in the past." Doreen Carvajal gave a small laugh here.

Burrell continued. "Mr. Blackwell has had problems with gas bills in the past. But that's not the issue in this campaign. The issue is talking about how we're going to solve the fiscal crisis, how we're going to get police officers into the street so we can address the issues of drugs and crime, and how we are going to have a mayor in there who can work in cooperation with the people of this city and convince them there's a partnership trying to solve these problems."

His strategy had obviously been plotted to raise personal financial issues about his opponents—stories that had once been in the news but had not been raised in a major way in this campaign—and then, once mentioned, to say that there should not really be discussion of either his accusations or those against him. It was a way of deflecting further attacks on his finances and slinging mud at his opponents, while appearing to take the high road by claiming that the city's problems should be the real issues in the campaign.

Poindexter mistakenly called on the next questioner without letting Burton have her follow-up, which would have been another tough question about Burrell's finances. Vernon Odom directed a question to Peter Hearn.

"Mr. Hearn, you've accepted $400,000 in campaign donations from one person, Elizabeth Woodward. That's legal, but since it's four hundred times what an individual can give a federal candidate, doesn't that raise some ethical questions, even as you've been preaching reform? A lot of the rest of your contributions have come from big law firms and from out of town. Isn't that business as usual?"

The question touched on an issue that had been a very sensitive matter for the *Inquirer* and the black community in Philadelphia in the last week. The Woodward donation had come up in an article in that Sunday's *Inquirer* profiling two large campaign contributors: Woodward, who had given to Hearn's campaign, and David W. Huggins, a New Jersey defense contractor who donated $135,000 to Burrell's campaign. The controversy began when Congressman Bill Gray attacked the article as racist in his sermon to his North Philadelphia church that Sunday. Barbara Grant of Channel 29 happened to be in the church that day researching a story about Gray, and she interviewed the congressman afterwards about his criticisms.

Gray charged that the *Inquirer* had implied that the black defense contractor was using his contribution to Burrell to indirectly gain influence with Gray and improve his chances of winning federal contracts. (The article had noted that the contractor's clients included NASA, the FAA, and the Department of Defense.) No such insinuations had been made about Woodward, Gray pointed out. He also wanted to know why the newspaper had used a picture of Huggins, who had wanted to retain his privacy, but had not printed one of Woodward. "That raises a very serious question in my mind about fairness, about prejudice—even really outright bigotry," Gray said in his interview with Grant.

Odom's question about Woodward's donation may have been more than a query for Hearn. It also signaled to blacks in the television audience that he agreed with Gray's attack on the *Inquirer* and that the white donator should get the same kind of scrutiny, the same consideration of influence seeking that Huggins had. As one of the most visible black journalists in town, Odom seemed concerned about his own constituency in the black community, and his question suggested that he was taking their interests seriously.

Hearn responded to Burrell's question. "No, it's not business as usual. I'm proud of my supporters. My supporters want nothing back, nothing in return. All they want to do is have a better city government. They want somebody to be an outstanding mayor, so that's what they're looking for . . . they are looking at me as somebody's who comes from the outside, who's not part of the political process that got us into this mess." To the very end, Hearn would continue selling himself as the outsider.

Lucien Blackwell fielded a question from Terry Ruggles. "Mr. Blackwell, it looks like you're the only candidate of the four that doesn't favor privatization. Why is that?"

"Well, I've learned through other cities that privatization does not work. In fact, two of the largest trash collectors in this country have been indicted for price fixing. I believe in modernization. I believe in the complete flexibility as far as the work force is concerned. And I believe if we do that we will save the money that is intended. In privatization you usually save money in the first year. After that, it goes to the company." Blackwell's comment about believing in the "complete flexibility" of the work force was interesting in view of his long history as president of the longshoremen's union.

Rendell was asked next which specific services he would cut. "I don't think it will come to that," he said, claiming that there were savings that could be brought about to balance the budget. "We can't raise taxes . . . we can't cut services. Services are at rock bottom level in this city right now. That doesn't mean there won't be layoffs. There may be layoffs, but they will be designed so as not to cut any specific city services."

When Cindy Burton asked Peter Hearn how he responded to her newspaper's poll finding that only 20 percent of the city's population favored privatization of trash collection, he defended the plan as the only way to bring about efficiency in services. Then he maintained that there would have to be layoffs involved in solving fiscal problems and that those layoffs would necessarily result in cuts in services. "I disagree with Mr. Rendell when he says we will not have a cut in services . . . as we go through the cuts that are necessary to balance the budget. That defies the law of gravity."

Stephen Collins asked Lucien Blackwell how he would "ensure protection for people and at the same time employ people with shrinking dollars," a key question facing the city.

Blackwell completely ignored the question. "First, I would like to inform Mr. Burrell that I do not have any problems with my gas bill. I received a $1,700 reimbursement because they had overcharged me. That was the problem. But I would say that in the last ten years we have lost $200 million from the federal government. We have raised taxes eighteen times in the last ten years, $260 million. The cost of all our social services has risen $400.4 million. We're talking about the shelterless, we're talking about AIDs, so as a result we've tried to fill the gap with local taxes, but we can no longer do that."

Collins repeated the question, since Blackwell had not answered it.

"We set the priorities. We still have a $200 million budget. But more than that, we need our fair share of revenues from the state . . . I for one would work with federal officials, state officials, along with involving people, labor, to identity creative ways to raise revenue in lieu of taxes." He also suggested an amendment to state legislation that would allow the city to charge user fees "that people don't mind paying."

Vernon Odom asked George Burrell about police brutality in the wake of the much-publicized Los Angeles case and the Philadelphia police commissioner's recent firing of officers for alleged brutality against a citizen. "What would you do as mayor to ensure that Philadelphia doesn't once again become one of the nation's recognized capitals of police brutality?"

Burrell responded by complimenting Philadelphia's black police commissioner, Willie Williams, on the job he was doing and by noting that crime and drugs were major problems in the city. "We've got to figure out how to get people out from behind their desks to fight crime," said Burrell, echoing a line from his campaign advertisement, without adding how he was going to do that or whether or not Williams was trying to do that now. Odom repeated the question, saying he had not heard anything about dealing with possible police abuses. Burrell responded that he would support a police commissioner who "responded aggressively to abuses." But then he used the question as a starting point for another answer.

"We need to find a way to solve the budget crisis that confronts this city so that we can actually increase the number of police officers that are in this city. We're not going to do it by the way some of my challengers have said in this election. We're not simply going to cut waste, cut spending, eliminate the deficit, by cutting the waste in this government. Reaganomics did not work for Ronald Reagan. They're not going to work for Mr.

Rendell or anyone else who is the next mayor of this city. We're absolutely going to have to confront the issues facing this city. We're going to have to work with our state legislation, work with city council to find the revenues, to make the cuts that are necessary to improve the delivery of services in this city."

When Terry Ruggles asked Peter Hearn if he favored selling city properties to raise revenues, Hearn talked about selling some of the city's parking garages, but once again returned to his message of the outsider. "One of the reasons that I would be the best person in looking at this problem, in selling city parking garages and the possibility of selling other assets, is that I come with a clean slate. I look at it from the point of view of what makes sense for the city of Philadelphia. In the case of the parking authority, with all the promises that are made along the campaign trail with politics as usual, many jobs are promised along the way in the parking authority, which is notorious as a patronage haven. So that some mayor who is addressing the question of whether to sell the parking garages has the problem of all these promises that were made. I haven't made those promises."

Doug Schlatter asked Lucien Blackwell about the criticism of his temper and his reportedly strained relations with city business leaders and how he would dispel that image.

"First, I think that it's been dispelled. I worked with business to build the Gallery. I worked with business to build the Liberty Place I and II, when the city and when Ed Bacon, chief architect of the Market Street East plan, said they did not want it, when the planning commission said they did not want it. I worked with Charlie Pizzi, president of the chamber of commerce, with Fred DiBona, Nicholas Benedictus, in regard to the business privilege tax. So we have worked extensively . . . I think it's a misnomer . . . Mr. Ron Rubin himself has said recently that Lucien Blackwell is probably one of the most qualified people at this point to lead the city because he has worked successfully with business. But I also have a history of working with the little old lady who has problems. And I think some people have a problem with that. And I do not apologize for that."

Stephen Collins asked Rendell how he would reconcile his election with the African American empowerment movement and how he would deal with the minority set-asides issue.

"Well, Steve, I think as Senator Hardy Williams [a black state senator from Philadelphia] said when he endorsed me, that minority empowerment really has occurred in Philadelphia . . . and as mayor I would work hard to see that there was no fall back from that. It's very important that we have a government that is made up of all the people and represents all the people. As D.A. I had a terrific record of doing that, and I intend to do it as mayor."

Moderator Malcolm Poindexter took over the program, posing questions to the candidates that other candidates could comment on. He began with Burrell and once again raised the finance question. "The loan defaults, the late revealing of the tax returns, the slip in the polls afterwards—is that good management to do what you did, or did we misconstrue?"

"Well, with respect to my school loans, the story wasn't really reported. I owed almost $26,000 that I had to pay to get myself through school. When I ran into a financial problem I paid back almost $20,000 of those loans. It wasn't like I was trying to avoid them. I had to make a choice between supporting my family or paying some obligations that I could not afford to do. I made the choice to support my family. But those loans are paid in full. There are no discounts. My taxes are paid in full. There are no discounts. And as I indicated earlier, Councilman Blackwell got a preference from the gas commission to cut $700 off his bill. Mr. Rendell has had those problems—and I point this out just as factual information—Mr. Rendell has had those problems with parking tickets in the past and was confronted by the city solicitor and responded to those. Anybody who has not had problems ought to be the first person to throw stones. . . . The issue that is important in this campaign is, what are you going to do to lead this city forward? What kind of record do you have? And I think I have a record on city council."

Poindexter then gave Blackwell and Rendell the opportunity to respond. Blackwell began: "I'm not going to dignify Mr. Burrell. It's obvious that he has nothing going for himself, he has no record in city council, he's never really done anything. As someone said, he passed half a vending bill, and that's true. The rest of the time he spent crying that we would not allow him to do anything. I have a record that I will stand on, and I believe that's what the people want to hear. He keeps going back to my gas bill, which is ridiculous. I was overcharged. I was given a reimbursement. It took me months of negotiating for that. Subsequent to that I became the chairman of the gas commission, and we have not had a rate increase in the last few years, and I think that speaks for itself. If I had owed the gas commission anything, if I had done anything wrong, after a thorough investigation I believe I'd have had to give it back. I still have my reimbursement. So I would not dignify that. I would rather stick to the issues."

Then Poindexter gave Rendell the chance to respond to the issue of the ninety-six parking tickets he had received while district attorney. Although Rendell felt that the media criticism he had received about the issue failed to take account of the money he had saved the city by not using a driver, he would mention none of that tonight. Here he would do his best to be nonconfrontational.

"Malcolm, I agree with Mr. Burrell as to one thing. I think that all of us who spend any long period of time in public service are going to make mistakes. We are, in fact, human beings, subject to the same frailties as everybody. But I would ask the voters of Philadelphia to judge me on my record of almost a decade and a half in public service. And I think I can say without fear of contradiction that as the D.A. of this city that I was the most effective executive that we have had over the past twenty-five years. Did I make mistakes? Sure I made some, but on balance I think my record is a terrific one, and I'm happy to stand on it."

Rendell had avoided attacking his black opponents, acknowledging his "human frailties" before saying he would stand by his record. He was out to avoid controversy tonight, and so far he was succeeding.

Poindexter asked the candidates how they would approach funding for the arts. Burrell took the opportunity to slam back at Blackwell. "Let me say that, in response to my friend Councilman Blackwell, I'm proud to have not been in the loop of leadership in the Philadelphia City Council that has led us to the brink of disaster over the last ten years, with the kind of fiscal policies that Councilman Blackwell has been in the leadership of. We are where we are today because of that kind of leadership, and I don't think the city is going to want it in the future."

Blackwell claimed he had made a promise to Councilman John Street and Mayor Goode that he would remain silent about what he thought was a conspiracy on the part of the banking community—that he thought there were people who wanted "to make this administration look bad, and the Council, as a result, they prolonged it to an extent that it appeared so. I was not going to sit by and negotiate with people who were not negotiating fairly."

Poindexter turned to Burrell for response. "Councilman Blackwell did not provide the kind of leadership that adopted a balanced and responsible budget that allowed us to address these issues. They adopted budgets that I voted against, that were clearly unbalanced on their face, that addressed priorities that we could in no way ever achieve, that accepted revenues that were never going to come to this city. . . . Councilman Blackwell, I believe, represents the politics of the past. I represent the politics of the future, of being able to reach out to the broadest coalition of people, bring them together, formulate solutions to problems."

In turning to the fiscal problems again, Hearn talked about the priority being to negotiate with the unions to reduce the benefits package, which he claimed could save $200 million. When Blackwell was asked whether the unions would accept a cut in their benefits package, he said, "Well, first, I'd like to go back to Mr. Burrell. It seems he's decided to take on Lucien Blackwell tonight, and I accept that. The one thing that I do, I take care of my finances, including my gas bill, including my taxes. I released my taxes for the last ten years. I believe Mr. Burrell did the same thing. I think he also ought to explain why in a year he made $40,000 a year, he said he made $36,000, why in a year he made $35,000, he ought to explain how he deducted $32,000. We can go on with this nonsense about what we did in city council. We had a people's council. That council was open to the public more than any other process . . . the tax increases that were sought were sought by the administration, not by city council."

When Rendell got his chance to comment, he said, "We do have to go after the benefits package. . . . Right now we could save almost $30 million if we required city employees to pay five dollars for each prescription. They now pay only one dollar. But I think the unions have a valid point. They have to give a little on this. But their point is that a lot of the city's fiscal problems come from management abuse, and these abuses have to be curbed . . . the inefficiencies are unbelievable. Mr Burrell has said that I'm talking about Reaganomics in talking about cutting waste. Does anybody out there really believe that we are getting our dollar's worth in tax benefits? The city wastes so much money it's unbelievable. . . . We can do so much more with the same amount of money. . . . I hope we'll be able to get concessions from unions, but I won't be afraid to take a strike."

After a few more questions, the candidates gave their closing statements and the debate wrapped up. Paolantonio turned off the TV, and the reporters and editors sat thinking for a minute. Another reporter passing by the group anticipated the first question they would discuss, and said sardonically, "The people are the winners." Everyone laughed, and then the serious discussion began. Will Sutton started it off. "This debate was better than the Republicans. There was more lashing out. For the analysis let's focus on where they lashed out. It should go in the sidebar, too."

Doreen Carvajal asked, "What was the gas stuff about?"

Sutton explained there was a controversy a few years back about whether Blackwell had received special treatment in paying his gas bills. "It was more of a *Daily News* thing than us," he told her.

And then Sutton offered his analysis. "Each candidate tried to get their points across about their campaigns, except Burrell. He was the only one who brought up the others' campaigns."

Carvajal said, "But Blackwell would do the same thing."

"Only in response. Burrell had a very different strategy from the other candidates."

"Rendell was Mr. Congeniality again."

"I was surprised at Hearn. He was more doing the image thing again. He took some potshots against Rendell, but not many."

Laurie Hollman walked up to the group at that point. She had been watching a TV across the newsroom. "Any winner, Laurie?" Sal asked her. "Yeah, Rendell. Hearn didn't take any shots at Rendell."

Bill Marimow entered with his interpretation. "Rendell acted mayoral. He stayed above the fray." Those were the kinds of phrases that were increasingly being used in political reporting—phrases that said nothing about substance but everything about strategy.

Paolantonio offered his own shorthand phrase: "Nobody landed a blow. When Cindy Burton asked that first question, it was like Burrell took a shot against the ropes and he tried to counter with the shots against Blackwell and Rendell."

Marimow said, "Burrell didn't have a good answer [for the questions about his finances] like Rendell."

Carvajal said, "He had a good answer, I think, about his family."

Paolantonio quipped, "Except it wasn't true."

"Burrell seemed to isolate it, as if to say, it's me and Blackwell. Like he knows that's where he has to draw his votes, from Blackwell's base, to win."

Seplow interjected, "I thought Burrell did a good job on the question about the arts. He gave a broad answer, almost as if he had been prepared for the question. I thought he looked good."

Paolantonio added, "If he hadn't been on the defensive all evening."

Amy Rosenberg walked up, and Paolantonio asked, "Amy, did you see any clear winner?"

She answered indirectly. "Burrell handled the questions on his loans well, I thought."

"Hearn was, like, whining off-camera the whole night. He just said his same old stuff," said Hollman, who had been covering Hearn in the stretch.

Carvajal responded, "Yeah, but you've got to remember, how does that appeal to the regular voter who hasn't heard him every day."

"That's true," said Paolantonio. "For the first-time viewer, that might really work. You can't call him a loser. He hit his base."

Sutton entered the discussion again. "Blackwell did well. He wasn't as angry as he could be."

"I think when he said he wasn't going to apologize for being for the little old lady, he sounded good," said Seplow. "I think he did that well."

"He made his point," Sutton agreed. " 'I'm for the little people.' "

"As far as my analysis, 'No blow landed on Rendell, stayed above the fray,' right?" Paolantonio asked the group.

Marimow answered with a question. "Does anyone think any of the four hurt themselves?"

No, as one person put it, the consensus was "No gaffes here, but no particular knock-outs, either."

Carvajal seemed bothered by the fight analogy. "Do we have to declare a winner?"

"You don't have to," said Paolantonio. "But in terms of my analysis, it's going to be that the front-runner didn't get cut."

At that moment, deputy editorial board editor Don Kimmelman walked by. "Hi, everyone, I'm the spin doctor. Well? Our guy looked good, right?" he said, smiling, referring to Rendell, whom the *Inquirer* had endorsed editorially. "Didn't drool or embarrass himself." Some in the group smiled, but mostly they ignored him. Clearly, none of the reporters or news editors present had been thinking of Rendell as "our guy" as they watched the debate.

Carvajal muttered, "The big loser was the game show set. 'And now the question for Mr. Hearn . . . ' " and she made the sound of a buzzer. "So the story should be the civility among the Democrats was shattered this evening . . . "

"They were lashing out at each other . . . " someone continued.

"But in a way that didn't draw blood," offered another reporter.

"Are we agreed on that? What do you think, Bill?" Carvajal addressed her question to Marimow.

He nodded. "No surprises. They all agreed the city has to tighten its belt."

"There were a lot of issues where Lucien Blackwell was out by himself on. He was the only one against privatization," said Seplow.

"If I were a voter, I'd trust Blackwell more on taxes," added Hollman. "He said very clearly that he would not raise taxes."

"Yeah, but where's he going to get his money? By going to Harrisburg? Sure."

Rosenberg said she was disappointed by Rendell's final statement. She thought it seemed a bit tired and didn't have much punch. But Paolantonio disagreed. "I liked all their final statements." The discussion petered out, as someone claimed that Rendell looked a bit like Richard Nixon at the beginning of the debate. "There was a tiny bead of sweat on his forehead . . . " But no one picked up on that as they regrouped to begin writing.

Sutton directed some of the reporters to use the *Inquirer*'s data base to

research the details on Burrell's charges against Blackwell for his gas bills
and Rendell for his parking tickets. He asked Hollman to compare Hearn
on the stump with Hearn tonight. Carvajal asked Rosenberg to transcribe
parts of the debate to get quotes she might need. "I'll try to get the biting
stuff," said Rosenberg. "Wherever there was an exchange," Carvajal responded.

Both Carvajal and Paolantonio started to type at their computer terminals at about 8:30, an hour or so before deadline. A few minutes later,
Carvajal's phone rang. It was Terrence Samuel calling from the debate.
"What's the deal, Castille?" she asked. "Did any of them talk about that
gas stuff anymore? That's the first time he talked about the gas stuff. . . .
Was there anything anyone said afterwards? How did Burrell and Blackwell deal with each other afterwards? . . . He did agree to pose for a
picture, right? . . . Was anybody sweating? . . . I noticed he did a lot of
chopping in the air with one hand. Rendell did a lot with two hands. I
noticed him shifting a lot on the balls of his feet."

When she got off the phone, Paolantonio asked if there was anything
good from the debate. She read him a quote from Blackwell. " 'I don't
know why he'd want to get personal because his personal problems super-
sede mine.' "

Paolantonio smiled. "Could I use that?"

Carvajal seemed a little put out. "I was going to use that."

Paolantonio persisted. "It'd be great in my story."

"OK, you can use it."

"Thank you, I just need that one quote."

"OK, fine."

A minute later, Paolantonio looked over with a smile. "Do you have any
others I can use?" Carvajal glared back at him, and they both went back to
work.

On his terminal, Paolantonio was filling in the one-line notes he'd written during the debate: Burrell smooth, sticks to the company line. Rendell
hasn't addressed others. Summarize that Rendell stayed above the fray.
Burrell on the attack. Burrell and Blackwell spar over council leadership.
Blackwell says Burrell did nothing. Key point came halfway through the
debate. But Rendell was unharmed. In fact, he was Mr. Congeniality.

As Paolantonio typed, his phone rang intermittently. To some of the
callers he said he would call back later, he was writing on deadline, but
other calls he took. One of the first was from Randall Miller, a political
science professor at a local university whom he'd arranged to call at 8:30.
As Miller talked, Paolantonio sat with the phone cradled in his ear as he
typed his comments into the terminal. Miller: format more conducive to

exchange this time, quite predictable in the beginning, coached candidates. Once Poindexter got a hold of things, it got interesting. What did each candidate achieve based on objectives—all the candidates did what they wanted to do. Rendell did well because his support is soft, and this showed what a good communicator he was.

Miller thought Burrell had done well, a statement which prompted Paolantonio to ask, "But did you think he rebounded?"

He began to type the answer into his terminal. "I'm not saying he rebounded, but he avoided getting hit squarely with it."

A few minutes later Paolantonio's phone rang again. It was David Cohen, Rendell's campaign manager. (Eventually, every campaign manager except Burrell's would call him to see what spin the *Inquirer* was going to put on the debate—an early review—and to try to get their own assessments in.) Paolantonio recited mechanically to him, "Rendell looked mayoral . . . nobody landed any clean blows . . . it didn't change the shape of the campaign."

At 9:30 he called out, "Anybody remember how much in gas rate increases Blackwell claims he didn't pass? I need the number."

A few minutes later, another reporter walked by and announced to all: "The record shows that Burrell supported two of the budgets he said he voted against."

At 9:50 Paolantonio finished his story, saved the file on the central computer, and sent it electronically to Marimow a few desks away for editing. After Marimow had had time to read it, the two men sat together discussing the phrases Marimow had highlighted for change. The changes they made were minor, phrases altered to be more precise, details added for explanatory purposes. Marimow and Paolantonio were much in sync working together. They discussed how Sal's story would run on 9-A, unlike the Republican debate analysis, which appeared on the front page. "Other things are happening today," the reporter acknowledged. "Jimmy Tayoun was indicted." By 10:30 he was done and ready to head for his home in the New Jersey suburbs.

The next day, there were three stories in the paper about the debate: the straight news piece by Doreen Carvajal, with assistance by Laurie Hollman and Amy Rosenberg, the analysis story by Sal Paolantonio, and the "color piece" by Terence Samuel. A day later, the *Inquirer* would run a fourth story about the debate, a follow-up piece analyzing some of the statements offered by the candidates. Together the four stories, involving the work of six highly skilled journalists, offered newspaper readers some four thousand words on the debate. But for all the effort that went into them, the stories in some ways illustrated what was wrong with campaign journalism in America. Taken together, the coverage cast the candidates in the most negative light possible, portraying them as sparring, mudslinging strategists who lied, distorted, and overpromised. The newspaper highlighted the most negative statements offered by and about the candidates and eliminated all that was well reasoned and thoughtful in what the men had said.

The first story ran on the front page with the headline "Debate Rhetoric Is Razor Sharp" and a smaller headline above the photo that read, "Democrats Attack Issues and Each Other." The lead stated:

"The four Democrats running for mayor, kinder and gentler in past joint appearances, met yesterday for their only televised campaign debate, one marked by cold, hard-edged disagreements over personal foibles and ways to erase the city's huge deficit.

"Much of the hourlong debate was devoted to Philadelphia's financial problems and cost-cutting notions about layoffs and selling off city assets. But at least three candidates sharpened their rhetoric, attacking their rivals for a grab bag of weaknesses: an abysmal Council record, a disputed gas bill, overblown campaign promises."

With sparring as the theme, the story focused primarily on Burrell's response to questions about his tax returns and his attacks on Blackwell and Rendell. The "cost-cutting notions" and "hard-edged disagreements over . . . ways to erase the city's huge deficit" were shunted to deep inside the story, where they received six short sentences. As was so often the case in the political journalism of the 1990s, the "personal foibles" of the candidates received far more attention and prominence than anything the contenders were saying about the city.

Sal Paolantonio's analysis, "Rendell Emerges as Mr. Congeniality," focused on the strategies of the candidates. "Democrat Edward G. Rendell, who has strengthened his lead in recent polls, needed to escape last night's television debate unharmed—and he did just that," the story began. Its language steeped in sports analogies, the story portrayed the candidates more as prizefighters than potential leaders with a vision for the city's future. One source characterized George Burrell as "on the defensive. . . . [H]e took a couple of jabs, but he turned out to be a fairly good counterpuncher."

Terence Samuel's color piece offered a different angle on the debate, focusing not on how it affected political fortunes but how the candidates appeared up close that night. He described Ed Rendell's nervousness as he stood at the podium: "He just couldn't decide what to do with his legs. He kept shifting his weight from right to left, hoping to find one more comfortable." He depicted Lucien Blackwell as "the only candidate daring enough to go on television without some red in his tie" and noted that the candidate "showed his nerves by bouncing so hard on the balls of his feet that at times it seemed he was running in place." It was another slant on the debate, but hardly more inspiring. Body language might have seemed an amusing focus for a story, but it was hard to say what it told the undecided voter about the candidates.

The final word on the debate came a day later, in a follow-up story by Dan Meyers and Terence Samuel. This story focused on the substance of the debate rather than the sparring, strategy, or color, but it too displayed the disturbing negativism of the new political journalism. Under the headline "From Democrats, Politics as Usual," the story began: "Ah, politics. An exaggeration here, a notion there, perhaps an outright misrepresentation and a fast flip-flop, and pretty soon you're talking about a good old election campaign."

The reporters focused on four statements made by the candidates at the debate and criticized them, based on follow-up research. "Edward G. Rendell wants to exhume Class 500 grants, a scandal-stained program that over the last four years was starved and finally killed because the city could no longer afford it," they wrote, before questioning Rendell's explanation for why the program had been halted and dismissing his contention that the city's deficit might be wiped out in twenty-four months so that funds might be freed up again. Next, the reporters knocked Peter Hearn, "who for months has talked tough about turning trash collection over to private haulers" because he "suddenly prefers negotiations with the city's blue-collar union." Then they noted that George Burrell had actually voted for two of three Council budgets he claimed he had opposed, and they mentioned that Lucien Blackwell believed a bank conspiracy was behind the city's financial problems.

In other words, the story took one candidate's proposal to reinstate discretionary funding for the arts once the city's budget problems eased and another's decision to moderate a stand on privatization and equated both with a third candidate's blatant misrepresentation of his voting record and a fourth's patently false assessment of the city's fiscal problems. Was it any wonder that the voters were having a difficult time distinguishing one candidate from another if campaign coverage failed to draw distinctions between controversial proposals, softening of positions, lies, and conspiracy theories? But perhaps worse than the blanket condemnation was the fact that the newspaper had chosen to write about only those proposals they could mock. The claims and proposals and assessments that made sense had been carefully omitted. In jumping on a minor, off-hand proposal by Rendell, for instance, the reporters had failed to highlight the most important statement Rendell made at the debate: that he hoped to win concessions from the unions, but was prepared to take a strike if he did not.

The reporters seemed to be trying to paint the candidates as negatively as possible in order to keep the tone of the story light and cynical. If some of the candidates were lying and fantasizing, but others were taking perfectly reasonable stands, it would be hard to say the candidates were just a bunch of good old-fashioned political hacks. It was as if only through a wholesale disparagement of the candidates did the reporters think they could get anyone to read their piece, as if they felt they had to disguise their focus on substance by laying on top of it a veneer of flippancy.

But what they really may have been trying to disguise was the fact that they so rarely looked at substance at all. If the candidates at times offered empty rhetoric or half-baked proposals, if they made false claims or shifted positions without explanation, it could be argued that the media were partly to blame. If it was only in the rare exceptional moment that reporters took time out from grading the candidates on their strategies to listen in on what the candidates were actually saying about the city, then they should not really have been so surprised by what they found. Lucien Blackwell had been espousing his theory about a bank conspiracy for months before the Democratic debate. If the idea came as a surprise to reporters—and was not written about in the *Philadelphia Inquirer* until one week before the election—there was a simple explanation. The paper had been so caught up with the drama of the three black candidates competing for the same voter base that they had not managed to figure out what one of those candidates thought about the worst problem facing the city.

In all the focus on making campaign reporting more interesting, the newspapers seemed to have lost sight of how much crucial information they were failing to report and how negative in tone was much of what they were choosing to write. If the major newspaper in town devoted four stories and four thousand words to painting the candidates as all personally flawed or crassly opportunistic, if they distorted the debate so that it looked like nothing more than "politics as usual," then why even bother to vote for one of these jokers, come election day? It was politics as usual, all right, but it was coming as much from the media as from the candidates.

23 Pumping It Up

May 16, 1991

In the last week of the campaign, the schedule was hectic for both the candidates and the reporters who were covering them. On this sunny Thursday, Ron Castille was winding up his morning's events at a senior citizens' center on Castor Avenue in the Northeast. The seniors in their pastel clothing sat leaning on canes and walkers, politely listening to Castille's rote talk about turning the city around. "I want to get things in this city back to the way they were when I first came here twenty years ago," he said in his low-key manner, "back when all of you were teenagers." The attempt at humor went unnoticed by the crowd. They seemed unmoved by anything Castille was saying, thinking perhaps more about the lunch they would be served when he stopped talking.

Dave Davies of the *Daily News* was the only reporter covering Castille that morning. In the last weeks of the campaign, he had been assigned to the Republican candidates, while Cindy Burton took the Democrats. Davies was in his late thirties, tall and thin, with straight brown hair that fell onto his forehead and a neatly trimmed beard. He often made it into television reporters' pieces at press conferences in his characteristic pose: slightly hunched over, his elbow resting on his other arm, hand stroking his beard, as if he were leaning in to discern what the candidate was saying.

Davies had started out in Philadelphia in the news department of public radio station WHYY and had covered city hall since 1984. In 1986, he had gone to commercial radio, working for KYW, the city's all-news radio station. It was the highest-rated radio station in the market and the station at which NBC White House correspondent Andrea Mitchell got her start. In 1990, he had made the unusual switch from broadcast journalism into print, jumping to the city hall bureau of the *Daily News*. In some ways, he still loved radio, the immediacy of it, the live reports as news happened, his resonant voice detailing the latest budget wranglings. But he had also found it frustrating, especially at KYW where his reports had typically been limited to forty-five seconds, with little time to do much reporting. He was constantly ad-libbing live reports and then going on to make prerecorded pieces that would be played throughout the day. In news radio, research was unheard of.

At the *Daily News*, all this changed. Suddenly, he could spend real time looking for stories and researching them, and now he had some space to write up the results. His pieces were edited much more closely than on radio, where the standards were fairly loose, and he liked that. But there were compromises to be made here, too. He soon found that *Daily News* reporters and editors were often driven by competition with the *Inquirer*, chasing after stories not because of their ultimate importance or even interest to the guy riding on the subway but so as not to get beaten by the *Inquirer*. Ironically, the competition seemed to be more intense by virtue of the fact that the two newspapers were owned by the same company. Editors at the *Daily News* had something of an inferiority complex when it came to the *Inquirer*. Partly it was because the larger paper got more resources from Knight-Ridder, but some of it had to do with the *Inquirer*'s high-brow status, as opposed to the tabloid's need to appeal to the row-house reader. While the *Inquirer*'s market was concentrated in the suburbs, with a high percentage of college-educated professionals, the *Daily News* reached more of a city audience, the blue- and pink-collar workers who picked up the tabloid on the newsstand on their way home from work.

It was the need to appeal to that audience as they passed by the newsstand each day, Davies soon learned, that led the *Daily News* to adopt a writing style that was distinctly different from the *Inquirer*'s tone, a style that was breezier, more informal, more colorful, at times outrageous. One of the first stories he had done at the paper, on his third day on the job, had turned out to be a front-page exclusive on a proposal by Mayor Goode for an unearned income tax, a story that the *Inquirer* had missed. Davies had finished his research on the tax proposal and written the lead: "Faced with the likelihood that city council will reject his proposed increase in the city wage tax, Mayor Goode yesterday sent council a proposal that would impose a tax on interest from bank accounts and other kinds of so-called unearned income." But his editor had turned thumbs down on it. "This is a good lead for the *Inquirer,*" he said, "but it won't work here. You've got to personalize it."

So Davies tried again. This time he wrote: "For years Philadelphians have been complaining about the wage tax. Now Mayor Goode wants to tax their unearned income." Again, he showed it to his editor. Needs to be pumped up a little, said the editor, who rewrote it himself this time. The lead became: "Mayor Goode has his eye on the interest from your savings account to balance the city budget. And the earnings from your money market fund. And the dividends from your stocks. And the profit you make when you sell your house. He even wants to get his hands on your winnings from the crap tables in Atlantic City, if you're so lucky."

The "pumping up" was something Davies sometimes had a problem with. To make it hard-hitting, he thought, you may have to make it unfair. The new lead had been technically accurate, he knew. But it had taken the complicated budget situation facing the city and simplified it, making it sound as if the problem was that Wilson Goode had his greedy eye on your pocketbook. Davies recognized that when a newspaper must sell itself each day as an impulse buy on the newsstand, that kind of writing was necessary, just as serial murders were always going to make page 1 and push out city budget stories. But he didn't have to like it.

He didn't necessarily admire the *Inquirer*'s brand of reporting all the time, either. Throughout 1990, Davies had often found himself covering the same stories as Sal Paolantonio. Back in September, they had both covered the press conference by George Burrell, where he proposed his fiscal plan for rescuing the city, the one where Burrell had called on Mayor Goode to fire the city's outspoken finance director, Betsy Reveal. Many of the reporters present had felt that this was a cheap shot, an attempt to get more media attention for his proposal and not at all central to the city's recovery. But the stories Davies and Paolantonio wrote about the press conference were noticeably different. Paolantonio made the story a political one, centering on how Burrell's call for firing Reveal fed into his political agenda and how the other candidates were responding to it. The bulk of the article became the dumping on the Reveal proposal and interpretation of Burrell's political motives in proposing it. Only in the last paragraph of the story had Paolantonio summed up the other elements in Burrell's plan for fiscal recovery. It had all been proposed before, Paolantonio claimed. Why give Burrell ink for old ideas?

Davies disagreed. He had been covering city hall and fiscal problems—not politics—for years, and he knew that Burrell's plan had not all been said before and that it deserved to be presented to readers, so that they could make their own judgments. Certainly, he wrote about the call to fire Reveal and the criticisms it received. He had found it a wacky idea and ill-conceived. But he decided to take Burrell's proposal seriously. Burrell was the first potential candidate to lay out a specific plan that he would take some heat for, and the plan actually contained numbers that would add up. That was the difference between Paolantonio and Davies: Paolantonio, the political reporter, would tend to interpret each move a candidate made for its political implications, how it fit into the strategy to get elected. But Davies felt more strongly that the proposals themselves, as politically motivated as they might be, deserved to be presented to the voter and examined.

On this day in May near the end of the campaign, Davies looked tired. He had come down with a devilish stomach virus during the Democratic debate, which he had covered because Cindy Burton had been a panelist, and it had knocked him out for several days. He had been working hard covering the campaign, doing stories day in and day out, and then having longer analysis pieces, like his examination of the leadership qualities of the Republican candidates, thrown on top of it. He felt like he never saw his wife and two children, and he missed them.

As Castille wound up his speech to the seniors, there was lukewarm applause. The candidate walked to the back of the room, where he stopped to chat with people and shake a few hands. One-on-one he seemed to impress the people he talked to more, coming across as warmer and more sincere than when he delivered a speech. One older man stopped him and said he would be voting for him on election day. "And you know," said the man in a conspiratorial voice, "when you get in there you ought to make Frank Rizzo your police commissioner." Castille smiled noncommittally and said he'd sure give it some thought.

Davies caught up with Castille's press secretary, Laura Linton, and checked the rest of the day's schedule. Castille was racing off next to a downtown fundraiser, but Davies would skip that. He believed that Castille would collect his dollars; he didn't need to be there. Before he left, he chatted with Linton about the campaign. "Did you see Katz's latest ad?" she asked him.

"No, I haven't seen it yet. What's it say?"

Linton described it. Katz was on TV again, with his last ad blitz of the campaign, and he had chosen a new direction. His ads talked about how Rizzo had been on the city payroll for thirty years and how Castille had been on the city payroll for more than twenty years. It concluded: "The only man in the Republican primary who has never been on the city payroll is Sam Katz." Linton smiled as she described the ad. She obviously thought it was a bust.

"Why would they do something like that?" Davies asked.

"They polled. They found some public suspicion of people being on the public payroll. The ad came right from their polling data, apparently."

Katz's ads were one of his weak spots. He was one of the few candidates who had not hired an experienced media consultant for his campaign. Castille had Chris Mottola, Rizzo had John Goodman, Rendell had Neil Oxman, and Peter Hearn had Saul Schorr. But Katz had balked. He himself was a consultant. He knew what consultants did. They took a lot of money to tell you relatively simple things. He knew what he wanted to say to voters. He had his polling data. He had his shrewd campaign manager, Bob Kutler, who had learned politics at the knee of Rizzo's long-time campaign advisor, Marty Weinberg. Kutler wrote Katz's first set of ads, which aired back in January, the "I know how to manage money. I will solve Philadelphia's fiscal problems" ads. And now in the clutch, instead of going on the air with ads that reinforced his "above-the-fray" image as the clean, issues-oriented candidate who could solve the city's fiscal problems, he was using spots that made him look like just another politician. All because he didn't want to hire a media consultant.

Davies had actually been trying to contact Katz for days, to write something about him, but Katz had been cutting himself off from reporters. It was rumored that he was plotting a massive street organization on election day that would challenge both the party organization's street forces and the Rizzo contingent. He wanted reporters to know only that he was marshaling his troops, but nothing more, so as to maintain the element of surprise on election day. But in the process, he had dropped out of view in both the newspapers and on TV at a critical time in the campaign, when many voters were making their commitments.

Linton went over the rest of Castille's schedule with Davies, then she took off with the candidate. Davies slipped into a luncheonette that was on the same strip as the senior center and took a break for lunch, ordering an Italian hoagie and a Coke, and reflected on some of the things he'd seen recently on the campaign trail. He was particularly disturbed by an event he had covered on Monday and what it revealed about the local press corps. He had gone out to cover the press conference that Burrell-supporter Congressman Bill Gray scheduled the day after he had used his church pulpit to attack the *Inquirer* for racism. At the press conference, Gray had renewed his charges against the *Inquirer,* but had also attacked Lucien Blackwell. He claimed that Blackwell's campaign had received contributions from "individuals" listed in the Pennsylvania Crime Commission report, and he asked how Blackwell could effectively fight crime under such a situation.

What had disturbed Davies was that of all the reporters present—three

TV reporters, two from the *Inquirer*—he was the only person to ask Gray if there were more than one "individual" (Gray had responded that there were two) and the only reporter to bother to ask Gray's aide, Jerry Mondeshire, to supply the names of the two individuals. Once Davies got the names, he went to get a response from Blackwell, who claimed that the Junious Blackwell listed in the Crime Commission Report was not the Junious Blackwell who had contributed to Blackwell's campaign. The second person listed in the reports turned out to be the brother of a contributor.

Davies went back to the paper and told his editor, Ron Goldwyn, about the story. Davies wanted to lead with Gray's error: he thought it was outrageous that a figure of Gray's stature should make this kind of attack on a mayoral candidate with only the flimsiest of evidence. But Goldwyn, who was the *Daily News*'s political editor, had disagreed. He wanted the story to be more a sign of Burrell's campaign foundering and calling in Daddy's help. And so the lead became a political one, rather than a question of the congressman's integrity. "Eight days before the primary, Democratic mayoral candidate George Burrell's camp rolled out the heavy artillery: U.S. Rep. William H. Gray III" was how the story began. It wasn't until the tenth paragraph that Davies discussed the validity of Gray's charges. Again, it was strategy versus substance. Davies's editor had wanted to focus on the strategic move and what it meant for Burrell's campaign. Davies wanted to focus on the research he had done to verify the substance of a public official's claims.

Davies often felt that he was being pushed to take the political angle on a story, rather than focusing on the more substantive issues. Like when he went out to cover the Republican debate. The reporter had a strong feeling about debate coverage. He thought it was the one time in a campaign when people had a chance to decide for themselves how the candidates handled themselves. He thought it was wrong for reporters to put their "spin" on a debate and, in fact, believed that was why debates had such powerful and undue effects on elections. Journalists were always having to declare people winners and losers. But his editor had disagreed, and Davies had to write things like "All claimed victory. . . . But there was no knock-out, no TKO, more like a three-way split decision."

Davies had a strong sense of how campaign reporting ought to be carried out, and in looking back at the hundreds of articles he and Burton had written since the beginning, he felt they'd failed more times than succeeded. He thought certain personal issues were important. Like Burrell and his tax returns. Looking back, he thought reporters should have hounded Burrell every day of the campaign until he released the returns, because he believed they were important for the public's evaluation of the candidate. He thought it was outrageous that Burrell had told reporters he would make his lawyer available to answer their questions, and then didn't. In a way, he thought the reporters had let him off easy for these kinds of things.

But when it came to the coverage of issues, that's where he saw their greatest failure. He thought there was a clear way to cover the substance of a campaign. He agreed with Paolantonio that it was not the journalist's job to go to press conferences and just write up whatever proposal the candidate was mouthing that day. That kind of journalism often gave more credence to ideas than they deserved. Like when Blackwell had proposed a plan for scholarships for public high school students when the school district had no money. Davies felt it was the campaign reporter's duty to cover those plans in detail, pointing up their weaknesses. The best way to cover proposals, he thought, was to be able to do enough additional reporting to tell the public whether they were good ideas or not, whether they made sense or not. He was proudest of the story he wrote when Rizzo was attacking Castille's claims about how he had raised the conviction rate while D.A. Davies had gone to criminal experts to get their opinions on which of the candidates was justified in his claims. He then had searched court reports to look at the numbers, and the results had made an informative story. He had shown that Rizzo's charges against Castille had not held up.

There were other stories he had wanted to do. He was appalled that so many of the candidates' proposals to improve city government were coming directly from city controllers' efficiency reports, many of which, he knew from covering city government for years, were virtually worthless. He'd have loved to analyze some of those proposals and show the voters how intractable were some of these problems and how simplistic were some of the answers. But the problem was time. There was simply no time to do that kind of reporting when you were expected to write a story about each day's campaign events. As a result, the coverage tended to stay on the horse race—who was winning, who was losing, and what every move meant from a political point of view. In the process, Davies thought, as he took his last bite of hoagie, the journalists were failing in their duty to inform the electorate.

He headed out of the luncheonette to catch up with Castille's next stop and try to hit a playground appearance by Katz later in the afternoon. He smiled sardonically, contemplating the candidates. "Whoever wins will be a liar. Taxes will go up and services will go down." But it would be hard for him or any other reporter to write about that.

And it would be hard for any of the political reporters, ingrained cynics that they had learned to be, to imagine that one of the candidates might actually prove more or less true to his word.

24 Fatal Attraction

May 21, 1991

❦ It was finally election day and most people had chosen their candidate. But the candidates were still out shaking hands, making a last-ditch effort to get their voters out. Turnout would be crucial.

Ed Rendell's campaign had picked the downtown Gallery shopping mall as his final campaign stop. The Gallery was the brainchild of Philadelphia's most influential city planner, Ed Bacon, an idea he had conceived in the fifties for redeveloping downtown Philadelphia to make it more competitive with suburban shopping malls. With the help of federal urban development grants, the Rouse Corporation's Gallery project had succeeded in transforming the seedy run-down area on Market Street east of City Hall into a sleek new office and shopping mall. But the in-town mall was never able to draw suburban commuters the way it had been intended. Instead, the Gallery became a magnet for inner-city residents, and its food court was a popular lunch spot for center-city workers. On this fine spring day, many of those lunchers were congregated on the outdoor steps and benches provided at the entrance to the mall, the spot where Ed Rendell was set to campaign.

Rendell arrived shortly after noon and headed through the glass passageways that connected the mall to the anchor department store, Strawbridge and Clothier's. He was looking for a men's room. He moved through the crowded mall by himself, virtually unrecognized. Some two million dollars in advertising had been spent thus far in the campaign to spread the Rendell message, but still Gallery shoppers passed him without a glance. When he emerged from the mall to start shaking hands, he paused to meet with a campaign aide who was carrying his literature. During the campaign, one of the *Daily News* columnists had nicknamed Rendell "The Energizer" because of his tireless energy in campaigning. But today he looked tired and restless, as if eager to have the polling in and the results finally counted. It had been a long primary campaign—six months since he'd announced last October—and a long time since he'd enjoyed his last election victory. It looked good for him this time, but he had the wary expression of a man who would just as soon have it in writing.

He was without much of an entourage this last primary campaigning day because his top aides were directing the field organization to get out the vote. And so Ed Rendell just started in. He went from bench to bench, from step to step, intruding himself into lunchtime conversations to introduce himself. "Hi, I'm Ed Rendell," he said, thrusting out his hand. "How are you today?" Some looked unimpressed, while others jumped up in recognition when they heard his name. To each he said, "Did you vote today?" If they said yes, they'd voted for him, he answered, "God bless you." If they said no, then he shook his head and said, "Well, go out and do it." As he made his way around the people on the steps, he came to a woman engrossed in a cup of frozen yogurt. He started to extend his hand but thought better of it. She was in a world of her own. He didn't need this.

After five or ten minutes of shaking hands, he was ready to leave, but he got word that Vernon Odom of Channel 6 was trying to catch up with him. Rendell's schedule for the press had indicated that he'd be at the Gallery from noon until two, but he was clearly anxious to move on. Still, he figured he'd give Odom five or ten minutes to show up. And sure enough, at 12:20 the Channel 6 news truck pulled up. Odom was working on a piece on the Democratic candidates for the six o'clock news. He'd already gotten Hearn and Blackwell, but he still needed Rendell and Burrell. He shook hands with Rendell. "I just saw Midge up in Roxborough," Odom told him, referring to the candidate's wife. "She bumped right into Hearn campaigning." Odom asked Rendell why he was wearing such a heavy suit—charcoal gray wool—on what was becoming a very warm day. "Yeah, I know," said Rendell, with a smile. "The trouble is I just don't have that many summer suits. However this thing turns out, I'm going to need to buy some summer suits, win or lose."

Odom asked Rendell if he was going to be there until two. "Nah, I'm just waiting for you. I was going to cut out when I heard you were coming, so I waited around."

"Oh, OK. Well, we just need to get some shots of you shaking hands." As was so often the case, pictures were the first priority of television news, not anything the candidate might say in an interview.

Odom hung back out of the camera's view while his cameraman shot Rendell shaking hands. While Rendell was actively approaching people to introduce himself, Odom needed no effort at all to attract the attention of a steady stream of people. "Hey, Vernon, how you doing?" "Vernon, I watch you all the time. Every Sunday morning I watch you on that show you do and all the rest of the time, too." "Hey, hi, Vernon, I knew I knew you from somewhere." Being a reporter for sixteen years for the city's most watched television news station gave Vernon Odom the aura of trusted friend and local personality that any of the mayoral candidates would have gladly paid millions of dollars of advertising to get.

After the cameraman had gotten the requisite video, Odom interviewed Rendell, becoming more formal for his audience. There was a degree of theatricality in the way television reporters interviewed the candidates that was missing with the print reporters. Off camera, the TV reporter was joking, friendly, and very much in charge; on camera, he suddenly took on an air of formality and supplication.

"Mr. Rendell, what do you hear about turnout?"

"I think turnout's good all over, which I think is a good sign. I don't know if it's a good sign for me or not, but it's important to send a message to Harrisburg and Washington that the people of Philadelphia really do care about this election and their city's future, and a good turnout's the best way to do that."

"I heard you this morning on Mary Mason predict . . . you implied that George Burrell is in virtual free fall . . . and that he's going to come in fourth . . . "

"Well, I said that I think George Burrell and Peter Hearn are going to come in close together. They both waged pretty good campaigns. Peter Hearn spent a million six, and they're both going to come in pretty close together. Vernon, my record at predictions is not so good. If I were so good at it, I'd have just finished two terms as governor." Rendell was dutifully following the orders of his strategists to steer clear from talking politics, adding his own brand of self-deprecating humor.

"But you said this morning that it's you and Lu—"

"I think that's right. At this point it looks like Councilman Blackwell and myself. But you know, voters are funny. I know George Burrell had a tough week last week, but he made a comeback at the end of the week."

Odom raised his eyebrows at the comment. In an aside not meant for the air, his voice lower and more conspiratorial, he said, "That's not what I hear." Then he continued in his on-camera voice: "But let me ask you this. You ran an attack ad on Peter Hearn last night. Some interpreted that as 'I better go for every white vote I can get.'"

"No, that was a mistake. It was a mistake in the trafficking. As you know, the stations usually have four or five ads, particularly in the last weekend because you don't have time to deliver them, especially on weekends, and they just got the trafficking instructions wrong."

"And you had the trigger waiting, you had it there waiting?"

"Yeah, we had it there waiting if anybody had done negatives. We had negatives responding to all of the candidates. You know, Peter Hearn did negatives against us in March, but nobody came out and did negatives against us this last week. But if they did, we were ready to respond in kind and, unfortunately, the station and the media people got the trafficking instructions messed up. But if we wanted to do a negative against anybody, we wouldn't have done it with one ad."

"Does that say anything about the ultimate insincerity of politics, that you had a negative sitting there waiting if he made the right move?"

"I don't know. Understand, there's nothing in there that's factually incorrect. I've said all along, Vernon, and you've heard me say this, that I was going to do a positive campaign, and I did it. I think the most positive probably in recent history in this city. But if I was attacked, I was going to strike back, no question. I took the first quarter of a million dollars of the negative TV he ran against me without fighting back. But, if attacked at the end, I was going to fight back."

"But last night was a mistake?"

"It was a mistake. It ran once. It was just a trafficking error."

Odom asked him again if he didn't think it was just him and Blackwell at this point, and Rendell said that Burrell had had a good weekend, that Mayor Goode was out campaigning with him, that he'd done first-rate direct mail to voters. Odom responded in his off-camera voice, "I think he's in free fall."

"Do you?" said Rendell. It was the interview-turnaround, an occurrence that sometimes happened, particularly among veteran reporters, where the candidates interviewed them on what they'd been hearing on the street and how they were interpreting events.

"My prediction right now is that he and Hearn are going to finish last. I think it's you and Blackwell."

Rendell responded, "Do you think Burrell's not going to slow him down?"

"Burrell self-destructed last week."

"Yeh, but remember they have an excellent street organization, so I'm not so sure," Rendell responded, referring to Congressman Bill Gray's organization. "I think I'm going to get about 15 percent of the black vote." Rendell was breaking with the rule set out for him—no talking politics to reporters—but he knew Odom would never use the comments for his piece. TV stations wanted pictures at this point in the campaign, little else.

Odom agreed. "I think you're going to do about 15 percent, but it's all coming from Burrell. He is in free fall."

The reporter wound up his interview, telling Rendell that he might try to catch him again with his campaign workers up in the Northeast at three-thirty to get more video. Then he asked Rendell if he'd come on Channel 6 between nine and ten when the station was doing its election night special. Only Channel 6 was preempting its primetime entertainment program-ming to report on election results. Odom would be stationed at the War-wick Hotel, Rendell's election night headquarters, and the reporter was eager to get the first interview with Rendell, ahead of his competitors at the other stations. Rendell's campaign manager had said earlier that they would pick straws to see which station Rendell would go on first that night.

Odom gave a stab at lobbying Rendell directly. "So why should we have to stand in line and draw straws? The other stations have abdicated. I mean, they're not doing a damn thing. And David Cohen says we're gonna draw straws to see who gets him first. Man, those guys decided to go with *Fatal Attraction* tonight, and we're taking the bite."

"Are they going to do cut-ins?" asked Rendell.

"They might be doing updates, but, hey, we're doing a one-hour special."

"But what about *Fatal Attraction*?"

"They'll do it during commercials. So who's taking the bite tonight for the good of the civic pride, Mr. Rendell?

"I agree with you. I'm not arguing."

"Mr. Mayor, huh? Will you come and be on TV with us, Mr. Mayor, since we're doing something good for the city?"

Rendell smiled affably. "All right. I'm going to lobby David Cohen."

After Rendell left, Odom continued to grouse about the election cover-age of his competitors. "The other stations are gonna come in like they're doing something. They've abdicated, abdicated . . . hey, buddy, how are you doing? . . . completely abdicated. The contrast is, four, eight, twelve years ago, all three stations were heavily covering the campaign. They had top-notch experienced people covering the campaign. Now, Channel 10's got some people out there . . . I'm not saying they're not doing anything . . . but to me it's too bad. Because I enjoy the competition and being a newsman I like to see more jobs and more competition in the job. But you see the other stations pull back because of the economics of the business today. And it's a sad thing. Last week at Channel 3 for the debate, I was expecting a gold rush of reporters after the debate. But there was a small crowd compared to the way it used to be. There used to be more newspaper journalists, more TV stations covering it, more radio stations covering it . . . hello, how are you? . . . it's frightening the way it's become. I hate to see all that news go." As Odom spoke, he was continually interrupted by passers-by who recognized him and wanted to say hello.

Odom's observation about his competitors' election coverage was right on the mark. New management at Channel 10 had come in and quietly eliminated most political and government news from the newscast, including Philadelphia's mayoral primaries. The station had drastically cut its coverage of the election back in April, down to an average of 37 seconds per day—and that was spread across three newscasts—which was less than a third of what its competitors were doing. At the same time, the station was accepting thousands of dollars in campaign ads. One night a few weeks back, Channel 10 had done no news reports on the election on its 5:30 or 6:00 newscasts, but in commercial breaks in the news it had run no less than six campaign ads for the mayoral candidates. While the other stations had at least kept up the facade of covering the campaign, viewers of Channel 10 were mainly learning about the candidates via the carefully constructed images of media consultants.

Odom and his cameramen stopped to discuss where they would go for lunch that day. "The Reading Terminal's been working for me all week," said Odom. So off they went in the van to drive the few blocks to the Reading Terminal Market, the century-old market under the now closed Reading Railroad suburban terminal. In the last decade, the market had been transformed into a popular spot where downtown workers could buy fresh poultry, fish, and produce, as well as Pennsylvania Dutch products, and where they could get trendy ethnic foods for lunch from the many stands. The Channel 6 van pulled up to the Arch Street side of the market and parked in a no-parking zone.

Odom circled the market like a veteran, still greeting passers-by as he went. He stopped first at Bassett's Turkey stand for a styrofoam container of turkey salad. Next he moved to a salad bar stand where he methodically moved from container to container, building a salad as he discussed the newspaper coverage. He talked about the recent article on the Burrell and Hearn contributors that had drawn the ire of Congressman Bill Gray. He agreed with Gray's points. Why had they used a picture of Huggins and not of the Woodward lady? "And then they implied that Huggins was getting something in return for his money and that Mrs. Woodward was just doing it for the good of the city. I'm not saying she was trying to buy anything, mind you. I'm just saying you could say it wasn't even."

He was also critical of the early endorsements of both the *Inquirer* and *Daily News*. "This is a one-company town," he said, as he added grated cheese and tomatoes to his salad. "I don't care what anyone says about separate editorial staffs. I think that endorsing a candidate that far before an election compromises the credibility of their reporters. Do you mean to tell me if Sal Paolantonio found out that Ed Rendell was a child molester—now, I'm not saying he is or anything—but do you believe if he found out something very negative about the candidate that the *Inquirer* endorsed weeks before the election, that they'd print something like that after they endorsed the guy?"

Back in the truck, Odom climbed into the jump seat behind the passenger seat so that he could put his food on the small fold-down table. He carefully tucked his tie inside his shirt and draped a napkin on his chest. He'd be on camera any number of times in the next several hours, and he'd take no chances of having blue cheese dressing on his tie in front of hundreds of thousands of viewers. As he ate, he talked more about the newspaper coverage. "The newspapers in this town want a white mayor so bad they can taste it."

He paused in his thoughts to check the time with his cameraman. Their next stop was in North Philly, where they would try to get some shots of George Burrell. They talked about whether they would have time to get back up to Rendell's Northeast headquarters to shoot him talking with his campaign workers. The cameraman reassured Odom; he was from the Northeast and knew exactly where they were going. The cameraman had worked at Channel 6 for sixteen years, his father preceding him in the same job at the station. He remembered shooting his first footage as a young boy at the Cornell-Penn football game in Ithaca, New York. His father had let him hold the camera, sure that nothing was going to happen, when the Penn lineman ran for a sudden touchdown. He grinned as he told the story, how his father had said to him, "You better have gotten that play, or my job's on the line."

He showed no such enthusiasm for the mayoral candidates, confessing that he was not planning to vote in the primary. "When you see them as much as I do, day in and day out, you see they'll say anything to anybody. One day, they promise something to one group, the next they say the opposite to another. I've seen them too close up to think much of any of them."

Odom picked up his thought. "You think any of them has a fiscal plan for the city? None of them has a plan. Not even Sam Katz. We sat down with his 'plan' at the station. There was nothing really there. The key is to get money from Harrisburg, and no one's been able to do that since Buddy

Cianfrani [former state senator] went to prison." It was an interesting observation, particularly since it had never made it into any of Channel 6's stories about the campaign. Whether any of the candidates had a credible plan for dealing with the city's financial crisis—the central issue facing the city—was simply not viewed by local television news honchos in 1991 as an interesting enough subject for a story.

Odom ate his last bite of salad and got ready to move again. It was going to be a long day and an even longer night.

As promised, at 9 P.M. Channel 6's Action News replaced its regular programming with election results. The first numbers came from only 1 percent of the precincts. Anchor Jim Gardner cautioned that the results should not be taken too seriously since it was "extraordinarily early." Nevertheless, these early numbers were flashed on the screen. On the Democratic side, the slim number of vote tallies showed Ed Rendell with a commanding lead, while on the Republican side, it was far closer. Frank Rizzo was in the lead, with 46 percent of the vote, Castille coming in with 34 percent and Katz with 20 percent. Gardner discounted the Rizzo lead, noting that the early returns could easily be from one of Rizzo's strongest precincts. Rizzo had always enjoyed an almost fanatical following in some Italian neighborhoods in South Philly. "To give you an analogy," said Gardner, "if this were the Superbowl, and I suppose in a sense it is for Philadelphia politics, we're at the coin flip right now."

When anchor Marc Howard came on the air to offer some analysis of the early results, he pointed out that Rizzo's lead over Castille was probably due to the fact that the first results were coming from the 39th ward in South Philadelphia, "which is clearly Rizzo country," so he, too, cautioned viewers not to take the results too seriously. But ten minutes later, when 7 percent of the vote came in and Rizzo's lead was holding—47 percent to Castille's 31 percent—Gardner began to change his tune somewhat. He went to reporter David Henry at Rizzo headquarters:

"David, we got to go to you because it's early, but 7 percent begins to become a reasonable figure, and Frank Rizzo has a big lead, not just a lead, but a big lead over Ron Castille."

"Well, Jim, there is optimism here in the Rizzo camp, even though no candidate has ever beaten the machine-backed candidate in a Republican primary," Henry answered.

Gardner went on. "We don't know, David, even with all our technology, just where this 7 percent of the vote is coming from at this point in time. We know that Frank Rizzo has passionate support in many pockets and sections of this city, but we don't know where these votes are coming from."

The next tallies came with 20 percent of the vote, and still Rizzo's lead held, 43 percent to 32 percent over Castille. "Let it be said," noted Jim Gardner, "that Billy Meehan—I don't like to use the word, but let us use it for the sake of communication—the boss of the Republican party, has not been defeated ever. If it's going to happen tonight, it would be the first time, by Frank Rizzo." Gardner seemed unwilling to believe that Frank Rizzo could actually win this election, since the conventional wisdom for months had been that the machine could not be defeated. On the Democratic side, with 20 percent of the vote in, Ed Rendell's lead looked solid. He led with 53 percent, followed by Lucien Blackwell with 26 percent. Trailing behind were George Burrell with 12 percent and Peter Hearn with 9 percent.

After a commercial break, Gardner came back with a smile. "It looks like we're going to settle in for an interesting horse race on the Republican side." With 39 percent of the precincts counted, Rizzo's lead had begun to shrink. Now he led Castille 40 to 34 percent, a mere six-point margin, and Gardner noted that Rizzo's dwindling lead might mean that Castille could pull it out after all.

"One of Castille's problems tonight is the very respectable showing of Sam Katz. Virtually all of Katz's votes, one could assume, would have gone to Castille, if Katz were not in the race." Katz now held 26 percent of the tally, with only four thousand votes less than Castille in these precincts. "On the Democratic side, not as interesting from our point of view, but from Ed Rendell's point of view, things are fine, thank you, as he leads with 52 percent, double the level of Lucien Blackwell, with Burrell and Hearn trailing behind."

At 10 P.M., when Action News was set to close its special report, it got reports from 50 percent of the precincts. "Rendell, now with a fourteen-point lead over Blackwell. We're not calling it yet, but if you want to, you may," Gardner said. "On the Republican side, four percentage points separate Ron Castille from Frank Rizzo, Castille trailing 35 percent to Rizzo's 39 percent, Frank Rizzo very angry this time around at Billy Meehan. Ron Castille is closing the gap as the votes are being counted."

But as the evening wore on, Ron Castille never succeeded in closing the gap. At 11:35, with Castille a mere thousand votes behind Rizzo, Ron Castille took to the podium at his election night headquarters. Every television station in town had sent a reporter and cameraman to every campaign headquarters, and they were all set to go live at any moment. When Castille managed to get the crowd's attention, he said that the election was too close to concede and he would wait for the final count.

Judy Castille stood behind her husband, her eyes glistening with tears, stroking his shoulder as he spoke. Long after the election, she would still find it hard to believe that it had happened, that Frank Rizzo had beaten her husband, that he would lose the primary and lose it in this way. She would be filled with bitterness toward Frank Rizzo, the man who had been unwilling to let her husband stand in the way of his desire to wipe out the past humiliation of being beaten by Wilson Goode ("Frank's got to go out as a man," one Rizzo aide had said to her before her husband had decided to run) and who had attacked her husband in the most personal, despicable way. She had known that running against Rizzo would not be a bed of roses, but she had never dreamed it would become so vicious. All those unattributed, unconfirmed stories that the media had willingly repeated day in and day out.

She was equally bitter toward Sam Katz for staying in the election and spoiling it for Ron. She believed the theory that the Rizzo and Katz campaigns were in collusion, linked through Katz's campaign manager, Bob Kutler, who had close ties to Rizzo's campaign manager, Marty Weinberg. She wouldn't even be surprised if Katz had been unwittingly manipulated by Kutler into thinking he had a chance to win, just so that he would stay in the race to help Rizzo.

She knew they should have gone negative on Sam Katz. She had been pushing for it. Not the sexual harassment stuff; she'd have never gone with that. The man had a family. He had children. She knew what kind of pain those personal attacks caused in people's families. No, that wasn't what she'd have gone for. She wanted them to bring out what kind of political ties Katz had in the past, that he was a Democrat in Republican's clothing, that while he was pitching himself as an outsider he'd had more inside political ties than Ron. She had been in favor of the idea of Chris Mottola putting together a ten-second spot at the end of the campaign that would have simply said, "A vote for Sam Katz is a vote for Frank Rizzo." But the negatives had gotten the kibosh.

And now the vote tallies were coming in and, unbelievably, her husband, who had entered the election with an unheard-of popularity rating, who with the party's help was supposed to have coasted to the nomination and on from there into the mayor's office, was losing by some mere thousand votes. And he was losing to the man he had gotten into the election to make sure wouldn't win, the man he would describe in the most contemptuous terms over the course of this bitter campaign: Frank L. Rizzo.

The results of the primary were printed in a neat box on page 3 of the *Daily News* the next day, based on 98.6 percent of the vote counted. In the

Republican primary, Frank Rizzo had won with 46,786 votes, or 36 percent of the total, to Ron Castille's 45,666, or 35 percent of the vote. Sam Katz was in third place with 36,902, or 29 percent of the vote. On the Democratic side, Rendell took first place with 143,479, or 49 percent of the vote, with Lucien Blackwell in second place with 78,807 votes, George Burrell in third place with 42,937, and Peter Hearn trailing in fourth place with 26,129 votes, only 9 percent of the total. Rendell was said to have pulled in about 15 percent of the African American vote. The paper also noted that voter turnout was at record lows: only 45 percent in the Democratic primary, 52 percent in the Republican.

When the overnight Arbitron ratings for that night's election coverage came in, they were less of a surprise. Channel 10 had been the hands-down winner with its airing of *Fatal Attraction,* while Channel 6, which had preempted entertainment programming to bring the audience live election coverage, trailed far behind.

25 What Did It All Mean?

May 22, 1991

❧ The day after the primary, the analysis of the stunning results began, in the *Inquirer*, in the *Daily News*, and on the radio talk shows. Why did Castille lose? Why did Rizzo win? How did Katz manage to get 29 percent of the vote? Why did Burrell do so poorly? How did Rendell get such an unexpectedly high slice—15 percent—of the black vote? What did it all mean? Many voices were there to answer the questions and to talk about "what this election was about." The prognosticators mainly thought the election was about the rejection of boss control. In both parties, it was said, people didn't like the idea that some high party figure was telling them who to vote for, whether it was the Republican party boss Billy Meehan telling people to vote for Ron Castille or U.S. Congressman Bill Gray telling them to vote for George Burrell.

But there was one factor that none of the commentators thought to mention that day: the role of the media itself, particularly television, in the election's outcome. If party leaders were having less and less of an impact on the voter's choice of a candidate, that was in large part because television was taking on a bigger role than ever before. Advertising dollars and street organizations may have influenced the outcome of this election, but they did not determine it. Rendell's sizable lead, Burrell's poor showing, Castille's loss to Rizzo, and Katz's strong but not-strong-enough showing—all could be linked to the news coverage the candidates had received in the preceding months, particularly on television.

It was all there in the pictures that had entered Philadelphians' living rooms as they watched their local news: Castille and Burrell continually denying claims that they were drunks or deadbeats, Rizzo merely raising questions about Castille's "character and integrity" as he peered in close to talk about getting tough with street thugs, Rendell rushing to forums where he talked only about the issues, and Katz earnestly describing reassuringly incomprehensible ways to save taxpayers money. Many of the images had been carefully constructed by candidates who understood how easily manipulated was the medium of local television—if you were willing and able to dish up blistering personal attacks or powerful endorsements by well-known local figures. But other images were foisted on the candidates by the media, such as the tableau of three African American candidates whose only apparent concern was whether their opponents would withdraw from the race.

The election results could also be understood by looking at quantitative measures of the news. In the two and a half months preceding the election, only 12 percent of all the time devoted to the election on the major stations had concerned the substantive issues facing Philadelphia, such as the fiscal crisis, crime, trash disposal, or transportation. Meanwhile, 27 percent was spent on the personal attacks made by Frank Rizzo on Ron Castille, charges that were never shown to have any substance. The rest of the coverage had focused on endorsements, poll results, campaign strategy, and the catalog of public appearances by the candidates. To the increasing number of voters getting most or all of their impressions from television news, the election had looked like it was about mudslinging and political horsetrading and little else.

And then there was the way television news treated the candidates themselves, giving wildly different attention—and time—to particular candidates. While over 60 percent of the electorate was voting in the Democratic primary, in March and April almost three-quarters of the TV coverage had focused on the Republican candidates, particularly Frank Rizzo and Ron Castille. Because of all the attention given to the slugfest, Ron Castille had received 22 percent of the time given to all eight candidates to speak on television news in the two and a half months before the election, while Mr. Sound-Bite himself, Frank Rizzo, weighed in with 20 percent. Lucien Blackwell, a candidate who was to receive some 79,000 votes to Frank Rizzo's 47,000, received only 8 percent of the time. And Ed Rendell, the candidate who would win the Democratic primary by a commanding margin, the man who would receive more votes than Ron Castille, Sam Katz, and Frank Rizzo combined, received only 7 percent of the total time candidates were shown talking on television news.

It was not because he was hiding from the cameras. Ed Rendell held press conferences to call for offenders to do community service cleaning dirty streets and vacant lots, to release a plan to combat drugs, to urge Governor Casey to appoint Philadelphians to a SEPTA board vacancy, to call for charter amendments on the budget process, to propose ten ways to increase the city's tax collections, to urge continuance of the abuse assistance unit, to release a plan for Fairmount Park, and to announce a housing strategy. But television news had not covered any of them. Instead, the stations chose to focus on the slugfest and the horse race. The easy visuals of Rendell being endorsed by black state senator Hardy Williams could be picked up by a cameraman and cut to thirty seconds. But a plan, a proposal, charter amendments, ten-point strategies—all that would take time that the stations were increasingly refusing to commit.

For Ed Rendell's staff, who were carefully putting together the plans and staging the press conferences with their scenic locales, this was all quite frustrating. But for the candidate himself, being ignored by television news was not all that bad. Ed Rendell had raised plenty of money to fill in the news vacuum with his own advertising message. From January through May 21, the voters had heard lots about Ed Rendell's accomplishments and plans, all, of course, framed by his own media consultant. Lucien Blackwell had not been so fortunate. He had not raised anywhere near as much money and so, unlike Rendell, he could not fill in the blanks left by television news.

Simply getting time on television news did not help the candidates, however, as Frank Rizzo must have understood when he set out to orchestrate the way his chief opponent would be covered. While Ron Castille actually got more time talking on television than Rizzo, what Castille was able to talk about clearly hurt him. As Castille and his campaign staff were disheartened to learn every night when they turned on the news, all statements by the candidate on substantive issues, whether made in trash dumps or campaign headquarters, were edited out of television news pieces. Only if Castille was complaining about Frank Rizzo would he be allowed to speak on television. And so it was that almost three-quarters of the sound-bites Castille received on TV news were spent responding to Frank Rizzo's charges that he was a drunk or a mental case or had made a deal with a law firm or had never wanted to be mayor to begin with. In only 7 percent of his sound-bites was he found talking about issues. Castille's chances were destroyed by Frank Rizzo not because voters believed Rizzo's charges but because the charges became the only thing about Castille that TV reporters were willing to cover in the campaign.

The picture was similar with George Burrell. Although he had lagged consistently behind Ed Rendell and Lucien Blackwell in the polls, he got 18 percent of the sound-bites awarded to all eight candidates—more time to speak on television news than Rendell and Blackwell combined. But as with Castille, the sound-bites did not work in Burrell's favor, either. Burrell was not covered for his positions and ideas any more than Castille was, but rather when he stirred controversy. Only 13 percent of the time that Burrell spent talking on television news did he discuss his positions on any issues facing the city. Although Burrell's campaign commercials had portrayed him in the most elegiac terms as the man who had climbed the steps of the college football stadium, overcoming adversity and racial prejudice to achieve his goals, his news coverage had painted quite a different picture: the deadbeat, the target of protests, the man who wouldn't be there without the help of his anointer.

Ed Rendell was different. His media strategy had worked. He didn't get covered all that much by television news, particularly in view of the fact that he was the front-runner and was constantly holding press conferences to unveil new positions. But when he did, it was just what he wanted. The polls that were consistently picked up had all given Rendell the lead, and each major endorsement that was dutifully covered, if only for twenty or thirty seconds, had made his election seem more inevitable. And when Rendell himself was shown speaking on television news, he was more likely than any of the other candidates, Republican or Democrat, to be talking about substantive issues rather than personal controversy. This was no accident, of course, but the result of a carefully planned campaign strategy to keep the candidate from talking about politics and only commenting about issues. The strategy kept him from getting much coverage—since the reporters were looking for controversy and political maneuvering—but when he did get covered he looked as if he were focused on the problems of the city. His campaign message went out largely in his paid advertising, but his "free media," as the consultants referred to television news, was consistent with and reinforced the message of the ads.

Sam Katz's fortunes were also partially told in how he fared on local television news. His visibility ebbed and flowed on TV and with it the viability of his candidacy. He had come onto the scene in January and February with an advertising campaign and news coverage that made him look like an attractive new commodity who could, very simply, solve Philadelphia's fiscal problems. But for the month of March, following Castille's endorsement by the Republican party, Katz received only 8 percent of the time for all candidates on TV news, as compared to Castille's 33 percent and Rizzo's 25 percent. He managed to get back in the race not because he held a press conference or succeeded in getting some reporter to reexamine his positions or chances, but because one morning on a local television talk show he found himself placed in a dramatic encounter that was deemed appealing to TV audiences. And so in April, when he got a piece of the Rizzo/Castille slugfest action by appearing "above the fray," he managed to get 21 percent of the sound-bites. In the final weeks of the election, however, when Rizzo stopped the fray and Katz disappeared to plan his street organization, his coverage once again ebbed.

Although his visibility rose and fell, Katz's image never changed on TV. He was always "the fiscal expert" and later the "issues candidate" who posed a stark contrast to Rizzo's and Castille's squabbling. Like Rendell, Katz learned to take a strategy question from television reporters and turn it around to a passionate plea to focus on the issues of the city. And, also like Rendell, when Katz was found talking on television news, it was likely to be concerning issues. In fact, Sam Katz succeeded in becoming the candidate who spent the most time on television news talking about issues, even if the television stations spent little time exploring what he was saying about those issues. It was his television image as the candidate who cared about the problems of his beloved city that helped Katz win 29 percent of the vote in an election in which the victor captured 36 percent.

And then there was the newspaper coverage. While the *Inquirer* could proudly hail itself as one of the finest newspapers in the country, the winner of seventeen Pulitzer Prizes in the last two decades, its coverage of the primary had displayed a decided preoccupation with the horse race and questions of "character" while downplaying the consideration of issues. In the period from January 1 until election day, 65 percent of the *Inquirer*'s stories had focused on the horse race, with 9 percent dealing with personal questions, while only 19 percent of the coverage focused on discussions of where the candidates stood on the problems facing the city. Even more telling were the placement decisions. Of all the stories appearing on page 1 of the newspaper, only 9 percent were articles about the candidates' stands on the city's issues; a full 82 percent of front-page stories were about developments in the horse race and personal revelations about the candidates.

There were also specific newspaper stories that played a major role in the campaign. Sal Paolantonio was perhaps proudest of the stories he had broken about George Burrell's past financial problems, not because he had any personal dislike for the candidate or because he thought he would be a bad mayor. Rather, it was because his investigative digging into Burrell's background to find the loan default stories—the classic stuff for which journalistic prizes are awarded—had proved to have real impact on the campaign. It was in such cases that Paolantonio felt he had served as a "lightning bolt," not as a stenographer. He gave less consideration to the *Inquirer*'s decision to give more attention to Burrell's past personal financial transgressions than to his positions and plans as a candidate or, for that matter, more focus to Burrell's loan defaults than to Rendell's skeleton in the closet, his unpaid parking tickets. Journalistic convention held that a story about a public figure reported years back—as Rendell's parking tickets had been—should not make headlines in the same way that a new revelation about a candidate's past did. But in the process, Burrell's failure to pay his back loans were given far more importance in this election than Rendell's decision not to pay parking tickets received on personal business. While newcomers were welcomed into campaigns by the media for the interest of their "fresh faces," there was one area in which they suffered a distinct disadvantage. Veteran politicians whose transgressions had already been uncovered in past stories would not suffer the same kind of coverage that any new scandal about an outsider would elicit.

Equally important in the election's outcome was the *Inquirer*'s decision to herald the results of polls on its pages, since polls showing Rendell in the lead helped his campaign get an early fundraising jump. In trying to provide readers with hard facts about the status of the campaign, the newspaper gave credence to the most unreliable of campaign surveys, directly influencing campaign fundraising and thus, indirectly, the course of the campaign. And then there was the way Sal Paolantonio's coverage had alternately ignored and demolished Sam Katz. The candidate, and even a senior member of the *Inquirer*'s editorial board, would claim the coverage was the result of a personal falling-out between the two men, while Paolantonio would maintain that every shred of evidence—including the polls and the results of the election itself—confirmed that Katz could not win. He would also note that until the last few weeks of the election, he was the only reporter covering the campaign of eight candidates. Even if he had the time to cover Katz, it was unlikely that the story would get into the paper, because there were only so many city election stories that the *Inquirer*, with its broad regional audience, was going to print. But despite these justifications for the coverage, the election results would show that the *Inquirer* for much of the campaign had dismissed as unelectable a candidate who was to capture almost a third of the vote in a three candidate election.

When Paolantonio did write about Katz, the stories were devastating—from the piece about Katz's supposedly offensive personal conduct in February to the "lethal blow" story in March. And the conclusions he reached in those stories—that Katz had boasted about raising more money than he had listed in his campaign finance reports, that Katz's campaign had "all but ended" because of the loss of his finance chairmen, that Katz had exploded in anger at Tia O'Brien, or that he had not been selected by Billy

Meehan because of his temper—were at times plain wrong, at times disputed by other sources and observers. Paolantonio's editors made decisions on what went into the paper and where it was played, but they left the business of interpreting the developments of the campaign to the person who was closest to it: their lead political writer. And because there were few competing media voices that approached his power—the *Inquirer* being the dominant newspaper in town, the print medium relied upon by other reporters as the gospel—his angles on stories had a ripple effect on the wider media coverage of the campaign. Once printed in the newspaper, Paolantonio's read on the campaign would be picked up and amplified by almost every television and radio reporter in town.

While it was Paolantonio's salesmanship and skill in creating angles that so often won his stories good play, like taking the news that Katz had lost one of his finance chairmen and making it seem as if it were a turning point in Katz's campaign, many other editorial decisions were not his. Rather, they were made by the city and metro desk editors, and many he had vehemently disagreed with. When he chose to write about issues, as he had in his early story about Castille's stand on the sales tax and the candidates' stands on women's issues, his stories had been buried. Where he had tried to get a story about Rendell in the paper, he had been stymied, while his stories about Castille had been played all too prominently. And it was the editors who decided to give better play to his story about a shift in Rizzo's campaign strategy than to another reporter's piece on Sam Katz's fiscal plan.

But whether the result of Paolantonio's or an editor's decisions, how the *Inquirer* played the campaign was crucial. If Ron Castille made the front page when he announced he would be a candidate, when every other candidate's announcement was placed inside the paper, that sent a message to city readers. They didn't understand that placement decisions reflected many considerations, from what else was happening that day to the simple fact that Castille, by delaying his decision, had made it more dramatic and interesting. To many city readers, the message was that the *Inquirer* was singling out Castille as somehow more worthy, more likely to be the next mayor. And as many a media consultant understood, the seeming inevitability of a candidate's election goes a long way in helping to fulfill the prophecy.

In contrast, the candidates who became invisible had a more difficult time making their case to the voters of the city. If Sam Katz were nowhere to be found in the headlines of the paper, except for the occasional negative story downplaying his chances, it sent a message to voters. Despite the fact that the editorial board of the very same newspaper was actively pushing the man, the news coverage was far more powerful in saying that he didn't have a chance. So why if you were a Democrat should you bother changing registration to vote for him and why if you were a Republican should you risk wasting your vote for Sam Katz, only to receive Frank Rizzo instead? The message was particularly potent because the television stations, which had no political beat reporters, frequently used the *Inquirer* more or less as their assignment editor. They dutifully picked up the newspaper's messages about who was worth covering, ignoring any press conference that Katz might call since the *Inquirer* didn't think he had a chance. In this way, a single reporter's opinion had a profound and amplified effect throughout the city.

Television news had been the playing field on which Frank Rizzo had largely made his gains, causing widespread disenchantment with the formerly popular Ron Castille, and television was the medium that had catapulted Sam Katz to respectability and ensured that Ed Rendell would triumph over his opponents. But it was the major metro daily which determined that the early front-runner would be able to raise enough money to advertise his way to victory and that the one candidate who had managed to surprise all analysts and entrance so many city voters could never win the election.

And it was the campaign coverage of both television and newspapers—each choosing to devote far more space to the horse race and personal issues than to the city's dire problems—that may have been one of the key reasons why a disenchanted electorate chose to stay home in such great numbers on election day. By spending so much of their time and space on stories that cast the candidates in a negative light—Frank Rizzo calling Castille a drunk or three black candidates trying to get their black opponents to withdraw—the media helped engender cynicism and disenchantment on the part of the electorate. Through the lens of the media, where substance was ignored and dismissed at every turn, none of the candidates seemed to be very concerned with the city's problems or to be proposing much of anything to combat them. The news coverage of the election had succeeded in enthralling the people of Philadelphia more than any other election in recent memory. But it had also unwittingly sent them a powerful—and mistaken—message: that there was little difference among the candidates and few compelling reasons to exercise their vote, come election day.

26 "Mayor? Mayor? Frank!"

July 16, 1991

❧ On a hot Philadelphia summer day, in the lull between primary and general election campaigns, Frank Rizzo returned at 1:00 P.M. to his campaign headquarters from a meeting with black clergy in Mount Airy. He laid out on his desk the turkey sandwich he had ordered for lunch and went into the men's room to wash his hands. When he did not emerge after ten minutes, his secretary sent in an aide, Tony Zecca, to check on the former mayor. After calling out a few times, "Mayor? Mayor? Frank!" Zecca entered the room to find his boss lying face down on the floor, unconscious. After paramedics failed to revive him, Rizzo was rushed to Thomas Jefferson Hospital, a few blocks away.

At 2:12 P.M., Frank L. Rizzo was pronounced dead of cardiac arrest, and the search for a new Republican candidate for mayor of Philadelphia began again.

PART II

The General Election

27 RIZZO IS DEAD

July 1991

❧ The day Frank Rizzo died, the media in Philadelphia were jolted out of a lethargy that had characterized the stultifyingly slow news summer. There had been the customary murders and fires for the TV stations to cover. There was the trial of the eighteen-year-old who had hacked at his teenage neighbor ninety-five times before finally killing her and Lenny Dysktra's return to the Phillies months after crashing his car while driving under the influence. The newspapers had been following Pennsylvania's attempts to pass a budget, and there was always the progress of the city's attempts to finance the new justice center. But none of these issues seemed to capture the imagination of the reporters in their desultory reports.

The mayor's race had been quiet as well. There was a brief difference of opinion over a city loan to build a new sports arena for the Sixers and Flyers. "The owners of those teams are zillionaires," Frank Rizzo was quoted as saying in an *Inquirer* story. "You can rest assured they're not going to get any money from me." But the story blew over within a day or two. Rizzo got more coverage for an antidrug march in a black neighborhood where he drew both endorsements and jeers. Rendell succeeded in getting the cameras out for a press conference with D.A. Lynn Abraham, where he attacked a court-ordered prison cap that was forcing release of criminals to avoid prison overcrowding. But each story blew in and out of the news like a quick summer thunderstorm. In early June, Rizzo went off on an uncharacteristic vacation to the Jersey Shore for ten days, and even Sal Paolantonio took off for a week at the beach in Avalon with his family.

The week Paolantonio returned, he had a hard time getting back in gear.

After the primary, he had been restless, bored by the lull in the action. He had missed the hectic, frenetic pace of the last weeks of the campaign and felt a letdown. "Political reporting is like having a mistress," he said one day a few weeks after the primary. "It's seductive. It's the same kind of sexual energy, the same kind of drive involved. You know it's bad for you, but it's a great temptation." Sexual energy was something that was on his mind these weeks after Rizzo's surprise victory, because his one consuming question about the coming campaign was the subject of sex. For years, there had been rumors about Ed Rendell and "womanizing," stories that went back to his time in the D.A.'s office. No one had ever gone on the record, even anonymously, to confirm any of the rumors, and yet the rumors persisted.

Now the question that consumed Sal Paolantonio was whether and how Rizzo would bring up the topic in the campaign and how he, Sal Paolantonio, could write about it. It was not so much that he thought a candidate's personal life had much bearing on what kind of mayor he'd be, although when pressed Paolantonio could make a case for what such "duplicitous" private behavior (as he called it) augured for a public official's conduct. It was more that Rizzo's playing the personal card, as he had with Ron Castille, could be the key strategic move in the election, and Paolantonio was determined to be out in front when it came to covering campaign strategy.

In June, he thought he might be able to do just that when he got wind of some new political activity. He learned that Rizzo's people, although not Rizzo himself, were peddling affidavits, just like the ones used to smear Castille, focusing on Rendell's relations with women. The affidavits were not given to him personally, but he heard that they had been sent to Tommie St. Hill of the *Philadelphia Tribune* and Chuck Stone, a columnist at the *Daily News*. For most of June, Paolantonio had worked to pin down the story about how Rizzo's people were trying to smear Rendell. He planned not to go into any of the charges made by the anonymous sources in the affidavits—affidavits he had not personally seen—but merely to state that the charges had to do with "indecent sexual activities." He had been researching Rendell's background for months and had not come up with a single, solitary piece of information that he could put into a news story to confirm any of the rumors about Rendell. But he thought it was a legitimate story that Rizzo's people were trying to smear Rendell by referring to the charges.

But while Sal Paolantonio had gotten the green light on just about every investigative and analytical piece he had conceived since the beginning of the campaign, when it came to this particular story he was stopped. One of his editors made it clear that the *Inquirer* didn't want this story. For the *Inquirer* to print a story about charges that, as far as they knew, were false was simply to give credence to the charges. If Rizzo had openly made the charges, that would have been different. Then the paper would have gone with the story because the allegations were coming from a public figure. But at this point the story was considered still too much in the realm of unsubstantiated rumor.

The *Daily News* had been after the story as well. Its journalists had also wondered how and when Rizzo might bring the matter into the campaign. Opinions were divided when it came to discussing a political candidate's personal life, particularly his relationships with women. Dave Davies had felt that a candidate's sexual affairs did not have much to do with what kind of mayor he'd make. On the other hand, if a candidate's sexual activities were such that they showed an extreme lack of self-control and poor judgment, then maybe they were a matter of public knowledge. That was his read on the Gary Hart case. Others at the *Daily News* had stronger opinions. At a dinner meeting of reporters and editors involved in the campaign coverage, one editor had said, "If there's going to be anything about politicians fucking, the *Daily News* had well better be out in front on it." And so they had pursued it, but had come up with little.

Paolantonio's concern with the story faded a bit after a week of relaxing and exercising at the Jersey shore, taking in a family barbecue in Manahawkin with his aunt and uncle, going off to see *Terminator II* with his wife one night when they got a babysitter to stay with the kids. When he came back, his mind was on bike rides with his three-year-old, Sarah, in back of him, how she looked up at him when he gave her a bath, and how much he was missing with his children with the late nights of covering politics. The only political story he wrote the first week back was about a comedy night for charity at which the mayoral candidates told jokes. It was to be Frank Rizzo's last public engagement.

But then Rizzo died, and the questions of how his campaign would attack Rendell and whether the personal attacks could ever be substantiated gave way to the pulsating excitement that had been missing since the primary. Rizzo in death managed to create the same kind of magical political energy, the same kind of wonderment and disbelief, that he did in life. Within an hour of learning of Rizzo's heart attack, the entire pack of reporters swarmed into Jefferson Hospital, where Rizzo had been rushed. All three local television stations broke into their regular programming to broadcast live from the hospital entrance, where Rizzo supporters began to gather, some to pay their last respects to the ex-mayor, some, it seemed, merely to give interviews to reporters about him. And one by one, the TV reporters let them speak their piece, giving testimony to the man who had meant so much to them and to so many in the audience and who was now unbelievably gone.

On that first afternoon, in the midst of the confusion and shock, most questions focused on Rizzo's health. It was revealed that the ex-mayor had diabetes and required daily shots of insulin. Channel 6's Vernon Odom asked Rizzo's top assistant, Sandy Fox, "Had there been any concerns about his health? I understand from a lot of people who didn't want to say it publicly that there were concerns about his heart condition?" Fox denied it, as others close to Rizzo would do in the following days. But the TV reporters felt no similar need to be discreet, describing, as they had failed to do before Rizzo's death, the obvious warning signs of the candidate's condition they had noticed in appearances in the previous few months: his excessive sweating, his wheezing at the Comedy Club, his need for help getting in and out of his car at the antidrug march. Not a word had been said in the media in the previous seven months that would have hinted that Frank Rizzo had any health problems that would affect his carrying out the job of mayor of Philadelphia. But now in the aftermath of his death, it was all pouring out.

The matter of politics, the question of who would replace Frank Rizzo as the Republican nominee, was handled gingerly by the TV stations in the hours immediately following his death. Jim Gardner apologized to his audience, "who are mourning very deeply the loss of Rizzo," before saying he thought it was not inappropriate to ask an elections expert what should happen next. "I hope this question does not offend you," he told his audience before interviewing Fred Voigt, carefully choosing his words, "but as all of you must know, this is a very important office." The law, Voigt explained, provided for a substitute candidate selection process. The Republican County executive committee would select the substitute candidate, and in Philadelphia that would boil down once again to one person: party boss Billy Meehan. The only limitations were that the person be a resident of the city for three years, over twenty-five years of age, a U.S. citizen—and not Ed Rendell. One of the anchors asked whether a candidate who had lost the Democratic primary, say Lu Blackwell, could be chosen. Anyone, Voigt answered.

But in the ensuing hours and days, politics took a backseat to the emotional outpourings that followed Frank Rizzo's death. TV anchor Larry Kane opened Channel 10's eleven o'clock newscast on July 16 by describing the flags at half-mast all over the city and the moment of silence observed by the Phillies at the game at Veterans Stadium. Reporter Meg

Grant was stationed at Rizzo's Chestnut Hill home, where friends and dignitaries were gathering to mourn the death. "Someone here tonight said, 'Frank would have loved this,'" noted Grant. Another reporter posted on Rosewood Street in South Philly, where Rizzo grew up, drew testimonials from people in the neighborhood. "He was a hero," said one man. "I've been followin' him since I was a kid. He always had an open door for the underdog. He was like a movie star. When people would see him he was like a magnet, he would attract people." A 91-year-old woman cried as she recalled young Frank running errands for the neighborhood butcher. "I'm shocked," she said. "I'll never get over it."

After several more reaction stories, from Rizzo's political opponents and supporters alike, Kane offered personal observations. "Over the years people would always ask me, what's he really like? And I would answer, what you saw was what you got. He did it his way, as Frank Sinatra would say, with no regrets. There was a side that few saw until later in his life. Amid the controversy, a wonderful warmth and love for people. Despite the controversies surrounding him, he was a pleasure to cover. And he had the most incredible sense of humor of any person I've met in this town in my life. It's something only a few people saw, until recently. Last week he joined the other candidates at a special comedy night, and that other side of him really came out." Then the tape rolled of Frank Rizzo, on the tiny stage of the Comedy Club, telling his joke.

> There once was a man named Rendell
> Whose ambition no one could quell
> He's got such a yen
> He's enrolled now at Penn
> Taking Campaign 101 with Burrell.

The crowd broke up and the tape stopped. In its place, a portrait of Frank Rizzo appeared on the screen inscribed with the dates "1920–1991."

The next morning's *Inquirer* featured a two-inch-high banner headline, "RIZZO IS DEAD." The newspaper was far less reticent than its TV counterparts in turning quickly to the political question. "Castille Seen as Likely Replacement in Election," was the headline of Sal Paolantonio's article, which was the other top story that day. "Pa. Politics Stunned a 3d Time," was the subhead. Paolantonio wrote: "Ronald D. Castille, the man Frank Rizzo defeated in the Republican primary for mayor, is his likely replacement on the November ballot, Republican officials said yesterday."

However, he also noted that "some GOP officials fear that Castille's selection would touch off a bitter war with Rizzo supporters and renew nagging questions about Castille's lackluster primary performance and his desire for the job." Later in the article he noted that "Castille ran perhaps the worst mayoral campaign that anyone in city politics remembers. . . . In public appearances he seemed nonchalant and unschooled in a key aspect of city government—finances, Rendell's strongest suit."

Paolantonio laid out Meehan's alternatives: Castille, who still had $30,000 left in his bank account, and Sam Katz, who was described as seeming "to catch fire at the end . . . but his latest campaign finance report shows he is more than $200,000 in debt from the primary. And Meehan may harbor resentment at Katz's refusal to get out of the primary and accept the endorsement for city council." He finished the story by suggesting that Meehan might choose a compromise candidate such as Councilman Brian O'Neill, Councilwoman Joan Specter, former city development official Joseph Egan, or Democrat Lucien Blackwell.

But even as Paolantonio went about his job, dispassionately laying out the likely scenarios to replace Frank Rizzo as Republican nominee for mayor, he was struck by a deep sense of loss, a loss that was both personal and professional. Since May 21, almost his every waking thought had been occupied with second-guessing the large and small elements of Frank Rizzo's strategy against Ed Rendell. He had been consumed with the question of whether Rizzo could possibly win against the long odds that faced him. And whether because he really believed it or because it simply would make the campaign that much more compelling for him to report, he had convinced himself that Rizzo could do it, that he was gaining credibility in the black community because of the crime issue. The Friday before Rizzo died, Paolantonio had covered the candidate's march with black antidrug leader Herman Wrice in West Philadelphia. Although he didn't get the sense of outright enthusiasm by the neighborhood for Rizzo, he hadn't gotten a sense of hostility, either. It was those little clues that he liked to pick up on and make his indicators, and the lack of hostility on that march said to Paolantonio that this was a turning point for Rizzo. Rizzo just might win it all or at least come within a few breathtaking points of catching Rendell. What an election that would be to cover, for a guy who had been given up for dead politically to make this kind of a comeback.

And then it was all snatched away, not just from the candidate and his devoted staff, but from the reporter who had covered the remarkable Rizzo campaign almost single-handedly from the beginning. All of Paolantonio's professional energies had been poised to spend the next four months answering the question of whether Rizzo could win, of whether the Big Bambino's wily and cunning strategies could defy these odds. He was as eager as anyone to see it all unfold and be the central person in describing the outcome. And now it was all gone. Like a nightmare that would forever torment him, he would never know whether Frank Rizzo would catch his rival and one last time capture the mayor's office. He would never see the game play itself out.

There was also a personal element that Paolantonio would almost not let himself admit, and because of the hectic pace of the next few weeks, covering who Billy Meehan would pick as the replacement candidate, he didn't have to think about much. But there was clearly a sense of personal loss for a man with whom Paolantonio could not help having developed a bond. Paolantonio would always remember the first time he had ever met Frank Rizzo. He had been thoroughly primed, having read all the clips and every book he could get his hands on about Rizzo. And then he met the man, almost on his first day on the job covering Philadelphia politics, February 5, 1990. There were rumors that Frank Rizzo would run for a fifth time for mayor of Philadelphia, and Sal Paolantonio had gone to check them out. What he had found had been a six-foot three-inch, 280-pound, barrel-chested guy, who had put his enormous hand on Paolantonio's shoulder while he looked him up and down. Paolantonio was thinking, thank God I've been in the Navy and I have my shoes polished, because he could see his face in Rizzo's shoes, that's how shiny they were. And Rizzo said to him, "I thought you were a little guy." *I thought you were a little guy.* How could he resist that? It was instant male bonding. It was amazing, Paolantonio thought, how this guy knew how to disarm a reporter.

Rizzo told Paolantonio that day he was indeed planning on running for mayor, and the story Paolantonio wrote about the decision made page 1, above the fold, the next day. His first day covering city politics in Philadelphia, Frank Rizzo had landed him in the premiere position in the paper. The next day Rizzo had been forced to deny that he was running for mayor, or else WCAU would have pulled him off the radio talk show he was hosting at the time. To keep that from happening, Rizzo went on TV and radio all over town saying he was not really running. Paolantonio had been sure his editors were going to make him write a retraction, tell him he'd screwed up. So he called Rizzo at ten o'clock the next morning.

"Mr. Mayor . . . "

"Call me Frank."

"You want me to retract the story?"

"No way," answered Rizzo. "We got these bastards on the run."

Paolantonio had eaten it up, even as he had told himself he had better really watch this guy, he was so good at charming reporters. He had known quite well that Rizzo, as the campaign went on, tried to stroke the sense that they had something in common, both being Italian-American. But even as he saw right through it, he couldn't help but respond to the Rizzo charm. And for months after he first heard the news of Rizzo's collapse, he would still feel sad.

Rizzo had a similar effect on many who had followed him in the media, and the coverage he got in the days after his death testified to the strong emotions he had evoked. The day after he died, the *Daily News* carried no headline on its front page, only a massive picture of Rizzo staring out at the camera with his thumb up. "Full Coverage and Special Photo Pullout Inside" was.all that was stated soberly on its cover. The headlines inside covered every aspect of Rizzo's life and death: " 'He Went Fast and Furious,' " "Larger than Life Rizzo is Dead at 70," "Not All Loved 'The Mayor,' " "Despite Vigor, Rizzo Bore Risk for Heart Attack," "He Was the City's Own Paul Bunyan," "The Life and Times," "Pals and Advisers Are Devastated," "Black Friends and Foes," "To Most Cops, Rizzo Was Tops," "Recollections of a Leader and Friend," "Quoth the Mayor, Never a Bore." The columnists, too, weighed in. Sandy Grady: "His death leaves a hole in the city"; Dan Geringer: "The guy was as real as real ever gets"; Jill Porter: "His presence was felt by all who knew him"; and Chuck Stone: "Rizzo wore new gloves but old voice heard."

Only one small story discussed the campaign: "Death Puts Campaign on Hold." "He's done it again, " wrote Dave Davies. "Even in death, Frank Rizzo has thrown Philadelphia politics into turmoil." Davies made it seem more uncertain who would succeed Rizzo, noting the split camp over Castille more strongly than Paolantonio had. His slant on Katz was similar to Paolantonio's: "Katz, the financial analyst who ran a self-made and strong campaign to finish third in the GOP primary, is another possibility, though most Republicans believe he would have a hard time winning Meehan's nod." But he added as Paolantonio had not: "Meehan has a history of laying aside old feuds and sometimes serving up surprises."

On July 18, Carmella Rizzo decided that her husband's casket would be open for a viewing at the Cathedral Basilica of Saints Peter and Paul, on the Benjamin Franklin Parkway in downtown Philadelphia. Three hours before the viewing was to begin, a line formed outside the cathedral, and eventually 14,000 people would withstand the 95 degree heat to file past Rizzo's casket. On Channel 6 that night, the "big story" was, in anchor Jim Gardner's words, "Philadelphia starting to say its goodbye to Frank Rizzo." The newscast opened with a live aerial view, taken from a helicopter, of the people winding around the block from the cathedral, standing in line for the chance to say farewell. While many of the city's dignitaries had come to pay their respects, the newscast captured many sound-bites from "the little people" to whom, it was said, "Frank Rizzo meant so much." One woman in line shook her head when the reporter asked for her reaction. "Where's the city gonna go now? We don't have anybody anymore." The long lines outside the cathedral, the emotion of the mourners, the pathos of the sudden death of the man perhaps best known in the entire area—it was a story made for local television, and local television was pulling out all the stops to cover it. The TV stations had beaten the newspapers to the momentous news that Frank Rizzo had died, and now they were beating them again by leading the public dirge for the fallen leader.

Two days after Rizzo's death, the *Inquirer* ran another front-page story about his possible replacement: "A Message to Meehan: Forget about Castille." Rizzo supporters had reacted to the story the day before with their own message, carefully relayed to the media by Marty Weinberg, Rizzo's closest political adviser for over twenty years. Weinberg was recommending that Sam Katz take Rizzo's place, but his statement did not make the *Inquirer*'s front page. Rather the lead talked about how "Rizzo supporters" were putting forth Weinberg's name. In the *Daily News* article that day, "Rizzo Pals Try to Cool Castille Fever," Katz made it to the second paragraph: "Martin J. Weinberg, Rizzo's campaign manager, put forward the name of Sam Katz, who finished a strong third behind Rizzo and Castille in the May 21 primary." Even after the primary, Katz seemed to get a better shake from the *Daily News* than from the *Inquirer.*

On Friday, July 19, Frank Rizzo's funeral mass was held inside the cathedral. At noon, his casket was lifted into a hearse, and his funeral procession began to move down the Parkway and to circle City Hall. Thousands of people lined the streets to watch the procession slowly move north on Broad Street to Holy Sepulchre Cemetery in Cheltenham Township. Channel 6 broadcast the funeral live, stationing its top reporters inside and outside the cathedral to report every detail of the outpouring of emotion that was Frank Rizzo's final farewell. Through the medium of television, Philadelphians shared a sense of sorrow and disbelief. The man who had been larger than life was dead.

28 By Unanimous Vote

August 1, 1991

❧ Although Frank Rizzo was laid to rest that Friday, the media—and particularly the television stations—seemed reluctant to let the saga end. It had been one of the biggest stories to hit Philadelphia since the MOVE disaster, and the local media had submerged themselves in every detail of Rizzo's life and death in the three days following his collapse. Television had been at the very center of the story, doing what it did best: putting drama and emotion on vivid and immediate display. But when all the pomp and circumstance was over, a vacuum was left. There was a sense that people wanted more of this story about the folk hero that was Frank Rizzo, more of the pathos and intensity that surrounded his sudden death in the midst of his final campaign. But with Rizzo dead and buried, there was only one real way to keep the story alive: by covering who would take his place. And so it was that, for however brief a moment, politics suddenly returned to being a big story on Philadelphia television newscasts.

The newfound respect for political coverage was nowhere more obvious than at Channel 10, the station that had largely ignored the candidates and the election during the last two months of the primary. And no one witnessed the abrupt change more clearly than anchor Larry Kane. Kane was something of a Philadelphia institution himself, a fixture on local television newscasts for over two decades, first as an anchor at Channel 6, and then, after a brief sojourn in New York, as top anchor at Channel 10 for over sixteen years. Kane had an intensity and magnetism that endeared him to his loyal viewers, a quality in his delivery that made him seem as if he were talking to each person individually, letting each one know whether this next story should make them laugh or cry. He also prided himself on being much more than a talking head or newsreader. He was at his best in times of emergency or tragedy when the newscast went live and he was called upon to report nonstop on breaking events and ever-changing news. Channel 10 was the one local station in 1985 to preempt prime-time entertainment shows to stay live with coverage of the MOVE bombing and the fire that had raged out of control as a result. Those involved in the reporting had won the Alfred I. DuPont Columbia University award for outstanding news coverage. It had been one of Larry Kane's finest hours.

Kane also regularly went out to cover stories, mostly about Philadelphia politics. Many of the stations liked to send their anchors out in the field from time to time to reinforce the anchor's image as a "serious journalist," and probably there was some of that at work when Larry Kane went out between 6:30 and 11:00 to catch a ward leaders' meeting or a party policy confab. But it was also true that he loved Philadelphia politics and liked to keep his hand in. He had even pioneered a feature on the news, called "The Political Notebook," which reported tidbits of political gossip about who might run for what and what their chances were likely to be. Kane had been happy in his many years at Channel 10, the CBS affiliate. The station was known for years as the intellectual ghetto of local news in the market—the station that had the longest pieces with the most depth and explanation—and Larry Kane had liked that just fine.

But in 1990, when general manager Steve Cohen was forced out, Kane watched with dismay the new direction taken by Cohen's replacement, Gene Lothery, and his news director, Drew Berry, in their quest to make Channel 10 a closer contender with market leader Channel 6. To the new management, news decisions had to be business decisions, bottom-line oriented, made with a clear understanding of who the audience was and what they wanted. Berry knew that only 23 percent of his audience lived in the city of Philadelphia, while 27 percent lived in New Jersey, 7 percent in Delaware, and the remainder in the Pennsylvania suburbs. While he realized that sometimes campaign news could be interesting even to people who weren't voting in an election, he believed that the more "insider" the news coverage, the more likely noncity residents would be turned off. And you don't want 80 percent of your audience sampling the competition, he would say, particularly as the choices of what they could sample were increasing. To Berry, Larry Kane's "Political Notebook" was just too much inside information—nobody knew what he was talking about—and in Berry's mind, the feature did not serve the viewer whatsoever. What viewers wanted, their market research showed, was more health and consumer reports, more on how to stay safe.

But to Larry Kane, the new direction was both a big mistake and an abdication of journalistic responsibility. He thought it was the dirty little secret of local television news that without much fanfare stations like Channel 10 were virtually eliminating their coverage of politics and government. And it was even worse to watch it happen, given what Channel 10 used to be: a first-rate newscast. What's more, he thought they were wrong. They might think their market research was gospel, but he had been in TV news and in Philadelphia long enough to know that it was not always reliable. A new format might win raves from twelve people sitting around a conference table, but it was hardly guaranteed to drive ratings points up a single point when the Nielsen people started measuring. And Larry Kane knew that Philadelphians loved politics, especially the kind of local political stories that involved Frank Rizzo.

Although the signs were clear in 1990, it was the 1991 mayoral campaign that became particularly painful for Kane to endure. He had seen early on that this primary was going to be a big story and that Philadelphians were going to eat it up. But his station was refusing to cover anything but the most grandiose of media events surrounding the election. All through the primary Kane had argued with the higher-ups about their decision to ignore the campaign. If only for Rizzo's amazing personality, he would say, they should be covering it. But he lost each battle. Eventually they even eliminated his "Political Notebook." But then Rizzo had died, and the reaction of the city was a spectacle that even out-of-town station management could not ignore. Finally, they got the message, Kane would think. Frank Rizzo's death was clearly the biggest story to hit the market in years, and they would be fools if they ignored it. And so, although a month before the primary election the station had averaged some thirty-seven seconds of campaign coverage across its three daily newscasts, now, after Rizzo's death, a new commitment to political coverage seemed to overtake them. They began to cover the replacement process not in thirty-second pieces based on press releases or cribbed from the newspapers, but with real reporters doing packages over a minute in length. And finally, Larry Kane got the green light to do some of his own reporting on the campaign.

Kane was fairly well connected in political circles in Philadelphia. He got calls constantly from people who hoped they might spin him to put this or that item in his "Political Notebook," and he had particularly good sources in the Republican party. And to the people Kane talked to, there was one strong and logical replacement to Frank Rizzo: Sam Katz. The week after Rizzo died, Kane did a story using file footage of Rizzo's last appearance on Kane's public affairs show, when the ex-mayor had talked about Sam Katz following in his footsteps. "I will support Sam Katz if I am around after this four years for anything he runs for," Rizzo had said. Kane added a note of his own: "A lot of politicians think that Sam Katz could defeat Ed Rendell because of his appeal to Democratic voters." All through the primary there had been talk of how much support Katz had in various segments of the Philadelphia population, notably among center-city liberals and the Jewish population but that those people were mainly registered Democrats. Kane was the only reporter who noted the strength that support could give Katz if he were the candidate in the general election.

Kane's use of Rizzo's own words on a choice for his successor was particularly important since it came on the heels of the tremendous public outpouring of emotion that had been so vividly played out on television. The irony was that a few months earlier these same TV stations were talking daily about how "ugly" the primary campaign had become because of Rizzo's unsubstantiated personal attacks. Their reporters had reveled in getting people on the street to talk with disdain about Frank Rizzo's "Gestapo tactics." But now, with his death, the man was transformed into a saint. Yes, it was noted, not everybody "agreed with him," but suddenly the line that captured the television sound-bite mentality and was heard again and again was "Agree with him or not, you had to admit that he loved Philadelphia."

Frank Rizzo in death was being exploited by the media just as surely as he had been exploited in life. He was turned into a local hero in a metropolis which didn't have all that many candidates for the title, outside of a winning quarterback or basketball star, and it was being accomplished by burying all recent memories of Rizzo that would have struck a harsher note. The dirty politics, the unsubstantiated charges that his opponent was a drunk and a mental case, were all forgotten. The folk hero and champion of the little people was the image that had been conjured up for his funeral and that lived on with the coverage of the replacement process.

The Rizzo campaign staff were prepared to use the media's exploitation to do a little exploiting themselves. They were determined to have some say in Rizzo's replacement and in the question of who became the next mayor of Philadelphia, and they would do so by relying on the revisionist view of Frank Rizzo that the local media were supplying. The Rizzo forces would use the sympathetic news coverage to their own ends. The only problem was a three-way split in the Rizzo camp over who would best carry forth Frank's legacy—the man he himself had said he backed, Sam Katz, the man who had been the political force behind him for twenty years, Marty Weinberg, or a man who actually had the Rizzo name and same row-house character, Frank's brother Joe, a former Philadelphia fire commissioner.

Sal Paolantonio wrote a story about how Joe Rizzo might be the best candidate, since he could play on the sympathy aroused by Frank's death. Certainly, the TV stations had seemed only too happy to cover Joe Rizzo's candidacy, mainly because it continued the melodramatic theme. Emotional stories were always an easier sell to TV news than cerebral ones, and Joe Rizzo was clearly the emotional choice. All the better when it was revealed that Joe Rizzo had prostate cancer, since then the TV stations could portray him as the man with "two battles."

While touting Joe Rizzo, Paolantonio mentioned little about Sam Katz and ignored a poll taken by KYW-TV and KYW Newsradio that had asked viewers to call in who they thought should be the Republican nominee. The response, reported on KYW's newscast, was said to be "surprising": 53 percent chose Katz, as compared to 13 percent for Castille, 11 percent for Joe Rizzo, and less than 5 percent for other candidates, including Joe Egan, the compromise candidate from the business community. The poll was hardly scientific. It relied on people calling in voluntarily, and the station noted that all of Joe Rizzo's votes came within an hour, suggesting a concerted effort to get his name bandied around. Also, response was not limited to city voters, since the TV station reached a wide suburban audience.

But still KYW's poll revealed one thing reporters wrote little about: Katz had built up a terrific TV image and outstanding name recognition from the primary, and when television news asked who should be the candidate, its viewers said Sam Katz. Ron Castille had come out of the primary only a thousand votes behind Rizzo, but his image to the population of television viewers had been battered. He was the man who had everything going for him, including party support, but he had blown it. His television image was that of a man who had stooped to fighting back dirty against Rizzo, who was never seen talking about issues, a man who seemed to take the election for granted and wasn't hustling enough—a man who, with all the advantages, had lost.

Katz, on the other hand, had come out of the primary in third place but smelling like roses. On television, he had been the candidate who had bucked the machine, who had stayed in the race because he loved his city so much, the man who had stood "above the fray" against Rizzo and Castille and had always been talking about how much money he could save the city. Before Rizzo's death, the ex-mayor's campaign staff had been amazed at the favorable/unfavorable ratings Katz had shown up with in their polls following the election—still along the lines of fifty-one to nine. They were unbelievable popularity ratings for a man who had just lost an election, particularly a man who had come in third. But he had come in third with 28 percent of the vote in an election in which he had been predicted to capture little more than 5 percent—with no machine backing him.

On July 22, the *Inquirer*'s editorial board endorsed Katz, with the headline "For Katz—Again" and the columnists began to weigh in. Steve Lopez of the *Inquirer* wrote a column called "The Billy Boys Blunder Onward." After knocking Billy Meehan for his choice of Castille first time around ("This was the right choice, given Meehan's track record, because Castille didn't have any qualifications, any plans, or any desire"), he turned to the people who had been named as possible successors to Frank Rizzo. "They don't have a prayer. Not one of them could beat Ed Rendell in November." He went on: "There's only one question the Republicans need to ask themselves: Who would Rendell least want them to pick? The answer is Sam Katz." As support, he described the factors in Katz's favor, from the "moral victory" of his strong showing in the primary and his financial expertise, to the fact that he could pull Democratic voters and he really salivated for the job.

Clark DeLeon, another *Inquirer* columnist, wrote a piece called "The Candidate: Why Not the Dead?" DeLeon suggested that, at any minute, Abraham Lincoln was going to be touted out as the Republican replacement candidate. "What do you mean, 'But he's dead?!' How can that matter when you look at the list of stiffs being touted by Republican power (hah) brokers in this anyone-but-Katz backroom primary?" DeLeon gave voice to the theory that Billy Meehan didn't really want to win general elections with his candidates, since that might screw up his lock on patronage jobs. "Run Sam Katz and Meehan risks the possibility that voters might actually pay attention to the mayor's race. Run Sam Katz and Philadelphia might suffer an interesting—gasp!—mayoral campaign, one marked by differing ideas rather than different promises, one in which the candidates are willing to discuss the painful options facing an overburdened city desperate for leadership.

> Run Sam Katz and Meehan risks a real race.
> Run Sam Katz and Meehan risks making sense.
> So what are the odds on that?
> (I've got a fiver riding on Lincoln.)

Inquirer cartoonist Tony Auth added his biting wit to the commentary with a cartoon showing a giant elephant wearing a large "Katz '91" banner on it, surrounded by tiny, blindfolded party hacks saying, "It feels like a Weinberg to me," and "I still think it's a Castille," and "It's a Joe Rizzo," "It is Joe Egan." The cartoon seemed to typify the columnists' feelings. With all these stories about who Meehan was considering picking, why wasn't the obvious choice, Sam Katz, being taken seriously? In one last column before Meehan picked his candidate, Lopez tried again. He said he had called Katz that week to see if he knew why he was so low on the list. Lopez decided it was because Katz played classical music on his phone while people were holding for him. And possibly because all of the people Lopez had interviewed found him smart, competent, and possessed of a knack for taking complicated fiscal matters and explaining them to the layman. That, Lopez concluded, made him all wrong for the city of hacks.

That same Sunday, in his weekly column, "Path to City Hall," Sal Paolantonio included an item that documented the Katz fervor. He wrote:

"Although Sam Katz said early last week that he was not 'campaigning at all' to replace Rizzo as the Republican mayoral nominee, by the end of the week he admitted he was lobbying ward leaders for Meehan's roll call vote Thursday.

"And Rizzo campaign aides supporting Katz made available data from the last Rizzo-Rendell poll conducted three weeks ago by Fabrizio and McLaughlin of Alexandria, Va. The poll showed 51 percent of the 500 voters interviewed had a favorable rating of Katz. Only 11 percent had an unfavorable rating—giving Katz an unheard-of 5–1 ratio in voter preference.

"More important, the same preference rating showed up among Democrats and among blacks—the two segments of the city electorate needed for a Republican victory.

"Another poll taken by a top fundraiser in the city after Rizzo died showed Katz would give Rendell a serious challenge. But top Democrats say Rendell, after he learned of the results, successfully lobbied to stop public release of the poll.

"Katz polled well elsewhere: In one out of three of the GOP ward leaders meetings chaired by Meehan last week, Katz won the straw vote. But before the ward leaders vote Thursday, Meehan will make his recommendation. That's one count Meehan's never lost."

But, as with most positive items about Sam Katz, the information was buried at the end of Paolantonio's column, the last of five items. The column itself was headlined, "Longstreth in '55, '71, and Maybe '91," with its first item about the suggestion that City Councilman Thacher Longstreth might make a "viable compromise candidate." Once again, Sam Katz had been buried by Sal Paolantonio.

But this time around it didn't matter much since the decision was up to

Billy Meehan, not the voters of Philadelphia. And Billy Meehan had never really seemed to care much what the *Inquirer* said about politics. (The old saw was that he liked to read the *Inquirer* because he made sure to do the opposite of whatever the paper said.) But Billy Meehan didn't have to care much about the *Inquirer.* He was not courting public opinion. Running a city might mean paying exquisite attention to what the editorial pages and columnists and TV anchors were saying about this or that, but running a big-city political machine was a very different story. Machine politics had to do with a whole web of complex deals—for support, for jobs, for contracts, for votes—and those deals were left pretty much untouched by the media. As a result, on this most central question facing the city of Philadelphia—the choice of a candidate who could be the next mayor—the media and public opinion would play no role. If other issues were more important to Billy Meehan than winning the election, then his decision would be untouched by the news stories and editorials, by the columns and cartoons.

And so, when the Republican ward leaders met to choose a replacement for Frank Rizzo on August 1 at Palumbo's restaurant in South Philadelphia, they followed the lead of a man over whom the media and public opinion had little influence. Although many of the ward leaders were privately supporting Sam Katz and were disgruntled at the performance of Meehan's last choice, Ron Castille, they nevertheless followed the boss's pick one more time. Deals meant more to ward leaders than the media and public opinion, any day of the week. By unanimous vote, they selected Joseph M. Egan, a developer and former head of the city's industrial development agency, to be their candidate for mayor.

29 The Search for Scandal

August 29, 1991

❦ The summer was drawing to a close. Joe Egan had been running for mayor for close to a month, but his campaign had created little excitement in the media. On the day Egan was selected, Sal Paolantonio broke a story that Egan's campaign manager had an apparent conflict of interest since he was serving as a member of a new state authority overseeing the city's finances. The story had precipitated the man's resignation and sent the campaign scurrying around for a new manager. Since then, the mayoral campaign front had been quiet.

But now Paolantonio had come across something that might cause bigger waves. He had found out about two audits of the Philadelphia Industrial Development Corporation (PIDC) by the U.S. Department of Housing and Urban Development (HUD). The audits had been carried out in 1986 and 1988, when PIDC was headed by Joe Egan. PIDC used federal community development dollars to make low-interest business loans and subsidize land purchases, with the aim of helping businesses create new jobs or retain existing jobs in the city. Paolantonio had learned that HUD had found problems with PIDC's claims about the numbers of low- and moderate-income jobs that had been created using federal dollars.

Paolantonio was working on a story about the audits for the Sunday paper, and on Thursday, August 29, he was going to interview Mayor Goode about the matter. A few hours before his interview he sat in the newsroom, feeling a bit down, despite the prospect of another investigative coup. Partly the feeling had to do with covering the Egan-Rendell campaign. Egan was likable and friendly and accessible to reporters, but the campaign was nothing like the primary and nothing like the fast-paced excitement of the Rizzo replacement process. Although he was trying to keep an open mind about Egan, Paolantonio had felt that for the last month the man was in over his head, that he wasn't quite engaged in the issues or the campaign. But it was early. Maybe the guy would still turn it around.

Somewhat listlessly, he traced out what Egan had to do to win, as he had so many times before sketched out candidates' strategies. Egan had to keep hammering away at Rendell, to make him look like an opportunist who was shifting his positions to mollify different segments of the city. Egan had to raise an awful lot of money, much more than he'd raised so far. And he had to hope that the new registration figures which had come out that day, showing huge numbers of people being purged from voter registration rolls, held true and that the Democratic party wouldn't start a massive registration drive.

But still the scenario of an Egan win felt farfetched. As disenchanted as Philadelphians were with the current Democratic mayor and city council members and as eager as they were for someone new to come in and clean it all up, Egan would have a hard time running as an "outsider." He had worked in city government under many a Democratic administration and he had been handpicked by the Republican party boss. And then there was the matter of the second congressional district election for an interim replacement for Bill Gray. Gray had shocked Philadelphians and the nation in June by announcing that he would be stepping down from Congress to take over as head of the United Negro College Fund. It was not yet decided whether the election for an interim replacement for Gray would be held on November 5, with the mayoral election, or at a later date. But if the congressional election were held the same day, the black vote would be reenergized. And the black vote in Philadelphia was overwhelmingly Democratic.

Paolantonio was not yet giving up on the story of city politics, however. He still clung to the notion that in the next couple of months two important stories would unfold. One would be about the enormous vacuum created by the deaths of Senator John Heinz and Frank Rizzo, the resignation of Bill Gray, and the departure of Wilson Goode from city politics. Who would fill the vacuum left by those major figures? Who would have the ability to unify the split black vote on the Democratic side and the different factions that had developed on the Republican side? And then, the campaign itself could be a really good story to tell. What would happen over the next few months? Would voters get excited? Would they feel energized by these people? It would be fascinating, Paolantonio seemed to want to convince himself, to tell these stories.

But even as he tried to come up with ideas to make election coverage more compelling, he knew it would be an uphill battle. And part of that had to do with the enormous changes going on at the paper itself. Not only was the design changing, including a more "reader-friendly" layout for the front page, but the focus was changing as well, away from the city and out toward the suburbs. As bizarre and entertaining as city politics was this year, still it just didn't fit in with where the paper wanted to be going. Softer coverage was the aim, he thought, soft features on the front page about sidewalks leading nowhere in the suburbs or a dog park in West Philadelphia. He couldn't help but wonder what those stories were doing on the front page. It wasn't that he thought he hadn't gotten good enough play for his political stories. He had gotten great play. But in the overall scheme of things, he knew what he was covering was not central to the change the paper was undergoing. For him to keep up, he had to push, push, push and run very hard, because basically no one was pulling him along. He felt as if he had been on a different track than everybody else.

And then there was the flux in editors. In the last four or five weeks of the primary, during the final descent when he was the busiest, city editor Bill Marimow was negotiating to become the *Inquirer*'s assistant publisher, and assistant city editor Will Sutton was negotiating with two different newspapers for new positions. There had been times at night when he couldn't even find Sutton to edit his stories. It was very frustrating for him. It wasn't that he hadn't had enormous leeway and support. Even though he knew the paper had gotten complaints about his stories from people in the campaigns, there hadn't been a peep of disapproval from his editors. But every reporter needed some guidance and editing. As convinced as he was that he understood what was going on in the campaign, he still felt he needed feedback. There had always been a balance between independence and guidance, but he was feeling that the paper had really gone adrift overall.

He looked up at the clock on the newsroom wall. It was time to leave for the interview with Mayor Goode about Joe Egan and the HUD audits. Although Paolantonio approached the interview with his usual dogged perseverance, it was clear that he was feeling somewhat disengaged. A few months back, he had been relishing every day of the mayoral primary coverage, but today the enthusiasm was nowhere to be seen. Frank Rizzo was dead and the prospect for a tumultuous political contest was gone. While earlier in the year he had anticipated with excitement the prospect of covering the presidential election in 1992 for the *Inquirer,* now he wasn't sure where he'd go after the mayoral election. "Whatever pays me the most money," he said dispiritedly, as he headed for City Hall.

He arrived early at the mayor's second-floor suite and waited until he was called into Goode's office. Although it was a scorchingly hot August day outside, in the inner sanctum the atmosphere was cool and dark, the drapes closed against the sun, the room lit with artificial light. Goode greeted Paolantonio from a chair at a highly polished round conference table. Beside him were his press secretary, Karen Warrington, and another aide. The mayor himself was looking thin and dapper, having lost several pounds since he first took office, and he was dressed in a fashionable double-breasted suit. He had even taken to sporting a small mustache in the last few months. Goode greeted Paolantonio affably.

"My apologies about that interview we did last week never making it into the paper," Paolantonio started out. "They decided to devote the whole review and opinion section to the coup in the Soviet Union, so my column got moved to the metro section and I had to cut it."

Goode listened noncommittally. "What interview?" he said.

"We did an interview last week about the congressional election? Never mind," he laughed. And then he launched into the real purpose of the interview.

"How would you characterize Joe Egan's performance at PIDC?" he asked Goode. As mayor, Goode had been Joe Egan's boss when Egan headed PIDC. In fact, Goode had been largely responsible for bringing Egan to the position in 1985. But they had had a falling out a few years later over the issue of minority set-asides. It was in the aftermath of that dispute that Egan became a Republican, and now the two men were on opposite sides of the political fence. Goode was a loyal Democrat and solidly in Ed Rendell's camp. It was unlikely that he would have much to say in Egan's defense.

"He was always a good operative, a good bureaucrat," began Goode without hesitation. He was sucking on a hard candy and did not stop for the interview. "He knew how to move paper from one point to the next point.

"He knew how to put deals together, to put all the pieces together so you had a deal that would work. He was a good technocrat. What Joe Egan was not was an overall visionary. He was not someone who was able to look at the city as a whole and know how his piece fit in with all the other pieces. He knew what his job was and did his job and got done what was needed.

"I would characterize his tenure at PIDC as more of the same as in the past, nothing extraordinary under his tenure. He kept PIDC running. Essentially the agency runs if you have a good technocrat."

Paolantonio took some documents from his bag. "Let me bring to your attention these documents, which claim that PIDC was not filling the federal requirements for low- and moderate-income jobs created under federal programs," he said.

Goode responded immediately. "I don't think Joe Egan or anyone at PIDC ever had as a goal the creation of low- and moderate-income jobs. I always saw PIDC as concerned about the total numbers, how many jobs they could say they created and take to their board. I heard no discussion by anyone at PIDC about creating jobs for low- and moderate-income persons. There is no question in my mind that the HUD assessment was accurate." Goode had not hesitated in response to the reporter's question. It was almost as if he had been briefed prior to the interview and knew precisely what he wanted to say to slam Egan.

Paolantonio continued. "They also questioned the accuracy of the numbers of jobs that were created."

"I don't think anybody will ever know that. Some of what PIDC did with numbers was a game, a game of smoke and mirrors. I raised questions, how can you verify these numbers? And a second question I raised was, how could you go back a year later and see if what people said was done, was done? How long did these people stay employed? That kind of analysis was not taking place."

"Was there any specific instance of minority set-asides you had a problem with?"

"I had a major problem with Joe Egan when I issued the executive order in 1988 to extend the set-aside order to quasi public agencies. Every agency but PIDC agreed. Egan didn't agree. My respect and confidence in Joe Egan diminished considerably based on the fact that he was getting federal funds for a major part of his program. The fact that he did not go out on his own and establish an affirmative action program, the fact that he would challenge my order, was outrageous. The way it was done was disloyal and insubordinate in my view."

"Should voters in the black community take that into consideration when evaluating Joe Egan?"

"Joe Egan should be rejected by the black community because the case of the set-aside program is an indication of his true feelings. When he had no reason to resist, even if he didn't believe in it himself, the fact that he resisted is an indication of where he stands. I would urge others who believe in affirmative action and set-asides to do likewise and not vote for him."

Paolantonio had exactly what he wanted. "Thank you very much," he said and stood up to go. In one half-hour, the mayor had given the reporter just what he needed for his story: criticism of the candidate and how that criticism might play with black voters. But the encounter was as interesting for the questions that were not asked as for those that were. It was the mayor who was responsible for approving the use of HUD money for city economic development programs, and it was the mayor's commerce department and commerce director who were directly responsible for monitoring the agency's compliance with federal regulations. If PIDC had not intended to create low- and moderate-income jobs, why hadn't the mayor taken action to change the situation? But clearly, those questions were not the purpose of the interview.

The mayor stood up to shake his hand. "So how are you?"

"Good. How about you?"

"I could be better," said Goode. "I could be making more money." Paolantonio laughed.

Goode continued, "So how are you enjoying the campaign?"

"I was just saying that it could be interesting to watch the rebuilding process in the city's leadership after the events of this year." Paolantonio turned the questions back to Goode. "Henry Nicholas is going for Egan," he said, referring to the president of the city's hospital workers' union. "You think any of the other unions will go for him?"

"They'd be crazy if they did. I don't see how he can win."

"Can Henry carry his union, or is it just him?"

"I doubt he can carry the union."

"And the Teamsters? Morris hates Rendell. He'd never go for him."

"He might go for him," said Goode. "We're still working on him."

"Have you seen the purge rolls yet?" Paolantonio was writing a story for the next day on how many people had been struck from city voter registration rolls this summer because they hadn't voted in the last five elections. "There were 190,000 voters purged."

"How many Democrats are left?" asked the mayor.

"Five hundred thousand."

Goode looked genuinely surprised. "Back when I ran in 1983, there were 800,000 Democrats."

"People aren't voting."

"Do you have the racial breakdown?"

"Black men were the highest of the numbers purged, followed by white men. Women are voting more regularly."

"They were always my best voters," Goode said, "Older women, over fifty."

"That's because they listen to Mary Mason," Paolantonio said, referring to the host on one of the city's key black radio talk shows.

Goode rolled his eyes. "Good-bye, Sal."

His press secretary echoed the thought. "He always overstays his welcome."

Paolantonio headed back to the paper. All he needed was Joe Egan's response now, and he'd have his story for the Sunday paper.

Joe Egan had started out his mayoral campaign with a flush of excitement. That summer night at Palumbo's restaurant, when he was formally selected by the Republican ward leaders as the nominee, he had delivered a speech so fiery it made the memory of Frank Rizzo seem pale. "You're gonna see the strongest and swiftest fourteen-week campaign in the history of Philadelphia," he had shouted to the cheering crowd. "And I'm gonna bring home a victory for the Republican party!"

The night at Palumbo's was the high point of a distinguished career. A product of a working-class Philadelphia neighborhood, Joe Egan had started out in real estate but moved quickly to a position of authority in the city's redevelopment authority. As deputy commerce director under Mayor Rizzo, he had led the efforts to bring the aircraft carrier Saratoga to the Philadelphia Naval Shipyard for repairs. As president of PIDC under Mayor Goode, he had successfully lobbied the state legislature in Harrisburg for funding for the city's new convention center. He was a development official who had gained the respect of private developers and city agency workers alike, known as a man who had command of the details of development work, a man who knew how to close a deal.

In 1988, he had left the public sector to return to commercial real estate, and two years later he accepted an offer to run as a Republican for an at-large seat on city council in the 1991 primary. With the party's backing, he had won the nomination and was headed for an almost certain win to a council seat when Billy Meehan had convinced him to take Frank Rizzo's place. It was in Egan's nature to accept. "Ask my sons what I'm about," he would say, "and they'll tell you what I always tell them. I believe in doing things, in leaving this earth a better place than I found it. And I believe in loyalty. The party asked me to run. I had to accept." Of course, there were other reasons. A man with Egan's experience in city government couldn't help but get a thrill at the thought of being the top dog and running the show. And no one with a healthy ego could turn down an offer to run for mayor of the nation's fifth largest city.

But when, on August 30, he got the call from Sal Paolantonio about the HUD audits, the excitement of stepping into the mayor's race gave way to pure rage. He'd gotten the call on a Friday afternoon, and when he heard Paolantonio's question, he responded that he'd like to have a chance to go over the documents. Unlike Wilson Goode, who, as a seasoned politician, had developed the ability to respond to a reporter's questions without hesitation (and who seemed to be completely familiar with the audits Paolantonio was investigating), Egan was still in the habit of briefing himself before responding to questions about a complex issue. In his years at PIDC, the agency had been audited any number of times by any number of agencies—every federal agency that gave the city money conducted yearly audits. And so he asked for time to go over the documents and reacquaint himself with the issues. But he heard Paolantonio say, "I want your response now. Either talk to me, or I'll do the article without your comment." (Paolantonio would claim that he had made two calls to Egan's campaign staff earlier in the week to get in touch with Egan and had made clear to them that he was writing a story about the HUD audits but that he was put off by Egan's staff until Friday afternoon.)

Egan couldn't believe what Paolantonio was choosing to focus on about his tenure at PIDC. He was proud of his record at PIDC. Yes, he had used HUD money for some of his programs to make loans to businesses, but it was money that came back to the agency, that revolved and revolved. And that money created jobs, lots of them. You only had to look at PIDC's record when he headed the agency to know that it was impeccable, Egan would say, impeccable. He had called companies in. He had said to them, "Hey, listen fellahs, what happens if we get audited by GAO and they find your numbers aren't right? They could put you in jail." He made them toe the mark. Why wasn't Paolantonio looking at any of that?

And then Paolantonio should have known, he thought, that there were always political forces that lay behind these audits. There were housing interests in the city who watched PIDC get all this HUD money and saw how well they were administering it, and the housing people were having a tough time administering their money. To Egan, that was completely understandable, because housing was a tough and complex business. But because you're doing so well, you become the guy who sticks his head above the water, you're the big agency, the chamber of commerce agency, so you have housing interests always aiming at you, a lot of jealousy. But if people went to HUD and looked at all the agency's audits, they would have seen that professional integrity and performance had always been his hallmark. And Paolantonio knew that, Egan thought. He had to know what a good reputation PIDC had under Egan. To have this reporter want to take one and a half seconds of his career and portray him as incompetent—it was unbelievable. But not knowing what else to do, Egan talked that Friday afternoon, trying to defend himself.

That Sunday, Sal Paolantonio's story about Joe Egan and PIDC ran in the *Inquirer*. It did not make page 1, but that was not surprising since most readers would not even know what PIDC was, much less understand that part of its charge was to create jobs for low- and moderate-income people. The story ran instead on the first page of the metro section, with the headline "PIDC Criticized by Auditors When Egan Headed Agency." It began: "When Republican mayoral candidate Joseph M. Egan was president of the Philadelphia Industrial Development Corp. federal auditors twice accused the agency of overstating the number of jobs it had created, and of failing to urge companies here to hire poor and middle-income people." It reported that in 1986 and 1988, HUD had asked the Goode administration to "suspend its economic development programs run by PIDC until the problems cited by HUD auditors were corrected." It noted, before the jump, that even though the city's commerce department responded to the first audit by claiming to correct the problems, a HUD 1988 audit had found the same problem. The audit was quoted as stating, "Sixty-two percent of the transactions which were funded . . . have actually provided no benefits to low- and moderate-income persons."

Egan's response, as described in the article, was that the HUD criticisms were "nitpicking." He noted that during his tenure as head of the agency, PIDC had arranged for $71 million in loans, with only a 2 percent loan failure rate, as compared with a national average for similar agencies of 22 percent. The audits, he claimed, were "not a major problem." But in the lengthy article his response got lost, followed as it was by Goode's criticism of Egan's affirmative action record. Though Egan once again defended his record, claiming that he resisted the set-aside rule being applied to the private portion of agency projects, the defense seemed weak.

Late in the article there were comments from unnamed officials in the Goode administration that the HUD audits were merely a sign of the national agency trying to tighten its control over local development agencies in the 1980s and there was praise for Egan's tenure at PIDC by a former city commerce director. But it was typical of much investigative journalism that the apparent scandal was played high in the story, while the consideration of the official's overall performance was buried. This was not a story about Egan's success in job creation, or his handling of low-interest loans, or his ability to make development deals. It was a story about an apparent scandal in a candidate's past.

Although the story did not make the front page and was never picked up by television, it was in its own small way a turning point in the campaign. Joe Egan was proud of his record at PIDC, and here this reporter had come along and taken what Egan considered a completely routine audit and turned it around to make it seem like Watergate. Egan had tried to refute the story as honestly as he could: pointing to his major accomplishments at PIDC and trying to show how unimportant was the audit.

But to no avail. The story seemed to press a button in Egan that would influence his relationship with reporters for the rest of the campaign. The reporters—or at least Sal Paolantonio—seemed just out to get him.

It was not until almost two months later, a few short weeks before the election, that anyone questioned the claims made in the story. And that person was not Joe Egan or any other member of his campaign staff, but another reporter, Dave Davies of the *Daily News*. When Davies first read Paolantonio's article, his heart sank. Beaten again, he thought, a sentiment shared by his editors. They decided not to bother following the story that week but to go into it when they did their Egan profile later in the campaign. And so in October, as part of his research on Egan's tenure at PIDC, Dave Davies acquired the HUD audits and monitoring letters Paolantonio had written about. In a document dated May 2, 1988, he found the complaint cited in the *Inquirer* story.

Although it did not jump out at Davies, the statement Paolantonio had quoted in his story left out an important phrase. A May 1988 letter from the HUD regional officer to the city stated, *"The information reported in the Grantee Performance Report indicates* that as many as 62 percent of economic development transactions in the city funded by the federal government provided no benefits to low- and moderate-income persons."* The first nine words in that sentence may have seemed trivial to Paolantonio, but they conveyed a different message than the reporter's quote. HUD was not making an assertion that 62 percent of the transactions had not benefitted low- and moderate-income persons. The agency was claiming that the documentation provided by the city was not sufficient to establish that goals were met. In the world of government programs that was an essential distinction, but Paolantonio had ignored it.

Davies came to a sentence that did catch his attention. The 1986 and 1988 HUD audits "focused on transactions that were funded in fiscal year 1985 or earlier years." In other words, the transactions they monitored had been completed in earlier years and were merely being reported in the 1986 and 1987 performance reports. The timing of the transactions was crucial to the point of Paolantonio's story. Egan did not become president of PIDC until late in 1985, well into fiscal year 1986. The transactions causing concern to HUD had been completed before Egan was president, Davies realized.

Davies read further and stopped again. The "transactions" that HUD was criticizing for not producing enough low- and moderate-income jobs were not solely PIDC transactions but those of several other agencies. In fact, he saw that only 149 of 613 transactions cited by HUD were PIDC's. The rest were carried out by other city economic development agencies, namely, the

Philadelphia Citywide Development Corporation and the Council for Labor and Industry. Yet Paolantonio's article had only mentioned PIDC, creating the impression that HUD had found that 62 percent of PIDC's transactions had not met their job goal. A more accurate statement would have been that PIDC failed to document the low- and moderate-income benefits for 42 percent of its transactions.

To Davies, the message was clear: Paolantonio's article criticized Egan for the performance of PIDC before he had been at the helm, and the criticism itself misstated the complaint about PIDC.

There wasn't a whole lot Davies could do with the information. He used it in his article, but not until the twenty-second paragraph. He wrote "By the mid-'80s, the U.S. Department of Housing and Urban Development was focusing on local development agencies' use of funds and PIDC came in for some criticism.

"But HUD audits released in 1986 and 1988 aren't nearly as damning as Egan's critics charged early in the campaign.

"The audits covered three agencies, not just PIDC, and the most serious findings concerned the other two. The most troubling findings—that 62 percent of projects offered no help to the poor—were based on an analysis of transactions before Egan became PIDC president in 1985."

When Paolantonio was later asked about Davies's interpretation of the audits, he would dismiss it with one word: Jealousy. They got scooped on an important story back in September, and this is their way of getting in a dig at me. Davies probably didn't intend it that way, he would say, but the city editors at the *Daily News* hated the *Inquirer* and they were probably behind it. Egan's name was all over those audits, he would say, he was responsible, and Paolantonio's sources at PIDC had confirmed the story. And then Paolantonio would note that Egan himself had never complained about the story. If he had gotten it wrong, Paolantonio reasoned, if Egan hadn't been head of the agency at the time of the transactions, why wouldn't Egan himself have brought it up, instead of bragging about his default rate and complaining about being called for an interview late Friday afternoon?

It was a little-noted episode in the campaign, and yet it said much about the media and the mayor's race. The aggressive reporter, reading the tastes of his editors, not for judicious stories assessing in a balanced way the performance of government officials, but rather for negative exposés about candidate wrongdoing, looking only far enough to find the scandal. An evenhanded story about Egan's strengths and weaknesses, or an examination of whether the tried-and-true strategies of economic development agencies really did benefit low-income people, or even an in-depth look at the pros and cons of minority set-aside requirements, would not excite editors the way a negative investigative coup could.

The story also highlighted the consequences of assigning political reporters to investigate candidate performance in substantive areas. The complex world of federally funded government programs was difficult for any reporter to comprehend in a few days, but it was going to be particularly problematic for a reporter whose main charge through the campaign was to chart campaign strategy. For Paolantonio, the approach to researching the HUD audits was to examine how the criticisms would play with an important voting bloc, namely, minorities and low- and moderate-income voters. Less time was spent investigating the substance of the charges themselves.

As a result, the reporter never pursued two essential questions concerning the audits. First, had HUD found problems with PIDC's job creation efforts, or was the criticism actually of the agency's monitoring and documentation of those efforts? If you were a low- or moderate-income voter in the city, that was an essential difference. Second, how was the complaint resolved? In his story, Paolantonio wrote, "In 1990, HUD found that PIDC had corrected most of its problems cited by auditors," but the statement left many questions unanswered. What exactly had been corrected? If HUD had found that federal dollars had been used to fund economic development transactions with no benefits to low- and moderate-income persons, they would have been required by law to demand that the funds be returned.

Had Paolantonio pursued these questions, he would have learned that HUD never demanded that funds be returned. He might have even located PIDC's year-end report issued December 31, 1990, which noted that the agency had developed and implemented new policies and procedures for documenting that its prior transactions did meet the requirements for low- and moderate-income benefits—and that HUD had accepted the city's findings with no further comment. In other words, nine months before the *Inquirer* ran its story claiming that HUD had found that 62 percent of PIDC's transactions had not produced any low- and moderate-income benefits, HUD had settled with the city that it was satisfied that those transactions had, in fact, met the national objectives.

But none of this information came out in the media. Even though a reporter at another newspaper uncovered what looked to him like clear errors and misstatements, he was constrained from making much out of it, particularly in view of the fact that the two newspapers were co-owned and rarely set out to embarrass each other. As in most cities in which there are newspaper monopolies and in which television stations spare few resources to allow their reporters to do any original reporting, there were

few corrective mechanisms when a newspaper reporter, for whatever reasons, didn't get it right. And that is particularly true in cases where candidates and officials don't possess the know-how or resources to point up
the mistake themselves. In this case, Joe Egan had not even handled the
city's response to the 1988 HUD audit and the negotiations to provide the
information HUD had required. That task had been handled by Wilson
Goode's commerce director, William Hankowsky. Egan had not known
enough to make the case himself that the story was inaccurate.

But there was an even deeper moral to the story, a lesson about how the
media, in their rush to reveal apparent wrongdoings by public officials,
often completely ignore the big picture. In the last decade, the city of
Philadelphia had lost 13 percent of its middle-class residents, the very
people the city depended on to pay wage and property taxes. At the same
time, hundreds of thousands of jobs were being lost as businesses moved
to the suburbs and other regions. Even the *Philadelphia Inquirer* and
Daily News had decided to move their new printing plant to the western
suburbs, to better meet the needs of their target market. And with each
lost business went city wage and business taxes, as well as jobs for residents. What was the next mayor going to do about the basic problems of
the city's economy? Wilson Goode had charged that Joe Egan had no
vision for the city's future, but did Ed Rendell? Was the city to become a
warehouse for the poor in the future, or was there a way to become
competitive for both middle-class residents and businesses? Which candidate was more likely to build the economy of the city and increase its tax
ratables?

The questions mattered to every resident of Philadelphia, including the
city's low- and moderate-income residents. But because there was no hint
of scandal associated with them, they were never posed by the media in
the 1991 mayoral campaign, much less answered.

30 The Big Question

September 3, 1991

❦ It was the Tuesday after Labor Day, the unofficial start of the fall campaign season, and the local talk show *AM Philadelphia* was set to give Philadelphia's mayoral campaign its send-off. Joe Egan and Ed Rendell were scheduled to come to the Channel 6 studios on City Line Avenue to answer questions from *AM* host Wally Kennedy in what would be the first live television debate of the Egan-Rendell campaign. That there was an *AM Philadelphia* and that it actually turned its attention occasionally to politics was something of an oddity in the world of local television. A decade ago, there had been any number of local morning shows in media markets across the country, each with its own matching set of "Ken and Barbie" co-hosts taking turns in the kitchen doing recipes and showcasing the latest fashions. But the economics of the business changed, and the local talk show had given way to the nationally syndicated superstars like Donahue and Oprah and Geraldo. It began to make much more sense for a local station to buy one of the syndicated blockbusters than bankroll its own local show.

Kennedy had watched over the years as his local competition had folded—first Channel 3's *People Are Talking* and then the *Jane Wallace Show*—and then as *AM* shows in other cities had also gotten the ax. But somehow Channel 6 had stuck by the show even though in 1987, when they bought *Oprah*, they had cut *AM Philadelphia* from an hour to a half-hour and changed its format. Instead of featuring cooking and fashion, the new format became news oriented, centered around live interviews with telephone call-ins. The show had a decided tabloid tilt to it, but that didn't bother Kennedy. He was a veteran of talk radio, where you had to have a well-developed sense of what kind of topics excited an audience, and he thrived in a live format, where he could sometimes catch his guests off guard and get unexpected responses. He also liked bouncing his shows from the latest headlines, and he had no small interest in using the show to break news.

As with most local television talent with any longevity in a market, Kennedy was a realist when it came to the bottom-line criteria of his business. Kennedy knew that the primary concern was ratings, and if *AM Philadelphia* had managed to survive when so many of its clones had been yanked, it was because the show had always yielded respectable ratings for Channel 6. For better or for worse, Kennedy would say, your efforts today are on the table by ten-thirty the next morning, in the form of the overnight ratings. And there was typically only one reason why the size of the audience for a morning talk show fluctuated: that day's topic.

And it was a simple fact that *AM Philadelphia*'s worst ratings came when they did politics. The only exception had been when Frank Rizzo was on. When political stories could feature Rizzo, they always did well. In fact, although Kennedy had never been one of Rizzo's fans politically, the ex-mayor was one of his favorite guests because he was never nervous on live TV and you never knew what he was going to say. There was an element of danger about having Frank Rizzo as a guest on live TV, and Wally Kennedy had always liked it. And the audience seemed to share his feelings. Ratings for the Rizzo/Castille/Katz confrontation in the primary had been somewhere around 5 or 6—high for a morning slot—while the Democrats had only captured a 3—among the lowest rated shows. Little wonder that local newscasts, obsessed with their ratings, would feature the Republican candidates far more than the Democrats back in the primary.

But Wally Kennedy was proud of the fact that, despite the sometimes low ratings of his political shows, station management supported the staff's decision to keep on doing them. As a result, *AM Philadelphia* served as one of the few vehicles that allowed candidates to speak for more than a few seconds and confront each other head-on. Kennedy felt he paid his dues with the lighter fare he was willing to do for the sake of the ratings, particularly during sweeps months when television focused heavily on sex or sensational crimes. (It would have to be a pretty exciting campaign to justify doing a show with local political candidates during sweeps.) But Wally Kennedy would push to keep doing political shows because he himself loved politics. He had grown up in Chicago, where city politics was practiced as a fine art by Richard Daley, who was mayor when Kennedy was a boy and who ruled the city until the time when Kennedy had children of his own.

Kennedy's agenda was clear. Politics may not have brought *AM Philadelphia* much in the way of ratings, but it could bring prestige. Kennedy wanted his show to play a unique role in the campaign, as it had in the primary when the confrontation between Rizzo and Castille had transformed the dynamics of the race. He offered a more revealing platform than the League of Women Voters debates, with their strict formats agreed upon by the candidates, leaving little room for follow-up questions and confrontations. The Republicans' appearance in the primary was just about all that you could want in a political morning talk show: great television—Frank Rizzo had taken care of that—but also revealing the candidates' personalities. Ron Castille had demonstrated that he could neither stand up to Rizzo's attacks nor convincingly discuss the city's problems, and Sam Katz had found a badly needed platform for his message. As Kennedy saw it, his job was to serve the candidates up on a silver platter for the audience to perceive and make judgments on.

And now on the first day of the fall campaign season, *AM Philadelphia* had gotten the two candidates for mayor in their first televised debate. Kennedy was well aware that Egan's chances of winning the election were slim. But he also knew that there was still a single outstanding question remaining in the campaign, a point of continuing drama. Kennedy had watched Frank Rizzo tantalize reporters with innuendos about how he was going to attack Ed Rendell after Labor Day, go after him with the personal stuff. "Just wait," Rizzo had said with a gleam in his eye, "I'll tell ya' why they call him Fast Eddie." Kennedy had known, just as Sal Paolantonio at the *Inquirer* and columnist Chuck Stone at the *Daily News* and Lisa DePaulo at *Philadelphia* magazine had, that the single most interesting question that would arise in the media in the general election campaign would have nothing to do with the city's finances or its massive job loss or its desperately troubled poor population. For these most sophisticated big-city journalists, the major question would have to do with whether and how Rizzo would play the personal card against Rendell. It was the consummate insiders' political question. It had nothing to do with the city's future but everything to do with who would win. And it was the unfortunate fact that in 1990s urban America, the most highly developed journalistic skills were often deployed to figuring out who would win, not who could solve the crushing problems of a city.

When Rizzo died, the question had been temporarily submerged beneath the drama of his sudden loss and the suspense over who would fill the Republican slot. But now with so little drama left in the campaign, the political reporters returned to the only big horse race question remaining: would Joe Egan take up Frank Rizzo's mantle? Would he attack Ed Rendell's character, with sly references to the rumors about womanizing? Wally Kennedy kept his ear to the ground about the big political questions, because to keep politics on AM *Philadelphia*, it had to have something of an edge. He wanted the show to be the place where something happened that couldn't happen in the pages of any newspaper or on the evening newscasts. It was a place where the candidates could reveal their personalities and where one could play a trump card on the other—as Frank Rizzo had done with Ron Castille—and watch what happened. Today, Kennedy wanted to make sure that the remaining question of the campaign—the last remnant of the horse race—would be answered on his show. But he would need to build up to it. One of the skills that Wally Kennedy had perfected in his years of doing live interviews was the ability to create momentum with each successive question until he reached the most controversial one, the big payoff question. At the same time, in a medium where ratings were measured every quarter hour, it was important that each question along the way piqued the audience's interest.

And so Kennedy didn't start out this day's interview by asking the candidates how each would deal with the fiscal problems, or how each would go about stemming the awful tide of jobs and middle class residents flowing out of Philadelphia, or how they would combat the alarmingly high rates of infant mortality or crack addiction or public school drop-out rates in poor neighborhoods in Philadelphia. Rather, he turned to Ed Rendell and asked him to refute Joe Egan's latest radio ad, which claimed that Rendell was just "the same old stuff."

"Can you give me one thing that contrasts that image. Why aren't you the same old stuff?" Kennedy asked.

Rendell, as ever, was prepared. He reeled off a convincing list of reasons why he was the candidate of change—how he had challenged Wilson Goode in the last election, how he was calling for changes in city council membership. And then he turned to consider his opponent. Without a hint of animosity or hostility, he noted that Egan was a part of the last four administrations in city hall, that he had endorsed Wilson Goode when Rendell ran against him, and that he had been handpicked by the boss of the Republican party. Rendell even referred to Egan as a "patronage employee."

Egan responded with what he probably thought was homespun bluntness. "That's horse dip, " he said. "Joe Egan was employed by the business community in this city. I was the part of the administration that shined. Joe Egan is not a professional politician. Joe Egan has not run for office before, not run for governor, not run for mayor. You will not change this city unless you reach down into the bowels of it and pull it out by its hairs." He sounded as if he were trying to combine Frank Rizzo's colorful language with Peter Hearn's "I'm not a politician" mantra, and add on an additional message about his own reputation in economic development. But from the minute he opened his mouth, it was clear that he could not make the combination work. He didn't possess Rizzo's ability to turn a phrase to make a simple point. Where Frank Rizzo's talk was picturesque, Joe Egan's was merely bizarre. Kennedy raised his eyebrows at the mixed metaphor of bowels and hair.

"Well, that's a vivid description of what you want to do . . . I guess," he said. "There is a question about your running of PIDC. Last week in the *Philadelphia Inquirer*, Sal Paolantonio wrote an article that questioned whether or not the government in the form of HUD and the mayor, Wilson Goode, were not constantly on you about the way you ran PIDC and whether, in fact, your administration of certain jobs conjured up visions of not being totally fair or equitable in the black community." Once again, the city's newspaper was setting the agenda for the broadcast media's questions. Paolantonio's article had suggested that there had been major problems at PIDC when Egan was president, and while the *Daily News*'s Dave Davies would take the time to go back over the original audits and sort out the validity of the *Inquirer* story, no broadcast journalist would take the time to do so. To them, by necessity, the *Inquirer*'s word was gospel.

Egan once again seemed to be verbally tripping over himself. "I'd put my reputation in job creation against Ed Rendell's as D.A. any day of the week," he said, without offering specifics. "That article . . . you're always going to have articles like that . . . I take HUD as a compliment. It was a scandal-ridden agency. And when you're in government and have a strong record you're going to have people coming at you. But when you look at my whole record . . . HUD gave me $70 million and I kept it. I still have it. I had only a 2 percent bad loan rate. If the savings and loan industry had had that kind of bad loan rate . . . they come from all over the world to look at PIDC . . . it's not just one article. And by the way, I was called at three-thirty in the afternoon to respond to that article."

Kennedy turned to Rendell. "Did he do a good job at PIDC?"

Rendell shifted in his seat before answering. "Well, I don't know the total facts at PIDC. I think Joe worked hard. I've had the opportunity to work with Joe, and I have a great deal of respect for Joe. I think there were problems with PIDC. Everyone in the public sector has their pluses and minuses . . . " Rendell was willing to say a lot of things about Joe Egan in order to win, even call him a "patronage employee." But he seemed reluctant to address this issue.

The questions continued. A caller to the show asked the candidates how they would do a better job of running utilities. Rendell claimed he would work harder to enforce bill collection at the Philadelphia Gas Works. Egan said, "First of all, why is the city in the gas business? I'm not sure we should be in the gas business." It was the first mention by a mayoral candidate of selling off PGW, and it had come on a morning talk show. Kennedy asked where the candidates stood on privatization. While Rendell talked about the need to "open it up to the competition," Egan called the concept a "gimmick" to disguise poor management.

Then Kennedy moved away from specific issues into a different realm. Were things so bad in the city, he asked, that it would be impossible to turn it around? "No," said Rendell decisively, ticking off the reasons why he thought one man—namely, himself—could accomplish change. He talked about the need to offer real leadership, to energize the city, to make some tough decisions. Egan spoke in different terms. "I don't look at the next mayor as being a strong person, but as being a facilitator, someone who steers government, who generates competence to help other people make change." Rendell retorted, "But one thing we have to remember was that Wilson Goode's main failure, I think, was his inability to be a strong and decisive leader."

It was a brief but revealing interchange on a subject rarely discussed in local news coverage of the campaign: an exploration not of personal scandal but of leadership styles, where one candidate called the other on his approach. Rendell had put his finger on one of the major weaknesses of the current mayor and suggested he could do it better. The exchange could have been an important takeoff point for further reporting, had journalists viewed the question of leadership as a legitimate area for investigation in a mayor's race. It might have been interesting for voters to learn about Joe Egan's leadership style at PIDC and hear a discussion of whether the same skills it took to see development deals through to completion translated into the qualities you needed to be a successful mayor. They might have found it interesting to hear more about Rendell's leadership as D.A. and whether he was successful in lobbying the state legislature for changes in the law as he would have to be as mayor if he wanted to gain more financial support for state-mandated services that the city had wound up covering.

But the question of the candidates' contrasting leadership styles and how they might relate to digging the city out of its hole was one that would largely go unasked by campaign journalists. The profession had carved out a narrow definition of what personal qualities were worthy of scrutiny, and they mostly had to do with sex and personal finances. And so it was probably not much of a surprise to either candidate when Wally Kennedy brought up the most controversial question of the program. "Before we continue," he said, "I have to ask this question, because it came up on this show about a month ago. *Daily News* columnist Chuck Stone, since departed [Stone had left the paper to teach in North Carolina], was on this show, and he said, and I quote, 'Ed Rendell makes Gary Hart look like a choir boy.' My question to you, sir," he said, turning to Rendell, "should your private life, or for that matter, your opponent's private life, be fair game in this election?"

It was, in its own way, a remarkable question. A newspaper columnist had come onto a local talk show and made a completely unsubstantiated claim about a candidate for mayor. The *Daily News* had given Chuck Stone a fair amount of leeway in the primary, but his comparison of Gary Hart and Ed Rendell would never appear in the newspaper's pages. On television, however, there seemed to be a much lower standard for substantiation. Once someone gave voice to the rumors, it was considered legitimate to repeat them. As long as one person with a high enough public profile went out on a limb to accuse a candidate of some personal scandal, it was deemed okay to parrot the charges—at least on television.

Ed Rendell didn't flinch. "Let me start out by saying that I've been in politics for sixteen years, and anyone who's ever run for office you hear all sorts of garbage rumors about from one source or another. You've got to sift through them for the garbage that they are. I think our private lives are fair game in the respect that they do or do not reflect on our ability to lead. Other than that, my wife is the one who I have to answer to on all questions, and I'm sure that's true for Joe as well."

Joe Egan also seemed prepared for this question, and no matter what some of his campaign staff might be advising him, he knew without a moment's hesitation how he would answer the question. "I don't think personal lives should be an issue," he said quietly.

Kennedy pushed on. He would not let the payoff question go by so easily. "Because there's been talk about The File . . . " One of the ways that the innuendoes about Rendell's past had circulated in the media was through the use of the code words *The File*. It was said that Frank Rizzo's campaign possessed a file of damaging information about Rendell's sexual activities and that he was planning to open the file to the media sometime during the fall campaign. After Rizzo's death, *Daily News* political editor Ron Goldwyn had written a column speculating about the contents of The File and what would be done with it, although no reporter had ever seen it or had any hard evidence that anything remotely damaging existed.

Rendell smiled and was quick to answer. "Marty Weinberg, who should know best about the so-called Rizzo file has said it was nothing more than a file of old newspaper clippings."

Egan added, "I think we have plenty in the file of the record on the past twenty years. I think there are enough issues out there in this campaign other than personal lives." While he may have been out of his depth on almost every other question that day, one thing he was absolutely certain about was his resolve not to follow his predecessor's example when it came to feeding the media's hunger for personal innuendo. Joe Egan was demonstrating his own form of personal character that day on AM Philadelphia, but that definition of judgment and integrity was given little credence by the media. He had answered the big remaining question for political insiders, but he had also sealed his fate for the campaign. By refusing to smear Rendell through unsubstantiated rumors and provocative innuendoes, he was virtually guaranteeing that the TV news crews would fold up their equipment and not even bother covering his first run for mayor of Philadelphia.

Wally Kennedy had tried his best to make sure that AM Philadelphia broke some news that day, and he had succeeded. That night on Channel 6, the newscast ran a story from the debate about Egan's suggestion that the city sell the Philadelphia Gas Works. In the following day's Inquirer Sal Paolantonio would focus his story on the candidates' agreement to refrain from raising personal issues in the campaign.

But over at the competing television stations it was as if nothing at all had occurred on the campaign trail that day. Channel 10 ignored the campaign entirely, which was not unusual since the station had reverted to its pattern of minimal campaign coverage. But KYW-TV had taken a different approach. Choosing not to ignore the campaign but refusing to acknowledge that the candidates had appeared on a competing station, Channel 3 used its "Issue Tonight" segment to hold its own debate. They had decided, in effect, to replicate the confrontation between the two candidates, so that they could claim any news that had broken on the other program as their own. The only difference, of course, was that instead of AM Philadelphia's half-hour, KYW was allotting three minutes and thirty seconds to their substitute "debate," and instead of having the candidates side by side in a free exchange, they were in separate remote locations with strict time limits for their answers.

The segment started out with KYW reporter Marge Pala alone in the studio. "This year we'll elect a mayor who'll have to deal with crushing problems," she said earnestly. "Among them, drugs and crime and a huge deficit. There are no easy solutions. From tax hikes to job cuts, all the potential cures will be painful for someone. The Issue Tonight: The future of the city and the men who want to shape it." It was a suitably serious introduction and an accurate rendering of what the next mayor would have to face. The only problem was that it was hardly suggestive of the tenor of the interview that would follow. Pala's five questions to the candidates might have been used in a primer for the new breed of TV reporters assigned increasingly at the last moment to cover politics.

Question one: start with the horse race. "Mr Egan," Pala began, "you've been running for thirty-three days. Your opponent has been at it literally for years. With money tight, low name recognition, and time running out, how can you hope to catch up?" The question was a little like asking a man if he had stopped beating his wife. It was hard to imagine what voters learned from Egan's answer that he still believed he could be elected mayor of Philadelphia.

Question two: bring up any personal scandals, including some element of sexual innuendo, if possible. "Mr. Rendell, you've been involved with a couple of public peccadilloes over the years, reports that you encouraged rowdiness at the infamous snowball game between Dallas and the Eagles. Also, there are some scandals surrounding your unpaid parking tickets. Also, one columnist once said you made Gary Hart look like a choir boy. How do you deal with the issue of character in this race?" It was Marge Pala cribbing from Wally Kennedy and indirectly from Chuck Stone, with all the messy business of attribution and validation sidestepped.

This time around, Rendell seemed irritated by the question; the third generation of unsubstantiated rumors was beginning to get to him. Even though he understood the media pretty well and was generally prepared for anything reporters might throw at him, even he seemed at this point to be stifling outrage. His response was terse: he thought his record as district attorney should provide voters with all they needed to know about his character.

This led the reporter to question number three: tie personal scandal to the horse race. "You're confident, then, that private issues—for example, the unpaid parking tickets—won't be an issue?" Rendell managed to say that he was.

With personal scandal and the horse race taken care of, Pala moved on to the "issues." Again, as if following a text, the reporter picked out the one simple question on which she knew the candidates would have opposing positions. "Mr. Egan, privatization of some city services—take, for example, trash collection—is often suggested as a possible way out of the financial crisis. You oppose it. Why?" When he had presented his stock answer that privatization was a way to balance the budget on the backs of the workers, she turned to his opponent. "Is it a buzzword, Mr. Rendell, or a way out?" Rendell, in turn, offered his standard statement that he favored competition, not necessarily privatization.

"In the few seconds left," Pala told both candidates, "I have to ask you one more question, which I hope you will give me a yes or no answer. Will you, if elected, raise taxes?" Both said no, but when Egan tried to expand on his reasons, Pala laughed. "Just no. That's good enough for me." It was the sound-bite reduced to its most absurd dimension. The cynical viewer, listening to the interview, might ask, what is next in the interest of brevity? True or false questions to mayoral candidates?

Pala turned earnest again to close the segment. "Election Day is November 5th. We've spent much of the last couple of weeks watching the Soviets putting their lives on the line for the right to vote. It will be interesting to see whether the example of the Soviet commitment will inspire more Americans to go to the polls to participate in a democracy that is too often taken for granted."

Even more interesting was the question of how much the exercise of democracy mattered when voters were being so poorly informed by local television, where personal innuendo, the horse race, and an ultrasimplified treatment of the issues merged into a brand of campaign journalism that was also accepted without protest.

31 Politics Is a Funny Business

September 6, 1991

❦ The press conference was called for 11:00 A.M. at Ed Rendell's campaign headquarters on the twenty-fourth floor of the Fidelity Building, one short block from City Hall. Rendell was set to announce what the *Inquirer* and *Daily News* had already reported that morning. Frank Rizzo's top lieutenants, including Marty Weinberg, Rizzo's trusted campaign manager and political adviser for two decades, had decided to switch parties to back Democrat Ed Rendell.

Weinberg had learned about city politics at an early age from his father, Emmanuel, who had served as a Philadelphia city councilman. Like his father, Weinberg had started out in the Democratic party, but had become a Republican when Frank Rizzo had switched parties. He had been at Rizzo's side in good times and bad. It was often said that a large part of Rizzo's electoral success had to do with Weinberg's political brilliance.

In that morning's *Inquirer,* the story about the Rizzo team's backing Rendell had made page 1. Nothing Rendell had said about the problems confronting the city had gotten him on the front page of the *Inquirer* thus far in the campaign, but this purely political story had carried him to the premiere spot. It was hard to say that the endorsement was all that important to the campaign or even as dramatic as Ron Castille's last-minute decision to enter the Republican primary, which made front-page news back in February. But it had Frank Rizzo's name attached to it, and that alone seemed to take a story to the front page these days. The news about the endorsement had been broken to reporters the night before, and many had hunted down Joe Egan at a campaign appearance for his reaction.

Egan had claimed that Weinberg was making the move solely to protect his law firm's contract with the city for legal work for the Philadelphia Gas Works.

Even though the news had already broken, the Rendell campaign was going through with its ceremonial media event, largely for the benefit of the television cameras for whom pictures were preeminent. Sure enough, cameras from all four television stations in town were out this morning, dominating the back of the small meeting room at Rendell campaign headquarters. But only two stations had actually sent reporters. Barbara Grant of Channel 29 and Suzanne LaFrankie from Channel 6 joined Dave Davies from the *Daily News,* a few radio reporters, and, wandering in a little late, Sal Paolantonio.

When Rendell arrived in the room at precisely eleven, Dave Davies reacted in mock shock. "You're on time. What is this? A press conference is actually going to start when it's supposed to?"

Rendell laughed. "You want me to go out and come back in again a little later? You know why we're on time? Because of the location. It's here for a change." All through the primary, Rendell's staff had been careful to stage press conferences on location, with the kind of visual backdrops that had worked a few years ago to gain television coverage. But they had learned the hard way that even having their candidate collecting dirty hypodermic needles from trash-strewn city lots was not going to get television reporters out to cover a position paper. Now, in the general election, they went to fewer lengths to supply backdrops.

Rendell was accompanied by Marty Weinberg; Jim Baumbach, another top Rizzo aide and partner in Weinberg's law firm, Tony Zecca, Rizzo's long-time press secretary; and about a dozen other members of the Rizzo team. Weinberg began. "We are all here united in support of Ed Rendell. The reason for that . . . the primary criteria that all of us had was the betterment of the city of Philadelphia, dealing with a number of issues. But an issue that was particularly close to the heart of Frank Rizzo was the crime issue. I know that when I met with both Joe Egan and Ed Rendell, the topic of conversation in my mind . . . my primary thrust was what was best for the city of Philadelphia. And I had a conversation with Ed Rendell, and I asked him specifically what was his plan for solving the horrible, horrible crime problem that exists in the city of Philadelphia. I knew Ed when he was a hard-hitting D.A. I know Frank Rizzo had a lot of respect for Ed as D.A. They worked together from the time Ed became D.A. There was a period of two years when Frank Rizzo and Ed Rendell worked together as mayor and D.A., and worked in simpatico, absolute agreement on the need to solve and handle the crime issue. And I questioned Ed about that and that was the thing I was most impressed by, Ed's dedication in terms of where he believes the issues are, and crime is, if not at the top, near the top. And I asked him about an issue that was dear to Frank Rizzo and that was adding police officers. And Ed told me that one of the first orders of business is to see to it that there will be one thousand more police officers. He has the money for it, he has the plans for it . . . I became convinced that the only choice for Philadelphia to solve the crime problem, solve the financial problem, and turn the city around is Ed Rendell."

After a few more of Rizzo's campaign staff spoke, Ed Rendell took the podium and thanked the people who had come out to support him. He said he knew that this was probably an emotional moment for many of the people who stood behind him who had been so committed to Frank. "You know, politics is a funny, funny business. This crew was dedicated as of June and the first half of July to beating my brains out." The Rizzo team standing behind him broke into laughter. "Notwithstanding that, even back then, I had terrific personal relationships with many of these people.

"You know, everyone who spoke today spoke with conviction about crime. Our campaign, we used to sit around occasionally and we'd look at Frank in the primary and we'd sort of get a laugh because no matter what issue you asked Frank about, he'd relate it to crime. And yet, when you think about it, Frank Rizzo was right. It doesn't matter what type of houses we try to build if we put them in neighborhoods that are unsafe, and people can't work in them and live in them, it doesn't matter if they're palaces, they're worthless. And education, we can improve our educational systems, but if kids can't walk to their neighborhood schools in safety, if many kids stay home and become truants because they're too afraid to go to school, it doesn't matter if you have the best schools in the history of man and womankind. And economic development. Frank Rizzo always cared very much about ordinary men and women getting back to work. But economic development is hindered—whether it's center city or neighborhood strips or shopping centers—by the notion or reality that we're not safe. And enterprise zones have not been nearly as successful in our city because they're afflicted with crime. So the only pledge I made to any person in this room and the pledge I make today is that I will work with all the energy I can muster to try to make Philadelphia a safer city."

The press conference was offering an ultrasimple pitch, aimed largely at the TV cameras. Frank Rizzo knew how to fight crime, and now his key campaign staffers were backing Ed Rendell because he, too, could fight crime. The simple beauty of the theme was a testimonial to the marriage that was taking place on this day between two highly skilled campaign forces. Each one knew that the media would do little research either on whether Rizzo's get-tough approach to fighting crime would have even made a dent in the gun-riddled, crack-addicted mean streets of 1991 Philadelphia or whether Ed Rendell's pragmatic proposals—like hiring one thousand new police officers—had any chance of being funded. For TV, the simple anticrime theme would be enough. And then for the newspapers, there was the all-important horse race angle. Weinberg and Co.'s defection was another strategic victory for Rendell.

Barbara Grant opened the questioning. "How big a political coup is this? Is this the last nail in Joe Egan's coffin?" Since Tia O'Brien had left town, Grant seemed to be stepping into her role as the aggressive television political reporter, willing to jump in first to ask the slightly overstated question that might elicit a good sound-bite. The assembled group laughed at the bluntness of her question. Rendell responded, "This is obviously important. Not so much for the endorsement, because you've all heard me say this for the last year. We all wonder about the value of endorsements in terms of voter persuasion. But I think it is extraordinarily valuable because of the talent—that's the key—and because of the issue that has led these people to be here. It is an issue that is one of the paramount issues of the campaign. To the extent that the decision was based on the ability to fight crime, it is very valuable. I'm not going to speculate on what its long-term political value is." Rendell always remembered the campaign edict: talk issues, not politics.

"Marty? Marty?" The question was coming from Vince Thompson from WDAS, a black radio station. "How much did this endorsement have to do with the perception that Egan is not going to win and that you don't want to back someone who has no chance of winning this election? Did that have any role in it, that you just said, 'God, Egan just can't win'?"

"Well," Weinberg answered slowly, "I have actually been in politics for forty-seven years, but one criteria that I never used was winning or losing. I have basically in my life made judgments on who I think was the best candidate for a particular office. I have backed a lot of losers in my time . . . they're not losers, but people who have lost elections. I never look at polls. I never ask people for polls. I haven't asked Mr. Rendell or Mr. Egan about polling. I suspect that Mr. Rendell is the favorite in this race. What I basically made my judgment on in dealing with two candidates is who could better serve the interests of the city of Philadelphia, I mean, who could make the better mayor."

Rendell jumped in. "I'm going to echo what Marty said. Frank Rizzo was a long shot in '87 and almost pulled it off. Frank Rizzo, despite what the people behind me think, was a longshot in '91." The Rizzo supporters laughed at this. "But these people didn't care about odds. They cared about commitment to someone they believed was best for the city. I don't think it has anything to do with standing in the polls or who's going to win or not going to win. Everyone here has fought a lot of battles. Everyone here has won some and lost some. Of all the people I met with, that never came up, that simply never came up."

Then Sal Paolantonio entered the discussion. He often bided his time through a press conference, letting the other reporters toss out their queries, before he produced the zinger, the question he intended to make his story of the day. And today he was going to pick up on the political attack that Joe Egan had made against Weinberg the night before. "Were there ever any discussions about keeping the PGW contract with Obermayer with Marty Weinberg?" he asked.

Rendell responded immediately, clearly prepared for the question. "Marty Weinberg has never—since the day Frank Rizzo died—Marty Weinberg has never mentioned that contract, city business, or anything of the sort. He has simply never opened up the discussion, nor have I talked about it. I have said universally that I am going to take a look at all contracts, to see, number one, whether they're necessary, whether we're paying too much money, number two, and number three, whether the people who are performing those services right now are doing a good job." He noted that he had talked about the possible sale of PGW, as a city asset that could generate revenues, and that if that were to happen, the contract wouldn't be in city hands any more.

"Look," he added, "all of you know I have respect for Joe Egan, and I know that with ups and downs in a campaign you have a tendency to try to put a favorable spin on it, but I don't think that that was worthy of Joe."

Then Weinberg responded to the question. "After Frank's death, I had conversations with both mayoral candidates, Ed Rendell and Mr. Egan. The only time the question of being rewarded for supporting a candidate ever came up was when Mr. Egan brought up the fact that he wanted me to be heavily involved in his campaign. In fact, he asked Jim Baumbach when he came to his office whether he could get me to run his campaign. And Mr. Egan said, 'You know, I remember my friends. And anything you ever need or want, if you do that for me, is yours.' That's the only time we've ever had any conversation with any candidate."

It was a well-executed one-two response from the new team of Rendell-Weinberg. When Rendell was asked the political insiders' question of the day, he managed to turn the charge around to the issues of the city's fiscal problems and how he would attack them. His response preserved his image as the above-the-fray candidate who was focused solely on the issues. When Weinberg took over, however, he not only responded to Egan's charge but attacked right back with the bomb that he knew would turn the headlines around. Not only had he not made a deal with Rendell, he claimed, but he had turned down a very crass political offer from Egan. In the classic Frank Rizzo tradition, albeit in a quieter, less flamboyant style, Weinberg was attacking Egan's character and integrity with a charge that would be very difficult for reporters to verify. Just as had been the case with Ron Castille, Joe Egan would be forced to deny the charges, thereby prolonging the media coverage of the issue. Rendell had a point when he claimed that endorsements were crucial "because of the talent." The highly developed "talent" of the Rizzo team had always been the ability to use the media to slam an opponent, to place an opposing candidate in a defensive position from which it was hard to escape—and today it was being put to use for Rendell.

Dave Davies jumped at the charge, as Weinberg had probably known that all the reporters would. "Marty, I just want to be very precise about that. That statement, as you remember it, was *what* from Egan?"

"Yes," he answered. " 'If you would do anything you can to help me, in any way or any form that you feel you can do it, I remember my friends and you can have anything you want.' "

"How did you respond to that statement?" countered Davies.

"I said, 'Joe, I don't really want to get into that. I want to talk about who I think would make the best mayor of the city, and we're sorting out the issues that have to do with that. First of all, I don't understand why you're even running.' I said, 'It's beyond me. I don't know where you're coming from on that.' "

Davies continued. "Do you think 'anything you want' could have meant the tools of the trade? I mean, campaign apparata?"

"I'm not speculating. I'm not saying what it meant. I'm just repeating, word for word, what he said," Weinberg answered.

Thompson joined the questioning. "But did Mr. Egan say to you anything like, 'If you join the campaign, I'll make sure that your law firm keeps the city contract'?"

"No. He said, 'Anything you ever want or need, you can have.' "

Paolantonio asked, "Were you left with the impression that he was talking about anything more than the campaign apparatus?"

"Oh, I think he wasn't talking about the campaign apparatus. Absolutely not."

"How do you know that?" Davies pressed.

"As a reasonable human being." (Laughter and clapping by the Rizzo loyalists greeted this comment.)

"Marty," WDAS's Thompson interjected, "some of us, in fact, spoke to Mr. Egan last night, and he said he never promised you anything. If he continues to say that, what is your response?"

"Well, as I understand what he said last night, he indicated that he never wooed me, that he never even tried to get me aboard. Unfortunately for Mr. Egan, Mr. Baumbach was also present in that situation when he came over to my law office to speak to me. I agree with Mr. Rendell that this should not really be a part of the campaign, but since he brought it up and since Mr. Rendell and I never had a word about anything other than issues having to do with being mayor of Philadelphia, and we had the discussion with Mr. Egan, I thought it probably would have been something that would add to the dialogue."

When the press conference ended, the reporters separated to interview the Rizzo people, Paolantonio to Weinberg, Davies to Jim Baumbach, and Barbara Grant to Tony Zecca. Channel 6's LaFrankie had left before the question-and-answer period began because she had to do a live shot for the noon news. In their quest to appear on top of every breaking news event, TV reporters sometimes had to leave the scene of a story to do a live shot in a good visual setting. LaFrankie missed the heart of Weinberg's charges—the big story of the day to the other reporters present—because of her station's need to give the illusion that they were aggressive news gatherers.

Dave Davies, meanwhile, asked one of Rendell's campaign workers if he could use the phone to call Egan's office. He knew he would need Egan's response to this latest charge from Weinberg, the accusation that it was Egan, not Rendell, who had offered Weinberg a deal, and he wanted to get hold of him as soon as possible. Davies put in his request for an interview and said he'd check back later for an answer.

Walking up Broad Street to the *Daily News*'s city hall bureau after the conference, Davies was torn about what he would make of the new revelations. It was the classic conflict facing a reporter on the campaign trail. The *raison d'etre* of the press conference—to announce the support of the Rizzo team for Rendell—had already been reported in that day's papers. For the TV reporters, the pictures were enough, but for the newspaper reporters, a new angle was required to make more news. And Weinberg had supplied that angle, with the accusation that Egan had tried to make a deal with him. Weinberg, the veteran of many tough-fought Rizzo campaigns, knew how to control what would become the day's news about the campaign, whether on television or in the newspapers.

And yet Davies was troubled about making that the angle of his story. If he had to choose which one of the two, Joe Egan or Marty Weinberg, was telling the truth, he thought, he would have picked Egan easily. He had covered Egan for years, and he thought that Joe Egan just wasn't the kind of guy who lied. Davies had seen him back little-known people running for office in remote localities because, it certainly seemed, he thought they were the best for the job. Egan was not the kind of guy who had been building himself a power base for years.

It was a telling fact about the local media that of all the reporters who had been present to cover the Weinberg charge, only Dave Davies had any lengthy experience actually covering the two men who were facing off. Only Davies had watched Joe Egan as he went about making economic development deals and Marty Weinberg in his years of engineering Rizzo's political campaigns. Davies was a member of a vanishing breed: a reporter who stayed with a single beat for more than a year or two, maintaining the institutional memory through which to make judgments about political acts. In local television, more and more experienced reporters with such memories were being given the ax so that younger, cheaper talent could be brought in from out of town. At the newspapers there was also increasing movement between markets and between beats. Many newspapers, including the *Inquirer,* consciously tried to rotate reporters after they were on a government beat for a year or two, concerned that the reporter might get too cozy with sources or become too focused on insider issues of little interest to the audience. With beat reporters rotating so quickly, however, the knowledge necessary to understand city governance and to evaluate the claims of candidates and officials was difficult to develop.

But while Davies was reluctant to blindly pick up on Weinberg's charge, he was afraid that he didn't have much choice. The trouble was, he thought, you have to report it because everybody else will report it. Because the TV cameras were there—particularly Channel 6, whose six o'clock newscast reached more than a half million households—the *Daily News* editors would expect the charge to be their lead story. Although TV often slavishly followed the newspaper's lead, sometimes the process was reversed. If TV reporters rose to the easy bait offered them at a press conference in the afternoon and ran the story at six or eleven, they forced the newspaper reporters—particularly at a tabloid like the *Daily News,* with a heavy television-viewing audience—to build their stories around the issue for the next day's paper. Notwithstanding their limited reporting staffs, their lack of beat reporters, and their inability to research stories, TV news departments often defined what was local news on any given day.

It turned out that Davies was not the only reporter who tried to reach Egan, and as a result the candidate called a press conference at his Locust Street campaign headquarters for 2:00 P.M. that afternoon to give his side of the story. While the reporters waited for Egan to appear, Channel 6's Suzanne LaFrankie asked Dale Wilcox what Weinberg had said that morning about a deal. Paolantonio turned to her and said, "Did you have to leave before he said it?"

"Yes, I had to do the all-important noon show." Her voice was dripping with sarcasm as she described having to leave Rendell's headquarters to do a live spot on Broad Street. Like many local television reporters, there was a large amount of cynicism in her tone when she talked about her job.

"That's better than the 'Issue Tonight,'" quipped Wilcox, referring to the new Channel 3 segment that was running in the revamped eleven o'clock news. The new show was a cheaper version of their old newscast, which had featured high-priced anchor Steve Bell. Now most of their news spots were voice-overs read by the stunning but lower-paid new anchor, Jennifer Ward, who had been imported from Canada. Once again, television news seemed to be trading in the craggy face of experience—Bell was a veteran journalist who edited the copy he read and liked to get out and cover the news—for the youthful beauty of the skilled newsreader. In Channel 3's new late newscast, which debuted in the days after Tia O'Brien left for San Francisco, the station was assigning three reporters to do a longer segment called "The Issue Tonight." Intended to be a hard-hitting in-depth look at important societal issues, the segments featured issues that were highly promotable, often with tie-ins to the network's entertainment programming. On the night that Johnny Carson hosted his anniversary show, KYW would claim that the big "Issue Tonight" for Philadelphia was the appeal of late-night talk shows; a few nights before the station ran the Miss America pageant, standards of beauty would be the issue.

The reporters continued to make small talk until Egan finally appeared and walked to the podium. "Today's press conference brought the campaign round to my strengths: integrity and character," he said, reading quickly from his notes. "That's what this campaign is all about: who can you trust? Ed Rendell and Marty Weinberg are the masters of let's-make-a-deal politics. This is just another example of Ed Rendell's politics-as-usual that's brought our city to its knees. Over the last four weeks, I met with hundreds of people and listened to their concerns and asked for their support. The only thing I have offered in return, if I am elected I will bring about fundamental change.

"It is apparent that Joe Egan struck a nerve with Ed Rendell last night because Joe Egan told the truth. The only deal that has taken place here is that Marty Weinberg gets to keep his sweetheart deal with PGW's contract, squash the famous Rizzo file, and conduct business as usual. The difference between Ed Rendell and Joe Egan is clear: he cuts deals in back

room meetings, I build coalitions of leadership. That's how I got the Saratoga here and its 25,000 jobs, that is how I got the funding for the convention center, that is how I will bring jobs to our city and make our city safe
again and clean again. Now the campaign has really begun because we are
talking about the main issue: that is one of Joe Egan's character versus Ed
Rendell's character. Thank you."

Egan was trying to bring the campaign discourse back to his expertise in
job creation and to get the media to make the simple leap that, because he
had been the point man on two highly visible employment-generating
projects, he could bring jobs to Philadelphia better than the former district
attorney. It was no more outlandish a notion than the idea that because
Sam Katz was a "municipal finance expert" he could solve Philadelphia's
fiscal problems. But Egan was not going to succeed in getting his simple
message across—or focus the campaign on the issue of which candidate
was more qualified to stimulate economic development—because he really
had no idea how the local media worked. They were not here today trying
to sort out the records of the two candidates; they were following the
latest charges of impropriety.

"Joe, are you saying Marty Weinberg is lying about the statements he
made?" one of the reporters asked. They didn't want to talk about the
Saratoga or the convention center or the nitty-gritty issues of job creation.
They wanted another slugfest.

"Yes. Period. Next."

"What went on in that room?" Paolantonio asked.

"We went in to discuss the campaign. We talked about Rizzo stories. I
hadn't seen or talked to Marty in a long time in a private conversation. I
was asking for his help, and that was *all* that happened. Period. And I've
met with a lot of people in this campaign. Find somebody else that said
that about me." There was an edge to Egan's voice that was missing from
the veterans Rendell and Weinberg, who responded in a dispassionate and
calculated way to charges of impropriety. Joe Egan could not keep his
emotions out of it when someone tried to attack his integrity.

Paolantonio continued. "Jim Baumbach was in the room and he cor-
roborates Marty's story."

"Not so. Jim Baumbach wasn't in the room."

Wilcox asked, "You've known Marty a long time, both in government
and privately. Why do you think he might be saying these things?"

"He's got a lot to protect. An awful lot to protect. The PGW contract.
Being on the inside. He went from inside to outside. You gotta remember,
fellas, when Frank Rizzo died, a lot of those people lost their American
Express card."

Davies jumped in. "How do feel about this kind of accusation coming out against you personally, Joe?" Davies knew that this was something new for Egan. In all of his years at PIDC, only on one occasion had Egan been questioned on the ethics of his dealings—and in that one case, Egan had gone all the way to the state's Attorney General to get his name cleared of any wrongdoing.

"Politics as usual in Philadelphia. I've learned a lot in this campaign, but to me . . . just look at my career. If there were a career, you could follow this kind of activity. There'd be a trail. I've been in public life for twenty years. There'd be something to distinguish how Joe Egan has conducted himself."

"You said you'd rather have the foot soldiers last night. Did you ever discuss with Marty Weinberg his coming onto the campaign or being the campaign manager?" Paolantonio asked.

"I didn't discuss being campaign manager. I asked him to be part of the campaign. We did discuss Bob Kutler, and he urged me to hire Bob Kutler, and I didn't do that."

Paolantonio continued. "So you did want Marty Weinberg to be part of your campaign?"

"Yes. The interesting thing is that I did ask Sam Katz to be my campaign chairman and I didn't promise him anything. Fellas, thank you very much."

Davies ignored his attempt to cut the press conference short. "Joe, Jim Baumbach said that he met with you separately and separately you made a similar statement to him, the phrase 'anything you want.' Can you comment on that?"

"I never said that. What can I tell you?" Egan was backing away to leave the press conference.

Paolantonio asserted himself. "You called a press conference, and you brought us here to say something. We have some follow-up questions. Can we just continue this a couple more minutes?"

Egan's press secretary acquiesced. "A couple more minutes because he broke his schedule to . . . okay, a couple more minutes, one more."

Thompson continued the questions. "What role did you want Marty Weinberg to play in your campaign, if not campaign manager?"

"I just asked him to be a part of the campaign. I needed his advice."

"What effect does this have on your hope to be the unifying candidate of the Republican party?" another reporter asked.

"It has no impact on it. He's a Democrat. He's always been a Democrat. It says nothing about unifying at all."

"Because of his statement, if you do become mayor, would you get rid of that contract that they have?"

"There's no question in my mind that I'll look into that contract in and out."

"Joe," Dave Davies asked, "when Marty made this statement, he didn't say you offered him legal work or money. What he said was 'anything you want,' which could mean a lot of things. It could conceivably mean campaign resources. Is there anything that you could have said that could have been misconstrued? Is there anything approaching anything like that?"

"Dave, there is nothing in anything that has come out that has that connotation. You'll have to ask him that. He's made that interpretation."

And with that, the press secretary led Egan away.

The two press conferences that day had been a study in contrasts. At Rendell's, the bombshell had been carefully saved for the question-and-answer session, to give it the most impact. Weinberg and Rendell had let the questions go on until the reporters were satisfied, fielding every query expertly, getting their messages across perfectly. Egan, on the other hand, had come prepared with a canned statement that he thought would turn the incident to his advantage but that left the reporters' questions largely unanswered. Like Ron Castille, he had not been able to turn around the personal attack from the Rizzo team. He had not been able to focus the reporters on the question of who was making the attack or the record of their credibility in the past. And like Castille, he had not been able to get the reporters to buy his simple message, which in Egan's case was that his experience in economic development gave him the capability to be mayor.

After Egan left, Suzanne LaFrankie pulled Dale Wilcox aside to get more on what she had missed that morning, trying to make sense of this press conference. As in so many other cases in the campaign, the TV reporter, shuffled from location to location and from story to story, was forced to get information from the beat journalists who followed the story much more closely. The other reporters headed for the elevator. "What a level of debate in this campaign," one said, shaking his head. " 'You're a liar.' 'No, you're a liar.' " They were right to be cynical. It was hard to imagine what this press conference would tell voters about their choice for mayor or about the nature of the compromises that would have to be made to bring Philadelphia out of its quagmire. What the reporters failed to recognize, however, was the role they themselves played in keeping the "level of debate" so low.

Paolantonio was thinking about something else. "Did anybody notice that the phone didn't ring once in Egan's office while we were there? At Rendell's, it was ringing constantly." Paolantonio was always into his indicators, and this was one more which said that Egan was in deep trouble.

That night on Channel 6, when Suzanne LaFrankie did her piece on the endorsement, she left out Weinberg's accusation that Egan had offered him a deal. But the next day both the *Inquirer* and *Daily News* stories did focus on the "deal." The bait had been thrown by one of the all-time great political anglers, and in the midst of a humdrum campaign it had proved hard to resist.

While the charges and countercharges never made it to television, their very public appearance before the local press corps had clearly rattled Egan—just as Rizzo's charges had so rattled Castille. Both men were personally injured by accusations that went to the very core of their sense of integrity. It was the new journalism of personal attack, orchestrated by political operatives who knew how to get the media to do their dirty work. The information that campaigns threw out rarely impugned their opponents' plans or positions or qualifications. Rather, the charges had to be personal in nature if they were to be picked up by the media—and if they were to knock the less-schooled candidates for a loop.

It was the veterans against the rookies, and the veterans were clearly winning.

32 The Dog and Pony Show

October 4, 1991

❦ Joe Egan's short campaign could not be said to be going well. At forums throughout the city, he seemed to reporters unprepared to lay out his plans for the city or to successfully differentiate himself—in any positive way—from Ed Rendell. In his public appearances, he stressed his rowhouse roots and noted that in the area of economic development he would "hit the deck running," but his failure to provide any details made his arguments less than convincing. *Inquirer* reporter Doreen Carvajal was now following Egan on the campaign trail, while Marc Duvoisin was assigned to Rendell. Sal Paolantonio was monitoring political developments, trying to give the bigger picture in the campaign.

For both Carvajal and Duvoisin, the campaign was turning out to be painful to cover, as Egan seemed incapable of mounting the barest challenge to Rendell. It was Marc Duvoisin's first political campaign, after years of covering city government, and he found himself in a continual quandary. He was covering a campaign in which one candidate's victory over the other seemed virtually certain, leaving him to constantly battle the "so what, why am I doing this?" feeling. He and his editors were struggling between two poles in their coverage. On the one hand, they didn't want to be in the position of writing Egan off and making what they wrote a self-fulfilling prophecy. On the other hand, they wanted to describe accurately what was going on. Everybody knew that Egan didn't have a chance to win. And what's more, it was clear to reporters that people all over the city, from the row-house guy trying to get a pothole fixed to the biggest powerbrokers seeking early ins, were turning to Ed Rendell, already considering him mayor.

Duvoisin had already written two stories from the "let's get real" direction, both suggesting the election was a foregone conclusion. A Sunday, September 22 story had described how Rendell was trying to fight a sense of complacency in his campaign. Five days later, Duvoisin wrote another piece that made the front page, headlined "Rendell's Tightrope Act: Aiding Oversight Board While Seeking Election." This story suggested that Rendell was already providing input to the state oversight board established to help the city sell bonds for operating expenses, under the assumption that he would be the next mayor.

Joe Egan, on the other hand, had not made the front page of the *Inquirer* since he was selected by the Republican ward leaders back in August, although reporter Sal Paolantonio had managed to make it there with stories about key Rendell endorsements. Paolantonio had been alternating between covering the big horse race stories—like Rendell's somewhat surprising endorsement by the police union—and doing some issues pieces. After covering the Fraternal Order of Police's endorsement, Paolantonio did a follow-up piece examining the obstacles that would face the candidate if, as mayor, he tried to fulfill the promises he made to the police union. "What Rendell did not tell the police officers," he wrote, "was that to achieve all those goals, it will take an act of the legislature, a ruling by the Supreme Court, a change in civil service rules, and the removal of a police department directive installed by the cop's cop of all time, Frank L. Rizzo." It was the kind of story that was all too rare in campaigns, and certainly in the primary: an incisive examination of a candidate's proposals and analysis of what it would take to implement them.

But on this day in early October a very different kind of story had landed Paolantonio once again on the top of page 1, with the headline "Ailing Egan Cancels His Appearances." Although Doreen Carvajal shared the by-line, the story was in some ways vintage Sal Paolantonio. As in his most controversial stories of the campaign, Paolantonio had pieced together a few isolated bits of information to come up with a story that he would claim was a major turning point in the campaign. Although he would criticize the candidates for reducing politics to marketing strategy, one of Paolantonio's marks as a reporter was his ability to come up with an angle that would be a sell to his editors.

The "Ailing Egan" story was one such piece. The story began when Egan failed to show up at a Thursday afternoon crime forum, with no explanation for his absence. Paolantonio decided to pursue it. He'd just gotten a copy of Rendell's latest polling data, and the results were devastating for Egan. They showed Rendell crushing Egan by 63 to 26 percent of the vote and, even worse for Egan, they showed that 48 percent of Republicans favored Rendell. Could it be that Egan was just giving up in the face of these terrible odds? Paolantonio decided to call Egan's campaign manager, John Denny, and check it out. He's gone home to rest, said Denny, without much elaboration. Oh, really, Paolantonio thought, and immediately picked up the phone to call Egan's home. Egan's wife, Pat, answered the call and told the reporter her husband hadn't been home all day. When Paolantonio went back to Egan's campaign staff with more questions, they hastily called a press conference and announced that the candidate would be canceling his appearances for the following day and possibly into the weekend because of his health, a combination of exhaustion and sinusitis.

To Dave Davies and the *Daily News,* the story that came out of the press conference was worth seven sentences on page 30 of Friday's paper. But to Sal Paolantonio, it was more than that, much more. The unexplained no-show at the forum, the latest crushing poll from Rendell, the attempted cover-up by Egan's campaign manager about where the candidate was—to him, it all added up to a big story in a campaign with very few big stories. It was not the easiest sell to the editors, who wanted to know why Egan's getting sick for a day should be a big deal. But Paolantonio wasn't one to shrink from a tough sell. An editor questioning him on what the big deal was just made him rise to the occasion.

"Why do we want to make a big deal about it?" he would later respond to a question about the story. "We just had a candidate, Frank Rizzo, who died of cardiac arrest. We had John Heinz, who was killed in an airplane crash in Lower Merion Township. Now we have a guy who doesn't show up for campaign appearances, and his campaign manager says he went home, but his wife says he's not there. Sources are telling us he's holed up in some apartment in Center City, flat out exhausted, and couldn't take Ed Rendell on in a Crime Commission forum at the Union League because he's basically wimping out. I think that's a major league story. This is a guy who's been running for mayor for thirty days, and he can't handle the pressure? How is he going to be mayor for eight years? Not only does it raise serious questions about the candidate, by his odd behavior and by their ridiculous answers to obvious questions about where the candidate is, but it raises questions about him as a character. And people want to know. This is not some guy running for Board of Revision of Taxes. This is a guy that's going to lead them out of the greatest hole in urban America. Does he have the right stuff? Or is he wimping out? I think it's an important story to tell people."

Paolantonio was suggesting that the real measure of the man could be observed from the prism of a single symbolic event—in this case, his failure to show at a forum on a day when he was found to be trailing in the polls. It was a convenient definition of character, allowing assessments to be made by reporters who possessed a keen eye for clues and a willingness to spend the afternoon on the phone. And it was a standard that was particularly useful in a business that continued to define news, including campaign coverage, as discrete events occurring in the previous twenty-four hours.

The front-page story that resulted from Paolantonio's efforts sketched out the details of the canceled appearance and the explanation by campaign staff and then noted, "The decision to temporarily withdraw from the campaign came on a day when his Democratic opponent, Edward G. Rendell, released new polling data showing him with a commanding lead. Even Republican voters preferred Rendell to Egan, the poll showed. Yesterday, Egan's staff gave mixed signals about just where the candidate had gone." The staff member in question, campaign manager John Denny, would be fired within two days of the article's appearance.

When Joe Sanchez, Joe Egan's press secretary, saw the story, he winced. Although not the most seasoned of political operatives—he'd served as press secretary only once before to a minor candidate in the 1987 Republican primary—his twenty years as a local television reporter had taught him well what a front-page story in the city's major newspaper meant. He knew that assignment editors at all the TV stations followed the front page of the *Inquirer* with a devotion that bordered on the religious. If a big local story made page 1 of the *Inquirer* in the morning, he knew, you could be sure it would make the six o'clock TV line-up that night.

Sanchez thought the story was just plain absurd. Joe had looked awful the day before, and Sanchez and others on the staff had ordered him to go lie down for the afternoon. And then that turd Paolantonio comes sniffing around asking questions about where he is. And soon he's calling Pat Egan at home and making a big deal about the fact that Joe wasn't there when John Denny had said he was. What was wrong with that guy? The campaign rented an apartment downtown for Egan to rest at between appearances, and that was where he'd gone that afternoon, instead of trekking all the way back up to his home in the Northeast. A front-page story all because John Denny said, "He went home," instead of, "He went to the downtown apartment we rent for the campaign"?

But it was hardly surprising from the *Inquirer,* Sanchez thought, the newspaper that loathed Republicans, and most particularly loathed Billy

Meehan, and that was not going to cut any breaks for the candidate who had been picked by the man they viewed as evil personified. In Sanchez's view, the *Inquirer* was trying to pan-broil the Egan campaign, and this was just one more example. Sanchez was also hardly surprised when that afternoon Channel 10 reporter Harvey Clark showed up at Egan's headquarters for the first time during the campaign. Sanchez knew Clark well, though they had worked in different shops. Sanchez had spent four years as a reporter at Channel 6 and then several at Channel 3, and he considered himself good friends with just about every TV newsman in town, including Clark. One of the main reasons he had gotten the job as Egan's press secretary was his ability to pull in the TV reporters, to get out the "free media," as it was known in campaign jargon.

And here was Harvey Clark, one of the senior broadcast journalists in Philadelphia, who had risked personal injury to broadcast live from the 1985 MOVE disaster in West Philadelphia, who had been part of the news team that won the prestigious Alfred I. DuPont award—this Harvey Clark was arriving with a camera crew to investigate Egan's health. Sanchez hadn't been happy with any of the TV stations' coverage of the campaign, but Channel 10 was the worst. Channel 10 had just about rolled over and died in this campaign. "Dammit, Harvey," Sanchez said to the reporter, "we're talking about the economy of this city, the University of Pennsylvania lending us money, stuff that's really really important, and you're coming up with this dog and pony show about Joe Egan being sick?" It was hard to believe that this was the one package that Channel 10 was going to do in the mayoral election. But it was not Harvey Clark who was making the decisions. He was just as disgusted with what was happening. He had watched as the station had done everything it could to pull the veterans away from the big races and use the new guys to do the job, to get their recognition level up, since all the focus group research showed that viewers tuned to stations when they felt some connection to the "talent." And the talent, both reporters and anchors, were getting younger and younger every year.

It was not just Channel 10, he knew, that was throwing out the experienced reporters and bringing in the young faces at lower salaries, people who cared little about journalism, as Clark saw it, but had gotten into the business for the prestige thing, the money. Clark had not been happy about the stories he was increasingly being assigned to cover. And he had been dismayed by the way the station had stripped the dignity from his award-winning public affairs show, *Channel 10: the People*, trying to turn it from a serious look at local issues into a clone of *America's Most Wanted* in what seemed like a shameless effort to boost ratings and cut costs. It was a particular rub to Clark that the station seemed to exploit the troubles of African American youth, rather than try to explain them.

There was not much Clark could do when the assignment editors sent him out for a story that he thought was a crock. On this day, he dutifully did his story about the questions raised by Egan's missed appearance, picking up on the point of Paolantonio's story by noting that "some political observers" suggested "it may have been recent polls that made Joe Egan sick." Even a reporter with the estimable talents of a Harvey Clark had been reduced to putting pictures on an *Inquirer* story. Clark did, however, start the piece with video of a fiery Egan speech from a few days earlier, noting that the candidate had certainly looked healthy and aggressive then. He had quoted Ed Rendell saying that Egan was "just beat," and he used a bite from Sanchez saying, "I'm absolutely amazed that a candidate getting ill is getting so much attention." It could not be said to be a positive story for Joe Egan, but at least Clark had made an effort not to swallow the *Inquirer's* slant whole.

The piece would, however, be one of the last stories that the reporter would do for Channel 10. A week later, Clark would be fired as part of his station's general cost-cutting moves. With one dismissal, they managed to get rid of an estimated $165,000 salary and a reporter who was complaining too much and too often about the direction local television news was taking in order to keep the rate of return high. More and more, the reporters who were remaining at TV stations were the ones who learned to give the executive producers and news directors what they wanted, with a minimum of backtalk or discussion.

For Joe Sanchez, the degradation of Harvey Clark was just another glimpse at the pathetic state of the profession he had not long ago practiced. Of course, part of his newly acquired view of what TV news was all about came from being on the other side of the microphone, on the receiving end—or nonreceiving end, in Egan's case—of television news coverage. But part of it was what was happening in the business. In his estimation, cable had kicked the hell out of broadcast television. When he had first come to Philadelphia, electronic journalists were kings. They had lots of money and some time for their stories. But now it was different. Cable had eaten into the ratings of the affiliates. The slices of the pie were getting smaller and smaller. And as a result, the staffs were getting smaller and smaller. TV had always followed the newspaper, it was true, but with reduced staff it was getting even worse.

In a way it was ironic that, as a TV reporter, Sanchez had avoided political stories whenever he could, hiding under his desk, he liked to say, whenever a president came to town. Even now, he didn't think of himself as a political animal. Political campaigns from the inside were fascinating to observe, but he had never had a taste for covering them as a reporter. And now he was getting to see firsthand what the TV reporters were looking for, and it was as demoralizing as it was understandable. He had been hired to get Egan on TV, and try he did. He pulled every favor he could. He begged, he borrowed, he pleaded to get coverage. He had priorities. If Channel 6, the ratings leader, showed up, that was all he cared about. Bingo, he had hit a home run that day. If KYW radio showed up, that was a two-bagger. And if he got Joe Egan's picture in the paper, no matter what the accompanying story said, then it was a grand slam.

But he'd hit all too few home runs or even singles in this campaign. Partly that was because of his candidate. This was Egan's first run for office, and he was a neophyte in every sense. But he was particularly inept when dealing with the broadcast media. Sanchez would look at him and know it was hopeless. His body language was all wrong. He had this habit of looking down his half-glasses at TV cameras in a way that made him look mean and angry, when he wasn't like that at all in person. Another problem was that he wasn't a slick talker. He kept talking in these twisted sentences that didn't quite make sense. He simply could not come up with the glib ten-second reply the TV reporters were looking for.

Part of the problem, Sanchez felt, was the structure of the campaign. The whole thing was being run by goddamn committee. Egan had brought in a Washington consultant, the Eddie Mahe Company, to run the campaign, and their operative, John Denny, as campaign manager. The Eddie Mahe people would come in on Wednesday, and by Thursday they were back in Washington. They were doing this campaign by remote control. Even though Sanchez was the campaign's chief press liaison, he had to have Eddie Mahe's approval and the campaign manager's approval and the party leader's approval before he could do or say anything of substance to the media. If Sanchez had had his druthers, from day one, Egan would have done a press hit each day, a well-prepared press hit, and begged for money the rest of the day and the hell with all these forums. The homeless, the battered, the Jewish League, the Mexicans, you had all these damn groups, you wind up talking to sixty people, it takes an hour and a half and what did you accomplish? Zip. In a traditional campaign, you could do it, but not in eighty-five days.

But he was not even sure that the press-hits would have accomplished much. Even gimmicks weren't getting TV reporters out if your guy was going to talk about the economy or health. In 1987, he had his candidate respond to Frank Rizzo's refusal to debate by staging a press conference with a cardboard cutout of Rizzo, placed at a podium. Back then, gimmicks had worked to get reporters out. But not in 1991. Sanchez kept telling Egan, "Joe, these people want a damn show. You give them a show, they'll show up like flies. You give them substance, talk about baloney budgets, the fiscal integrity of this town, they're not going to be there." But is Ed Rendell a bad guy? Does he have a sordid past? Does he have a couple of skeletons in his closet? That's what they wanted.

The show they were being pushed to deliver to the reporters was about Rendell and the much alleged womanizing. They were under constant pressure to go negative on Rendell with the personal rumors. What else were you supposed to do when you were in a football game and it was 32 to 0? Throw the bomb, throw the bomb, people were saying. People would continually walk up to Egan, put envelopes in his pockets, talking about Ed's so-called illicit relationships. But getting Egan to attack Rendell was like pulling teeth. It was against his very nature. There was always a conflict between what the political strategists wanted to do and what was in Joe's heart. The day after Joe announced, he said to Sanchez, "We're not going to do it." Sanchez thought that Egan's refusal to exploit personal innuendo said volumes about his character and integrity—certainly much more than his failure to show at some forum one day because he was sick and exhausted. But he also knew all too well that to reporters covering the campaign, that kind of character never entered into the equation. As Sanchez would say, it was the ability to produce a "goddamn dog and pony show" that much of the media seemed to value in a candidate.

Although no dog and pony show was being put on public display, behind the scenes of the lackluster Egan-Rendell campaign, there was much investigative activity that voters would never learn about. As Egan was being bombarded with advice to attack Rendell with rumors and innuendo, the *Inquirer* was methodically investigating with renewed energy whether any of those rumors and innuendo could be substantiated. Editor Max King had given the go-ahead to the investigation because he felt that his reporters were being told enough things to raise the questions as a legitimate issue. The issue that King believed was valid to pursue was not one of marital infidelity but of sexual harassment. That is, reporters were investigating whether they could substantiate rumors that Rendell had misused the power of his office as D.A. As King would later describe it, the paper felt an obligation to report the issue, but not to write about it unless they could obtain substantiation. And though much time and effort were spent on the investigation, substantiation was never found and not a word was written about it.

As careful as the newspaper was being in not printing rumors, the truth was that if Joe Egan had made the rumors public—as Frank Rizzo had done when claiming Ron Castille had a drinking problem—those stories would have been reported even without substantiation. For the newspaper, a candidate's personal attacks on his opponent transformed rumors into fair game for reporting, a legitimate campaign issue on which to report. In a way, the newspapers were caught in a difficult ethical dilemma. If they refused to print the charges made by one candidate on another, they could be said to be hiding important information from the public. But if they did print the attack, they could be said to be giving credence to the charge itself. In this case, however, they would write nothing because their investigations had failed to confirm the rumors and Joe Egan would not levy the attack himself. The television newscasts would also report nothing of the rumors. With few reporters or researchers to spare to do anything resembling the *Inquirer*'s investigative reporting, the newscasts were forced to merely wait, as Sanchez would put it, to see if Egan would put on the necessary dog and pony show.

While Joe Sanchez understood what his former colleagues needed to excite their managers, he would not realize that it was going to take more than an ex-TV reporter who knew about pat media events to get a candidate elected mayor of Philadelphia in 1991. It was going to take the understanding not of a Joe Sanchez but of a David Cohen, a man who knew that the *Inquirer* was not an evil monolith and that it didn't "pan-broil" candidates because they were Republicans. Cohen would understand that it was not political affiliation that mattered to reporters but good stories, and that the winning hand would go to the campaign that was smart enough to hand out the intriguing angles while helping their candidate look good. Although David Cohen had only worked in one other campaign since his college days, as press secretary in Ed Rendell's 1987 primary challenge to Goode, and although he had never worked in local television news, he understood more fundamentally than did Sanchez how both newspapers and television worked.

Had he stopped to think about it, David Cohen would have realized a certain irony about Joe Egan's campaign. Although campaign reporters would have dismissed the notion outright, in some respects candidate Joe Egan was not that different from candidate Frank Rizzo. In campaign appearances Rizzo had really offered no more specific plans than Egan about how to solve the fiscal crisis or any of Philadelphia's many other problems, including crime. And after the primary campaign, polls had showed that Rizzo trailed Rendell by numbers that were not all that different from the ones facing Egan now. But there was one big difference. Frank Rizzo knew how to give the media what they hungered for. Rizzo had offered TV reporters funny and outrageous sound-bites, instead of Egan's stumbling and confusing aphorisms, and with each appearance he had tantalized them with the promise of more juicy tidbits in the future. And unlike Egan's almost total lack of a game plan, Frank Rizzo's campaign had presented to newspaper reporters the labyrinth of strategies and scenarios they thrived on, suggesting he just might be able to turn the numbers around.

As he had traveled the campaign trail, Frank Rizzo had really had few more specific plans than Egan to offer reporters regarding the city's problems. The difference between the two men was that Frank Rizzo knew just what to offer up to the media instead.

33 Voicing-over the Election

October 15, 1991

❀ It was ten-thirty on a wet Tuesday morning and a group of retired employees from the Atlantic Richfield Company had gathered to hear Ed Rendell speak in the Pickwick Room of Strawbridge and Clothier, one of Philadelphia's few remaining downtown department stores. This morning's group numbered about two hundred, mostly older white men, with a smattering of white women and one or two black men. Only one reporter was covering the speech, Barbara Grant, a black reporter from independent station Channel 29, the local Fox affiliate, which produced a one-hour news show at ten o'clock. Channel 29's newscast was only five years old, but already was considered a serious challenge to the three network affiliates' eleven o'clock newscasts. Aside from offering the news earlier in the evening, Channel 29 was developing a reputation as the least sensational of the local news shows, submerging the traditional fare of fires and crimes to more serious local and national issues.

Barbara Grant, like Tia O'Brien and Dave Davies, had started out in radio, first at the University of Pennsylvania's public radio station WXPN and later at black station WDAS, where she had been news director. She had made the move to television in 1986 to join Channel 29's fledgling newscast. Unlike Tia O'Brien, she had not had to submit to the make-up and fashion consultants. About the only concession she had made to the fashion morés of television was to straighten her hair after she was told that her Afro bush on her audition tape looked dated. (Also, there was the fact that her mother, whom she loved dearly, said to her around that time, "If you ever make it onto television, please straighten your hair.") It was not uncommon to see her dressed for success from the waist up, but wearing pants and running shoes on the lower half of her body, which could be hidden from the camera.

With O'Brien's departure, she had become the only television political reporter in town, and she was a worthy successor. Like O'Brien, she cultivated her own sources, particularly in the black community. Partly because Channel 29 attracted a more upscale, educated audience than the network affiliates, Barbara Grant had the luxury of putting together pieces that were often longer and more substantive than her competitors'. Of course, another reason Channel 29 did longer stories was because they had smaller resources than their competitors. With fewer reporters and fewer camera crews, they couldn't be everywhere in the region, as the ratings leader, Channel 6, tried to be. But they could do a more in-depth job on what they did manage to attend.

Grant had recognized early on, after Joe Egan had been appointed Frank Rizzo's successor, what was likely to happen with television news coverage of the mayoral election: it was going to disappear. She knew the polls were not even close, so there was going to be little in the way of an exciting horse race. And she knew that Joe Egan did not have the television appeal of a Frank Rizzo, whose popularity would encourage the TV stations to cover his campaign even in the absence of a close race. But she thought that was all wrong. Even without a close race and dirty personal attacks, there was a mayoral election in the midst of a terrible crisis. It should be covered, she thought. The problem was, would people want to watch the station follow candidates around for two months when there was no real race?

So, early in the campaign season, she met with her news director and producers to lay out a plan. They decided that instead of following the candidates and producing twenty-second voice-overs, as the other stations would churn out, they would do longer in-depth pieces. They would pass up covering the daily forums and decide for themselves what kinds of pieces they thought were important for voters. They would put together features on the major issues facing the city: the budget, crime and drugs, privatization, and sexual harassment. And, rather than wait for the candidates to hold press conferences on those issues, Grant would initiate interviews with both Rendell and Egan and combine what they said with what they put into their position papers. It was a straightforward attempt to gather the information voters might find useful about the candidates— noteworthy only in how very rare the approach was at the other television stations in town.

On this October morning Grant was following Rendell, trying to put together her issues pieces. She was also working on "A Day in the Life of the Campaign," in which she would try to capture what Rendell's schedule was like, what kind of personal characteristics he exhibited, and who his supporters were. But she had to admit that this morning her mind was less on the mayoral election than on the Clarence Thomas hearings. Thomas's appointment to the Supreme Court had been threatened by the eleventh-hour allegations of law professor Anita Hill, who had charged him with sexual harassment. National and local news had been focused on the congressional hearings, which had continued throughout the weekend. In the process, the Philadelphia mayoral campaign had faded even further into the media background.

Grant chatted with her cameraman about the hearings as she waited for the event to begin. Rendell was running late as usual, the result of a campaign schedule that crowded as many as ten events into one long day and a candidate who liked to linger at appearances to answer questions. When he finally arrived, he gave his usual energetic presentation, putting himself forward as the man who could make the tough decisions. After his standard rendition of his qualifications and proposals, Rendell opened it up for questions from his audience of retired ARCO workers. "You can ask me anything, even how I feel about Clarence Thomas. I won't necessarily tell you," he said, to their laughter. "No, but I'm serious. I'll try to answer anything."

A hand went up immediately in the back of the room. The questioner said he thought the police were doing a good job, but it seemed every time a criminal was locked up he was let go again and did more harm than he had done before. He asked why the city couldn't "put them in jail or something or shoot them."

Rendell repeated the question for those who couldn't hear, hesitating a second before repeating the idea of shooting the criminals. "While I share all your frustration, I'm not sure a return to the firing squad is such a good idea," he said. He explained the federal court order that capped the number of prisoners who could be jailed and said he was working to get the order revoked to keep more prisoners in jail.

The questioner was not impressed with the answer. "Why not bring back the whipping post?" he asked, to the obvious agreement of many in the crowd who laughed appreciatively.

"I don't think we need the whipping post. I think that we need strong administration of justice. I don't think we need anything that is going to give the bleeding hearts an issue. I think we need a criminal justice system that works swiftly and justly and strongly. All the deterrent we need is prison. Let me ask you this. A rapist—you wouldn't want to just whip a rapist, would you? You'd want him off the street, wouldn't you? The best protection against hardened criminals is to incarcerate them. Get them off the street for a significant period of time."

The questioner would not be stopped. "How much does it cost us to keep these guys in jail?"

"Over $20,000 a year," Rendell answered. "But let me tell you this. The harm that they do if they're not in jail is infinitely more costly."

"Why don't we change the goddamn laws?"

"We don't need to change the laws. They need to be enforced," Rendell responded. "Look, I would love to grow hair, but it can't happen." He often used a self-deprecating reference to his balding head to get laughs and make a point about political realities. "I can only tell you what we can do, and what we can do in law enforcement could be very, very effective."

Rendell answered several more questions before winding up the session and moving on. The next stop, a press conference, had been scheduled in front of the gas commission's headquarters, but the driving rain had forced it inside to Rendell's campaign headquarters. At the podium in his campaign headquarters, with the small press crew, some of whom had been covering him for almost a year, he was far more informal than with the assembled group at Strawbridge's. "Do you actually want me to read this?" he asked the reporters, pointing to his statement. "Where's Barbara?" he asked a minute later, looking for Grant before starting, remembering that she was trying to get his day recorded and not wanting to start without her. When she called out from the back of the room, he said "Barbara, shall we tell them about the ARCO retirees who want to bring back whipping posts and firing squads?"

Then he got serious and moved on with business. Rendell was calling for an overhaul of the management structure of the Philadelphia Gas Commission and Water Department, which he claimed would yield a savings for the city of $39 million and move the city closer to wiping out its deficit. To symbolize the savings, he had next to his podium a giant check made out to the taxpayers of Philadelphia, to the sum of $39 million, the obligatory visual for television cameras. As he read his statement, Rendell called for creating a new authority that would combine the gas commission and the water department to produce economies of scale and more effective management, switching from quarterly to monthly billing, and lobbying the state to continue funds to help low-income home owners with their energy bills.

There were a number of print and radio reporters present. One from talk radio station WWDB made a joke before the press conference began about how many reporters had turned out. "It must be a slow news day if we're all here for this," he said. Dave Davies was covering the event for the *Daily News*, accompanied by Bob Warner, an investigative reporter for the *News* who had specialized for years in the coverage of the Philadelphia Gas Commission. Marc Duvoisin was covering the event for the *Inquirer*, and Dale Wilcox from KYW Newsradio and Vince Thompson from WDAS were also there.

Television cameras filled the back of the small conference room, but, as was becoming typical of this campaign, not many TV reporters were in attendance. While Robin Mackintosh was covering the conference for Channel 3, Channels 6 and 10 had sent only cameramen. The network affiliates had more or less decided to "voice over" the election. They continued to send cameramen to cover the media events, but rarely would a reporter go along. What resulted were thirty-second voice-over pieces, in which the candidates' proposals were summarized in one or two sentences taken from the press releases that the campaign staffs faxed to the stations.

Barbara Grant would probably not have been at the event if she had not been following Ed Rendell around that day for her "day in the life of the campaign" story. Any press conference on PGW was likely to be fairly "dry," in her terms. "It's a losing proposition for us," she said to a Rendell staffer who asked her what she thought of the press conference afterwards. "The newspapers have the luxury of all that space to explain the details of the plan in. But all our viewers care about is whether their rates are going to go up." At the press conference, the print reporters asked most of the questions. The TV reporters remained mute, since as general assignment reporters they did not have the time to specialize in one area of government. And they also knew that their news directors didn't want substantive pieces on campaign proposals but, rather, some color with which to create the illusion that the station was covering the election. Dave Davies asked the first questions. "What would happen to the city's $18 million subsidy from PGW if these savings were enacted?"

"Still be there," answered Rendell.

"Why?"

"Why? Because it's needed to help the operating budget," Rendell responded.

"Why should gas customers pay higher bills to help the city? Isn't that a regressive form of taxation?"

Rendell answered that he didn't think it was a terribly large amount of money and that he was trying to equalize the rates people would pay.

Davies next asked if utility rates for businesses would go up. Rendell said no. Bob Warner asked if any new authority would have the capability to float bonds. Rendell said it was possible. Marc Duvoisin asked if

Rendell's plan was at all similar to Mayor Goode's failed attempt to sell the gas works to get an infusion of cash for the city as it faced its extreme shortfall. Rendell said it was nothing like that plan, which he claimed was a bad idea, providing an "illusory shot of revenue."

Dale Wilcox mentioned Joe Egan's proposal that morning that the city should sell certain assets to hire more police officers. Rendell responded immediately. "If you did that, you'd run out of money pretty quickly. Say you sold some asset for $70 million, and you hired one thousand additional police officers. That would get you about two years, and then you'd be out of money. You need a permanent long-term solution. That's the problem with the sale of assets for any long-term solution. And I don't think it's good to sell assets in that way for another reason. People would look at it as a fire sale, as evidence that we're up against it and we need cash, and they'd try to steal our assets."

Rendell was then asked whether he thought the new city council would go along with his plans. "Sure," he answered, "because the new council has to deal with the overwhelming problems of the city. We're $200 million in the hole. There are three ways to address that: raise taxes, massive layoffs, or do everything in our power to save money. You know, I was asked by one of the editorial boards, do I have nine votes on council for privatization, because they had figured that I didn't. And I said, I'm sure if I did a head count now, I wouldn't have nine votes, but that's because they're being asked in a vacuum right now. But if you give council a choice, privatization or tax increases, privatization or layoffs, I think it would be a different story."

The press conference wrapped up with the television reporters having not asked a single question.

Barbara Grant went to check the schedule with Rendell and found that things had gotten rearranged. She had been scheduled to interview Rendell at four in his office for her issues pieces, but he wanted to try to catch his son playing football, so he suggested they do it immediately. It was typical of Rendell to give up eating lunch or having a short respite from the campaign to oblige another reporter. His office was a perfunctory one, with a small desk, a large black leather executive's chair, and two leather chairs for visitors. He had some pictures of his family on the desk, but his framed art work lay on a table in the back of the room. "It's funny," he said as Grant sat down and her cameraman set up for the interview, "I haven't felt settled in enough to hang pictures." Behind him stood the commanding tower of City Hall, as if beckoning to him through his window.

Grant had a good idea of what she would wind up with for her issues pieces from having observed both candidates on the campaign trail: Rendell would have a far greater command of the issues and have many more ideas than Egan about what to do about the city's pressing problems. And as she pressed Rendell on the key issues, that is what she heard. She asked about the terrible crime problems facing the city, and Rendell ticked off the things he would do to reduce crime: hire more police, in part by adding a ten-cent surcharge to lottery tickets; go to court to have the prison cap lifted; and set up a narcotics court that would try those accused of drug trading within ninety days.

She asked about the people on the streets, and he reeled off how they needed to be differentiated—how the aggressive panhandlers needed to have their source of cash removed by a citywide voucher system, how the mentally ill on the streets had to be put somewhere where they could be helped, by changing commitment laws, and how the city had to do the best with meager resources to help its homeless families. She asked whether the oversight board could force him to raise taxes, and he said they could only force him to balance budgets, and he would try his best to do that through downsizing government. He went through what he would cut—the overtime, the benefits.

To each question there was an answer. He talked to her for forty-five minutes before he finally cut her short to hurry on to his next campaign event in the far Northeast at a Jewish community center. When he finished, he smiled amiably and said with a shrug, "And this will wind up being all of two minutes, right?" It was still hard for Rendell to swallow, after all these months, how much time he would talk and talk about his plans for the city to television reporters and how little of it they would wind up using. But what he would get on other stations was even more dismal. The network affiliates wouldn't even bother to do a piece on where the candidates stood on the issues. And in the world of local television news, two minutes on issues was an eternity.

They decided that the Channel 29 cameraman would ride with Rendell at some point in the day to get pictures of the candidate traveling. Still on his agenda was a stop at the food distribution center in the far southern end of the city, then back up to the Northeast, and several fundraisers in the evening. Grant and Rendell agreed to try to finish the interview sometime around 4:00 P.M., if the rain kept Jesse Rendell from playing football. As Grant walked to the elevator with Rendell, a man stopped the candidate and after they had exchanged pleasantries, he told the candidate how good he looked. "I look better than I feel," said Rendell with a smile. "I tell that to everybody," he said, turning to Grant. "Everybody tells me how good I look, and I tell them I don't feel that way, I feel terrible."

"You're tired," she said.

"I am. I'm physically tired. But it's more than that. I'm mentally exhausted. I've given these answers six thousand times."

They all got into the elevator, and a man smiled at Rendell and asked, "Should I say, 'Hello, Mr. Mayor'?" Rendell smiled and demurred.

Grant asked him how it felt to have everyone treating him as if he were already mayor. "It's funny," he said. "Midge and I got an invitation to be honorary chairmen to some function on New Year's Eve. I think it was the American Heart Association. I said, 'Listen, we've been going to the home of a friend of mine on New Year's Eve for twenty-five years. If it's a half hour, OK, but no more.' He said, 'Fine, we'll send the invitation to Mayor-elect and Mrs. Rendell.' I said, 'You do that and I'll personally come down and murder you.' "

"It's tough," said Grant. "We're all struggling with how to cover the election when it doesn't seem like much of an election." Rendell could not let this go by. "But that's where I think Joe is wrong. He should be scheduling events all over the place, and what's he doing? He's pulling out of things right and left. That's a mistake, in my opinion."

Barbara Grant agreed. "I'd heard rumors that he wasn't showing up places."

But Rendell would not concede he had it sewn up. "You know, I still remember back in 1973 when Arlen Specter was running and everybody assumed he had it by 100,000 votes, and then he lost. So nothing's a sure thing."

What Rendell would have probably been more comfortable predicting was the way his press conference—and the one held that day by his opponent—would be covered by the media. The *Inquirer* devoted some twenty-seven inches to the two press conferences. Marc Duvoisin's story summarized Rendell's plan for the gas works and the water department, noting that the proposed changes would require changing the city charter. Sal Paolantonio described Joe Egan's crime plan, pointing out that most of the points were taken from a plan advanced by Rendell. He also noted that Egan's plan to fund the hiring of one thousand new police officers, by using 15 to 25 percent of the city's newly enacted sales tax, was impractical. The city needed every penny of that new tax, Paolantonio made clear, to balance the budget. Dave Davies's story in the *Daily News,* while shorter than the *Inquirer*'s, was substantive as well. He wrote that Egan's crime proposal "is based on revenues from a sales tax [Egan] has denounced and future spending cuts he can't yet name."

The newspapers were finally covering issues and raising important questions about the candidates' plans, as they had rarely done in the primary.

The only problem was that the substantive coverage was a little late in coming. In the primary, a focus on the issues might have changed the election's outcome, particularly on the Republican side. But in the primary, the ad campaigns, the back room meetings, the ever-shifting poll results, had all made for such good reading that the question of which man might be most qualified to be mayor had been shunted aside. Now, in a lopsided general election, the focus on issues would matter less.

But it was a different story with TV. With no horse race or personal attacks to make the election entertaining, the local stations had decided to ignore the campaign. They would be present at only the most important of the press conferences, and even then they would send only cameramen— people with no reporting capabilities—to cover major campaign propos- als. That night, only Channel 6 would find the thirty seconds for a voice- over report on the two press conferences. Anchor Jim Gardner would announce, "Democrat Ed Rendell and Republican Joe Egan took turns speaking about health issues tonight before the Delaware Valley Hospital Council. Both candidates had major announcements earlier today. Egan unveiled an eight-point crime and drug action plan which included hiring former D.A. Ron Castille as deputy mayor of drug enforcement and hiring up to an additional one thousand police officers. Rendell proposed com- bining the water department and Philadelphia gas works. Rendell said the move could save Philadelphia $40 million a year."

The story could have been a model for the new local television cam- paign reporting: half-minute stories that did not use reporters and that did not allow candidates to speak. While, in presidential elections, scholars would be decrying the networks' eight-second sound-bites, on local televi- sion mayoral candidates might as well be mimes. Increasingly, the words of the popular local anchor were substituted for the speeches of the local candidate. And video of campaign appearances, combined with tidy cam- paign press releases, replaced investigative reporting.

Three weeks later, Channel 29 ran Barbara Grant's issues piece on where Joe Egan and Ed Rendell stood on the budget crisis. She talked about how both candidates were against raising taxes or engaging in mas- sive layoffs, both looking to cut waste. For Rendell, she said, the answer lay in using privatization as a bargaining chip in negotiations with the city's unions. For Egan, the way to cut costs was to decentralize city ser- vices to the neighborhoods. She noted that all too many candidates in the past had promised to balance the budget by cutting waste but had failed to do so, which had led to the massive deficits of the 1990s. And she closed by holding up the volumes of Rendell's position papers on streamlining government, as compared to a handful from Egan. Egan's ideas, she noted, have been found by critics to be "thin," while many of Rendell's have been termed impossible to implement.

The piece, as Rendell had guessed, was just a little over two minutes in length, and it could not compare with the detail of the story the *Inquirer*'s Marc Duvoisin had done on the same topic or the sources he had contacted to review the plans. But it was a piece that, for local television news, was an utter rarity: independently researched by a beat reporter, focused on the issues, and trying to assess where the candidates differed and how effective their plans would be, if implemented. In the course of the campaign, no other station would even attempt it.

34 Have You Had Enough?

November 1, 1991

❧ Four days before the election, the Republicans held a pep rally on Dilworth Plaza on the west side of City Hall. A flatbed truck had been driven up onto the plaza and a makeshift podium placed on top of it. At noon a small crowd of about fifty die-hard Republican regulars gathered, and one of the Mummer's string bands performed until it was time for the speeches. The media "pack" this day included Dave Davies from the *Daily News,* Doreen Carvajal from the *Inquirer,* a few radio reporters, and Vernon Odom from Channel 6. The other television stations were represented by cameras, not reporters.

Dennis O'Brien, a Republican ward leader, walked up to the podium carrying a megaphone. It was emblematic of Egan's poorly funded and managed campaign that, rather than a microphone, each speaker would talk into a hand-held megaphone that kept losing its amplification. O'Brien gave it the old college try:

"Have you had enough?" he shouted into the megaphone. "I'll tell you, I am fed up. Driving down here on I-95, for the first time this year I saw bags of trash along the highway where they finally cleaned it up. Why? Because there's an election for mayor comin' up. Have you had enough of that?"

"Yeah," was the weak response of the meager crowd, a few claps heard in the background, the cameras recording the pallid show.

"When you talk to people about the city of Philadelphia, what do they talk about? They talk about crime. They talk about dirty streets. They talk about a lack of city services. Why is crime on the rise in Philadelphia?

Because the Democrats put a prison cap on and let violent offenders out on the streets. Have you had enough?"

This time the crowd was a little louder in replying yes, as if they were finally getting it.

"Have you had enough of dirty streets? I can remember, Ladies and Gentleman, over a decade ago, when Frank Rizzo was mayor, the streets were safe, the streets were clean, and people felt they were getting a fair share of their city's services for their tax dollars. That has to come back, Ladies and Gentleman. We have to bring back integrity, services, and pride to Philadelphia. There is only one man who can do that, and that is Joe Egan."

The line was greeted with anemic applause.

As O'Brien spoke, Sam Katz made his way to the front of the platform, to wait for his turn. Katz had served as Egan's campaign chairman for the duration of the short campaign, but he had done little to guide it. Although he had stood up with Egan at public appearances, he had looked less than enthusiastic. In the last few weeks, however, he had been attending more and more party functions on behalf of Egan, and he seemed to be the one Republican who drew any enthusiasm from voters. Doreen Carvajal, who was covering the Egan campaign for the *Inquirer*, had observed the response Katz was getting at these campaign events, and she had written a story on the subject for that morning's paper, suggesting Katz was already running for mayor in the next election.

Katz had found it somewhat amusing when he got the call from Carvajal about the story. "You guys already did the story about what Sam Katz is doing after the election," he reminded her sarcastically. "I was playing golf, remember?" He was talking about a story Paolantonio had done about him after the primary, suggesting that instead of playing a power role in the Republican party, Katz was persona non grata and could find nothing better to do with his time than play golf. But metropolitan newspapers did not speak with one voice, and they were not necessarily consistent over time in their assessments of politicians. While Sal Paolantonio could write one day that Sam Katz's political career was over, a few months later Doreen Carvajal could turn out a story painting Sam Katz as the rising star of the local Republican party. And Katz was prepared to revel in the turnabout. He didn't want to be seen as crassly taking the limelight off Egan, whom he was supposed to be pushing for mayor. But he was not terribly disappointed when Carvajal went ahead with the story, despite his mild protestations that she should wait until after the election to write it.

Katz looked out of place standing on the podium with the Republican leaders. There was Joe Rizzo, the ex-fire commissioner and Frank's brother, and Franny Rizzo, Frank's son. There were the Irish and Italian ward leaders and, of course, Joe Egan, all of them symbolic of row-house Philadelphia and the tough talk of "have we had enough?" But Katz, in his navy suit and horned-rimmed glasses, looking and sounding the financial consultant, did not fit the picture. Just a few days before, he had sat with Republican leaders in a strategy session and had been amazed at the way they thought about the campaign. They were debating whether they should spend their limited money on television or radio advertising. But they hadn't said a word about what they should be saying on either. He was astounded that they were paying so little attention to the message they needed to send to the electorate.

O'Brien introduced Katz as "someone who knows the fiscal side of government, someone who cares about Philadelphia, and someone who wants to see Joe Egan elected as the next mayor of Philadelphia."

Katz took the megaphone and blew into it sardonically, as one would play wine glasses filled with water. It was a trick he had picked up on the campaign trail, how to take something that might make him look silly and play with it. The strange sounds he made with the megaphone drew laughter from the crowd, as did his follow-up line to O'Brien, "And someone who wants an invitation to Denny O'Brien's wedding." Bob Kutler had taught him how to always open with a joke, and Katz had learned the lesson well.

"When Joe Egan came to me in August and asked me to serve as the co-chairman of his campaign, there wasn't but an instant of hesitation. And I recognized that the person I had known for sixteen years, who has been responsible for so much good that has happened in this city, the return of the Saratoga, the resuscitation of the Navy Yard, the delivery of $180 million in funds to build a convention center, which will mean jobs for so many people and will help the tourist industry, a guy who has cared about small business . . . "

Dave Davies leaned over to Vince Thompson from WDAS. "Did he say there was not an instant of hesitation, or there was?" The reporters all knew that Katz was hardly the most enthusiastic supporter for Egan and that what he was saying was pretty much bull.

" . . . a man who all through his life has demonstrated integrity and commitment to this city, was a man I could not turn down. And as Denny said, we had a tough primary, but we've come together, and it's taken us a while, but our message is being heard, Philadelphians can only blame themselves if after forty years of rule by Democrats, we decide to try four more. We have an extraordinary slate of candidates, for council at-large, for common pleas, municipal court, for traffic court, district council candidates, and we can make a difference on election day from top to bottom. I'm proud to be here to support Joe Egan, and on Tuesday night I look forward to standing with him and Pat, and his family and I'm proud to present to you the next mayor of Philadelphia, Joe Egan."

The string band began playing "Happy Days Are Here Again." "This is kind of pathetic, isn't it?" said Davies, surveying the crowd. He could detect no popular enthusiasm for the Republican candidate—only Republican hacks trying to look like a rally.

Egan took the megaphone. "Thank you very much. We've had a generation of corruption and incompetence. HAVE YOU HAD ENOUGH? DO YOU WANT RADICAL CHANGE?" Yes, chanted the crowd. "Vote Republican next Tuesday if you want it." Unfortunately for Egan, the megaphone had failed when he said, "Vote Republican," and it had been almost inaudible until the sound came back with "next Tuesday."

"Ed Rendell has been on TV every day, every night, for the last four months, saying he wants change. It is the biggest lie in Philadelphia history." Once again the megaphone had died, this time on the word *lie*. He repeated the line when he realized it hadn't come out. Unlike Katz, Egan didn't know how to transform mechanical failures into self-deprecating gestures for the crowd and the television cameras.

"He will not represent real change for this city. Ed Rendell has raised almost $6 million."

"It's up to six million now, is it?" murmured Davies sarcastically. The official count was $4.4 million, but each time Egan talked about it, he seemed to inflate Rendell's tally.

"Campaign contributors, think about it. And he says, no special privileges. The biggest lie in Philadelphia's political history." This time the line came out in full over the megaphone, but Davies was not impressed.

"Well, which one's the biggest, dammit?" he asked, quietly deriding Egan for making the same claim twice.

"Four months ago I stood with Ed Rendell at the first forum, and he said, 'I will not raise taxes.' Four weeks ago he started to waver. 'Well, maybe.' Last Sunday it was, 'I think I will.' Joe Egan will not raise taxes. We have had eighteen tax increases in the last ten years. We can't stand it anymore. This city will not survive another—" The last words got lost as the megaphone died. "Six million dollars in campaign contributions."

"There's that six million again," said Davies to Thompson.

"Ed Rendell has put this city up for sale. Joe Egan will not put the city of Philadelphia up for sale. Joe Egan is not for sale. Thank you for your support. I need it badly." With his last lines, campaign supporters had hoisted a sign high enough to be captured by the television cameras. The sign said FOR SALE, and when he had said "Joe Egan is not for sale," they unveiled the first word in the sign, NOT.

Thompson and Davies laughed contemptuously at the sign. "Oh, well," said Thompson, "we've got to appeal to that television, don't we?"

"No kidding," responded Davies.

When the rally was over, the Republicans scattered and answered questions from the reporters. Davies went to talk to Denny O'Brien. Later that afternoon he would head to Egan headquarters to watch the candidate's new ad spots. He was writing for the Saturday paper, which had relatively low circulation and a small news hole, so he didn't need much for his story. Vernon Odom headed straight for Sam Katz and began interviewing him. "I don't want to respond to that question right now," Katz could be heard saying, "Right now we want to concentrate on working for Joe Egan." Odom, it seemed, had asked him about his future plans to run for mayor. Even a story on page 6-B of the *Inquirer* could catch the attention of television reporters and sway their line of questioning.

Dave Davies had read the story about Katz and liked it, wished he had gotten it. As he headed off to a Vietnamese restaurant where he was meeting Cindy Burton, the reporter he had been sharing campaign coverage with for the past year, he talked about the sorry state of Egan's campaign. He had had a great deal of respect for Egan going into the campaign. Covering him in the past, when he had been a development official, Davies had always found him intelligent and effective. But as a candidate he had been a disaster. Davies almost wished he had thrown in a few paragraphs in his Egan profile about what it said about Egan's management skills that his campaign staff was so bad. When his campaign manager had resigned after Paolantonio's stories about the perceived conflict of interest, he had been replaced by a Washington operative who had been a disaster. And Davies had found Joe Sanchez, Egan's press secretary, impossible.

When Davies was researching his profile about Egan, he had found in one of the press releases the statement that Egan had created 140,000 jobs at PIDC. He had called Sanchez, wanting to know where that figure had been drawn. What years did the jobs come in? Where was the evidence? Sanchez said he'd try to track it down, but he never got back to him. Davies kept pressing, calling again and again, but never got a response. He was close to writing in his profile that the number was apparently pulled out of the air and was a sorry act for a candidate trying to represent his record to the public. But two days before the story ran, Davies pressed Sanchez for the name of somebody who could explain the number. Finally, he suggested Davies speak to Walter D'Alessio, a long-time development official, who very effectively and convincingly explained how the number had been derived.

But the incident nevertheless had pointed up to Davies just how ineffective Egan's campaign staff was. Here they had a legitimate number that made a convincing case that Egan had played a role in creating a great number of jobs for the city. But the campaign staff was so inept that they couldn't explain the number and had been this close to having the *Daily News* reporter write that it was completely bogus. It was just the opposite case with those many officials and candidates who made convincing cases for what later turned out to be truly distorted numbers. In fact, Davies sometimes thought that was the case with Rendell's staff: they were very effective in presenting numbers to back up claims for how much Rendell could save the city, and the numbers were fairly convincing on first blush. But Davies suspected that, with any in-depth probing, they might fall apart.

Thinking about the Egan profile reminded Davies not only of the ineptitude of Egan's staff but of the pressures of his own news organization when it came to covering politics. Davies had devoted a good two weeks to researching his profile, which would run as two stories, one about Egan's "political development," which was part personal profile and part assessment of campaign skills, and a second piece about Egan's performance at PIDC. He had worked hard, trying to strike a balance between making the stories interesting and fairly assessing the candidate and his performance.

And he felt he had succeeded. In the first story, he began by describing how Egan's skills as a deal maker had helped bring to reality the elegant Four Seasons Hotel on the Benjamin Franklin Parkway. He went on to discuss how Egan had not found the same success on the campaign trail. But part of Egan's failure to present an answer to every question about issues, Davies wrote, was his reluctance to offer glib solutions that would "provide a facade of substance." He added, "A man who had prided himself on being prepared couldn't bluff answers like an experienced pol." Egan had difficulty speaking effectively on the campaign trail, but "he was effective in small groups, and one on one." In the second story, Davies addressed Egan's claim that he had helped create 140,000 jobs in Philadelphia. With D'Alessio's background information and other interviews, he was able to conclude, "Campaign boasts aside, the record suggests that while there are legitimate policy questions about the development strategies that Egan helped shape, he was good at what he did and his agency performed well by industry standards."

But while Davies felt satisfied that his research had produced a balanced perspective on Egan's job performance and his campaign, he knew all too well that such even-handed stories were not always big hits with newspaper editors. The placement of the two articles said it all. The personal profile made page 4, while the assessment of Egan's performance at PIDC was placed on page 20. Davies was even glad to see the headline on the second story, "Good Job or Snow Job?" since it gave a little more of a hard (read negative) edge to a story that the reporter worried was a little too soft. Davies understood the pressure on reporters to come up not only with exclusives but with negative exclusives.

Just a few weeks earlier, he had come up with one such story about Egan, a story that raised the question of whether there had been a conflict of interest on Egan's part when, while head of PIDC, he had held onto an interest in a large commercial site in center city. Davies had gotten the story by analyzing Egan's tax returns, which the reporter had repeatedly requested. (Egan's campaign staff was so inept that they had failed to follow the candidate's orders to release the tax returns to the press generally. Instead, when Davies persisted, he alone was given the returns.) The reporter found that Egan had made a small investment in the now-cleared site of the old Penn Center Inn, an investment which held at least the potential for conflict of interest on the part of a city development official.

The story was by no means a major scandal, but still it made page 4 with the headline "Egan Reveals Taxes, Holdings / As PIDC Chief, He Held Stake in Center City Building Site." Sure enough, the day after the story appeared, Davies received a copy of the article with "Nice job" scribbled on it by editor Zack Stalberg. While Davies had been pleased by the piece and by the note—he had gotten the story through his own digging into documents, not through some leak—it was not lost on him that no similar feedback had come after the considerable work he had done on the Egan profiles, where he had found no wrongdoing but rather that Egan had been a fairly effective government official. No doubt about it, negative stories advanced reporters' careers, and the temptation to push the negative angle was always there.

It was not surprising that reporters responded, salivated even, when sources offered them tantalizing tips about possible negative stories about candidates. The source's motivations in offering the tips were not mysterious. They would far prefer to have a reporter reveal something negative about their opponents in the seemingly neutral guise of an investigative newspaper article than to have to call a press conference where they appeared down and dirty by making the charge themselves. And for the reporter on the lookout for negatives, the temptation was always there to pick up the tip and not investigate too deeply.

Davies had resisted one such tip in his assessment of Egan's job performance. He had been leaked information that showed that the number of jobs PIDC claimed to have created dropped during Egan's tenure, from 6,951 in 1985 to 1,879 in 1988. When he looked into it, Davies found that the numbers were indeed accurate and he knew he could have done a story about the drop that the editors would have loved and that might even have led the paper—a story that would have been absolutely accurate. But he had looked deeply enough into the case to know that there was a simple explanation. A federal tax law change had sharply limited the most common type of PIDC loan financing, which had resulted in the reduction in jobs created. As much as newspapers loved negative stories about public officials, he could never bring himself to do that kind of one-sided reporting.

At the restaurant, Davies caught up with Cindy Burton. They often took a break for lunch together and with other reporters on Fridays, before going back to finish their reporting and writing their stories late in the afternoon. Today, they looked surprisingly relaxed for the two reporters responsible for covering city politics a few days before an election for mayor and congressman. The primary had been so different. Before the primary, they had been overwhelmed with activity, which had been crazy but exciting, too. The primary had been invigorating, but that energy had been completely missing from the general election campaign.

"It's been so depressing to cover," said Burton. "It's like this one incredibly well financed, well positioned candidate just beating this other guy to death, and the other guy just keeps taking it without doing anything."

"Yeah, like one of those bullfights where the bull just keeps taking the swords and staggering around," added Davies.

One of the other reasons it was becoming very depressing to cover the election had nothing to do with Egan and Rendell, but rather concerned what was going on at the *Daily News*. Circulation had been way down in the last several months, dipping to 200,000 from a high of close to 250,000 a few years before, and the top editors had become worried. The gamble they had made earlier in the year to raise the price of the *Daily News* from thirty-five to fifty cents may not have paid off. People picking up the newspaper as an impulse buy were sensitive to the price increase, and although the paper had tried to get out early in the morning to be read on the way to work, they just hadn't been making it consistently. The top brass at the paper were huddled that very day in meetings to think how to restructure the paper, how to change beats and shift people around. Davies and Burton were not optimistic about the outcome. There was talk that the city editor might go, that the political reporter would be reassigned, and that city politics would be eliminated as a regular beat and that the two of them might be assigned elsewhere. It was the trend in journalism, they knew, away from hard news, into the *USA Today* type of softer lifestyle pieces, but it was not their view of what the *Daily News* should be doing.

They were also depressed about competing with Sal Paolantonio. They viewed him as a reporter who continually hyped stories, distorting information to get good play for his articles. Although they acknowledged that many of the stories he got were good and that he was a prodigious worker, they increasingly resented the stories that they felt he invented, because the stories made the two of them look bad for not having gotten them. Both Davies and Burton felt that their campaign coverage had been unappreciated, because their editors were unconsciously comparing what they were doing to what Paolantonio was writing. The editors weren't out covering the campaign, and so they didn't know—as Burton and Davies did— whether his stories were accurate or not. And so their attitude was kind of, well, we want that. In a sense, the *Inquirer*'s aggressive political reporter was not simply calling the tune for the television and radio stations, he was also putting pressure on the other newspaper in town to follow his coverage.

Davies also felt a strange sense of dissatisfaction with his role in this election. "But I think you've done a lot of great stories," Burton protested. "And I think you've done a lot of great stories, too," Davies returned the compliment. "But somehow, here the election is winding up and I should be feeling good about how we've covered the election and how it's contributed, but I don't. Somehow I don't think it's made much difference."

35 The Men from the Boys

November 5, 1991 2:00 P.M.

Election day 1991 was unseasonably cold, but the skies were clear and turnout was expected to be good. The question was whether the increasingly tight senatorial contest between Harris Wofford and Dick Thornburgh and the Second Congressional District election to replace Bill Gray would draw out voters in the city of Philadelphia, where the mayoral election had been a foregone conclusion almost from the outset. Sal Paolantonio had been out roaming around the city since early in the morning. He loved election days. In the nine elections he'd covered since he started doing political reporting, he had always gotten a charge from the electricity of the day, and he liked to be out on the street, checking polling places, getting a sense of turnout, getting a feel for the mood of voters. He liked to see for himself which campaigns had a presence at the polls and which ones were nowhere to be seen. To Paolantonio, being out on the streets was what separated the men from the boys in political reporting. Most of his colleagues, he figured derisively, were probably still in bed.

It was hard to believe that in a few short hours it would all be over, the frenetic activity of the last year, the excitement and also the sense of power of being the lead political reporter for the city's paper of record. Over at the *Daily News,* Cynthia Burton and Dave Davies were already planning stories on how Ed Rendell would take over the reins of city government, but for Paolantonio, the question of how Rendell would govern was irrelevant. He couldn't care less. He was a political reporter, not a city hall reporter, and his questions would all be answered in the next twenty-four hours.

But the day itself still held a certain thrill. He had been out at polling places all morning. By mid-afternoon he was ready to catch up with David Cohen, Rendell's campaign manager. Cohen had agreed to Paolantonio's request to ride around with him, as he wound up the final hours of a yearlong campaign that had been marked by shrewdness and luck. In large part, the shrewdness had been Cohen's. A quiet, unassuming man, he had known precisely how to respond to reporters' inquiries throughout both campaigns, getting back promptly to every journalist who called, offering an answer that was always articulate but never self-righteous. Dave Davies had compared Cohen to a basketball player who always knew where he was on the court, a point guard who's dribbling around the defense but sees right where the forward and center are.

Cohen and Rendell had been brought together in 1987 by a partner in Cohen's law firm, Arthur Makadon. Cohen, who had distinguished himself at Ballard, Spahr, Andrews and Ingersoll as a brilliant attorney and unequalled workaholic, turned out to be the perfect alter ego to Rendell. Although marked by very different personalities—Rendell charismatic and emotional, Cohen, low-key and dry—they shared common political values and a sense of political pragmatism. During the campaign, they had played distinctly different roles with the media. Rendell talked about policy, Cohen handled questions about politics. But there had been another sort of division of labor as well. Rendell dealt with TV reporters, who, when they deigned to cover the campaign, wanted the high-recognition candidate, while Cohen dealt more and more with the newspaper reporters, who wanted the detailed information about campaign strategy and background on positions. While Rendell painted with a broad brush, it was Cohen who always mastered the details, Cohen who put together the meticulous background book with supporting evidence for every single position the campaign took. Although not many of the campaign journalists had spent much time with the binder, Cohen knew the importance of looking—as well as being—prepared.

David Cohen also appreciated the importance of developing relationships with reporters. He happened to like them, particularly newspaper reporters. He had been editor-in-chief of his high school newspaper and editor-in-chief of the Swarthmore College paper, and he had continued to hold a certain affinity for the world of journalism. One of the reasons he was so good at dealing with the media was the way he was able to develop a rapport with reporters and meet their needs for information. And one of the reporters that he particularly enjoyed talking to was Sal Paolantonio. He understood that Paolantonio had a tendency to interpret his way onto the front page, and he knew that other candidates, like Sam Katz, had been infuriated by some of the reporter's stories in the campaign. But Paolantonio's writing had never harmed the front-running Rendell, and Cohen was more than willing to have Sal ride along on this final day of the campaign.

Paolantonio waited for Cohen's car on the windswept plaza on the northwest corner of City Hall, the site of many political rallies in the past year. He wasn't wearing a coat, and for the first time that day he felt the cold. A car pulled up. It was not Cohen who emerged but Bob Kutler, the one-time campaign manager to Sam Katz, who in June had joined the Rizzo campaign. With Rizzo's death he had gone to Rendell with his mentor, Marty Weinberg. He smiled at Paolantonio as he handed him sample ballots he was distributing. Along with Rendell, Chaka Fattah's lever in the Second District Congressional race was marked with a big X.

"You're working for Chaka?" Paolantonio was incredulous. Fattah was a black state representative challenging Lucien Blackwell and John White for the congressional seat.

"It is indeed strange where people end up on election day," Kutler said with a smile, before getting back into his car and speeding off. Kutler and Paolantonio, political operative and political reporter, were part of a small fraternity in a city. All through the campaign, they tried to use each other and outsmart each other, but when the campaign wound down, they seemed to simply want to touch base and share a laugh.

David Cohen soon arrived, driving a rented Ford Taurus equipped with a mobile telephone system, through which Cohen could respond to his beeper. He was accompanied by Bob Barnett, executive director of the state Democratic party. Paolantonio got into the back seat. "Everything you hear in here has to be off-the-record, OK, Sal?" said Cohen, as he picked up his car phone to return a call.

"OK," agreed Paolantonio. "Off-the-record until after the election."

"Off-the-record," shot back Cohen.

Almost immediately his beeper went off and as he headed the car toward I-95, he began returning calls. "Hi, Chaka," he said on the first one. "We're trying to track some turnout." He listened for a minute as he turned down Race Street. "No, we're not doing any exit polling. What are exit polls for? They just make candidates feel better." He listened for a moment. "Well, I'll put a call in to her, but I don't know about street money. OK, I'll let you know."

He hung up, only to have the beeper go off again almost immediately. "What'd I tell you, Sal? You can run, but you can't hide."

"Who was the 'she' in that conversation?" the reporter asked.

"Lynne Abraham," Cohen replied, referring to the district attorney who had been appointed when Castille resigned and who was now running unopposed for re-election. "Chaka wants to know whether we can get her to give him some street money." (He never made the call.)

The beeper went off, and Cohen returned a call to Robin MacIntosh from KYW-TV, who would be covering the Rendell celebration that evening at the Warwick Hotel. "When did he announce? October 29." He paused to listen. "I hope he'll do it early, but a lot is in Joe Egan's control tonight. OK, see you there."

Paolantonio laughed. "Robin MacIntosh called you to find out when Rendell announced last year?" Sometimes he couldn't believe television reporters and how little research they did. An announcement date was the most rudimentary bit of information, but here the man was calling Rendell's campaign manager on his car phone to find it out. Cohen's prompt and matter-of-fact response was one of the many reasons that reporters had great respect for the man. He was always reachable by car phone, and he got back to reporters quickly, about both big and small questions.

"Yeah, and when he's going to give his acceptance speech. That's what everybody wants to know," Cohen said.

By now, the car was on I-95 heading for the Northeast. "Bob Kutler had a funny story today," said Cohen. "He said that if I had a dollar for every sample ballot out there on the street with Rendell's name on it, I'd be able to retire for the rest of my life. Everybody, everybody has Ed on their ballot." The sample ballots were telling voters how to vote, and Rendell was seen as the inevitable winner who would help the lower candidates ride along.

"So do you have your people manning many divisions?" Paolantonio asked.

"I hope we're not manning any divisions. We've spent $3 million getting our message out. If people aren't convinced by today, some little piece of paper telling them how to vote isn't going to do it. Every one of our people is supposed to be knocking on doors, just dragging people out of houses to the polls, not handing out pieces of paper."

"Where's Ed?"

"He's wandering. In the 37th ward, I think, in a car."

"Who's driving him?"

"Dave Montgomery," Cohen answered, "who I believe drove him on election day in 1977." That was the day Ed Rendell had won his big upset against the party-backed Emmet Fitzpatrick to become D.A., and there was a certain superstition in campaigns about lucky omens.

"Where are we going?" asked Paolantonio.

"Up to the Northeast headquarters, and then we'll check out a few divisions," said Cohen. "The Northeast is not a very mysterious place," he added with a small smile.

Cohen turned the questions around to the reporter. "Now that you've been out all day, what do you think turnout's going to be?"

"Forty-eight, low, maybe up to 55 percent," answered Paolantonio.

"That's higher than you used to think. What do you think about black turnout?"

"I don't think over 50 percent. I haven't seen a lot of Blackwell people."

KYW Newsradio was playing on the car radio, and Cohen would stop and listen when reports on the mayor's race came on. One piece on Rendell announced that the candidate was talking as if he were mayor-elect already, announcing targets for January. "The fiscal crisis is essential," said Rendell.

Cohen chuckled. "They say they're gonna talk about targets, and then they let Ed say all of five words. 'The fiscal crisis.' " He started to tell Sal about how good Rendell's coverage had been on the Channel 6 news last night. On the six o'clock newscast, Rendell had gone first, with his appearance at the Wofford rally downtown. "The rally looked great," Cohen added. "Much better on television than in person."

"So after the Warwick, are you going to go to the Diner on the Square?" Paolantonio asked, referring to a small upscale diner down the street from the Warwick that stayed open all night. The reporter was going to try to wind up his night's coverage by following Rendell and his key advisers after the hoopla had faded.

"There's almost no other place to go. I'll talk to Ed."

At that point they had arrived at Rendell's Northeast headquarters, which was on Frankford Avenue in a blue-collar section of the Northeast. It was only blocks away from the United Skates of America, the roller rink where Frank Rizzo had announced that January night ten months ago. The headquarters were on the second floor of a storefront next to a tire store and the Pennsylvania School of Dog Grooming. The main room featured a phone bank run by volunteers. "Hello, I'm calling for the Rendell campaign to see if you voted yet today" said one. "You did? Well, I'm certainly glad to hear that. Thanks very much." David Cohen made the rounds, talking to campaign workers about turnout and getting the word on who he should try to contact in the field. Paolantonio called his office.

When they left the headquarters, they walked across the street to a firehouse that was a polling place. Paolantonio went to the tables in each division, introduced himself, and asked what the count was. At the first it was 225. "Out of how many total voters?" he asked the poll worker. She fumbled with her sheets and finally found the street list: 557. Paolantonio did the math quickly in his head. "Almost 50 percent," he told Cohen, who had trailed behind him.

The ritual would be repeated at polling place after polling place that afternoon. Paolantonio did not really need the numbers for the story he would write that night. By the time he went to write about turnout he would have more accurate and final numbers, but he got a kick out of finding out what was happening midday. It was part of the excitement to try to predict final turnout and then theorize about which candidates that turnout would help and hurt. It was a little like being a sports reporter, trying to figure out what the score was in the first and second quarter, so he could predict and later explain victory or defeat. Cohen, on the other hand, was tracking the turnout to see if there were any major surprises, any places where extra manpower might be needed to bring out the vote. But since turnout was looking good for his candidate, he seemed to be simply keeping occupied on this last day as the votes were being made, keeping watch on the tight ship he'd run throughout the long campaign.

From the Northeast, they headed for divisions in the Northwest, a black middle-class section of the city. "So, we looked for you last night at the Melrose Diner," Cohen said to Paolantonio as they drove down Roosevelt Boulevard. Rendell had been out shaking hands at midnight at the popular South Philly diner.

"I never made it. I was at the Eagles game, and I went out with some people afterwards." Paolantonio had bought tickets for a skybox at Veterans Stadium the night before to watch the Eagles in a surprise victory against the New York Giants in Monday Night Football. It had not been a good season for the Eagles, since quarterback Randall Cunningham had been sidelined by an injury in the first game, but they had miraculously trounced the Giants, 30–7. "Best football game I ever saw," he said. He talked about how much he'd paid for the tickets. "It's terrible. I'm such a sports fan, and there are always these tickets to games floating around, but I can't accept them."

Paolantonio talked about how he had a policy never to eat at campaign events he attended, although not all reporters held the same credo on food and drink. "I drink a Coke, but that's about all. I figure nobody can say they buy me for a Coke."

Cohen smiled at this. "You mean they can buy you for a pig-in-a-blanket?" Paolantonio laughed in response.

"That's the trouble, Sal," Cohen said sarcastically. "How do you draw the line?"

Cohen continued to get beeped and to return calls. "We'll try," he said to one. "But Ed's schedule is not his own tonight." When he hung up, he said to the reporter, "We've got a lot of big contributors taking suites at the Warwick tonight, and they're all expecting Ed to stop by before going to the floor."

They checked another polling place in a black neighborhood and found turnout running closer to 30 percent. Paolantonio was curious about how the Second Congressional District election would go, and he noted that while candidates Lucien Blackwell and John White had street workers out, the third candidate, Chaka Fattah, didn't, and he talked about it with Cohen and Barnett when he got back to the car. As they headed down Broad Street, they passed John White's North Philadelphia headquarters, a dingy row house covered with White's campaign posters. "Imagine what it would feel like to see that many pictures of yourself," observed Paolantonio.

They decided to stop off at a polling place in North Philly, one of the most depressed areas of the city. They stopped the car outside an elementary school that housed a polling place. The campaign street workers, all of whom were black, eyed the three white men stepping out of the new white car. "What's wrong?" they asked alarmed. "Something happen?" They assumed that the men were police or FBI, to be in this neighborhood.

"No, no," Cohen hurried to reassure them. "We're with the Rendell campaign and he's from the *Inquirer.*"

The workers smiled then and handed them their literature. Inside the dilapidated school, Paolantonio went up to the head poll worker, a black woman in her sixties, explained he was from the *Inquirer,* and asked for the numbers. "You got credentials?" the woman asked suspiciously. "People been in and out of here all day wanting to see the numbers, every two minutes asking me for the numbers, people trying to mess with my machines, all these guys warring with each other when they should be in it together, and us, we're supposed to be neutral down here. I am not in a happy humor today."

Paolantonio showed her his press pass, and she begrudgingly read him her tallies. He thanked her politely and said he wouldn't be bothering her again. She gave him a second look and began to warm a little. "It's just this is the first time we ever had press down here. I like the *Inquirer.* I read it all the time. You all from the *Inquirer?*"

Cohen and Barnett smiled. "No, we're from the Rendell campaign. We just drive him around."

"I like the *Inquirer,*" the woman repeated. "I like that Chuck Stone. He's got some good things to say. But didn't he up and leave? Where'd he go to?"

Paolantonio didn't bother to tell her that Chuck Stone had been with the *Daily News,* not the *Inquirer.* Instead he informed her that Stone had left to teach in North Carolina.

She continued to chat. "Who I miss is Mr. Rizzo. Now there was a man who could get things done. He gave his word, he kept it. The day he died I almost died myself. I'd a given a few years of my life if he coulda lived."

When Paolantonio got back into the car with Cohen and Barnett, he was still thinking about what the woman had said. He'd believed all along, as others had not, that Rizzo had a good chance of getting the black vote. "David, what a fight this could have been if Rizzo had lived," he said almost wistfully. But then he laughed. "But I sure wouldn't be in this car today if he had."

"Where would you be?" Cohen asked.

"If Rizzo had lived, you guys would have hated me at this point in the campaign."

Cohen scoffed. "What do you mean, we would have hated you? It would have been a fight. We knew that."

Paolantonio wouldn't let it drop. "You would have gotten Wilson Goode to get out the black vote for Ed, and he would have hit you with Wilson in the Northeast," he said with relish, thinking how Rizzo would have adeptly turned the mayor's support for Rendell against him by playing on anti-Goode feeling in the white Northeast. Paolantonio was still planning out potential campaign strategies, even for a candidate lying in his grave.

Periodically Cohen checked in with Rendell, car phone to car phone. "Hi, Ed. David. It looks good, more of the same. We've just been up in the Northeast and they're sure they'll break 60 percent. The Northwest numbers are 25–30 percent. . . . Sal's in the car . . . "

"Hi, Ed," Sal shouted so that Rendell could hear him.

Cohen kept talking to his candidate. "KYW still has Fred Voigt saying turnout's going to be 60 percent." Voight was head of the Committee of 70, a civic watchdog group that monitored elections. "I talked to Neil. Neil's happy." Cohen was referring to Neil Oxman, the campaign's media consultant. Cohen told Rendell he'd check in with him later and hung up.

"Are you going to get the numbers tonight at the *Inquirer?*" Cohen asked, referring to the immediate poll results when the polls closed.

"We get them, but they aren't worth anything. The city and the *Inquirer* hate each other so much that the numbers are always fucked up, and every year they're worthless. I've been what the paper calls 'quarterback' for four elections now, and not one time have we been able to use the numbers we get from the computer hook-up. I told them, 'Don't give them any money until after you get the numbers,' but they never listen to me. We always wind up getting the numbers from Channel 6. It's unbelievable. We'd be nowhere without Jim Gardner and Marc Howard. That's why I have a television on my desk."

Cohen told Paolantonio about arrangements for the celebration at the hotel. "I've got podium passes and fourteen security guards. That should do it."

Paolantonio arrived at the *Inquirer* offices at four-thirty, ready to start writing his early story and step into the "quarterback" role. "See you at the hotel," he said to Cohen and Barnett.

Cohen looked at the car clock. "Three and a half hours," he said with a sigh, measuring the time left before the polls closed.

Barnett smiled. "You worried?"

"I just want it to be over," said Cohen.

36 The Night the Reporters Danced

November 5, 1991   *8:00 P.M.*

Election night headquarters for the Joe Egan campaign was set up in the Benjamin Franklin Hotel at Eighth and Chestnut Streets. Although the venerable old hotel had been refurbished three years ago and turned into an apartment house, there was still a somewhat drab air about the build-ing. At seven-thirty on a Tuesday night, the streets outside were deserted. By day, the area witnessed a brisk business, as the center of the jewelry trade in Philadelphia. But by night it was a tomb. Inside the Ben Franklin, it was little different. The massive lobby was practically deserted, except in one corner where a polling place was set up.

The party was set to begin in the grand ballroom on the mezzanine at 8:00 P.M. but at 7:45 the room was filled with no one but reporters. It had been a foregone conclusion for months that Egan did not have a chance and that the election was likely to be a landslide, but still the reporters were out in force, a part of their election night ritual. The three major TV stations all sent reporters, cameras, and live hook-ups to every headquar-ters in town, and Channel 29 had a producer and cameraman there. A number of radio reporters were also in the room, along with Doreen Carvajal and Dave Davies, although Davies would soon leave to spend election night in Egan's suite above the ballroom.

The presence of all the TV reporters was a spectacle not lost on the print reporters present. All through this campaign it had been rare to see a television reporter covering any press conference or forum where issues of substance would be discussed and ignored. But here on election night, the stations were going all out to cover a relatively meaningless ceremonial

event. Suddenly, they were "live on the scene," pretending that they were
the vehicle that brought election information to the voters, all the high
price talent out, sitting around waiting to cover the concession speech.
Kevin Boyle, reporter for talk radio station WWDB, was there, too,
dressed more formally than usual in a gray suit with loafers and no socks.
"I'm doing penance tonight," he said. "They're mad at me. That's why I'm
here." When he saw Dave Davies walk in to cover the event, he shrugged.
"I wonder who's mad at him." It was hardly the first-string television
reporters who were present at the event. The showcase reporters and
anchors were all at Harris Wofford's headquarters or Ed Rendell's. Egan
had gotten Robin Garrison from Channel 6, who regularly anchored the
early news and did "health checks," Joyce Evans, a low-profile black reporter from KYW, and Bill Baldini, a veteran from Channel 10.

At eight o'clock, the room looked even emptier as the reporters gathered
around the small television monitor that was showing Channel 10's election night coverage. The anchors broke in with an update but had no
results to report. Instead, they began to roll with their movie of the night,
Posing, about three women who let themselves be photographed for *Play-
boy* magazine. It was sweeps month, and the stations were not going to air
much of the election results since it would cut into the ratings that would
determine their advertising rates for the next quarter. Even Channel 6,
which had done an hourlong election special the night of the primary, had
cut back to a half-hour at nine-thirty this evening.

The reporters chatted idly as they waited for something to happen.
They had organized a pool to guess when Egan would concede. Boyle had
taken 8:25 and 9:26, thinking Egan would either want to be out of his
misery early or get coverage live on Channel 6's election night special.
Shortly after eight, Bill Baldini did his first live report. Standing on a piece
of masking tape laid down on the rug so he'd be in the right position for
his camera, with the other reporters out of view, he said, "Well, Diane,
everybody's optimistic here. They're handing out sponges that say 'Egan
for Mayor' to show how they'll clean up City Hall if they get in. But I'll
tell you, if Egan wins tonight, it'll be the biggest political upset in sixty
years."

The reporters were hoping that there would be some interesting people
to interview in these live spots, but for the first hour there was almost no
one in the room, except for a few campaign organizers and family members. The word was out that there would be very few Republican biggies
there tonight with Egan. Party boss Billy Meehan wasn't even there. He
was staying out of the limelight, as was his tradition, at the Bavarian Club
in the Northeast. Ron Castille wasn't expected. Council candidates were

all at other headquarters, possibly to dissociate themselves from what was happening with Egan.

But then at 9:00 P.M. Sam Katz walked into the ballroom. The reporters had wondered if he'd show up because that day his nine-year-old son had been mugged by kids wielding knives on the playground. But there he was, and immediately he was besieged by reporters. Bill Baldini landed him first, throwing out questions he would ask when he got his next live cut-in report in a few minutes. "Would it be fair to ask you what you would have done differently than Egan?" he asked. Katz said it would. For the last week Katz had been preparing for a new opportunity for himself to challenge the Republican party and use popular disenchantment with the results of this election to his own advantage. This might be a crucial night to get wide media coverage as passed-over hero and future savior of the Republican party, so even though his son had been badly shaken up that morning, he'd gone out for the night.

And it was true. He was the hot ticket for the many reporters camped at the Benjamin Franklin, the only person worth interviewing aside from Franny Rizzo, Frank's son. And so they lined up one after another to get him and put him on prime time. Bill Baldini was first. "Well, Diane, outwardly, people are optimistic here tonight, but privately people are admitting that a win is not going to happen tonight. The person standing next to me right now is a man some people think should have been the candidate in this election, Sam Katz. Mr. Katz, what would you have done differently if you had been the candidate?"

When Baldini was done, Robin Garrison got him, and then Joyce Evans, and then he moved on to the radio and newspaper reporters. When Katz had made the rounds, done all his interviews, and shaken a few hands with party faithful, he put his trench coat back on and headed out of the hotel. He would not be at Joe Egan's side that night when the candidate conceded, even though he had served as campaign chairman. It appeared that he had come to the Benjamin Franklin that night to give interviews, and when he had done that, he headed out to the next appearance, as a guest analyst on the Bernie Herman show on WWDB and later for commentary on Channel 6's late news.

At Rendell's election night headquarters at the Warwick Hotel at Seventeenth and Locust Streets, the scene was very different. At 10:00 P.M. the softly lit mezzanine ballroom was cloudy with cigarette smoke and mobbed with Rendell supporters, both the powerful and the rank-and-file. Two large television sets had been mounted above the stage so that election results could be followed. With every election update, Rendell's lead grew and the excitement of the crowd seemed to mount. Rendell was triumphing over Egan, as expected. Equally heady for the crowd gathered, Harris Wofford was showing a strong lead over Dick Thornburgh in the race for Senate.

Across from the stage on a large podium set up for the television equipment, even the reporters were caught up in the excitement of the evening. Barbara Grant was dancing barefoot to the sounds of the six-piece band that entertained the crowd as they waited for Rendell to appear and claim victory. Rendell's campaign had been so well planned that even the election night fete, orchestrated by the city's premiere events planner, Fred Stein, was perfect, a rollicking good party in and of itself. "How do you like the band?" Stein was heard to ask. "They played at my son's bar mitzvah. They're great, aren't they?" It was somehow fitting that Rendell's campaign had managed to get the reporters dancing on election night, since in a way it had kept them dancing all through the long campaign.

As supporters drank their cocktails and schmoozed, David Cohen and Neil Oxman took turns making their way from Rendell's suite to the bank of reporters in the ballroom to give interviews about what their own tallies were showing and to keep reporters apprised of when Rendell was likely to make his acceptance speech. Shortly after 10:00 P.M., the television screens on the podium flashed with Joe Egan's face. The volume came up and the crowd quieted. "I have just called Ed Rendell and conceded the election, and I wish him the best," Egan was shown saying. "I want to tell the people of Philadelphia that we have to get behind Ed Rendell."

The crowd cheered at the announcement and immediately began calling for Rendell. But plans were plans. The victory speech had been calculated to make the eleven o'clock news, so the crowd waited another forty-five minutes for his appearance. The television screens showed the tally with 88 percent of the votes. Rendell had 67 percent to Egan's 33 percent. As the band played "Happy Days Are Here Again," and the crowd clapped and cheered, Rendell finally appeared, walking through an opening in the crowd that was created by the security guards. He climbed to the podium and was surrounded by his wife, Midge, his son, Jesse, and key supporters like State Senator Hardy Williams, George Burrell, and Sandy Fox. "Well," said Rendell, with a broad grin, "it was a long, long, long, long road to get here, wasn't it?" The crowd cheered in response. "I know I've said on the campaign trail this last two or three weeks that we had miles to go before I sleep, but tonight we have about 6.3 miles to go before I sleep." The distance he described was from the hotel to his home in the East Falls neighborhood. He went on to thank his wife, congratulate Joe Egan for the dignified campaign he ran, and call for unity in trying to govern the city.

In the back of the room, behind the platform holding the bank of television reporters, David Cohen stood alone, allowing himself a moment of quiet emotion. His work on the campaign was finally done and he had accomplished what he had set out to do. Ed Rendell had won and won by a huge margin, some thirty-four points. It was a victory that had come as a result of hours and hours of strategizing, churning out position papers, and meeting with party leaders, the unions, the business community, the community groups, the real-estate sector. It was also a victory that could be said to have resulted from all manner of chance events and uncontrollable moves—from Lucien Blackwell's decision to stay in the primary and challenge George Burrell, to Frank Rizzo's death and Billy Meehan's decision not to pick Sam Katz as his successor.

But David Cohen would be the first to acknowledge that it was also a victory for a campaign that understood perhaps better than any of its competitors how to use the local media to its own advantage. More than anything in 1991, it was understanding the weaknesses of local reporters—the newspaper's fascination with strategy and the horse race, television's need for simple themes and sound-bites and its inability to scratch very far beneath the surface of a plan or proposal—that spelled victory for a candidate. While the newspaper reporters would pride themselves on their intricate analyses of strategy and their issue-based stories down the stretch and the TV stations would claim they were managing to capture the high points of the campaign, they would all wind up being used at crucial junctures by the campaign of the most media-savvy candidate.

In the end, Ed Rendell's victory would have more to do with how well he understood and controlled the local media than with the case he was ever permitted to make on how he would govern the city of Philadelphia.

Conclusion

❧ This book has told the story of how newspapers and television stations covered the 1991 election for mayor of Philadelphia. But it was meant to be more than the saga of one city's election and one particularly colorful group of politicians and reporters. It is offered as a cautionary tale about the new direction of local campaign coverage in cities throughout the country. All too often in local elections, journalists are not providing voters with enough information to evaluate candidates and make sense of the issues confronting their cities. While devoting much attention to the horse race and personal scandal, the local news media offer disappointingly little reporting on approaches to policy and governing.

This fundamental failing in campaign coverage is not the result of the laziness or incompetence of reporters operating in a journalistic backwater. To the contrary, the journalists described in this book were considered at or near the top of their form, working in the nation's fourth largest media market for news organizations that routinely receive national accolades. If they failed to provide city voters with important information, it was not because of personal weaknesses but systemic ones. They failed because of the system of rewards and constraints set up by their news organizations.

Some of these constraints and rewards have existed since the emergence of the mass circulation newspapers of the nineteenth century. Daily journalists have always faced deadlines that limit in-depth reporting, and the need to capture mass audiences has often tempted them to use personal scandal to capture attention. But, as this book has tried to show, other forces are new. The changing economic realities facing metropolitan newspapers and local television stations have led to a major restructuring of the news product, with important implications for the way city elections have come to be covered.

For metropolitan newspapers, the new challenges are coming from many directions. Where once network television posed the major threat, today direct mail, cable television, and suburban newspapers compete for consumers' time and advertising dollars. Although metropolitan newspapers in most media markets are still producing high rates of return, management has been rightfully concerned about the future. The long-cherished separation of editorial and business operations is fading, as newspaper editors have been forced to pay more attention to circulation and advertising trends and market research. Editors know that to survive they must make major changes, although they are not always sure which strategies will work.

Some of the changes have been to make the newspaper look better: introducing color, increasing the use of photographs, and shortening stories. But other changes have been in the news itself. Newspapers have increased their coverage of national and international news, expanded regional business sections, and added specialty areas such as science, health, and the environment. At the same time, an increasing percentage of resources has been withdrawn from city coverage and put into reporting on the suburbs, where more and more readers now reside. Another focus for major change has been the front page. Editors have experimented with new designs and more "reader-friendly" writing styles. They have gone after a new mix of stories, including the weighty examination of a scientific breakthrough alongside the lighter feature on a quirky sociological trend. But in this attempt to come up with a more marketable product, straight news pieces on subjects like a city political race have fallen in priority. In 1991, it would be telling that only nine stories about the Philadelphia mayoral election would make the front page of the *Inquirer* during the fall campaign.

Such placement decisions are important not simply for their ability to attract readers, but for the signals they send to reporters—providing immediate feedback on what kinds of stories are most prized at any point in time. It was remarkable how many of the reporters interviewed for this book remembered precisely where stories they had written months before had been played in the paper. The front page or first page of the metro section made an indelible mark, as did being above or below the fold, with a single column or banner headline. In the 1991 campaign, the placement decisions of the *Philadelphia Inquirer* would send a clear message to the paper's reporters. Only the most dramatic stories about the campaign—a surprise entrance into the race, an unexpected endorsement, the apparent collapse of a campaign—would make the front page, while stories about issues would be pushed much further back. In the primary, only three of the twenty-two stories that made the front page would be about issues, while in the general election, it would be only one in nine.

In the face of such a reward structure, it is not surprising that much of a newspaper's political reporting has come to focus on the horse race or that campaign coverage has devolved into the sophisticated dissection of campaign strategy. Political reporters pride themselves on their aggressiveness in getting the inside scoop on key endorsements and backroom deals and new ad campaigns, and they take satisfaction from the fact that such stories win them good play. The only problem with the new political journalism of strategy is that it offers so little of value to the readers who will actually be voting in an election. It was telling that in Philadelphia's primary elections, the *Inquirer* devoted almost 65 percent of its coverage to the horse race, information that had nothing to do with the candidate's plans or proposals or positions or qualifications. Only 19 percent of the stories focused on issues.

Even when issues were considered, there were glaring omissions, in particular the failure to examine a candidate's performance in past positions. It was the most obvious question to ask about the contenders, and yet in Philadelphia's elections, the least examined. While reporters alternately touted and ignored Sam Katz, and while some tried to decide whether his sexual harassment case would affect his election chances more than his marijuana smoking or his questionable land dealings, most paid virtually no attention to his actual qualifications for managing city government. As a member of the School Board, had he been a force for fiscal responsibility or had he sat back ineffectually while the school district continued to run deficits? Did his experience running a small professional consulting firm qualify him to manage the complex affairs of the nation's fifth largest city? Did his work helping cities finance capital projects justify the claim that he knew how to manage money and would solve Philadelphia's fiscal problems? The questions were essential in evaluating Katz's candidacy, but they were never posed in his news coverage.

Other crucial substantive questions were also largely ignored. What were the candidates proposing to do about the problems facing the city, and what information supported or contradicted their approaches? While privatization received some attention, the larger question of how Philadelphia—or any city—could reverse the trend in declining employment and tax revenues was rarely mentioned. Late in the campaign, Rendell's and Egan's proposals to add police officers to the force received some critical scrutiny, but dozens of other proposals and plans were tossed out through both primary and general elections with little probing. Did Frank Rizzo's plans to restructure the health department make any sense? How did Lucien Blackwell's scholarship plan or Sam Katz's proposals for educational choice jibe with fiscal realities? Ed Rendell's campaign had an answer for every problem, a laundry list of programs thrown out for every dilemma. But reporters made few attempts to dissect the list and contact independent experts to evaluate the wisdom or feasibility of the plans.

The reason such important questions were ignored was, in part, that reporters were not asked to address them nor were they rewarded with prominent play when they tried. But it was also because it takes more time to report on substance than strategy. Charting which candidate is most likely to get the mayor's endorsement can be teased out by an afternoon on the phone to well-placed sources. Investigating personal scandal may be accomplished by responding to leaks or conducting electronic searches of past news stories. But reporting on substance often requires poring over the fine print of many complex documents, not just the segments highlighted by a political enemy, and examining in detail the records of candidates in past positions, not simply speed-reading old newspaper clips. And it necessitates digesting the often long-winded evaluations of technical experts, rather than just collecting the glib sound-bite of the day from the willing and eager media consultant.

And that is the problem. Beat reporters are given no time to research the issues, particularly given the fact that they are under constant pressure to produce stories about the campaign from events that occurred in the previous twenty-four hours. While the *Inquirer* would release reporters to track down rumors of sexual improprieties, no such equally determined and concerted effort was made to find out which plans made sense. The irony is that the *Inquirer* has a history of long-term, in-depth reporting on important issues, one of the few newspapers in the country that has given reporters months at a time to investigate issues of public import and hundreds of column inches to report the results. In the year before the mayoral race, the paper had even turned out an incisive series on the underlying structural problems facing Philadelphia. The problem was that city political coverage was seen as a mission separate from long-term substantive projects, so much so that campaign stories never mentioned the earlier series that had so cogently laid out the dilemmas facing the city.

When Sal Paolantonio stepped into the job of covering the 1991 mayor's race, he would be made forcefully aware of the newspaper's reward structure and how city politics fit into it. Paolantonio was young, ambitious, and aggressive, the kind of person who quickly mastered the rules of any game and always played to win. Paolantonio not only remembered what page his hundreds of campaign stories landed on, he practically memorized the type face of the headlines. He watched as his coverage of announcement speeches, the kind of stories that made the front page back in 1987, were pushed back into the metro section. And it was not lost on him when his probing piece on Castille's sales tax proposal was buried on page 12-B behind pages of display ads or when an enterprising story on women's issues made only 6-B. It was quite a different story, however, when he focused on the elaborate twists and turns in the horse race. When the reporter offered his interpretations of the polls and endorsements and campaign finance reports and the insider information he managed to unearth, he would get far more prominent display.

And some of the best play for his stories would come when he stepped out on a limb to create angles, piecing together seemingly disparate pieces of information to come up with a story full of drama and intrigue. When he took the news that Sam Katz's finance chairmen were abandoning him and combined it with other clues to suggest that Katz was about to withdraw from the campaign, his story made page 1. He used the same technique in the fall campaign when he took Joe Egan's failure to appear at a forum on a day when devastating poll results were released. In each case, the angle was responsible for the play, because increasingly a story about a mayoral campaign had to have some extra element of drama, some novel twist, to appear on the front page.

The problem was that while the angles and interpretations won good play, they sometimes proved wrong. Sam Katz's loss of his finance chairmen did not "all but end" his campaign. Ron Castille turned out to be not particularly "cool under fire." And Joe Egan's bout with sinusitis and exhaustion was no more indicative of his weakness as a candidate than his simple answers to questions on the campaign trail. While Paolantonio would argue that every interpretative story was backed up by informed sources, it was also true that often other sources were making quite divergent assessments and not getting covered for them. The important point is that the newspaper provided little check on the reporter's penchant for taking interpretive reporting to the edge; instead, it actively encouraged it. The city politics reporter, like so many of his counterparts, was being rewarded for drama, not substance.

That Paolantonio may have brought a slant to his reporting on the campaign—or that sometimes in the course of writing hundreds of stories, he would read the signs wrong—would not have been a problem if he had been one of many voices interpreting what was happening to the candidates. But the simple fact was that he, like so many political reporters at metropolitan newspapers around the country, had almost a monopoly on political interpretation in the city and came to play a major role in influencing broadcast journalists in the market. As a result, his reporting—interpretations and all—influenced important decisions on fundraising, voter registration, and actual voting. The irony, of course, was that Paolantonio wrote many solid stories throughout the campaign that would never be picked up by broadcast journalists. No TV reporter would ever crib from the pieces he wrote about reactions to Castille's sales tax or how Rendell's promises to the police union would be difficult to fulfill. Instead, his most interpretive pieces on the horse race would have the most amplified effect.

In an interview after the election, Paolantonio offered an interesting observation about his role in the campaign. He acknowledged his power as lead reporter for the largest newspaper in town and realized that broadcast journalists sometimes took their cues from him. But he contended that the hundreds of column inches he wrote about the campaign didn't have a fraction of the impact of reports on local newscasts. While political insiders were reading every word he wrote, he noted, it was the pieces that made it onto the top-rated Channel 6 news that would really hold sway with voters. It was probably not lost on Paolantonio that Frank Rizzo's entire assault on Ron Castille was largely carried out on local television news and that if the newscasts had not been so willing to revel in the slugfest, Rizzo probably would have lost the election. The newspaper reporter who took such pride in his role in the campaign and held TV reporters in such disdain would readily admit that the role of the print media in campaigns has been overshadowed by TV.

And that, of course, is the other major new factor influencing local political coverage in the 1990s: the growing importance of local television news as a source of information about politics and government. The power of local TV has been growing not just in Philadelphia but throughout the nation. In 1990, the Roper Organization found that more Americans said they became best acquainted with candidates running in local elections from television (43 percent) than from newspapers (40 percent). In Philadelphia in 1991, the circulation of the two major newspapers combined was approximately 700,000, while more than one million households were tuned to the three local newscasts at six o'clock. Hundreds of thousands more viewers watched those same newscasts early in the morning, at noon, at five, and late at night. By 1992, the Times-Mirror Organization found that voters were relying on local television newscasts, almost as much as network TV, as a major source of news about presidential elections. Clearly, local newscasts are fast becoming a major vehicle for the communication of political messages in America, trusted by the public and taken very seriously by public officials and candidates alike.

What is troubling about this trend is that, as more and more citizens are relying on local television for their news, the coverage of politics and government by local newscasts has become progressively weakened, abbreviated, and more susceptible to manipulation. In part, the change has resulted from mounting pressure from corporate owners to keep profit margins high, which has led to a stronger emphasis on the bottom line. To keep ratings up, station managers have come to demand that news be fun to watch, not necessarily informative to the electorate. Increasingly, the goal is to find new and different visual gimmicks to catch the attention of the errant viewer and convey the illusion that the stations are delivering news.

At the same time, cost-cutting moves have slashed what were already small staffs. While the *Philadelphia Inquirer* employs hundreds of journalists to report the news each day, each local newscast typically relies on fewer than a dozen reporters to cover the very same region. At the same time, older, more experienced—and higher-salaried—reporters are being replaced with younger, cheaper talent. The departure of veteran political reporter Tia O'Brien from Philadelphia's KYW-TV in 1991 was emblematic of a disturbing pattern at stations around the country. Increasingly, local television reporters who try to present an alternative media voice to a city's newspapers find their reporting efforts undercut at every turn. Because their stations seem more concerned with entertaining than informing the audience, reporters are forced to substitute glitz and sensation for substance, even when reporting about governmental issues and campaigns for local office. Each time a reporter mounts a fight against a news decision, she gives her news directors one more reason to offer thumbs down at contract renewal time and turn to a more docile talent willing to work for less money.

Whether veterans or newcomers, the reporters who remain at local television stations are faced with the same prospect. They are forced to abandon the coverage of government and politics in favor of more crime stories and more consumer and health features. Again, individual television reporters are not ultimately responsible for downplaying and trivializing local politics in favor of more sensational fare. Station managers make these decisions, maintaining that their focus group research tells them this is what viewers want. But the deeper truth is that this is the kind of news that is cheapest for the stations to produce while still attracting viewers. If only a few hours are being put into any story, then it is not surprising that gruesome murders are what local television news is best at covering. With no beats, little time for research, and constant pressure to come up with dramatic video and sound-bites, is it any wonder that the shallow government coverage TV reporters produce wins few accolades from focus groups?

The upshot is that, increasingly, local TV will cover only those political campaigns that feature a close horse race or savage personal attacks. And even then they will ignore what the candidates are saying about problems and solutions. In Philadelphia's 1991 mayoral primaries, the TV stations were only too happy to cover Republican Frank Rizzo's provocative personal attacks on Ron Castille. Meanwhile, they virtually ignored the Democratic candidates and the substantive issues facing the bankrupt city. The major TV news stations devoted a full 27 percent of their primary coverage to Rizzo's unsubstantiated charges against Castille and Castille's countercharges, while only according 12 percent of their time to the issues. Collecting Rizzo's latest outrageous sound-bite about Castille was clearly easier for time-pressed general assignment reporters than making sense of the candidates' position papers. It also tended to be just what the managers back in the newsroom wanted: shocking, sensational fare with which to emulate *A Current Affair* and *Hard Copy* and compete with all the other entertainment shows on all the other channels. But as a result, the public learned shockingly little about the issues facing the city—or even that the candidates were talking about those issues. Out of 504 half-hour newscasts in the primary, only thirty-four minutes touched on the issues facing Philadelphia—only four minutes more than the typical situation comedy.

Even more disturbing is that when it comes to elections where frontrunners lead by large margins and candidates refrain from personal attacks, the television cameras, and particularly the television reporters, virtually abandon the race. When Frank Rizzo died and Joe Egan was selected to replace him, camera crews across the city folded up their equipment and went home. In Egan's case, it was not that he stood much less of a chance to beat Rendell than Rizzo would have. It was that Egan was unable to duplicate the Frank Rizzo show for the cameras. In response, the television stations drastically cut back on their coverage. In the general election, network affiliate newscasts devoted seventeen seconds per broadcast to the campaign, less than half the limited time they had devoted to the primary. Meanwhile, the stations were accepting over a million dollars in advertising from the candidates, most of it from Rendell's well-funded campaign. More and more, television news has come to tell people about bizarre crimes, and television commercials to tell them about their options for elected office. Media consultants, rather than journalists, have assumed the job of informing the electorate about their choices.

When Philadelphia's television stations did cover the mayoral race, their few reporters, working without specialized beats and under severe time constraints, could offer little depth. They were expected to turn the campaign into a mini soap opera, where the premium was on drama and emotion, not information for voters. Candidates were cast into convenient dramatic roles, with little probing into the validity or relevance of the characterizations. Ron Castille was conveniently hailed as a "war hero" at a time when the United States was at war, despite the fact that fighting on foreign soil could not be said to have much to do with governing a major city. Sam Katz neatly fit the bill of the "municipal finance expert," although the stations never examined his qualifications for the title. And Frank Rizzo was cast as "tough cop" with little analysis of whether he could make the streets safer than his predecessors. While these political mini-series made for entertaining viewing, they provided viewers with little useful information and ensured that candidates who could not be easily typecast would be essentially ignored.

Another disturbing new trend was the assignment of cameras alone to cover campaign events, as a way to create the illusion of covering civic affairs while working within a severely limited budget. In Philadelphia's general election, almost three-quarters of the affiliates' stories on the election did not use reporters, relying instead on video and campaign press releases for their stories. Television stations today seem content to merely show their viewers what the candidates look like. They rely on press releases as a substitute for independent reporting and allow themselves to be subjected to the almost complete influence of campaign organizations. In the 1991 Philadelphia mayor's race, it was clear time and again that a newscast was failing to do even the most rudimentary research on even the most outlandish proposals. Instead, they parroted the words prepared by the candidates' aides. While not every candidate understood how to control TV news and it was no simple feat to get on local television in 1991, a few shrewd politicians knew precisely how to get the increasingly docile local news operations to follow their tune.

Many campaign organizations have figured out how to operate in this new media environment, manipulating not only local TV but also newspapers. If the newspapers now care mostly about strategy and the horse race, then some campaign managers will orchestrate poll results that show their candidate in the lead and spin out scenarios under which they can triumph. If TV is looking for simple, emotional sound-bites, then some candidates are only too happy to attack their opponents or set themselves up in the pose of local hero, knowing the TV reporters of the 1990s will do little to check the veracity of the charges or the soundness of the image. For some candidates, the increasing withdrawal of local television news from the coverage of local elections has become an advantage. Well-financed politicians can use television advertising to get their message across without fear of contradiction by a local newscast.

In contrast, other local candidates have little idea about how to orchestrate their news coverage in the new media environment. They still think that calling a press conference with a visual backdrop will win them news coverage and that a straightforward approach to the issues will gain them recognition. They mistake the overtures of the schmoozing journalist as the approach of a fellow traveler, and give little thought to delivering potentially damaging information to an audience of hundreds of thousands. Candidates talk to reporters when they shouldn't, but they become inaccessible when they ought to be spoon-feeding facts and figures. They think that the way to neutralize a bad story is to call a press conference to talk about it and that the way to reverse negative coverage is to march into newspaper offices and raise hell with editors. As a result, the field of candidates becomes divided not just into "new faces" and "old faces" but, more fundamentally, into "users" who know how to exploit the media and "nonusers" who blunder their way into embarrassment or oblivion. As a result, the victor in too many local elections is not the person who has demonstrated the most decisive leadership in past positions or who has presented the most convincing plans and strategies for the future of the city. It is the candidate who has understood how best to exploit the weaknesses of the local media.

That the public loses out from this kind of coverage is not hard to see. The continuing overriding emphasis on poll results and the horse race by both television and newspapers has several negative effects on election outcomes. Early polls that show the candidate with the greatest name recognition in the lead have almost no reliability in predicting the outcome of a race, except as self-fulfilling prophecies. And yet they send important signals to contributors, allowing the early front-runners to successfully raise funds and purchase television advertising to maintain their lead. On the other hand, the candidates who have not yet established themselves and thus trail in early polls are ignored by the media and have a harder time raising money or increasing their support from voters. It is understandable that in campaigns with multiple candidates, particularly primaries, the media would be tempted to focus their limited time, space, and reporting staff on only the leading candidates. But from the voter's perspective, such selective coverage does great disservice. Results of primary elections often determine outcomes of general elections, particularly in cities like Philadelphia, where one party dominates.

Preoccupation with the horse race and personal attacks is also harmful in that it drives out consideration of substantive questions. The time spent covering the Frank Rizzo-Ron Castille "slugfest" meant that very little television reporting would even mention that the candidates spent most of their time out discussing issues. The *Inquirer*'s decision to cover the KYW radio debate as a story about Ron Castille's failure to attend resulted in the omission of any information on the substantive differences that arose between the two candidates who did debate. And the continued focus by both newspapers and television on whether one of the three black candidates would drop out of the Democratic primary kept reporters from finding out that one of those candidates thought the city's financial problems were the result of a bank conspiracy. Thus, Philadelphia voters chose candidates based not on who was most qualified to lead but on who had been most successful in manipulating the media.

Another result of the news coverage may be even more important than obscuring the differences that exist among candidates. An emphasis on the horse race increases the cynicism of voters who come to believe that candidates are not even talking about the issues. Sometimes, they aren't—particularly if the objective of a campaign is to avoid controversy or to discredit an opponent or to get a message out unimpeded through advertising. But all too often candidates voice a range of opinions and positions during campaigns. The problem is that most of it is ignored by television stations, and often by newspapers, in favor of a "slugfest" or one more racial analysis of voting patterns. The resulting image of the politicians is that of pure political opportunist. Candidates seem to care only about winning and losing, garnering endorsements, raising money, and assessing different voting blocs. Whatever substance is put forward in a campaign is carefully edited out of the picture by reporters, editors, and news directors. As a result, voters become disenchanted and detached from the electoral process, they fail to understand crucial distinctions among the candidates, and on election day they are less likely to exercise their vote.

In thinking about remedies for these weaknesses in campaign coverage, the responses of two key decision makers in the Philadelphia media are enlightening. Maxwell King, the editor of the *Philadelphia Inquirer,* was asked to comment on the conclusions of this study, specifically the findings that his newspaper devoted 65 percent of its 1991 primary coverage to the horse race and only 19 percent to issues, and that most front-page stories focused on the horse race, not on issues. "If your statistics are correct," he responded, "that so much of it was not on issues, then I think that's a failing. It wasn't intended to be so heavily horse race." He added that there has been an historic tendency by newspapers to play dramatic stories rather than issues stories related to a campaign on page 1. "It takes a little more thought to see and develop the potential of issues stories for the front page," he said. But he added that he would like to see the paper's political coverage become more issues-oriented. "I think that's something that we have a growing awareness about, among editors and reporters: that there's a real opportunity for us to be more issue-based in our coverage of politics." He also said that while newspapers may "connect viscerally" with readers by means of dramatic stories, the long-term success of the newspaper depends on connecting with readers via substance. "Our distinctive strength," he said, "lies in our ability to explain things well. We need to move toward more issues coverage."

King's response is revealing for two reasons. First, it shows that emphasizing the horse race over issues is not necessarily a deliberate objective. Rather, it is the result of day-to-day decisions by a complex cast of actors. Second, it shows that often the key decision makers at a paper are unaware of the extent to which the horse race has dominated coverage. Focused as they are on the redesign of the paper as a whole, the top editors have been caught unaware when it comes to the direction in which their election coverage has been moving. But it was also significant that when made aware of the findings of this study, the editor agreed that it was a failing. King claimed that it was increasingly important for a newspaper to recognize the importance of covering issues as a means of "connecting" and retaining readers. In other words, many newspaper editors may not realize the extent to which their political coverage has moved away from substantive concerns. But when provided with hard data about the patterns, they may be moved to change.

The response of television news director Drew Berry from Channel 10/WCAU was noticeably different. Berry expressed little surprise that his station had devoted dramatically little attention to either the primary or general election campaigns. His response to the data was, "Quantity is not necessarily quality." He maintained that his station had done a completely adequate job of covering the campaigns and suggested that while "it is an obligation to cover a mayoral race," in the future there would be a continuing de-emphasis on the news of those campaigns which affected only a segment of the regional market. In responding to the question of why so much of the news was concerned with the Rizzo-Castille "slugfest," he answered that television is a "visual medium" and that "people are interested in controversy." He said that he thought the Sunday morning public affairs programs gave ample attention to the issues in local elections, but that newscasts have only a finite amount of space. He offered little sense that television news was spending much energy trying to develop new ways to better communicate important civic information to viewers. Rather, Berry offered a profile of the new local television journalism, which would stress new marketing strategies and provide audiences with more stories about personal health and safety.

These responses suggest that the prospects for the improvement of local election coverage are very different for newspapers than for television. Newspapers have always had a strong commitment to providing their readers with the substantive information they need. But with the major structural changes of the last decade, they seem to have lost sight of how their election coverage has veered off course. Newspapers need to recognize that all their focus on strategy and personal scandal not only fails to provide voters with the information they need but actively increases voter apathy and cynicism and unfairly stereotypes the candidates.

Newspapers have been inching closer to bolstering their coverage of issues, but they must learn to do it better and at the point in time when it makes a difference. In the Philadelphia mayor's race, the *Inquirer* showed in its coverage of the general election that it was committed to examining the candidates' positions on a series of issues facing Philadelphia. But there were two problems with the approach to such coverage. The first has to do with timing. Issue-based coverage is usually done least in primaries, since that is when horse race questions are typically most exciting. But issues coverage matters most during primaries, since the candidate who emerges victorious from a primary often goes on to win a general election. Issues coverage in newspapers also tends to come later in campaigns, when voters have already formed opinions of the candidates based on all the horse race and personal character journalism. A few weeks before election day, newspapers tend to "dump type" on all the candidates' positions on the issues. They clump together more information than readers can understand in a short period of time, well after financial contributions have been made and many voters have already decided.

The second problem lies with how issues are approached when they are covered. All too often, issues coverage takes the form of a tedious rendering of the candidates' position papers and little more. It is not that such information is unimportant, but it should be the starting point, not the ending point, of a news story. Journalists need to invest their energies not merely in summarizing plans but in gathering the additional information necessary to help readers make sense of those plans. They should be looking not for more political operatives to ask about game plans but for more independent experts to interview about the feasibility and soundness of plans. Reporters need to cast the underlying problems, in all their complexity, before the readers and then explain how the candidates' plans may or may not succeed. Although not simple or quick to report, this kind of information is precisely what voters need to make reasoned decisions about the candidates and what newspapers need to try to answer if they want to be relevant or useful to the electorate.

The structure of newspaper reporting also needs to change so that the biggest kudos and most prominent placement are not awarded solely to stories that uncover something negative about the candidates. Reporters need to know that they will be equally rewarded for pieces that help voters judge which candidate is better qualified to be mayor. A model of campaign reporting needs to be put forward in which reporters are neither passive stenographers—merely transcribing whatever programmed message a campaign is transmitting—nor cynical deconstructionists of campaign strategy. Instead, they need to be active inquisitors about the plans, proposals, and qualifications of the candidates. They need to turn their skills in creating drama and interest to questions of substance rather than to amusing trivia. As editor Max King noted, the survival of newspapers will depend on the ability to clearly and compellingly explicate complex matters for their audiences. Smaller suburban and community newspapers have already learned that there is ample demand for news coverage of government issues that directly affect the audience. In the near future, as metropolitan newspapers explore new methods for delivering information, including the all-important electronic pathways, they may find that they will be better able to supply substance targeted at different audience segments.

When it comes to local television news, the prospects for change are mixed. Newspapers seem committed to experimenting with new formulas for conveying information while maintaining audience excitement. But the typical local television station appears less concerned with social responsibility and less willing to spend the money necessary to improve the quality of information provided to voters, as increasingly news decisions at local television stations are being made by businessmen, not journalists. While newscasts are constantly trying out new formulas, the innovations tend to center on visual techniques, not better ways to convey important information. Since the 1991 election, the low-budget approach to local television news coverage seems to have grown even stronger, resulting in more tabloid-like coverage of sensational crimes, more canned reports picked up from the satellites, and less local campaign coverage than ever.

And yet there are two trends on the horizon that offer hope. One concerns the dramatic innovations in television political coverage that occurred in the 1992 presidential election. Through the vehicle of television talk shows and other so-called new media, Americans showed that they were hungry for information about the problems the country faced, not more stories on personal dirt or the latest poll results. And the national media got the message. The networks did not abandon the coverage of the horse race, but they began to run longer segments examining where Bill

Clinton and George Bush stood on specific issues and what they had done in the past. The news programs also used "truth squads" to check the validity of claims candidates made in public forums. These innovations demonstrated that the medium of television is capable of presenting substance, if reporters are given the assignment and provided with the time and resources with which to follow through. The change in the tenor of the news also showed that there is an apparent link between substantive news coverage and political participation, since voter turnout in the 1992 presidential election was at its highest level in thirty years.

While the lesson of the 1992 campaign does not seem to have to registered much with the local stations, there are signs that substance is filtering into local television news in another venue: through the twenty-four-hour local cable news channels that have been cropping up throughout the country. From News 12 Long Island and New York City's Channel One to Washington, D.C.'s Newschannel 8 and the Orange County Newschannel in Southern California, new vehicles for local television news are offering less murder and mayhem and more substantive information on government and politics. More and more of these upstart operations are proving that, in the future environment of the so-called information superhighway, some important local niches may be created to deliver on substance, not sensation.

But in the end, it is the public who must drive the process of change. People need to recognize the emptiness and negativity of what they have been getting in the way of political coverage and demand something more. Voters have become accustomed to thinking that what they need to know about a campaign is who is ahead, who is behind, and by how much. They have become too accustomed to election reporting looking and sounding like sports coverage, with all the talk of strategies for offense and defense, prospects for victory, and tales of off-the-field scandals. Both television viewers and newspaper readers need to stop and think about how little such play-by-play coverage tells them about their choice of a candidate and the challenges facing their localities.

In the end, the public must demand something better from the media, and the media must rediscover their ability to demand something more from the candidates.

Epilogue

In his first two years of office, **Ed Rendell** obtained major savings by renegotiating municipal labor contracts and privatizing some city services. He succeeded in balancing the budget without tax increases or drastic service cuts. He was, however, unable to fulfill his campaign promise to hire one thousand new police officers.

David L. Cohen took over as Ed Rendell's chief of staff and was viewed by many city reporters as the most effective media source the city had ever witnessed. Instituting a policy limiting the ability of other administration officials to talk to the media, Cohen was able to orchestrate a media honeymoon for Mayor Rendell that carried into the third year of his first term.

Ron Castille worked as a private attorney until 1993, when he was elected to the Pennsylvania Supreme Court. His coverage in the Supreme Court primary election prominently featured his personal background and experiences in the war. In the general election, he received the endorsement of the *Philadelphia Inquirer*'s editorial board.

Sam Katz entered the 1994 Republican primary for governor, but failed to win the endorsement of Philadelphia's Republican City Committee, still headed by Billy Meehan. A few months earlier Katz had celebrated his daughter's bat mitzvah, inviting Sal Paolantonio and his family to attend.

Sal Paolantonio covered the 1992 presidential campaign of Pat Buchanan for Knight-Ridder, before taking a leave to write a biography of Frank Rizzo, which became a local best-seller. When he returned to the *Inquirer*, he was assigned to the sports department to cover the Philadelphia Eagles.

Dave Davies returned to covering city hall for the *Philadelphia Daily News*. In 1993, he was given his own column to write analysis and commentary of local policy issues.

Tia O'Brien continued to work at KRON-TV in San Francisco, breaking a story, largely ignored by the newspapers, on how car dealers in California were violating the state's lemon laws.

Larry Kane left Channel 10 in 1992 after a bitter contract dispute. He was replaced by anchor Ken Matz, who was estimated to receive a salary of close to $130,000 as compared to Kane's reported $600,000. Kane was hired by KYW-TV in 1993 to host a new local newsmagazine, *The Bulletin.*

Drew Berry, news director of Channel 10 News, was relieved of his duties in 1994, a few weeks after the release of ratings data from the most recent Nielsen sweeps period. With its lower-salaried anchors and glitzier approach to the news, Channel 10 had declined dramatically in ratings from the previous year.

Scott Herman, news director at KYW-TV (Channel 3), resigned to return to news radio at WINS in New York City.

And the city of Philadelphia by 1994, with a balanced budget and improved bond rating, would continue to lose jobs at a rate of one thousand per month.

Appendix: How the Book Was Researched and Written

❧ This book had its roots in the fall of 1990, when I became increasingly aware of new forces that were sweeping local television journalism. Local newscasts were facing new pressures from bottom line-oriented corporate ownership and from increasing competition from cable, and those pressures were beginning to change the way news departments approached local election coverage. A growing body of research was pointing up the weaknesses of national political reporting—particularly television coverage of presidential campaigns—but relatively little study had been devoted to local television coverage of local election campaigns. I set out to do such a study, through the prism of the rich and colorful case of Philadelphia's 1991 mayoral race. I chose a case study method because I wanted to understand in as much detail as possible the underlying structure of media organizations and the processes through which they interacted with political organizations. While I would be looking at only one case, I had two reasons to believe that news coverage of this political campaign would not be very different from what I would find in other cities. First, the economic pressures facing television stations in Philadelphia would be similar in other media markets. Second, the continual movement of news directors, producers, and reporters across media markets and the reliance on formulas supplied by a small number of news consulting firms servicing stations throughout the country guaranteed a degree of uniformity across cities.

My original plan was to study the way local television news covered a political campaign from the vantage point of a single reporter. I was fortunate to gain the cooperation of Tia O'Brien, political reporter for Philadelphia's KYW-TV (Channel 3). O'Brien had visited my classes on the news media and urban policy, speaking trenchantly about the hurdles of covering politics for local television. I knew she was a veteran reporter who cultivated her own political sources and that she was regarded as a force to be reckoned with by both local newspaper reporters and politicians. My objective was to follow O'Brien for the next year as she went about the job of covering Philadelphia's mayoral race. I wanted to witness firsthand how external and internal forces influenced the way she covered the campaign. By December 1990, I had received the consent of O'Brien and her news director to follow her on the beat and in the newsroom.

But my plan had to be altered almost immediately. In February 1991 Tia O'Brien announced that she was leaving KYW, because the station had failed to meet a better offer from a news operation in San Francisco. That a television station would let one of its best reporters go—and that they would not take steps to keep their political ace from departing in the middle of an important campaign—said much about the state of local television news. But it also left me with a major problem. How could I follow one reporter and one station when that reporter was leaving town with no clear successor? My answer was to shift the focus of my study to a small number of key reporters and their news organizations. In particular, Sal Paolantonio of the *Philadelphia Inquirer* agreed to engage in periodic long interviews with me throughout the campaign, to explain why he and his newspaper were making their news decisions. Dave Davies of the *Philadelphia Daily News* cooperated in a similar way. The new focus of the study came to rest on the economic forces that were affecting both local television and metropolitan newspapers and how those forces were influencing city political coverage. The study was not meant to grade the efforts of individual reporters; rather, I wanted to understand the underlying processes that influenced their coverage. Ultimately, I wanted to examine whether news coverage was providing voters with the information they needed to make choices between candidates in local elections.

With this focus in mind, my case study relied on three research methodologies: participant-observation, content analysis, and interviewing. The participant-observation component involved attending campaign events and following reporters on the campaign trail. For as long as Tia O'Brien remained in Philadelphia, I followed her to selected campaign events and observed the raw event—e.g., Frank Rizzo's announcement speech, Ron Castille's anointment by the Republican committee—and the way the reporters in the small "media pack" related to each other and to the candidates. Some of the events I attended were public appearances or forums at which a number of reporters were present. In other cases, I observed only one organization or one reporter. For example, I observed O'Brien in her newsroom and editing booth as she wrote and selected video for her story about the Republican endorsement meeting. I joined Sal Paolantonio and a team of reporters at the *Inquirer* as they watched the Democratic candidates' debate on television and afterwards discussed the angle they should take on its analysis. As the campaign progressed, I would also accompany Dave Davies, Cindy Burton, Vernon Odom, and Barbara Grant as they covered specific events or conducted interviews with the candidates. On election night of the primary, I watched the results in my living room, as any city voter might. On the night of the general election, I went to both Joe Egan's and Ed Rendell's headquarters to observe one of the city's premiere media events.

At each event, I audiotaped the proceedings so that I would be able to record word-for-word what both candidates and reporters talked about on the campaign trail. I also wanted to be able to compare what I observed about a raw event with the way it was eventually covered by newspaper and television reporters. In addition, I wanted to understand how reporters went about the task of deciding what was news and what wasn't and how they chose the angle for their stories. In the course of the campaign I acquired some of the secondary materials from which reporters drew their stories, such as campaign finance reports, position papers, press releases, and background material on the candidates and campaign issues.

While I traveled the campaign trail to observe public appearances and the interaction of reporters and candidates, I was also collecting the raw materials for my content analysis. Every newspaper story about the campaign was filed and, with the help of the Annenberg School's audiovisual department, the weekday evening newscasts of the three network affiliates in Philadelphia were taped. I used these articles and television news pieces first for a qualitative analysis of how the event I had attended had become transformed into a news story, e.g., looking at what the reporter decided to quote or what angle on the story she or he had taken. Second, I carried out a content analysis on both the newspaper articles and television news stories, to understand the nature of the coverage in a comprehensive way. For the primary, I examined the 5:30, 6:00, and 11:00 P.M. weekday newscasts of the network affiliates (KYW-3, WPVI-6, and WCAU-10) from March 1 until May 17, 1991. The total number of half-hour slots included in this analysis was 504. I watched them all. Every story about the primary election was measured for length of time and categorized by subject into one of twenty-five subcategories, then aggregated into five broader categories. In addition, each candidate's sound-bites were timed and categorized by content, such as issues or strategy. In the general election, I examined the same network affiliates' newscasts from September 2 until November 1, 1991, a total of 360 newscasts. Television news pieces were again measured for length and type (such as voice-overs as compared to packages) and categorized into three broad groups: positions on the city's issues, horse race/campaign appearances, and personal issues.

I carried out a similar analysis of the coverage of the primary in the city's major metropolitan newspaper, the *Philadelphia Inquirer,* with the excellent assistance of my students. Sarah Dupret measured stories in the *Inquirer* from January 1 until May 21, 1991, to determine the extent to which the coverage focused on three major categories (issues, horse race, and personal/character) and the location of stories within the paper (e.g., to what extent did stories about issues make the front page?). For the general election, a similar analysis was carried out by Patty Chang and Jefrey Dubard, using stories from September 1 until November 5, 1991.

The third leg of the analysis came from interviews with journalists as well as with candidates and their advisers. With a small number of journalists—namely, Tia O'Brien, Sal Paolantonio, and Dave Davies—these interviews took the form of ongoing conversations throughout the campaign. Other informants—including other reporters, editors, and news directors, as well as candidates and their staffs—were interviewed either during or after the campaign, including several who answered questions posed by students in my course on the news media and urban policy. With the journalists, I examined the reasons for the reporting decisions they and their news organizations were making and how the candidates and their campaign staffs were interacting with them. From the candidates and their staffs, I wanted to learn how they were going about trying to get media coverage for their campaigns and how they thought they were faring in the media. Many of the people I interviewed were willing to share their thoughts and feelings as they proceeded along the campaign trail, allowing me to blend those ideas into the narrative. Other interviewees, however, were more guarded, and their thoughts remained shielded from my view.

In these conversations and interviews, I was often faced with the same problem confronting the journalists I was writing about: how to separate the facts from the interpretation of events by my informants. As people talked more or less freely with me about the media coverage, I was aware that some were trying to "spin" me—calculating how they would appear in print, or how they might want to cast aspersions on someone else's motives. In general, my solution was to use the observations of my interviewees—reproduced as much as possible in their own words—to provide a sense of how different players were interpreting what was going on. But I would try to base the "facts" of the book on the results of my content analysis and direct observations.

When I began actually writing this book, I decided to draw together these three different techniques—participant-observation, data collection/

analysis, and interviewing—into a narrative writing style. I would use the events that I was able to attend as the window through which to make my observations about how the local media were changing and how they were covering the mayor's race. I made several decisions along the way that bear noting. While I could not cover every event that occurred on the campaign trail, I did try to be present at a sufficient variety to provide readers with a sense of the nature of the exchanges between reporters and candidates. I tried to use each event I witnessed as a dramatic episode with which to make a broader point about how the local media have come to cover political campaigns. Each depiction of a particular scene, therefore, was used to convey a lesson about the general nature of the interaction between media and campaign.

Other literary devices employed in the book are also worth mentioning. The descriptions of people's motivations and thoughts and beliefs were derived from my interviews. However, I made a key decision in writing up the results of those interviews: I chose not to quote directly the words of the people I interviewed. Rather, for the sake of maintaining a narrative flow, I chose to present their words as though they were merely reflecting on these issues as they went about their business on the campaign trail, rather than responding to my questions. My intention was in part to re-move myself from the story, so that the reader would see the participants and not the interviewer, and in part to make the book read more as a story than as a series of interviews. In no case did I project or imagine what a journalist or candidate or other actor was thinking. In some cases, com-ments from interviews undertaken at different points in time were blended into a description of an individual's personality and motivations, as well as their views about the media and the campaign. Whenever possible in de-scribing a person's thoughts, I tried to keep the language as close to the person's own spoken language as possible, so that individuals would come across with distinct voices.

Also blended into the narrative, along with a description of actual events that I observed directly and the reflections of participants on those events, was an assessment of the coverage itself. For example, in the chap-ter on Lucien Blackwell's entrance into the race, I combined an account of his speech in city council's chambers (based on events I had witnessed) with a description of how Lucien Blackwell regarded the media's coverage of him (obtained in an interview with Blackwell), as well as with a descrip-tion of the actual stories that greeted his announcement speech (based on my analysis of the tapes and newspaper stories), while also weaving in the findings of scholarly research on the media's portrayal of black politicians. Similarly, when I described Vernon Odom's comments about how his competitors had dropped out of covering the election, I brought in the numbers from my own content analysis to support his observation.

The actual words of the participants, the finished stories and pictures, and the interactions along the campaign trail were therefore meant to reinforce each other, providing a vivid portrait of the process through which the campaign received news coverage from start to finish. At the same time, the narrative was informed by many books and articles about the media, politics, and Philadelphia, although this book does not contain a single footnote. For those readers who would like to make use of those secondary sources, I have included a selected listing at the end of this appendix.

Ultimately, my intention was not simply to measure and analyze the news coverage of one particular race but, more importantly, to shed light on the underlying processes and organizational structures that influence news coverage of local elections. While the book pointed up some of the weaknesses of such news coverage, the criticisms are reserved largely for the structure of the system and the nature of the process, not the individuals who worked within them. In the course of this study, the journalists and candidates I observed and interviewed worked long and grueling hours practicing their craft and, in my view, were sincerely trying to produce the best quality work under the constraints that they faced.

Selected Bibliography

Adams, Carolyn, David Bartelt, David Elesh, Ira Goldstein, Nancy Kleniewski, and William Yancey. *Philadelphia: Neighborhoods, Division, and Conflict in a Post-industrial City.* Philadelphia: Temple University Press, 1991.

Adatto, Kiku. "Sound Bite Democracy: Network Evening News Presidential Campaign Coverage, 1968 and 1988." Research Paper R-2. Cambridge, Mass.: Joan Shorenstein Barone Center for Press, Politics, and Public Policy. June 1990.

Berkowitz, Dan. "Assessing Forces in the Selection of Local Television News." *Journal of Broadcasting and Electronic Media* 35 (Spring 1991): 245–51.

Berkowitz, Dan, and Douglas B. Adams. "Information Subsidy and Agenda-Building in Local Television News." *Journalism Quarterly* 67 (Winter 1990): 723–31.

Bernstein, James M., and Stephen Lacy. "Contextual Coverage of Government by Local Television News." *Journalism Quarterly* 69, no. 2 (Summer 1992): 329–40.

Boorstin, Daniel J. *The Image: A Guide to Pseudo-Events in America.* New York: Harper and Row, 1964.

Chaudhary, Anju. "Press Portrayal of Black Officials." *Journalism Quarterly* 57 (Autumn 1980): 636–41.

Daughen, Joseph R., and Peter Binzen. *The Cop Who Would Be King.* Boston: Little, Brown, 1977.

Entman, Robert. "Blacks in the News: Television, Modern Racism and Cultural Change." *Journalism Quarterly* 69, no. 2 (Summer 1992): 341–61.

———. *Democracy without Citizens: Media and the Decay of American Politics.* New York: Oxford University Press, 1989.

———. "Modern Racism and the Images of Blacks in Local Television News." *Critical Studies in Mass Communication* 7, no. 4 (December 1990): 332–45.

———. "Super Tuesday and the Future of Local News," in *The Future of News: Television-Newspapers-Wire Services-Newsmagazines,* ed. Philip S. Cook, Douglas Gomery, Lawrence Lichty. Washington, D.C.: Woodrow Wilson Center Press, 1992, pp. 53–67.

Epstein, Edward. *News from Nowhere: Television and the News.* New York: Random House, 1973.

Ettema, James, and Dwight Pallmeyer. "Race and the Horse Race: Newspaper Coverage of the 1989 and 1991 Chicago Mayoral Primaries." Evanston, Ill.: Institute for Modern Communications Research Monographs. April 20, 1992.

Gans, Herbert. *Deciding What's News: A Study of CBS Evening News, NBC Nightly News, Newsweek, and Time.* New York: Vintage, 1980.

Graber, Doris. *Mass Media and American Politics.* 4th ed. Washington, D.C.: Congressional Quarterly Press, 1993.

———. "Media Magic: Fashioning Characters for the 1983 Mayoral Race," in *The Making of the Mayor,* ed. Melvin G. Holli and Paul M. Green. Grand Rapids, Mich.: Eerdmans, 1984, pp. 53–84.

Hallin, Daniel C. "Sound Bite News: Television Coverage of Elections, 1968–1988." *Journal of Communication* 42 (Spring 1992): 5–24.

Jamieson, Kathleen Hall. *Dirty Politics.* New York: Oxford University Press, 1992.

Kaniss, Phyllis. *Making Local News.* Chicago: University of Chicago Press, 1991.

Kern, Montague. *30-Second Politics.* New York: Praeger, 1989.

King, Erica G. "Thematic Coverage of the 1988 Presidential Primaries: A Comparison of *USA Today* and *The New York Times.*" *Journalism Quarterly* 67 (Spring 1990): 85.

McManus, John. "How Local Television Learns What Is News." *Journalism Quarterly* 67 (Winter 1990): 672–83.

Mann, Thomas E., and Gary R. Orren, eds. *Media Polls in American Politics.* Washington, D.C.: Brookings Institution, 1992.

Ostroff, David H. "A Participant-Observer Study of TV Campaign Coverage." *Journalism Quarterly* 57 (Autumn 1980): 415–19.

Ostroff, David H., and Karin L. Sandell. "Local Station Coverage of Campaigns: A Tale of Two Cities in Ohio." *Journalism Quarterly* 61 (Summer 1984): 350.

———. "Campaign Coverage by Local TV News in Columbus, Ohio, 1978–1986." *Journalism Quarterly* 66 (Spring 1989): 114–20.

Patterson, Thomas E. *The Mass Media Election: How Americans Choose Their President.* New York: Praeger, 1980.

Robinson, Michael J., and Margaret A. Sheehan. *Over the Wire and on TV: CBS and UPI in Campaign '80.* New York: Russell Sage Foundation, 1983.

Roper Organization. *America's Watching: Public Attitudes toward Television.* 1991.

Smith, Conrad. "News Critics, Newsworkers, and Local Television News." *Journalism Quarterly* 65 (1988): 341–46.

Times Mirror Center for the People and the Press. "The People, the Press, and Politics: Voters Say 'Thumbs Up' to Campaign, Process, and Coverage." Survey XIII. Washington, D.C. November 15, 1992.

Westin, Av. *Newswatch: How TV Decides the News.* New York: Simon and Schuster, 1982.

Index

PHYLLIS KANISS is Assistant Dean of the Annenberg School for Communication at the University of Pennsylvania and author of *Making Local News*.